SOCIAL FEMINISM

SOCIAL
FEMINISM

NAOMI BLACK

Cornell University Press

Ithaca and London

First published 1989 by Cornell University Press.

International Standard Book Number (cloth) 0-8014-2261-2
International Standard Book Number (paper) 0-8014-9573-3
Library of Congress Catalog Card Number 88-47937
Printed in the United States of America
*Librarians: Library of Congress cataloging information
appears on the last page of the book.*

*The paper in this book is acid-free and meets the guidelines for
permanence and durability of the Committee on Production Guidelines
for Book Longevity of the Council on Library Resources.*

This book is dedicated to

S. P. ROSENBAUM

Contents

Acknowledgments

Over the ten years it took me to write this book, many people have helped me. The organizations I studied were all extraordinarily welcoming, as were those few scholars who have worked on them. For information about the Women's Co-operative Guild, I owe the most to Jean Gaffin, who knows more about the Guild than anyone else in the world and who made available to me copies of material the Guild had forgotten it ever had. I was helped at the Union féminine civique et sociale by Thérèse Doneaud, Jacqueline Godet, and especially Suzanne Viaenne; Andrée Michel was also exceptionally kind, going out of her way to assist me in refuting her interpretations. At the national office of the League of Women Voters, I interviewed Madelyn Bonsignore, Marie Lisi, Martha Mills, Nancy Robberson, and Ruth Wolverton, and was greatly assisted by Felice Sorett.

My participation in the Ontario Committee on the Status of Women and the Toronto Business and Professional Women's Club was important for this book, as were the two years I spent at York University as advisor to the president on the status of women. So also were my three years on the board of the Social Sciences and Humanities Research Council of Canada, especially as chair of the Committee on Nonsexist Research. I thank friends and colleagues in all these groups. I appreciate also two sabbaticals supported by Leave Fellowships from the Social Sciences and Humanities Research Council of Canada; other travel for research purposes was supported by funds provided by York University.

Friends and collaborators in the women's movement and in academic projects have influenced my ideas about feminism. I am particularly grateful to Christine Donald, Lorna Marsden, Thelma McCormack, Johanna Stuckey, and the Women's History Collective—Paula Bourne, Gail Cuthbert Brandt, Beth Light, Wendy Mitchinson, and Alison Prentice.

All my life, Max Black has provided the example of lucid and morally committed scholarship. When I was a graduate student, Karl W. Deutsch taught me that theory is a tool and not an end in itself; he opened up for me the possibilities of a rationally conceived and probabilistic social science. The person to whom this book is dedicated has worked beside me for thirty years and has always taken my work as seriously as his own.

I also thank my students who over the years have been exposed to the ideas that come together here. In particular, several graduate students both encouraged and challenged me: Sandra Burt and, in a more recent generation, Carolyn Baxter, Louise Carbert, Barbara Crow, Barbara Falk, and Deborah Stienstra.

Finally, I am grateful to the rest of my family, always the justification for social feminists and in this case all that any feminist could want. Michal Black was the first feminist I knew. Samuel and Susanna Rosenbaum give me hope for the future; they have always encouraged me to be more radical, more activist, and more feminist.

NAOMI BLACK

Toronto, Canada

SOCIAL FEMINISM

Introduction

This book is about feminism as it is shown in feminist organizations. The subject is an actual historical system of beliefs shared by specific, identifiable individual women in three organizations discussed in detail—and also shared by many other women in a large number of other, disparate groups. My initial task, therefore, is less one of definition than of finding a description of feminism which includes all those who consider themselves or are considered to be feminists. What these women have in common is something both real and significant. Feminism, as I understand it, is the desire for increased autonomy for women. Feminist groups are women's groups that are motivated by such a belief; men's groups or mixed-sex groups can support increased autonomy for women but cannot themselves be feminist.

Any rationale developed to support the general belief in feminism must necessarily include an awareness that women's situation and experience differ from men's. It must also imply that women should not be judged inferior by male standards; the policy implication is, at a minimum, that women should not be disadvantaged in comparison with men.

"Social feminism," the subject of this book, is a particular version of feminism whose most important characteristic is a focus on values and experience identified with women. By contrast, numerous versions of "equity feminism" extend existing belief systems to include the women previously excluded. The belief systems conventionally labeled "liberal," "Marxist," and "socialist" feminism are all varieties of equity feminism, while the so-called maternal feminism of the past and the radical feminism of the present are both versions of social feminism.

I argue that the inexact but recognizable term *feminism* serves to identify all these traditions and to chart their likely future impact. A major theme of this book is the common elements among the varying ideas and practices of women's activism. Today, "feminism" is itself a common term, often used pejoratively. We are still within the "second wave of

1

feminism," a designation that recognizes continuities in both organizational practice and ideology through close to two centuries of women's
active aspirations for autonomy. In this post-1960s' phase, feminists expect activists to identify themselves as feminists and also as part of some
narrower, exclusionary segment of feminism itself. My most important
goal in this book is to replace the current, restrictive definitions of kinds
of feminism with a classification of its subcategories which will serve
women better than what we have now.

I distinguish among versions of feminism in terms of beliefs about the
significance of women and women's experience. I am not neutral among
these ideologies, of course, any more than I am either indifferent or
disinterested in relation to the choices between feminism and other belief systems. Furthermore, the version of feminism I find most persuasive—social feminism—places considerable emphasis on the values of
subjectivity and specificity. Such an approach is in no way incompatible
with the possibility of truth, with understanding the concrete features of
human existence, or with communication among scholars. But it gives
added weight to problems always present for a social scientist: Who is
entitled to speak for another and to interpret her or his experience?
What data can justify such representation?

My own experience is as a white woman, middle-class, Jewish, heterosexual, with children and grandchildren and a long-established marriage; I grew up in the nonfeminist 1950s in the United States and am
now, in Canada, well into middle age. I have been professionally trained,
and then employed, within the academic establishment. My experience
in women's organizations is related. In the 1970s I was an active member
of a new women's organization resembling those I study; I still have
associations, some of them close, with past and present members of that
organization. My own history thus overlaps that of the members of the
groups I am studying. It does not coincide in every detail, because of the
diversity among groups in three nations—England, France, the United
States—during a period of more than a century. The groups I discuss in
this book differ substantially in origin, in structure, in political and social
context.

Yet among feminist organizations, my subjects share an exceptional
number of similarities. They are all European or North American, with
mainly white and middle-aged membership. Their leaders are middle-
class, though members of at least two of the groups are working-class.
One group was initially Catholic but, like the others, is now secular.
None of the groups is actively lesbian; only one was intolerant about
variations from sexual norms, and none has shown much policy interest
in issues of sexual orientation. All three of the groups are still active,
although their foundings range from 1893 to 1925.

The questions I need to answer here are these: On what basis can I
speak for even this limited and apparently unrepresentative sample of

women's organizations? On what basis can I reasonably generalize further about feminism and feminist organizations?

What these groups hold in common, I propose, is a set of beliefs they share and I share with them—a view of women as valuable because different. Furthermore, all derive a public role for women from the private role of women. I argue that their shared feminist perspective is significant, and the more significant for their diversity in other respects. I argue further that many other, dissimilar women's groups share such beliefs. Such beliefs, and groups using them, exist in cultures that are not just white, or middle-class, or Jewish, or modernized—or black, or impoverished, or Christian, or developing. And this set of beliefs also differentiates such groups from other women's groups and, more important, from most men's or mixed groups.

Because women share situations, especially their universal involvement with domestic activities and relative lack of public power and authority, the bundle of beliefs that makes up social feminism is one of women's most important bases of empowerment. Armed with such beliefs, women have been able to select and work for their own goals—which is the core of the feminist quest for autonomy even if it has not been recognized as such. Women activated by such ideologies have, in the past and the present, constructed an effective political role for women. I expect them to continue to do so in the future. Some of this feminist work I have been lucky enough to share in.

Social feminist analysis directs our attention to the ways in which women differ from men and in the process helps direct our research. The most obvious differences are biological, but although they are the easiest to see and the most persistent, they are also the most problematic. Today we can see pervasive equivalences in the physical lives of men and women—if not for individuals then for populations. Socially constructed modes of behavior and perception are by definition malleable, even if for given individuals or for whole societies they seem immutable. By contrast, women's disadvantage, visible in every social and political context, has a logical coherence that has made it the subject of most equity feminist research. But such research, directed at origins and explanations for relatively unchanging conditions, can give little guidance about possible sources of change. Finally, women's resistance to male domination, logically distant from what men and women share, provides the record of women's assertion of their autonomy and of the impact of their wishes on society. This is the account of how, because of women's efforts, change has in practice occurred. Women's groups focused on women's difference from men, as well as on women's values, are to be found at the heart of these efforts. These groups contain the social feminists who are my topic, a topic chosen in part because of my belief in change and my hope that it can continue.

One motivation for this book is my strong feeling that the accepted categories of feminism have no place for my beliefs or the beliefs of those I worked with on projects we were convinced had the potential to transform the world. In 1977 Jo Freeman asked a conference on the Canadian women's movement who among those present considered themselves "radical" feminists; I was one of those who raised their hands as self-identified radical feminists watched us with disbelief and hostility. It is as a feminist that I assert I can most usefully do research by beginning where I am, with groups I can understand because they are not impossibly remote from my own situation and experience. It is up to others to challenge or support my interpretation, beginning where they are themselves.

In this book, my specific subjects are the Women's Co-operative Guild (WCG) of England, the Union féminine civique et sociale (UFCS) of France, and the national League of Women Voters (LWV) in the United States. I draw also on my own experience as an early member of the Ontario Committee on the Status of Women, a small Canadian pressure group founded in 1971, and in general on my contacts and personal experience with the second-wave women's movement in Canada. My interest is in the shared ideology of such groups and how it made possible an expansion of women's political role in very different countries. I use the notion of *ideology* here in a Weberian rather than a Marxist sense, being unwilling to make assumptions about what is someone else's "false" consciousness or "objective" interest. My attention has been directed toward the policies derived from the ideology by those who accept it. In particular, I am interested in how social feminism served to establish a relationship between activist women and "normal" male politics. As a feminist, I have to start with the existing powers and power structures, accepting that taxes are as real as death even if social welfare and birth are more promising.

Because of the nature of this project, my use of sources has been somewhat different from what a complete historical account would require. "Appropriate" material is what establishes the content of beliefs and demonstrates the practical consequences that follow in relation to possible political roles. All three of the groups I examine have as explicit goals the education and organization of women for effective political participation. The ideological bases of this goal are best sought in material explicitly prepared for members and potential members; the ideal source would be a newsletter covering the entire existence of the group. I have used such periodicals as my major sources where they exist, supplementing them with other group publications for members and, in some cases, with interviews with members and staff. (See Appendix for information on sources.)

For each organization, I focus on features relevant to the issues of women's political participation. I am especially concerned with the charge—indeed, the widely held belief—that women's political participation tends to be conservative and the related notion that women's groups have hindered the development of women's political effectiveness. Accordingly, I have concentrated on issues that show how each group developed political awareness and progressiveness, both in terms of the women's movement and more widely. For the Guild, I concentrate on the group's relationship to the Co-operative Movement and to feminist pacifism. The facilitating effect of co-operative beliefs and structures is in conflict, as I show, with the WCG's feminism and its desire for independent action. Loyalty to party and movement finally destroyed feminism in the organization. For the UFCS, which had its origins in social Catholicism, I look at a range of domestic issues but particularly paid labor, municipal politics, and reproductive freedom. These are all areas where Catholicism is generally believed to impose a crippling constraint; I show how the UFCS became steadily more feminist, more secular, and more overtly political. For the League, I discuss nonpartisanship and changing views of the Equal Rights Amendment. The LWV always combined social feminist views and goals with a rhetoric that was, at best, equity feminist and that often denied any feminist tradition. Nevertheless, the organization was able to create a supplementary forum of political activity for women and has served as training ground and support for an amazingly large group of politically active women. In general, then, I attempt to demonstrate the impact of a particular political culture and time on social feminism.

This book presents detailed studies of three feminist organizations, at least one of which would often have rejected that designation. The long histories of these groups show the way in which women developed a political role out of what they perceived as their female identity. Such groups still assist women to move from their homes into what even they have understood to be the male sphere of politics. In the process, they help to erode the conceptual and practical boundaries that have restricted women's scope of activity. I argue that such organizations have therefore had—and will continue to have—a radical impact on society, changing the basis of participation in policy formation and expanding the agenda for social change. These are changes that affect not just women but all citizens and the general nature of politics.

I do not pay much attention here to the extent to which such organizations have also contributed to the ideology of "privatization," the notion of femininity as both an internal and an external justification of the restriction of women's opportunities. Women's reported uninterest in and uninvolvement with conventional politics is, I believe, best explained by the very real obstacles placed in the way of political activity that would be meaningful to them. It also seems clear to me that many activities of the women's groups I study should be classified as political, even though members and most analysts would exclude them from that category. They extend the range of political options open to citizens rather than provide women with a nonpolitical substitute.

This analysis absolves the activities or arguments of women's groups from any significant responsibility for the continuing disadvantages of women, which some see as the consequence of earlier feminists' failure to evolve an adequate theory of liberation for women. On the contrary, I am sure that the extension of women's activities and expectations, for which women's groups may claim some credit, has played a large role in improving women's situation. The lives of women have changed and, to some extent and in some ways, even improved. I do not think, for instance, that anyone can make a serious case for the argument that women in North America and Western Europe now have fewer opportunities than they had in the early nineteenth century. That the situation of women in the developing world has deteriorated is also undeniable. In both cases, feminist dissatisfactions must come from comparisons with men's situation and in terms of possible improvements that have not occurred or seem unlikely to occur soon. My focus here is on change, particularly political change, and on the part that women themselves played in the process of expanding opportunities. For the developed world, women's impact has been substantial; for the developing world, which I discuss only tangentially, it has great potential.

Although I shall not discuss the nature of women's continuing disadvantages, I do not wish to minimize or seem to condone the situation of the especially and shockingly deprived groups of women whose continuing plight reminds us of how much more change is still needed even in societies relatively responsive to such needs. Elderly women, particularly those who are single or widowed, sole-support and particularly adolescent mothers, women from racial or other castelike minority groups— the plight of these and others demonstrates the continuing defects of all social systems. Nevertheless, only a sentimental myth of the golden age of the family can present these women as worse off today in the developed world than their counterparts were in the days before the active women's movement. I would argue that even these women are in fact somewhat better off today, although they remain the casualties of patriarchy. That they form a larger segment of society now than in the past is not the fault of the women's movement. Then as now their suffering is part of what motivates feminists. Surely it is due in large part to the efforts of feminists—and particularly feminists of the sort I shall be discussing—that the most victimized of women have moved closer to being a public rather than a private scandal.

In this book I attempt to demonstrate the role played in such changes by the feminism characteristic of the organizations I study. I find hope for the necessary future, provided that social feminism continues to motivate large numbers of women whom most theorists dismiss as intrinsically, hopelessly locked into passivity and domesticity.

This book's working title was *Four Guineas*, in recognition of the way in which the author of *Three Guineas* expressed the reality and the possibilities of social feminism. Virginia Woolf was lovingly but dismissively described by her politician husband as "the least political animal that has lived since Aristotle invented the definition" (L. Woolf 1967:27). Her "Society of Outsiders" was partly a parodic response to the request that she publicly enlist in the cause of preventing war, a ridiculous request if she was indeed the apolitical being that Leonard Woolf described. But the Society of Outsiders can also be seen as a model for the social feminist organizations described in this book. "The Society of Outsiders," Virginia Woolf told the imaginary interlocutor of *Three Guineas*, "has the same ends as your society   freedom, equality, peace, but . . . it seeks to achieve them by the means that a different sex, a different tradition, a different education, and the different values which result from those differences have placed within our reach" (1938:206). This is a political goal, one whose pursuit made women into political actors; it is the subject of this book.

PART I

THEORY

This book is concerned with feminism as it operates to motivate organized groups of women activists. Feminism, a loaded and often disputed term, is not easy to define, and even more difficult once it is understood that the definition must include a set of beliefs existing in many different places and over a long period of time. As a belief system, feminism is located in the minds of individual women. I propose, however, to examine it in a group context, as the shared beliefs of women in a number of women's groups. My goal in this book is to identify and to classify feminism, and to do so in a way that will contribute to feminist progress. Autonomy, the central impulse of feminism, is adaptable to many systems of belief. It is probably best understood as self-determination, in contrast to the notion of "heteronomy," the condition of being regulated by some other's law (de Lauretis 1986:10).

Clearly there has been a continuing impulse toward autonomy for women, an impulse felt by many different women in many different national and historical settings. Embodied in the organizational efforts of groups of women, this impulse has also been characterized by recognizable institutional and, above all, ideological patterns. These patterns have not yet been adequately identified or classified, although the notion of a "second wave" of feminism usefully represents the continuity of the women's movement; the marine imagery catches the way in which troughs of apparent inaction have repeatedly been mistaken for the termination of something identified as feminism (Sarah 1982).

Many among today's public understand the meaning of the term "feminism" in spite of problems of definition. This ideology is regarded as a form of radicalism peculiar to women who are hostile to men, so that beauty-contest winners continue skittishly to deny that they are such freaks. But feminism also has a somewhat broader meaning, for a substantial group of women are now prepared to identify themselves with it. In 1979, for example, a newspaper poll found that 42 percent of urban

9

Canadian women accepted the designation "feminist" (*Weekend Magazine* 1979). In 1986 a poll for the Canadian women's magazine *Chatelaine* gave almost the same results—47 percent of those surveyed were prepared to call themselves feminists, while 40 percent identified themselves as "traditionalist" (Womanpoll May 1986). And Canada, although it has a flourishing women's movement, is not known for its radicalism (Prentice et al. 1988).

Poll data suggest further that, even if a majority identification with feminism is unlikely, disavowals are fully compatible with support of women's organized campaigns for policy changes intended to improve the situation of women. Fully 62 percent of those responding to the 1979 Canadian poll said they supported the less threatening "women's movement." Indeed, substantial majorities register support in all countries where relevant questions have been asked in polls (Black 1980). In addition, they agree that women activists—if not feminists—have in fact improved the situation of women. In 1976 Gallup reported that nearly all respondents who thought the situation of women had improved in the United States during the previous five years, 85 percent of those polled, also believed that "women's organizations" had made a significant contribution (Gallup 1976:24, 25). It seems clear that the majority of women prefer to say "I am not a feminist, but . . ." and then support equal pay, or freedom of choice regarding reproduction, or any of the wide range of issues that have concerned women activists. Such a position responds, explicitly or otherwise, to the efforts of earlier feminists, recognizing their value even while dissociating the speaker from any organized social movement. Feminism is thereby distanced, identified as a minority ideology or set of organizations, possibly valuable but socially unacceptable.

Discussions of feminism are shaped today by an established tradition of studies of suffragism and a generally accepted classification of the varieties of second-wave feminism. These modes of analysis assume a discontinuity between first- and second-wave movements and beliefs; both also reject social feminism. Beyond that, the two have little in common except their powerful influence on current analyses of feminist ideology and organization. Central to their impact is the interpretation of feminism in terms of mainstream politics and political beliefs, an interpretation that denies legitimacy to all forms of feminism but particularly to social feminism.

The earliest and most influential analysts of feminism used the American suffrage movement as their data base. They were, by and large, critics of the existing American political system, hence their interest in earlier reform movements. To the extent that any version of feminism accepted or worked within the existing political system, it was suspect to such scholars. But feminism was truly damned when it rejected the conventional analyses that "progressive" politics shared with the American mainstream—analyses that saw feminists as simply another pressure group. These historians established the contrast between "justice" arguments and what they called "expediency," along with the notion that these arguments defined two different varieties of feminists.

I accept a division among feminists but not these labels or the judgment they express. I suggest the term "equity feminism" for all those many belief systems which focus on women's similarity to men and demand equality for women on that basis. Equity feminism can exist in relation to any ideology, and it has argued for assimilation into fascist as well as democratic systems, collectivist as well as individualistic societies. By contrast, I focus on the "social feminism" that derives from women's specificity an argument for wider public action on the part of women.

Chapter 1 discusses definitions of feminism. Chapter 2 criticizes the work of those historians who have developed the tradition of disparaging social feminism. Chapter 2 also discusses the current classification of feminism as liberal, Marxist, socialist, and radical; I argue that the division between equity and social feminism is both more accurate and more useful for feminists. Chapter 3 describes the analytical and historical content of social feminism. Chapter 4 turns to feminist critiques of social science and argues for the necessity of a social feminist approach. The final chapter in this part discusses how social feminism can direct the researcher to a focus on women's organizations as a usefully feminist subject of enquiry.

CHAPTER 1

Defining Feminism

In 1987 Quebec farm women who accepted nearly all the goals of the contemporary women's movement commented that they were not happy about the way in which some women "demanded" them.[1] They refused to identify themselves as feminists. Such attitudes dismay many women who consider themselves feminists. Yet they often define feminism in terms unlikely to attract majority support. Within the women's movement it is common to insist that no one is a feminist who will not agree that women are "oppressed." Similarly restrictive assumptions operate among those few feminists who are prepared to make a public analysis of the present state of things. In 1982, for example, "Voices from the Post-Feminist Generation," a lead article in the *New York Times Magazine,* reported with some distress that successful career women in their early twenties were rejecting the term "feminist" because for them, or at least for their associates, feminist meant bitter, isolated, unhappy, and lesbian.

The article's author, who had been a feminist rebel at Cornell University in the 1960s, was appalled at the rejection of an identification that was very dear to her. But her own definitions do not invite large-scale participation, for she identifies "the philosophical core of feminism" very narrowly as "equality of economic opportunity" (Bolotin 1982:103). Furthermore, her article implies a restrictive understanding of feminism as including, necessarily, a personal commitment to militancy and group action. It is not surprising she found so little "feminism" among the young women she interviewed; what she sought was remote from the beliefs shared by the large numbers basically sympathetic to changes in

1. Discussions in December 1987, at St. Etienne de Beauharnois, Quebec, with members of the Cercles de fermières about a Eurobarometer question posed in 1983. In English the question read "Do you agree or disagree with women who claim that there should be fewer differences between the respective roles of men and women in society?" In French, however, the "femmes *réclament*" role change, which the respondents understood as "demand" and therefore rejected (Rabier 1983:A6).

women's situation. In fact, she noted, even the most conservative women she interviewed showed some appreciation of the efforts of earlier feminists, and all supported some equality issues, especially those relating to work.

Scholarly analysts of feminism rarely identify more than very small numbers of feminists.[2] Historical studies until recently discussed only suffragists under the rubric of feminism and recognized only a few of them as having relevant beliefs (Evans 1980). Even now the title "feminist" is likely to be reserved for the few suffragists whose public efforts were oriented explicitly toward changes in women's political status.[3] A careful recent study even confines the term "feminist" to American "women's rights" leaders in the years 1910 to 1930, on the grounds that the term is anachronistic unless used by activists themselves (Cott 1987).

At the same time, however, some empirical evidence suggests that the relatively few groups labeled feminist are part of a much larger whole. When sociologist Alice Rossi tried in 1977 to classify the women who attended the Houston Women's Conference, she could not find agreement among them about labeling anyone feminist in terms of issues; one in three of those she questioned felt that even an opponent of the Equal Rights Amendment or of abortion could be a feminist (1982:91, 93). Rossi herself felt no uneasiness in distinguishing among "feminist" groups like the National Organization for Women, "traditional women's organizations" like the Young Women's Christian Association and the League of Women Voters, and those groups focused primarily on ethnic, racial, and religious communities (65). The overlap of issues and attitudes among members of all these sorts of groups suggests why those polled were so reluctant to exclude any individual from the community of feminism. Rossi was struck by the extent to which the various groups seemed to be both expanding their own agendas and increasing their toleration of groups with other priorities; she finally concluded that they were all feminists.

Rossi did not minimize the differences dividing the women present at the Houston Conference; indeed, one of her major findings was that radicals had deceived themselves about the extent to which conservatives had changed their views about such issues as abortion and lesbianism. But she showed, within a microcosm of the middle-of-the-road women's

2. A rare attempt to identify feminists empirically singled out only that small though growing minority of women who, on the basis of belief in equality, voted in support of policies related to women's status (Fulenwider 1980:59). Again the feminists were a marginal group, though the analysis could not indicate the negative loadings of most uses of the term. Nor could this analysis make anything out of the larger group who supported prowoman policies but not because of what was identified as feminism.

3. Olive Banks, who extends the definition of feminism past suffragism, nevertheless restricts its application to those who made "a critique of the traditional subordination of women, enshrined as it was in law, custom and religion and a claim for a new relationship between men and women which would give women greater control over their lives" (1986:2). However, she looks only at individual leaders and includes men.

movement in America, that alongside each identified or self-identified feminist were other women who had similar beliefs and activities even though they did not belong to groups usually labeled feminist. Furthermore, many of these women explicitly rejected the term "feminist."

Nevertheless, it is possible to discern a coherence of practice and belief among women activists over both time and space, and "feminism" still seems the best designation for this coherence. In the past as in the present a wide, overlapping range of group activity and belief includes what is recognized as "feminist" and shares its characteristics in significant though unclear fashion. Women from all along this feminist spectrum often find themselves in sympathy and are able to co-operate on feminist action in spite of substantial disagreement in many areas.

The evidence for a feminist continuum is largely historical: the co-operative campaigns mounted in many countries and at many times on such issues as suffrage, mother's allowance, contraception, liberalized marriage and family law, and constitutional change. Also, a small amount of evidence is to be found in studies of American women. For example, a substantial similarity appears in the political attitudes of different sets of "grass roots" women—League of Women Voters members, registered voters, party officials—and national convention delegates, most specifically on the belief that women are as capable of being politicians as men are (Baxter and Lansing 1980:125, 133). Other studies have found a similar agreement among women convention delegates who disagreed on all other elements of political belief (Kirkpatrick 1976). Outside electoral politics, members of the Parent-Teacher Association supported many of the feminist social policies advocated by members of the League of Women Voters and the National Organization for Women (Bers and Mezey 1981). Even more to the point, women hostile to the women's movement often support the majority of issues associated with the movement, and a significant number of women in public office are in effect "closet feminists" (Carroll 1985:152).

Precisely these feminist commonalities are reflected in the reports of contemporary activists, including the pugnaciously liberal and Democratic Bella Abzug who insisted that the National Women's Political Caucus (NWPC) support women only selectively as candidates for office. The NWPC was founded in 1971 by unchallengeable feminists such as Abzug herself, Gloria Steinem, and Betty Friedan; its supposedly restrictive platform enabled it to support Republican Millicent Fenwick in her unsuccessful 1982 bid for a Senate seat. Abzug's appreciative discussion of Fenwick's feminism is illuminating, and her description of the Houston conference is very close to Rossi's (Abzug with Kelber 1984: 189–192).

Further support for a broad definition of feminism is to be found in discussions of activist women's organizations which present not a definition but an inventory or typology of groups and their beliefs. Recent

studies of the British suffrage movement, for instance, describe an astonishing variety of women's groups, as disparate as the Women's Social
and Political Union, the virtually anarchist Women's Freedom League,
which pioneered refusal of tax payments, and union-based working-
class groups such as the Lancashire and Cheshire Women Textile and
Other Workers' Representation Committee (Liddington and Norris
1978). These groups co-operated to a degree we have not appreciated,
with the mainstream National Union of Women's Suffrage Societies sub-
sidizing the organization of working women at a significant level (Holton
1986). Similarly, descriptions of the modern women's movement find a
vast proliferation of groups, each carefully defining its distinctiveness
but many often co-operating in practice. For example, Ann Oakley's
account (1981, following Amanda Sebastyen) has ten categories, and she
omits anarchist, lesbian, Third World, and Christian feminisms. Janet
Flammang, who includes all these categories in her inventory of feminist
discussions of power (1983), elsewhere recounts the practical political co-
operation in Santa Clara County, California, of women's organizations
from almost all categories (1984).

Hair-splitting distinctions among forms of feminism make sense only
if all can be fitted into some overlapping category. In fact, feminism has
always exhibited wide variety along with an underlying unity. One interesting question is why so many observers fail to see both the diversity and
the unity. I believe that observers have been trapped by inappropriate
theoretical schemas and unwilling to give sufficient attention to the actions and demonstrated beliefs of women in feminist organizations.
Seeking leaders and formal statements, in the pattern established by
male organizations, analysts have paid insufficient attention to what
women activists have actually said and believed. When they did consult
the statements of activists, it was only to reclassify and reinterpret them
inside the existing categories of mainstream politics and political theory.

Groups of woman active for social change began to organize in Europe and North America in the early nineteenth century. Only through
these organizations do we have access to the belief systems that make up
feminism. Until recently there have been few women theorists as such
and even fewer who are feminists, because of the virtual exclusion of
women from the means and the motivation for producing explicit theory, particularly theory about themselves. As a result, feminism developed most often as the logic of women's action, especially their group
action. The search for articulated theory leads to a focus on individuals,
as in Dale Spender's useful *Feminist Theorists* (1983).[4]

Spender rightly stresses the importance of her book's subjects, many

4. Spender feels no need to define feminism in this volume and no need to make
comparative judgments of value about the many women included.

of whom inspired women's group action. Nevertheless, I look elsewhere for the belief systems that characterize feminism. A focus on individual leaders brings out the distinctiveness of strong women with personal differences of perspective. It is unlikely that their views were fully understood or shared even in the groups so many of them led.[5] It is necessary instead to seek the collective, shared beliefs of group members, including the leaders. Such beliefs are to be found less in individual statements by leaders than in the continuing flow of communications to supporters and potential supporters. These messages were the justifications that seemed necessary to the activists, what in fact activated them.

As organizations, women's groups rarely provide statements of underlying philosophy. Characteristically, such groups have been action-oriented and pragmatic, with only the sparsest terms of reference. Projects are more common than programs, let alone manifestos. As a result, even sympathetic observers have said that feminism was a movement that lacked an ideology (see Degler 1965). Yet the documentation of women's groups implies consistent belief systems that served as guides to action, which is certainly ideology in Weber's sense. Whether it is also ideology in the Marxist sense of false consciousness is another question, and not necessarily the central one.

A very few historians explicitly studying women's organizations, usually suffragist groups, have suggested definitions of feminism based on the actual stated views of group members. The most influential are Aileen Kraditor (1970, 1981) and William O'Neill (1971, 1986), whose interpretations contributed to the narrow and restrictive definitions that are now widespread. By contrast, a few historians, usually explicitly identifying themselves as feminists, have recently begun to establish a more accurate representation. The most important of these analysts have focused on specific segments of nineteenth- or twentieth-century activism in the United States (Gordon 1976, Berg 1978, Du Bois 1978, Hayden 1981). All of them incorporate into their understanding of feminism Daniel Scott Smith's "domestic feminism," which he defined as "the extension of autonomy of women within the family and the gradual enlargement of the social territory assigned to the domestic sphere" (Smith 1973:239). But their broad, inclusive understanding of the essence of feminism has not been widely accepted. It has remained a relatively unnoticed part of the background of the birth control movement, of the early movement for moral reform, of the post–Civil War suffrage movement, or of the movement for co-operative housekeeping.

This lack of impact was in part due to the authors themselves, who had been influenced by more widely accepted estimates of feminism. They have tended to see only their own specific subjects as moving

5. On the basis of leaders' affiliations, Banks finds socialism the dominant ideology among British feminists of the later nineteenth and early twentieth century (1986:159–60).

beyond the common, narrower definitions.[6] A few exceptions, such as J. Stanley Lemons's study of women's organizations in the postsuffrage era (1975) and Susan Ware's more recent work on the same period (1981, 1982), have been prepared to generalize about feminism on the basis of actual organizational records, but they have not had the influence they deserve.

I cannot begin this book by simply stating agreement with the definitions given by historians such as Smith and Berg. Instead, I must start by examining the reasons why historians were not able to see the broader implications of their work and why their definitions have not been more influential. Only then will it be possible to suggest a more helpful classification of feminist ideology. Feminism needs to be identified accurately, so that it can then be properly subdivided—in a feminist fashion.

The disparagement of feminism comes, I believe, because feminism has been defined so as to recognize as legitimate only a limited sector of it. As a result, much of the reality of feminism is either ignored or condemned. Linda Gordon's definition of feminism is one of the few that does not fall into such a trap. Like me, Gordon seeks a usage that would avoid the anachronism of terms such as the nineteenth century's "woman movement" and yet allow for similarity, and sometimes continuity, across time and space. For her, feminism means "sharing in an impulse to increase the power and autonomy of women in their families, communities, and/or society." Gordon also writes of "women trying to create the conditions of their lives in their own interests" (1976:xiv); more recently she has presented a definition of feminism as "a critique of male supremacy, formed and offered in the light of a will to change it" (1986:29). In addition, she suggests a distinction among the "strains" of feminism very close to the one I use here. Only one variety of beliefs was originally labeled "feminist" in the United States, she says, that which "asserted the uniqueness of women, the special joys and even mystical experience of motherhood." Clearly a contrast, but also included by Gordon's definition, were those feminists who "tended to emphasize the basic similarity between women and men" (1976:xiv).

My own definition is a variant on Gordon's. To repeat, my goal here is a definition that will include all those women who, historically or currently, work or worked within women's groups on the basis of a shared

6. For instance, Berg (1978) concluded *The Remembered Gate* with a lament that, toward the end of the nineteenth century, American women activists moved away from genuine feminism as they concentrated their efforts on suffrage. In much the same way, Karen Blair's excellent study of the women's club movement recognized some of the complexities of the actual ideology of feminism but concluded with a statement of the limitations of the clubwomen's version of feminism, by implication an inferior one (1980, cf. Epstein 1981). Only in 1987 and 1988 has Karen Offen's published work expanded from descriptions of French women's history to an attempt to define feminism. Her analysis, developed from a comparative study of women's history in Europe, has much in common with mine (Offen 1988).

belief system that allows for felt commonalities and some degree of co-operation across groups. Feminism, as a belief system operating within groups, thus means the desire for increased autonomy for women. Feminist groups are women's groups motivated by such a belief. Any rationale developed to support this general belief necessarily includes an awareness that women's situation and experience differ from men's. It will also imply that women should not be judged inferior by male standards or in comparison with men. The policy implication is, at a minimum, that women should not be disadvantaged in comparison with men. Such a definition encompasses all women identified as feminists by themselves or by others, as well as those with beliefs sufficiently similar as to include them.

Such a definition and the related analyses imply a view of the nature of the social systems within which feminists express the aspirations of women. They immediately raise the issues of public versus private spheres and of the nature of patriarchy. My assumptions here are that feminism as an organized social movement emerges only within relatively modernized societies in which voluntary associations are viable. Such societies have a public sector in the sense that at least some of the activities of production and governance operate outside the home. On the ideological level such societies make some distinction between family and state, drawing lines that correspond to physical and analytical distinctions. I assume, further, that women in the "public sphere" are relatively uncommon and relatively low in authority—as they are in the household to the extent that status distinctions exist there.

I am convinced, on the evidence available, that the imbalances of authority outside and inside the home are connected. In such societies the public realm is the more authoritative, but an area of private life is thought of as separate; the latter point provides the basis for a private authority both derived from and independent of the public authority. This system I refer to in shorthand terms as "patriarchy," avoiding the many questions concerning its origin, function, and detailed operation. In the three countries I discuss, both the reality and the ideology of separate spheres and of male domination have been very powerful. I consider them paradigm cases of patriarchy.[7] Feminism as a movement toward autonomy exists in such a context.

The few attempts to define early feminism, and the many more attempts to define its contemporary versions, may help us understand why, with few exceptions, feminism has been defined in a way that excludes the majority of women activists of both the present and the past. As the quintessential establishment source of usage, the *Oxford*

---

7. I doubt whether such a thing as a "matriarchy" or a fully egalitarian society has ever existed. In any case, such social systems would have been possible under technological and social conditions that cannot be replicated today, however much we reduce the scale of family, state, or nation.

English Dictionary provides a good starting point; its definitions can usefully be compared with those supplied by the more influential academic analysts of nineteenth- and twentieth-century feminism.

The main text of the original *Oxford English Dictionary* (*OED*), published in 1889, suggests how slowly the word "feminism" became current in English. For the *OED*, "feminism" was "rare" and meant merely "the qualities of females." The dictionary also included the term "womanism," unknown today but then meaning what we might have expected to be called feminism: "Advocacy of or enthusiasm for the rights, achievements, etc. of women." By the time of the 1933 *Supplement*, the *OED* had settled on what is probably the most widely accepted definition even today: "Advocacy of the rights of women (based on the theory of the equality of the sexes)." Janet Radcliffe Richards used a recognizably similar notion in her explicitly commonsensical 1982 book, defining feminism as the belief that "women suffer from systematic social injustice because of their sex" (13–14). Close to the other end of the feminist ideological spectrum, Alison Jaggar employed a different vocabulary for a similar concept: feminists are "all those who seek, no matter on what grounds, to end women's subordination" (1983:5). That identification with such beliefs should be minoritarian and controversial is perhaps an indication of the continuing situation of women. It also indicates that, if common, such a definition is nevertheless incomplete.

A definition focusing on inequality between men and women was cited as standard in 1968 by Aileen Kraditor: she writes of "the theory that women should have political, economic, and social rights equal to those of men" (1970:7). Kraditor's discussion appeared just as a new wave of feminist activity began to come into public view. Her work was widely read and reprinted, and she clearly contributed to the academic use of a definition similar to her own.[8] Looking only at nineteenth-century American suffragists, she found the commonly accepted definition inadequate. At issue was "something more fundamental than any specific set of rights or the sum total of all the rights that men have had." Kraditor suggested that "autonomy" was what women wanted, what was implicit in their organizing to make demands; it was therefore the core of feminism (1970:8).

Kraditor in effect returned to the "feminism" Gordon noted, with its implications about the value of women's self-definition in terms of their distinctive experience. She also echoed the antiquated "womanism" of the original *OED*, including some notion of "enthusiasm" for the "achievements" as well as the "rights" of women. In this account feminism in the sense of equal rights meant, at the same time, both the accepted definition of a wider belief system (a definition Kraditor found

8. Books and reviews published in the 1980s continue to cite Kraditor's analysis (Degler 1980, Deckard 1983, Giddings 1984, Fowler 1986).

inadequate) and also a description more properly limited to the demands made by a particular segment of the movement.

This double meaning of the definition is clear in the *OED Supplement*'s illustrations of the term, which date from 1895 to 1930 and focus on suffragism and women's access to political participation.[9] The examples seem anachronistic; women in Britain were legally full citizens by 1928. The *Supplement*, which traces usage, was in fact recording what the most conspicuous early feminists demanded: political standing, including the vote. This demand expressed at a certain time an underlying philosophy of equal rights for women. Historically, however, the group the original *OED* identified as "womanists" had also demanded political standing—but not on the basis of an entitlement to equality.

We may expect the "equal rights" version of feminism to change as historical and other context changes. None of its successive versions can correspond to the whole of feminism, though they may be thought to do so. The other sort of feminism would also present an incomplete version of feminism, representing it as the whole ideology. Instead of equal rights, however, women would seek a proper appreciation of womanhood in order to have women's achievements and values evaluated positively. Here also their specific demands would vary over time and place.

Like equal rights, this very different ideal fell far short of the basic and inclusive goal of autonomy. In both cases the women activists insisted on women's entitlement to choose their own goals; their demands were no more than partially vitiated by, on the one hand, claiming for women the goals men had reserved for themselves and, on the other, glorifying the roles men had assigned to women. In the early phases of organized feminist activity, the two incomplete versions agreed that enfranchisement was the necessary if perhaps not the sufficient means to achieve their goals. In most countries their coordinated efforts then focused increasingly on the vote, an issue that could be articulated in terms understandable to the media. As a result, suffragism became—and unfortunately remained—the prime example of feminism. Along with it came the philosophy most clearly identified with feminism, that of equal rights. The vote, after all, was a right men already had. And the rhetoric of equal rights was easily assimilated into the commonplace rhetoric of modern politics.

It is not difficult to understand why so many people believed that feminism died when women were enfranchised. Suffragists had persuaded their public that the vote was identical to equal rights; once it was gained, why should feminism continue? Even if feminism also meant the possibility of celebrating and promoting women's own values—and this dimension was largely unrecognized—again the vote had been pre-

9. There is also one charming example of someone being so feminist as to declare George Eliot equal to Thackeray.

sented as *the* necessary precondition. In practice, the public and analysts alike accepted the feminists' explanations of what they were doing. Feminists could hardly complain of such interpretations, which were an implicit recognition of at least some degree of autonomy.

Olive Banks, who has since recorded much of the continuing history of feminism, was prepared in 1964 to state that "feminist movements, if they continue at all today, can only be counted alongside vegetarianism and nudism as bordering on the cult" (Banks and Banks 1964:350). Certainly this was the generally accepted view. Only today are we beginning to recognize that the suffragists did not cease to be feminists. Activist women quickly discovered further changes that were necessary for true autonomy, and these extended as far as constitutional remodeling and world peace. Such issues were clearly not identical to the vote, and very little beyond the Equal Rights Amendment could comfortably be included in the discourse of equality to men. Neither the welfare state nor peace, the overriding concerns of women's groups in the interwar period, could be presented as related to equal treatment of women. The public had every reason to be convinced that feminism no longer existed.

Toward the end of the 1960s a whole range of new feminist groups emerged into public notice. Although second-wave feminism had a substantial equal rights segment, the self-styled women's liberation movement was the most conspicuous agent in formulating the new demands of women. Liberationist arguments did not seem to bear any relation to earlier ones; equal rights could not easily be redefined to include challenges to beauty pageants and to wife-battering. Autonomy was not explicitly recognized as a goal by the liberationists, and the renewed praise of female qualities did not seem to be related to a struggle earlier epitomized by the demand for the vote.

In response to the new women's movement, classifications widened. By 1981 Banks felt obliged to extend the term feminist to include "any groups that tried to *change* the position of women, or the ideas about women" (3), and her *Faces of Feminism* included what little was known about the feminist activities of the interwar and immediate postwar periods. Banks's new definition erred by being too extensive; it could include reactionary, antifeminist groups hoping to remove some of women's newer bases of autonomy, as well as groups with male-only membership. Nevertheless, her interpretation reflected the existence of the women's movement and acknowledged that the notion of feminism must include a range of rationales and of goals. But even those analysts who recognized the "womanist" dimension of postsixties' feminism still failed to understand that it had predecessors and continuity, as well as an underlying commonality with equal rights versions.

And how are we to explain the contemporary proliferation of groups that call themselves feminist in different ways and their insistence on the uniqueness of each set of views? Part of the answer is implied by attempts to define feminism made by another influential historian, Gerda Lerner.

In 1971 Lerner noted the important distinction between what she called "women's rights" ("woman's rights" in its nineteenth-century version) and "emancipation." The first, she said, represented a relatively narrow focus on legal and political equality justified by "appeals to justice and equity" (corresponding to the *OED Supplement*'s definition). "Emancipation" referred to a broader, more inclusive set of goals that she summed up as "self-determination and autonomy." Within this category she included freedom, for both men and women, from the male-dominated and archaic "division of labor" and, for women, "from natural biological restrictions due to sex as well as from socially imposed ones" (237). In this way she incorporated all dimensions of equal rights feminism as well as the goals of those feminist groups which did not see women's political equality as their primary concern. In 1986 she expanded the description of emancipation to include "the freedom to make decisions concerning one's body" as well as financial independence and "freedom to choose one's lifestyle and sexual preference" (236). By implication she included the justifications used by those feminists whose goals she now included within emancipation. "Appeals to justice and equity" are characteristic neither of the Marxist feminists who focus on changing the current division of labor nor of the radical feminists whose goal is to transform of the whole system of patriarchy.

Lerner did not discuss the content of the alternative justifications for emancipation. She also left unexamined the question whether efforts for legal and political equality are inseparable from appeals to "justice and equity." But she made it clear that the encompassing notion of emancipation—autonomy—included a variety of objectives and also, what is not usually noticed, a variety of possible rationales. The practices of second-wave feminism are implied in her formulation: certainly, by 1986 arguments other than justice and equity were being used in support of equality, while arguments invoking justice and equity were being employed in the attempt to end biological and productive servitudes.

In practical terms, as Lerner's description of the different elements of emancipation implies, the separate sorts of feminism divide over what they perceive to be the crucial obstacles to women's autonomy. What they share is the insistence that women identify those obstacles themselves ("self-determination"). Emancipation is the imagined situation when no such obstacles remain, even though feminists disagree about which obstacles will have to be removed. Divisions among feminist groups become more precise and more numerous as groups focus more closely on the areas they feel must be changed: sex roles, the family, capitalism, male values and male dominance, the division of labor, heterosexism, natalism. Each such area generates specific demands, priorities for action, and possibilities of co-operation: abortion, daycare, equal pay for equal work and then for work of equal value, control of pornography, admission of women to skilled trades, lesbian rights and separatism, acceptance of childlessness and celibacy. The separations multiply. Yet underlying all demands and the analyses that justify them, we find the shared impulse for women's self-determination. As Kraditor put it in 1968, "the essential change demanded has always been that women's sphere be defined by women" (1970:8). Lerner's "emancipation" corresponds to this notion and identifies what I call feminism.[10]

The shared goal of autonomy or self-definition is what makes "male feminism" a logical impossibility.[11] Feminism amounts to a demand for freedom from gender-based control. It is not parallel to anything men have had to achieve or could want, and it is not a demand that can be posed by men on women's behalf. In no modern society have any human beings but men delineated men's personal needs, ambitions, and obligations. Depending on the society concerned, each man has more or less freedom to make the relevant decisions. But women as a group have never had authority over adult males in such matters. Many specific feminist goals can be shared by groups of men, who may have achieved them earlier, as in the case of access to education, to employment, and to religious, sexual, and other liberties. But the crucial feminist demand is the abrogation of men's authority and control over women, for it is the demand that defines feminism. One analyst sums up by observing that woman is "a gendered, heterogeneous, and heteronomous subject" (de Lauretis 1986:11).

It is possible, and indeed necessary, for men to support those particular changes which women at specific times identify as important. Women need to form coalitions not just among themselves but also with men. Certainly men may suggest to women the desirability of their having more freedom. Men may act, with or without the co-operation of women, to reduce the barriers to that freedom. But the crucial element in feminism is the effort to identify and eliminate those barriers. Even with the best will in the world, such efforts cannot be carried out by one

10. Unfortunately, her old-fashioned term "emancipation" is too closely related to the suffrage battles to be widely usable; in addition, it implies, restrictively, that the goal is freedom *from* something rather than the freedom of positive empowerment.

11. Ethel Klein notes only the lesser "intensity" of male as compared to female feminism; she attributes the difference to women's feminist consciousness being derived from experience whereas men's is based on intellectual sympathy for feminist ideology (1984:122). But many women also become feminists because of vicarious experience, or intellectual response, or in reaction to conditions other than the strains between work and home. Some men support feminism because of the experience of women with whom they imaginatively identify, their wives or sisters or more likely their daughters. The crucial consideration is the position of men, as compared to that of women, in the structure of gender-based power.

group on behalf of another. Male authority cannot deny its own legitimacy.

Feminist activism has solid, practical reasons not to include men. Men's unthinking assumption of authority over women is an added burden that feminists should not have to sustain. When and how male allies are needed, when and how groups can or should be integrated—these are questions of strategy or even tactics within a given political situation. The Stone-Blackwells and Taylor-Mills are good models: both husbands renounced dominance within their marriages. John Stuart Mill encouraged the suffragists to organize their own groups, giving generously of his expertise and his access to power; Henry Blackwell enabled his wife to return to her feminist tasks and helped when wanted, not when he himself thought best.

A relevant analogy is imperialism and decolonization. The term "women's liberation" applied to women the logic of one particular revolutionary brand of anti-imperialism much as the 1848 Seneca Falls Declaration adopted the rhetoric of an earlier generation. The historian of British imperialism A. P. Thornton made the comparison in more general terms, saying that women have been "colonized" by men. For him, the liberation of women was the "anti-imperialism with the longest future . . . since it seeks to liberate one half of the human race from the colonial rule of the other half" (1979:309).[12] The term "self-determination" applied to both sorts of decolonization; the rulers had difficulty understanding that the issue was authority, not just conditions of life. In both cases, enfranchisement became a crucial symbol, because participation in public policy was the clearest assertion of status. The following passage describes the impact of decolonization, but it could just as appropriately refer to the impact of feminism: "The assertions of the spirited and the ambitions of the nonconformists transferred themselves as practical possibilities into the awareness of at least some of the conformists. . . . Privilege became uneasy and began to blandish. Assertion, once so risky, became more commonplace and took a more truculent form, since it expected to be appeased" (Thornton 1979:309).

If the core of feminism is women's rejection of male direction, its general impulse necessarily is profoundly radical in a patriarchal society, however restrained are the demands made by a particular variant of feminist action. But the variants of feminism certainly differ, and the differences matter if they represent different possibilities of mobilizing women for the essential projects of feminism. What is lacking is a feminist classification of feminism, one that corresponds to women's experience and particularly to their experience in women's organizations.

Because this organizational tradition itself represents generalizable

---

12. Another of Thornton's book titles underlines the relevance to feminism of what he calls "habit of authority" and—not referring to feminism—"paternalism" (1965).

experience, the ideology derived from it has coherence as "a subjectivity that, however diverse its sociohistorical configurations and modes of expression, has come into its own as political consciousness" (de Lauretis 1986:17). On those occasions when feminists feel called upon to describe or justify the divisions among themselves, however, the explanation is not framed in terms of salient issues or desired changes or in terms of other dimensions of women's shared organizational experience. Instead feminists, to the extent they pay attention to such problems, understand themselves to be divided in terms of their analyses of the nature and origins of women's disadvantages. Their typologies are organized in terms of theoretical approaches or frameworks presented as true and therefore likely to produce successful feminist action.

This analysis, I suggest, is a misunderstanding of just what "success" for feminists might be. And success is action itself—autonomy. In relation to feminism, abstract judgments about underlying theory are less important than understanding what sort of logic most effectively produces women's group action. The available analytic groupings of feminism are unhelpful, for they fail to identify the significant bases of women's group action. Although each sort of feminism has mobilized groups of women at some time, as currently defined they do not correspond to any greater or lesser general likelihood that women will become active.

I propose a classification that corresponds roughly to the two strands of belief found over time in diverse discussions of feminism. Two elements of the definitions we have reviewed can also be found in the earliest evidence of how feminists actually justified group action: the activities and views of suffragists. Suffragism has been given quite disproportionate attention in the study of women, probably because it brought women into public view with goals that were recognizably part of "normal" politics. Nevertheless, suffragism serves as a surrogate for feminism, for in every country it has a historical continuity that grows out of previous women's organizations and is inherited by feminist successors. Further, we can see similar patterns in women's groups that were not suffragist, sometimes because of their historical timing, sometimes for other reasons.

Let us begin with the distinction usually made in relation to the suffragists. The American and British feminists who used arguments based on notions of justice and entitlement were referred to as "political feminists," and the others, who used arguments related to women's obligation to provide social services to an extended family, were called "social feminists." Typically, the first sort of feminist concentrated on getting the vote, while the second sort remained active in other social reform activities and groups for which the vote was wanted. This last difference is not an effective basis for classification, however, for considerations of strategy also divided suffragists in all countries. Thus, for example, the American Woman Suffrage Association, headed by Lucy Stone, which is usually seen as oriented toward social action, concentrated on suffrage activity during a period when the National Woman Suffrage Association, committed to equal rights, continued active on such issues as access to the skilled trades (Du Bois 1978; Fowler 1986). In analytic terms, however, there was a key dividing line among suffragists which corresponds to the distinctions evident in the very earliest English definitions: a demand for equality versus an insistence upon the worth of women's experience and values. Underlying each major category were beliefs about the similarities of women and men and about the value and appropriate role of women's distinctive qualities or experiences.

The terminology is unsatisfactory, and I see no solution other than neologism. I propose to identify two strands of feminism, which reach from the origins of the movement into the present and the future: *equity feminism* and *social feminism*. These are identifications in terms of the belief systems of organizations, which can also be seen as either equity feminist or social feminist groups.

The original contrast between political and social feminists is both inaccurate and unfortunate. All of the suffragists were political because they were concerned with issues of power and public policy. All of them were also political in the more conventional sense that they were involved in pressure-group activities and concerned with electoral outcomes. To restrict the term to those who used existing public rhetoric is to trivialize all other feminists and particularly the social feminists. "Social" feminism in turn is unsatisfactory because of its echoes of "socialist" and of "social" in the sense of leisure activities ("social drinking," "socializing" in the nonacademic sense). The suggestion of collectivism (socialism) is inaccurate, though all feminist activists have necessarily had to turn to state action for support against the power of individual patriarchs. The second echo is even more unfortunate, because it seems to support the notion of middle-class women motivated toward feminism in the nineteenth century because of their increased leisure: feminism as an alternative to sewing circles or bridge (Conway 1971). Most important of all, "social" seems to remove feminism from the realm of deliberate public policy and change. In general, our tradition of political theorizing understands society as prior to and separate from the organized state. Society often means merely the family and, in any case, the private as opposed to the public aspects of human life. Social feminism in fact had its major impact in helping erode that public/private boundary—but the very term denies the importance of such effects.

Yet the term is worth retaining precisely because the social feminists' argument was implicitly for the integration of the social and the political, the movement of women into the public sphere in the extension of their domestic role. The arguments of obligation and duty they presented were indeed new for public life. This novelty does not mean that such arguments were consequently inferior or irrelevant.[13]

The sort of "political" feminism which made the vote a direct symbol of equality has most often been called an "equal rights" feminism. When the reference is to nineteenth-century American suffragists, the term sometimes becomes "women's rights" with the same meaning (Lerner 1979, Hole and Levine 1971, Freeman 1975, Gelb and Palley 1982).[14] The term fits into the Anglo-American tradition of natural rights, as identifying the logical goal of those feminists who were convinced that women are or could be essentially like men, at least in all publicly rele- vant respects. With this tradition are associated the arguments of justice and fairness characteristic of this sort of feminism.

But equal rights feminism is highly specific in terms of time and place. In Barbara Berg's definitions of feminism in early nineteenth-century America, for example, feminism, at least at its origins, was "a broad movement embracing numerous phases of women's emancipation" (1978:5). This excellent general description, however, is then reduced to culture-bound specifications: "The freedom to decide her own destiny; freedom from sex-determined roles; freedom from society's oppressive restrictions; freedom to express her thoughts fully and to convert them freely to actions. Freedom demands the acceptance of woman's rights to individual conscience and judgments" (1978:5). This individualistic con- tent for "women's emancipation" fits Jacksonian America reasonably well, though it fits the United States of the 1960s even better; but it does not correspond to the views of many of the American suffragists who, Berg consequently mourned, had discarded the true core of feminism. Berg's basic description does, however, undercut male domination: "With autonomy the leitmotif of the many varied demands, the femi- nism that evolved . . . encompassed numerous phases of women's free- dom" (268).

The individualist natural rights tradition needs careful reinterpreta- tion if it is to apply to women (see Wolgast 1980, Midgely and Hughes 1983). Moreover, a feminism based on women's similarity to men can be imagined in traditions very different from that of natural rights. In a collectivist society or one based on a notion of a natural hierarchy of abilities and needs, arguments based on women's resemblances to men could be both feminist and profoundly radical without invoking notions of individual entitlement. Plato's female guardians can be reinterpreted

---

13. Dolores Hayden objects to the related distinction between "women who worked on public, or social issues, [and] those who worked on private, or family, issues" (Hayden 1981:4). She sees her subjects, whom she calls "material feminists," as "at the ideological center of the feminist movement," and she notes that in their campaigns "votes, higher education, jobs, and trade unions for women were demanded in the name of extending and protecting, rather than abolishing, women's domestic sphere" (1981:5).

14. Olive Banks uses "equal rights" and "women's rights" interchangeably (1981). I have previously used the term "equal rights feminist," but I am now convinced it is too narrow.

in just such a way, and Plato could not be more remote from a commitment to natural or equal rights (Vlastos 1978). In any place or time a collectivist society would see little value in the notion with which Berg ends the passage just quoted: "[feminism] postulates that woman's essential worth stems from her common humanity and does not depend on the other relationships of her life" (1978:5). In fact, such a society might well see relationships as the most important dimension of the life of all human beings.

Hence I opt for the new term *equity feminism*, drawing on Joyce Gelb's and Marion Lief Palley's discussion of the contemporary women's movement in the United States (1982). Of the many different goals of the women's movement, they note, some could be labeled "role equity" because they seem to "extend rights now enjoyed by other groups . . . to women," while role change appears to "produce change in the dependent female role of wife, mother, and homemaker, holding out the potential of greater sexual freedom and independence in a variety of contexts" (Gelb and Palley:7, 8). Role change, they believe, is more likely to encounter resistance and is also more important.[15]

Shifting the focus to the beliefs of feminist groups and away from the likely or perceived consequences of their actions, I borrow the term "equity" to identify all of the many feminisms that wish to "extend rights now enjoyed by other groups . . . to women." I include under equity feminism the many demands for equivalent status for women in societies that do not formulate their beliefs in terms of rights. Some equity demands are formulated by women's groups explicitly demanding role change; all equity groups are implicitly claiming a change of roles, since it is not part of the female role to band together to change women's status even in the direction of equality. What I call social feminism would fit into the category of role extension if such a term existed. Its arguments extrapolate from the accepted domestic role of women. Of course, because these arguments were made by organized groups of women, initially at a time when organized public activity by women was not accepted, in practical terms they represent role change, an adoption of activities not usually accepted as appropriate for women. But they can be presented and perceived as simply a maintenance of the status quo, since they rely on arguments (about male/female differences) that are

15. The distinction between role equity and role change is not as unproblematic as the authors assume. Not all observers agree that the domestic role is perceived as dependent. Nor is it obvious that sexual freedom is the most relevant area of autonomy. Moreover, the perception of the effects of reform is not as unambiguous as is assumed. The most prominent reform justified by role equity arguments—the vote—was widely perceived by contemporaries as likely to produce role change. In any case, it seems logically necessary to add a third category, with some such label as the clumsy "role extension," in order to refer to goals whose achievement would in fact produce role change because the implied extension was so great as to change the nature of the original activity. Here we move from how feminism is perceived to how it works.

anything but novel. The women making these arguments can be untroubled by accusations that they advocating anything as radical as role change. If they are sufficiently careful about style and pace in their efforts, they can get agreement from their main audience, the men of their society.

I shall not be looking at the circumstances under which social feminists produced hostility and resistance from those who in some way recognized the radical impact of their activities. My interest, rather, is in how such beliefs served to mobilize women and to move them into the practical carrying-out of political activities. I retain the term "social feminism" on the assumption that all the societies we know accept the distinctiveness of a social (domestic, nonpolitical) female role. I shall show through the three groups discussed in this volume how the extension of that role could work, with similar arguments, in very different political and cultural systems.

A similar study could be made of equity feminisms, showing how within societies as diverse as fundamentalist Islam, traditional Judaism, and German fascism, as well as the liberal-democratic societies previously studied, equity arguments have fueled feminism. Such a study would, I believe, also show that equity feminism has little impact in societies that do not have a tradition of individual rights and citizen action. I shall show, in passing, something about the limits of this sort of feminism even in societies relatively hospitable to it. But my main focus is on social feminism as a mobilizer of women and as the creator of a political role for them—tasks difficult to achieve even in those societies least hostile to women's activism.

It is understandable why those who studied the suffragists and their successors divided them into two categories. But we must still wonder why they dismissed one of the versions and why they criticized the other in ways they usually did not criticize their equity sources. For answers to these questions I now turn to analysts who established the tradition, small as it is, of interpretation of the beliefs of actual feminists.

CHAPTER 2

Traditions of
Analyzing Feminism

Writing in the middle of the 1960s, Aileen Kraditor first established
the assumption that feminism had no ideology, only "ideas" whose best
explanation is the personal and tactical needs of a specific group of
women.[1] She also established the notion that "justice" and "expediency"
define two different varieties of feminists. The first sort emphasizes "the
ways in which men and women were identical" and "based their demand
for political equality with men on the same ground as that on which their
men had based their demand for political equality with their English
rulers two generations before" (1981:44). Her description delineated the
elements of equity feminism: similarities or identities between men and
women and the direct application of arguments from mainstream theories. The American setting made this a natural rights or equal rights
feminism because of the individualistic arguments used about entitlement.

The "other" feminists were initially described as focusing on the ways
in which "woman suffrage would benefit society" (1981:45n.). Although
logic required that Kraditor notice social feminists' insistence on female
differences from males, she did not refer to that insistence in defining
their belief system. As a description of their suffragism, "expedient" has
a double meaning. First, the vote itself was sought as a tool for the
service of others rather than as a means of self-advancement. For Kraditor, service of others, characteristic of women, was inferior to the self-
advancement characteristic of men or at least of American men. In
addition, Kraditor argued that, for some of the suffrage leaders, "the
link of woman suffrage to reform seemed the best way to secure support

1. Kraditor's study, first published in 1965, showed no awareness of the beginnings of
second-wave feminism; in a 1981 reissue she added some introductory remarks that explicitly dissociate her from intending any "contribution to a cause" (Kraditor 1981:v). Her
work is a striking contrast to Constance Rover's 1967 study of the British movement.
Rover, who had been a militant suffragist, treated the suffrage campaigns as rational
political activities (Spender 1983).

30

for their principal goal: the vote. To these women the expediency argument was itself an expedient" (45). The second meaning implied that equal rights arguments were not expedient (instrumental), even though they also were intended to be persuasive and could be expected to be effective in a political culture based on a theory of equal rights. Kraditor's analysis was the start of a pattern of disparaging considerations of political effectiveness among feminists and another pattern of preferring imputed motives to those stated by the activists themselves. The scholars who adopted her distinctions incorporated their derogatory implications, together with the assumption that only equal rights feminism was authentic.[2]

Paradoxically, Kraditor's influential criticisms transformed social feminism into an equity version. When she did note social feminist insistence on the importance of women's differences from men, she interpreted it as a claim to domination. Hers was in part a simple inversion of that aspect of the "separate spheres" arguments which had been used to restrict women's activities. Conventionally, men were assumed to have the superior capacities that justified their ruling women. Reversed, patriarchy would become matriarchy, as hierarchical as its alternative; it would represent a change in personnel but would have nothing distinctive or valuable to offer public life. Surely the suffrage leaders realized that most women were ignorant and conventional but that they themselves were exceptional and entitled to a commanding position? If this was how the social feminists really felt, then their claims for women were equivalent to claims for a female share in the elite, possibly even an all-female elite. Their underlying attitude must have been disdain for the masses, whatever their sex. Kraditor saw such an elitism as increasingly characteristic of American Progressives in the late nineteenth and early twentieth centuries. In her interpretation, expediency or social feminism thus became the appropriation by women of the more unpleasant arguments of a declining American Progressivism.

This analysis ignored the statements of the social feminists that their claim to a hearing was based not on superior force or even on superior intelligence but on different values based on different experience. Their only advantage was a moral one that contradicted accepted notions of political power. At the center of these values was denial of the very desirability of control, competition, and hierarchy in favor of morally based persuasion. In a related analysis, scholars have accepted suffragist statements about feminine virtue as sincere but see them as an acceptance of self-limitations that crippled from the start any project of social change (Elshtain 1981). Like Kraditor, they find implausible the social feminist claim that social change is possible through the distinctive

2. When Sylvia Ann Hewlett, in 1986, wished to praise social feminism, she could find no tradition of it in the United States.

modes of female culture. Instead of seeing such feminists as deliberately misleading their audiences, however, they interpret the process as self-deception and a rejection of any possibility of social change.

In Kraditor's analysis of the social feminist arguments that votes for American women were desirable because they would counterbalance those of the recently enfranchised black and foreign males, she took the accusations even further, accusing social feminists of being not just elitist but also racist and xenophobic. These serious charges have been widely accepted, most damagingly by black feminists (Giddings 1984, Hooks 1984). The actual lives of the accused social feminists cast doubt on this interpretation, however. Although Henry Blackwell made the earliest and most notorious "counterbalance" statement, he and his wife, Lucy Stone, entered public life as abolitionists and were leaders of the suffrage faction that supported the abolitionist Fifteenth Amendment in spite of its omission of woman suffrage; Stone and Blackwell also quarreled with equity feminists Elizabeth Cady Stanton and Susan B. Anthony over the latter's association with the racism of George F. Train (Wheeler 1981:222–25). Suffragists genuinely believed that women's particular qualities would be a change for the better from the characteristics shared by men of all races, classes, and ethnicities. By definition, they had already rejected domination by their male counterparts who were like them in terms of race and class.[3] Even the more bigoted among them believed that enfranchised black, working-class, and immigrant women would to some degree offset their men. Given their political sophistication, the most serious charge against those making the counterbalance argument is that they knew how it would be understood by the elitists, racists, and xenophobes among the men who would decide on the enfranchisement of women.[4]

Kraditor's comments about exclusion related, however, most specifically to the suggestion made by some suffragists that a literacy requirement be added to the qualifications for voting. Such policies resonate unpleasantly with the disenfranchisement of freedmen in the South by discriminatory tests allegedly based on qualifications such as education. As Kraditor pointed out, an English literacy test could also be expected to exclude many newly enfranchised working-class, foreign-born males. Yet the suffragists themselves put significant energy into the cause of literacy and elementary and civic education; the very women Kraditor condemned, such as Carrie Chapman Catt, were later to be deeply in-

3. Barbara Berg (1978:250–51) has explicitly challenged Kraditor's assertions of the class biases of the bulk of the suffragists.

4. There were, of course, undeniable bigots among the Southern suffragists, but Kate Gordon of Louisiana and Laura Clay of Kentucky, leaders of the Southern white-supremacy suffragists, have never had a place in the suffragist pantheon. What is at issue here is an underlying reactionary element in the views of usually revered suffrage leaders, especially those who were social feminists. Suffrage leaders certainly tolerated, for tactical reasons, segregated suffrage groups.

volved in the voter education projects of the League of Women Voters. There is an irony here: in later years the League, as successor to the suffragists, was to be criticized for focusing on voter education instead of partisan politics.

In any case, it is possible to give credence, as Kraditor did not, to the commitment of the social feminists to an expanded electorate of educated voters. The urban political machines that exploited new ethnic voters were part of the environment of the suffrage campaigns; the New York State referendum on women's suffrage was won only when Tammany Hall stood aside. The suffragists had seen ignorant voters manipulated by party machines, most damagingly in the Kansas constitutional campaign of 1867 (Peck 1944; Rossi 1973:430–70). The social feminists meant what they said. They were rejecting not change itself but accepted ways of producing it. Such a context alters our understanding of the feminists' self-imposed limits. For instance, they often denied interest in holding office—not for them the reputation-oriented search for a monopoly over the use of force. Nor did they find partisan politics appealing. But they were not renouncing influence or the expectation of change. The newest of feminist analyses have begun to take seriously these women's beliefs that nonauthoritarian methods of influencing public policy might exist and that ambition is not the only basis for commitment to what is often called the "public service" (Flammang 1984a).

Kraditor was hampered by lack of sympathy with the perspective of the social feminists, who trusted women voters more than men and literate voters more than the illiterate. In part because most of her successors have had the same failure of imagination, she generated a lasting image of the social feminists as mere adjuncts of the men of their own class and ethnicity, more or less knowingly using spurious arguments to cover their own elitism, racism, and nativism. Neither gender nor education is, it seems, an acceptable criterion for a political role.

This first analysis of the ideas of the American suffragists also contributed the persistent interpretation that an "expedient" move away from equal rights feminism was a suffragist decline from the high standards of those who had earlier used arguments based on justice. The social feminists were thus criticized, by Kraditor and those following her, not only for serving class interests but for another sort of expediency. They allegedly abandoned feminist and progressive values in the search for political allies—a search mistakenly focused on conservative soulmates. Even within the male bourgeois establishment of presuffrage days, there were relatively progressive elements who might have been expected to respond to equal rights arguments. These, Kraditor was the first but not the last to suggest, the social feminists ignored, to join instead with those groups who opposed social change. Here the issue is not implicit racism and class bias but an interpretation of social feminism itself as, deliberately or not, showing an affinity to conservativism. Arguments based on female values are themselves labeled conservative and, again, seen as either mistaken or hypocritical. Social feminism, because its logic is instrumental, is made to appear particularly liable to compromising alliances. That the vote was won by social feminist arguments is the clinching proof, for how could the vote have been won except by appealing to ignoble elements in an ignoble public? The conclusion follows that gains made possible by the vote were already fatally compromised by social feminism's doctrine and allies. By contrast, equity feminism is seen as pure and progressive, untainted by political expediency—or success.

This interpretation was plausible for Kraditor because she believed that equity feminism characterized the early days of the feminist activism but was uninfluential in the later stages of the suffrage campaigns. This view, still widely accepted, cannot survive a careful look at the American setting of suffragism. To begin with, the suggestions about political alliances are patently absurd. All feminists were influenced by the need to seek support from men hostile to everyone except other men like themselves: all politicians and all voters were men, and they alone could decide on suffrage legislation and constitutional amendments. The most painful and disappointing suffrage negotiations were with the Republican abolitionists after the Civil War and with the National Labor Union a short time later. Both social and equity feminists attempted these alliances, and both found that in respect to woman suffrage the "progressive" Republicans and the labor movement were in practice as conservative as their opponents (DuBois 1978). Worldwide, truly conservative forces have only rarely supported feminist efforts.[5]

Belief in the conservatism of the suffrage movements as organized groups has, in fact, had less impact than the rest of Kraditor's argument. It is in a related tradition, interpreting the political behavior of individual women voters as conservative, that Kraditor's interpretation has been most damaging, for she is believed to have established that the struggle for the vote—usually, incorrectly, seen as women's earliest political action—was conservative. That conservatives often failed to recognize this alleged affinity has no impact on the argument. Again, the basis for the imputation is an incomplete analysis of feminism in the United States. The alleged contrasts and discontinuities of American equity and social feminism diminish when examined more carefully in the context of the American political tradition. There can be no doubt that many American suffragists wished for change in women's roles and saw political rights as constituting such change. Nevertheless, their demands were couched in terms of equal rights and were thereby located squarely

5. Richard Evans (1977) argues the opposite, but what he labels "conservative" is most often a welfarist or social purity element; his account demonstrates repeatedly the disinclination of "progressive" forces to support women's enfranchisement.

within the established tradition of political discourse. Louis Hartz has established how relatively radical values could, in "fragment" America, be espoused by conservatives (1955). Equal rights suffragists were able to use a familiar set of doctrines that counteracted any impression of female appropriation of nondomestic roles. As for social feminists, the use of acceptable, explicitly domestic arguments masked possible radical implications. A combination of the two sorts of arguments, with social feminist statements accompanying equity ones, was the most persuasive of all to men raised in the American political tradition. It was both genuine and expedient in various positive senses.

The two sorts of feminist rationale did in fact coexist, both in individual suffragists and within the suffrage movement. It is not the case that social feminist arguments became important only late in the suffrage struggle, in response to changed attitudes or as concessions to some perceived political necessity. The 1848 Seneca Falls Declaration of Sentiments, the movement's first public document, was a deliberate adaptation of the Declaration of Independence and therefore the preeminent example of equity feminism. But the accompanying resolutions included large and significant doses of social feminism, as did the assembly's debates. Resolution Ten gave the clearest possible statement of equity feminism in an American context: "That the equality of human rights results necessarily from the fact of the identity of the race in capabilities and responsibilities" (quoted in Rossi 1973:419). Even here we should note the claim for responsibilities along with capabilities. Resolution Three supported the statement "That woman is man's equal" by a social feminist assertion that "the highest good of the race demands that she should be recognized as such" (418). Even more important, on the crucial issue of the double standard of sexual behavior, the demand was not for women's (equity) right to do as men do but that men should be required to act as virtuously as women. Women's standards were to be applied, and men were to be punished like them for "the same transgressions." In addition, the right of women to "speak and teach . . . in all religious assemblies" was justified by women's "moral superiority." The controversial demand for the vote was indeed described as a "right," but women were told it was their "duty" to obtain it (418). Although discussions concerning the franchise were set within the overall equal rights frame of the meeting, some speakers argued—expediently—that asking for enfranchisement would make feminists appear either foolish or radical, hindering their pursuit of other change. The persuasive points were social feminist in their focus on the purposes for which women, as contrasted to men, would use their votes.[6]

6. The convention was not centrally suffragist, though it marks the beginning of the suffrage battles in the United States; as a result, like many other activities of the early feminists, it has had little careful analysis.

The continuing impact of Kraditor's distinctions and judgments has been quite remarkable,[7] but the selective interpretation of "social" and other feminists owes more to William O'Neill, who influentially adopted many of Kraditor's ideas.[8] It was O'Neill who termed "social feminists" those women who "while believing in women's rights, generally subordinated them to broad social reforms they thought more urgent." For him, the contrasting group was the women he identified as "hard-core," "extremist," or "extreme" feminists, those "chiefly interested in women's rights" (1971:x). He was less concerned with the two groups' ideas than in their specific programs for reform, for he did not consider that either version had an ideology.

Writers on feminism in the 1980s still accept and cite O'Neill as authoritative, incorporating Kraditor's distinctions in the process even though analyses focusing on the years after suffrage have recently become more sensitive about the multiplicity of successor groups (Cott 1987; Rupp and Taylor 1987). Carl Degler, for instance, adopted O'Neill's terminology and identified Eleanor Roosevelt as a "social feminist" while stating that "she asserted no feminist ideology or outlook" (1980:438). He was one of many to quote approvingly a key passage from O'Neill: "The chief feature of social feminism was that it created roles for women that militated against their full emancipation. Their benevolent enterprises met women's desire for useful and satisfying work without touching the sources of their inequality. It was in this sense an all too rational accommodation to the needs of its participants" (O'Neill 1971:143).[9] In 1986 O'Neill himself reasserted the same evaluation, centering it once again on the absence of explicit ideology among the successful social feminist leaders of the suffrage movement: "Ironically, because feminist leaders made suffrage a substitute for feminist theory and ascribed to it benefits it manifestly lacked, gaining the vote helped put an end to feminism" (109).

7. Kraditor's widely used anthology (1970) reiterated the distinction between justice and expediency, starting the latter section with selections on "racism and xenophobia enlisted in the cause of woman suffrage" (253–65).

8. *Everyone Was Brave* was first published in 1969 with the elegiac subtitle "The Rise and Fall of the Women's Movement in America." It was reissued in paperback two years later, reflecting the impact of the second wave of feminism with its new subtitle, "A History of Feminism in America." In his new "Afterword" the author expressed his surprise at the survival of feminism. And he thanked "my wife Carol [who] did not help me write this book. Instead she gave me love, happiness, and two beautiful daughters, for all of which I am grateful beyond words" (1971:xi).

9. In 1982 Nancy Cott again used Kraditor's concepts to question the identification of New Deal activists such as Eleanor Roosevelt and Molly Dewson as feminists on the grounds that "social welfare took first place among their concerns." The criterion of feminism was "to challenge explicitly the stereotype of woman's place at home" (898). Reviewing books written about women in the 1930s, she notes "for the professional and educated stratum . . . a change in vision rooted in the Depression experience. That change—to call on the language used by Aileen S. Kraditor to describe an evolution in suffrage ideology—was one from 'justice' to 'expediency' in arguing for women's due" (1982:900).

Where was feminist theory to be found? Not among even the equal rights feminists, for O'Neill as a socialist urged feminists to adopt an appropriately adapted socialism:

> Extreme [equity] feminists were too emotional to appreciate the logic of their situation. Social feminists lacked the motivation to undertake a radical analysis of the woman question. They had, after all, resolved their own problems by becoming reformers. They therefore enjoyed all the freedom they could use and, except for the ballot, were essentially satisfied with their status. Those who required socialism were incapable of understanding it, and those who were best able to appreciate it had no need for it (1971:144).

This analysis amounts to an endorsement of equity feminism—of the right sort. It makes clear the importance of distinguishing equal rights versions of equity feminism from other derivations of mainstream theory.

Two other persistent themes in the analysis of feminism are present in the quotation: the insistence on an "objective" logic of women's situation which is more compelling than women's own perceptions or preferences, and the attribution of women's preferences to their individual or class-related situation, with a subtext interpreting feminism as therapy. Especially when articulated by a man, these themes constitute a denial of the legitimacy of feminism's basic goal, women's self-determination. Together, such interpretations deny that women can rationally evaluate a political situation or that they can evolve any group interest based on gender.

In its most benevolent version, such a view attributes women's lack of political capacity to their better nature. It is ironic to see O'Neill, who regards himself as progressive, even feminist in his views about women, echoing the restrictive assumptions of the most conservative notions about women's nature. The perspective then shades over into disapproval of those women who did undeniably demonstrate political competence. For instance, O'Neill admires Florence Kelley, a social feminist and a major figure in the interwar movement; the epigraph for his book, the source of its title, was a statement by another feminist that "Everybody was brave from the moment [Kelley] came into the room." But Kelley was also a former socialist who had been one of the translators of Marx, and O'Neill was not praising her when he wrote that she was "drawn away [from socialism] by the practical urgencies of reform" (145). At the same time, he liked the social feminists: they were nice, womanly women, warm-hearted and practical. It was a shame, he felt, that the characteristics that led them, foolishly, to reject socialism also drove them to participate in mainstream politics in an inappropriate way. Carrie Chapman Catt, who led the suffrage forces to victory, comes in for the heaviest criticism, for having been too rational and pragmatic and "having made feminism too much like another interest group, trading a principle here for an advantage there" (126). Catt, according to O'Neill, should have listened to her heart more and her head less—been more feminine? less successful? or just more socialist?

Equity feminists, in contrast, were "self-destructive," neurotic, ineffective, even harmful to feminism (as in the interwar conflicts over the Equal Rights Amendment). Nevertheless, for O'Neill as for many others, Alice Paul, their leader, "cannot but inspire admiration" (129). Equity feminists get the greater praise, however grudgingly, while social feminists receive only the condescending tribute that "the subjective consequences of social feminism were very good indeed" and "the women themselves were better" for it (354). In both cases, the assessment is in personal terms, and the women closer to the personal or ideological styles of normal radical politics receive more praise.

Most seriously, social feminism is blamed for destroying the radical potential of feminism in America. O'Neill insisted that the bourgeois family was the key to women's subjection and that women who failed to diagnose it as such were less than true feminists. The test was not what women believed but what the "progressive" elements of mainstream politics decreed: the recipe for equity feminism. When Degler followed O'Neill to define the central problem of feminism as "the recognition and the realization of women's individuality in work" (1980:471), he too was recommending to feminists the priorities of radical and socialist politics. The combination of American individualism and socialist emphases on paid labor as the arena for liberation was certainly not accepted by all feminists, as their own statements make clear. But the most authoritative commentators on feminism have denied feminists' ability to articulate their own wishes or condemned them for expressing goals not derived from established theories.

More recently, Barbara Deckard explicitly relies on Kraditor for analysis of the suffragists and extends the definitions to the interwar period. Social feminists are accused of having "largely ignored the two areas of labor and family relations" (1983:266).[10] The author thus blithely disregards her own earlier discussions of the work of the Women's Trade Union League and both Lucy Stone's and Elizabeth Cady Stanton's ideas about the status of women in the family. In this example, once social feminists have been dismissed, the equity feminists get equally short shrift, for they also are analyzed in terms of their "objective" needs for access to education and protection of property, achieved by American feminists by the middle of the nineteenth century. As a result, they "mainly wanted formal equality with men in the Constitution" (266). Even Alice Paul is condemned because her unrelenting concentration on

10. *The Women's Movement: Political, Socioeconomic, and Psychological Issues* has gone into three paperback editions.

women's rights (in response to her own class interest) prevented feminist coalitions with the progressive forces of the American Left. This is O'Neill's point: that feminists should have understood that they belonged with the socialists. Deckard accepts his assessment in spite of her recognition that social feminist concerns about work and the family focused not on status but on the implications of women's reproductive role. Social feminists were therefore necessarily concerned with issues that could not be dealt with in equity terms.[11]

A persistent theme in the analysis of feminism after and following O'Neill is the attribution of irrationality and failure to the decision of so many feminists to avoid the embrace of leftist parties and groups in favor of their own autonomous organizations. Such arguments overlook the fact that the reformist or revolutionary socialist movements that formally supported the "woman question" gave no concrete priority to women's own formulations of their concerns, mainly because of the difficulty of conceptualizing women as a class or classlike group that could then have class consciousness. Yet in the context even of politically marginal groups such as socialist parties in North America, analysts persist in blaming feminists for attempting political independence. The feminist analysis of women's situation is rejected as ineffective (or too effective), unguided by a correct ideological assessment (so not ideological at all), and just plain wrong. Equity applications of socialism are acceptable; other feminist ideologies are not.

The accumulated tradition of analysis of feminist organizations, ideas, and campaigns which stems from Kraditor's and O'Neill's work was synthesized by Olive Banks in 1981. Banks drew on published materials to compare the historical development of the women's movement in the United States and in Britain, accepting newly developed views about a continuing tradition of feminist organizations and, above all, feminist thought. For her, feminism had a number of "faces" resulting from the interplay between three "intellectual traditions" and a variety of political and personal situations. In other words, she saw all feminism as equity feminism. She thereby rehabilitated social feminism but at the cost of denying it any autonomous standing or coherence. In the process, she also demonstrated the extraordinary ethnocentrism of accepted accounts of the development of women's activism.

Banks defined feminism in terms of English intellectual history, as

---

11. Deckard dismissed social feminist arguments about male-female differences or the value of women's experiences as "Victorian sexist stereotypes," which the suffragists both accepted and used as arguments because "they felt that it was not 'natural' for women to work or to be equal in the family" (1983:266). In general, her discussion, with its scornful quotation marks and its dismissal of contemporary context, denies social feminists the ability to develop a coherent justification and program of social change.

deriving from evangelical Christianity, "the Enlightenment," and utopian, communitarian socialism.[12] Like O'Neill, she saw the personal characteristics and situations of the feminists as providing any necessary resid-
ual explanation of particular feminist groups or campaigns: Elizabeth
Cady Stanton had an unsatisfactory marriage, and both Charles James
Fox and John Stuart Mill could have benefited from more liberal divorce
laws. Citing Kraditor, Banks saw the feminists of the later nineteenth
century as more conservative; like her source, she attributed this shift to
both the need to find middle-class allies and "their own attitudes" (59).

The most important part of Banks's account was her firm insistence
that both the doctrines and the organizational origins of feminism were
to be sought solely within the belief systems and mixed-sex organizations
that preceded them. In this context, she used O'Neill's term "social feminism," renaming it "welfare feminism" and making it into an equity
adaptation of ideas central to evangelicalism. Notions of the moral superiority of women, she explained, represented the extension to women of
the vocation of community service, a role that in its origins was not sex-
specific at all. The "reforming zeal" of social feminism "sprang directly
from the spirit of the evangelical revival anxious not only to save souls
but also, and in a sense even more importantly, to destroy sin" (46). Such
an interpretation ruled out social feminism in any but an Anglo-American cultural context, and above all it denied any autonomy to feminism
or its beliefs. Related explanations locked feminism, in institutional
terms, into the reform movements of the nineteenth century.

Banks presented the account of the development of the organized
women's movement that women's historians generally accepted at the
end of the 1970s. In this interpretation, feminism existed prior to the
nineteenth century only in the form of the beliefs of isolated individuals
such as Christine de Pisan and, later, Mary Wollstonecraft. The nineteenth century produced a few, relatively isolated socialist feminists as
well as individuals who espoused theories of individual rights. In addition, it produced the women's reform groups that eventually became in
one way or another suffragist. The process was spelled out precisely: it
began with religious revival, which both motivated and legitimated wom-
en's participation in mixed-sex charitable or pressure activities. These
reform groups then turned to abolition of slavery, using equal rights
arguments about race next applied by women to themselves. At this
point they became feminists and left male-dominated reform groups to
form their own, equal rights groups. They thus learned to serve their

12. Banks's book was mainly a summary of the field, but she added some interpretations
of her own, particularly an emphasis on the evangelical rather than simply Protestant
dimension of the influential religious tradition and an attempt to take the socialist tradition
back before Marx and Engels without denying the role of contemporary Marxist feminists.
Here she followed other English analysts, reflecting English experience. She found the
Enlightenment influence in ideas about equality, equal rights, and the application of
rationality to politics and to reform—equity feminism in its equal rights version.

own instead of others' interests and eventually become suffragist. They selfishly abandoned original reform goals in favor of women's rights; those goals reappeared only as part of an "expedient" strategy to get the vote (Rossi 1973: 248–50). Kraditor's sequence of justice to manipulation was central, as was O'Neill's reinforcing disapproval of the techniques and issues characteristic of the social feminists.

The sequence described what happened to feminists in both Britain and the United States, and it fitted equity feminists better than social feminists. It was thoroughly misleading as a generalized account of the development of feminist groups internationally. Solid evidence now opposes the suggested sequences of equity and social feminism even in England and the United States. Most often, for both individuals and groups, equity and social feminism went hand in hand, with social feminism preceding and outlasting the equity version and the two reinforcing each other. A case in point is the agitation led by Josephine Butler against the Contagious Diseases Acts in Britain. Here equity feminism insisted on the right of women to be exempt, like men, from unreasonable searches; it joined and reinforced a religious conviction of women's superior moral vocation and obligation. These beliefs also produced an extraordinary practice of sisterhood between middle-class activists and prostitutes, a sisterhood familiar from Berg's analysis of benevolent and charitable reform in the United States (Boyd 1982, Uglow 1983, Forster 1985).

Even for Britain and the United States, as Banks noted, there are problems of timing for her theory that evangelicalism had the major responsibility for social feminism: the appearance of women's charitable and reform groups sometimes preceded religious revival. If feminism was limited to equity or suffrage groups, of course, the problem does not arise, since such groups appear only later in the nineteenth century. But if we look at the origins of even these latter groups, we often discover founding organizations that did not in any simple sense have evangelical roots, such as the Langham Place Group, whose role as an employment agency Banks had difficulty in explaining. We also find earlier women's organizations that never transformed themselves into equity feminism and that did not have their origins in mixed-membership reform organizations.

Banks's analysis, derived from work on English groups, made it clear how the peculiarities of feminism in specific countries have shaped analysis of the women's movement in general. Her emphasis on evangelicalism did not fit well with American feminism, although she argued that the Great Awakening and Quakerism performed the same function in North America. Both evangelical and Quaker milieux were relatively supportive of feminism, as is indicated by the disproportionate representation of members among the founders of the women's movements in Britain and North America. But the logic of Quaker women's assertive role was one of difference and separate spheres, based on an established tradition of single-sex groups. There is no Quaker history of women's revolt into feminism (Dunn 1979); the celebrated Grimké sisters were adult converts to Quakerism, as Banks herself noted (21). Thus feminist women's groups did not always grow out of mixed-sex organizations. Nor did the ideology of social feminism derive from radical Protestantism in the way in which equity feminism grew out of utopian socialism or the Rights of Man.

These transmitted interpretations show their limits most clearly when an attempt is made to extrapolate from them. Banks asked naively why France had been "characterized by the absence of a feminist movement"; she wondered why the Enlightenment tradition and utopian socialism, both French in origin, should have had so little influence on French feminism (262).[13] But other, indigenous traditions had in fact created distinctive forms of feminism in nineteenth-century France. Protestant feminists such as Maria Deraismes (and later Cécile Brunschvicg of the Union française pour le suffrage des femmes) were actively anticlerical in orientation, drawing on a Freemason tradition not relevant for British feminists (Brault 1967). The socialists among the French feminists were not utopian socialists, with the major exception of Flora Tristan, but activists within a strong though schismatic socialist movement (Sowerwine 1978). The French social feminists, for their part, had nothing to do with evangelicalism, which was not a French phenomenon, but were associated, in at least one important case, with the reform tradition of social Catholicism. When we know more of the history of feminism in France,[14] we shall be able to work out the influences on it of various indigenous intellectual traditions. But we will not find the Anglo-American variant. Perhaps Banks was unable to recognize feminism in France because it did not fit the pattern she expected.

Even the history of Canadian feminism, far closer to the model Banks summarized, casts doubt on the sequence of development she outlined (see Prentice et al. 1988). Canada did experience an evangelical revival and was also subject, though less than the United States, to the influence of both utopian socialism and Enlightenment equal rights theories. All of these came to Canada relatively late, however, if only because substantial female immigration and settlement came late. It was not until the last

13. In part Banks's account simply reflects paucity of evidence: when she wrote less information was available about French than about British or American feminism. But she could have consulted Alain Decaux's massive popular *Histoire des françaises* (1972), which does refer to feminist groups before World War I and in the interwar period, ending with a long chapter that makes it clear that French feminism began long before 1968. Decaux summarizes parts of the important volumes by Andrée Michel and Geneviève Texier, published as early as 1964; Richard Evans (1977), cited by Banks on other topics, gives a summary of Patrick Bidelman's important dissertation (published in 1982). Banks apparently did not use Bidelman's articles, published in the late 1970s, but even Evans's brief account is informative.

14. As for instance through the research of Stephen Hause and Anne Kenney (1984).

decades of the nineteenth century that Canadian urbanization was sufficiently advanced to provide the urban stimulus that Berg (1978) sees as the immediate cause of the earliest feminist organization in the United States. But in Canada a female tradition of charity and also of "civilizing the wilderness" can be identified well before either religious revival or urbanization (Gorham 1976). The Protestant churches seem to have been important, but not in the same way as elsewhere; here, for instance, the Protestant missionary societies seem to have been important legitimizers of organized female charity on a very large scale (Mitchinson 1979). Similarly, organizations of alumnae seem to have been among the most significant feminist groups in a country where female entry into higher education was rather different from the process in Britain (Mac-Gill 1981). A recent history of the women of Quebec demonstrates yet another pattern of development, in which an early social feminist Catholic impulse was destroyed by a conservative and nationalistic Catholic church (Dumont, Jean, Lavigne, and Stoddart 1982).[15]

France and Canada alone are adequate to cast doubt on the universality of Banks's model.[16] They add weight to the suggestion that an autonomous social feminist ideology generated feminist groups in different countries and at different times. A range of cultures accept for women a charitable and philanthropic vocation, linked to some notion of special capabilities and obligations, in turn linked to the domestic role usually performed by women. Private, individual tasks of charity and social service easily become public, collective ones. A civilizing mission in the wilderness or the city, the need for national unity, international cooperation as a cure to war, social Catholic designs for a secular city, fear of ecological or nuclear threats—all reinforced the mission, all helped to produce an environment favorable to the action of women's groups. But the belief system antedated them and was largely independent of them.[17]

Banks's reductive analysis interpreted feminist ideology and feminist

15. The Canadian analyst who most explicitly applied O'Neill's analysis to Canadian feminism has now equally explicitly revised her critical judgment of the main current of social feminism (Strong-Boag 1986:189).

16. Studies more ambitious in scope than Banks's continue to be similarly constrained. For instance, in 1977 Richard Evans's study drew together the existing secondary material on feminism in twenty-two countries in Europe, North America, and Australasia. Evans cited O'Neill's definitions only to reject them explicitly on the grounds that "feminism *progressed towards* demanding the vote" (1977:39). Nevertheless, he followed in the pattern established by O'Neill and Kraditor, characterizing the earlier, more appealing stages of feminism by their commitment to equal rights, the later ones by arguments based on moral superiority, leading to racism, xenophobia, and so forth.

17. Five years after Evans, in 1982, after vastly more research had been done, another attempt to survey feminism worldwide reported little more progress in analysis but was able to find social feminism active and distinctive in a variety of ways and settings (Sarah 1982). In this collection, for instance, Forbes's (1982) discussion of Indian feminism showed a set of beliefs that was clearly responsive to Indian ideologies but that strongly emphasized women's specificity.

groups as dependent developments of mainstream reform movements and ideas. Any gap in the resulting explanation was filled in a way characteristic of the literature she was summarizing: by reference to the leisure of the middle-class woman and her need to find an occupation (Conway 1971). Such an interpretation makes feminism an individual response, a hobby. The political activities of middle-class men are never so characterized, even when prosperity and mechanization generate leisure for them. Time-budget studies should by now have destroyed the illusion about the free time available for the mistress of even a well-served household. The lives of the feminists themselves, so often invoked to explain their personal motivation for reform, also argue against such an interpretation. The self-supporting Lucy Stone and Charlotte Perkins Gilman do not fit such a pattern, nor do the difficult achievements of those like Elizabeth Cady Stanton who had large families and extensive household responsibilities. Single women such as Anna Howard Shaw or widows such as Emmeline Pankhurst needed to make a living; the income they got inside the movement was far less than they were able to earn as lecturers or journalists in less controversial areas. These women were hardly filling idle time with their feminism.

Banks's study at the end of the 1970s was a reasonably good summary of the state of the art in English-language analysis of feminism. Although she went beyond the studies of suffragism that for so long dominated and limited the analysis of feminism, her discussion was still constrained by the categories developed in the first studies of feminism-as-suffragism and, even more, feminism-as-equal-rights. She thus continued to accept limited and limiting ideas about the nature and potentiality of feminism. Historians in general have done little better; few have even attempted such synthesis and generalization. And as historians, they have been reluctant to incorporate into their analyses the experience of the second wave.

Alternative classifications are presented by second-wave feminists, based on their own perceptions of the movement's operations. As I have already suggested, in the context of group activism the different classifications of feminism represent competing identifications of the crucial constraints on women. Because such distinctions correspond roughly to priorities, delineating a range of shared rhetoric, affiliation, and recognized frameworks of discussion, they are effective predictors of the most likely alliances between groups. But they do not indicate with any precision the ideological differences between those groups.

When today's feminists exclude others from the movement, they are rejecting analyses of obstacles to women's autonomy. Although activist women's groups may not be accepted as feminist even when they join the specific campaigns of an era, those groups which oppose or refrain from such action will certainly be rejected. This is especially true when the campaigns concerned have gained key symbolic importance—hence the hostile analyses of antisuffrage feminists such as the young Beatrice Webb and the other signatories of the notorious 1889 "Protest" against woman suffrage (see Strachey 1978:285). Similarly, many observers still assume that the American women's groups opposing the Equal Rights Amendment in the interwar period thereby forfeited any claim to feminism (Rothman 1978). Among contemporary feminists, exclusions are based on estimates of likely impact, of what future changes will make a meaningful difference. Such estimates typically grow out of personal, usually organizational, experience and are also differentiated in terms of specific campaigns. In this way, campaigns such as the struggles for access to abortion become a litmus test for a generation of activists.

But such action-oriented definitions are not adequate for understanding the differences among and the different values of versions of feminism. Nor, unfortunately, are the more abstract analyses that academic feminists generate when they turn their attention to women's organizations. The need for a feminist classification of feminism is made glaringly obvious by probably the most sophisticated discussion of the typology of feminism, Alison Jaggar's *Feminist Politics and Human Nature* (1983). In it Jaggar examined the categories she and Pauline Rothenberg (Struhl) used in a widely distributed reader (1978, 1984). Their *Feminist Frameworks* summarized and illustrated the categories Jaggar then justified, and that most analysts of contemporary feminism now accept with more or less hesitation. Liberal feminism, Marxist feminism, radical feminism, and socialist feminism are all surprisingly familiar in rhetoric and structure.[18] What is specific about feminist theories seems to be simply that they are about women and, increasingly, by women. Admittedly, the creation of theory by women can itself be seen as a feminist activity. But the proposed fourfold classification is itself not feminist, even if feminists have developed it and it classifies the belief systems of feminists.

Jaggar and Rothenberg identified categories of feminism by reference to long-established intellectual traditions. Liberal feminism they described in terms of its origins in British theory about equality and entitlement to opportunity for self-development, as presented by Locke, Wollstonecraft, and Mill; education and civil liberties were the remedies for the disadvantages of women as of any individual. Nearly all historic feminists are assigned to this first category, with some few Marxist exceptions such as Nelly Roussel and Emma Goldman.

Marxist feminism for its part could call explicitly only on Engels but

---

18. The terminology varies slightly from source to source; these terms, used by Jaggar and her coeditor, are reasonably widely accepted. To capitalize all the adjectives would avoid confusion about "liberal" and "radical" while giving appropriate honor to the followers of Karl Marx, but this is not usual practice.

drew in general terms on Marxist notions about the material bases of social arrangements, incorporating women's oppression as a special case. The initial remedy was the involvement of women in the paid labor force and thus into the mainstream of change. More generally, the solution was revolutionary change; women's oppression would end with all other oppression when capitalism was finally displaced. Both liberal and Marxist feminism, thus defined, were reasonably venerable, having begun in the nineteenth century when feminists drew out the implications for women of the classic doctrines of political philosophy.

Radical feminism, by contrast, was entirely new, and it denied that existing belief systems could be adapted to explain and improve the situation of women. Perhaps as a result, Jaggar and Rothenberg had difficulty defining radical feminism, and Jaggar herself was reluctant to give it status as a theory. Nevertheless, they felt able to sum up the shared beliefs of radical feminists, as the "insistence that the oppression of women is fundamental" (1984:86). In a parallel to the Marxist emphasis on the class system, gender relations were equivalent to relations of production. Because radical feminism gave priority to issues that cannot concern men, or in relation to which men cannot be disadvantaged, it emphasized such consequences of women's physical specificity as female sexuality, abortion, rape, wife-battering, childbirth, and maternity. Prostitution, pornography, and a range of pay and occupational issues were also given priority because in a patriarchy they victimized women. The notion of "patriarchy," a term both descriptive and denunciatory of male domination, was central to radical feminism; it made little or no sense to either liberal or Marxist feminism.

Socialist feminism, the category in which Jaggar and Rothenberg placed themselves, was also difficult to define. Its central feature is an attempt to articulate "the inseparability of gender and class oppression as they affect women" (152). A traditional Marxist would place such feminists among the liberals, and liberal and radical feminists might well classify them as Marxist. Yet the socialist feminists saw themselves as a separate group and have generally been accepted as such. The question is whether they have any more theoretical standing than, say, the women of color to whom Jaggar and Rothenberg gave a place in the second edition of their collection or the lesbian feminists subsumed there as part of radical feminism.

The problems of defining these categories are obvious even in the titles, and the boundaries are necessarily fuzzy. If feminist theorists accept them, feminist activists are hesitant. Most second-wave feminists in Britain call themselves socialist feminists or simply socialists, and so do a large number in Europe and North America; they retain close connections with the social-democratic Left. But many other feminists who are convinced of the importance of socialism are unwilling to identify with those who call themselves socialist feminists. At the same time, Marxist and socialist feminists are sensitive to their mutual disagreements and to their differences with the groups they label liberal. In addition, although the ambiguities of the term "radical" are obvious under patriarchy, the postsixties' radical feminists are understood to be a distinct group.[19]

The identity of socialist feminism was the central concern of Jaggar's own book, which attempted to demonstrate, as she candidly stated, "that socialist feminism constitutes [not just] a distinctive approach to political life, [but the] one that offers the most convincing promise of constructing an adequate theory and practice for women's liberation." Described as "a political theory and practice that will synthesize the best insights of radical feminism and of the Marxist tradition," this form of feminism was to be distinguished from radical feminism by its "method"—historical materialism. When radical feminism adopted that method, any difference between it and socialist feminism would cease (123). The four categories therefore collapsed into two, with the key division being between socialist feminism and its predecessor theories, namely Marxism and (radical) feminism.[20] The dialectical patterns of Marxist analysis are obvious.

Jaggar defined the situation of women in terms of their oppression, which made them the most inclusive group of disadvantaged human beings. Logically, then, the "standpoint of women," central to socialist-feminist theorizing, was "the basis for a more comprehensive representation of reality than the standpoint of men . . . [and revealed] more of the universe, human and non-human, than . . . the standpoint of men" (385). Thus far socialist feminism resembled radical feminism, although it focused on women's work rather than on their bodies; Jaggar rejected as "biologism" any attempt to place primary emphasis on reproduction or women's related capabilities or qualities, even if socially shaped. At this point, however, as the project of building theory became primary, socialist feminism parted company with radical feminism. Historical materialism itself dictated the necessity of a "comprehensive" theory as the

19. Jill Liddington and Jill Norris (1978) identify Britain's (socialist) trade-union suffragists as radical feminists; Judith Hole and Ellen Levine, among others, have given the same label to elements of the program of the American suffragists (1971). In a second edition Jaggar and Rothenberg add a fifth category, different even in formulation: "Feminism and women of color." It is, the reader is told, not "a coherent theoretical framework" (1984:xiv). This addition seems to reflect U.S. experience, including leftist perceptions of a worldwide extension by means of American hegemony of the racist aspects of American society. The logic that includes Afro-American feminist responses to racism could equally embrace other specific feminist responses to religious bigotry, as well as feminist critiques of heterosexism and of the social pressures for child-bearing and indeed for female sexual activity in any form (Gimenez 1980). All of these are, as Jaggar and Rothenberg put it, "conditions that prevent us from freely choosing which of our potentialities we wish to fulfill" (1984:xvii). They are not, however, theoretical constructs conventionally used to classify forms of feminism.

20. Zillah Eisenstein's (1981) attribution of radicalism to liberal feminism would be useful here, to incorporate that set of beliefs into the schema.

first political priority: "Women who can theorize together can work together politically" (387). In principle, women are uniquely placed to
escape the myths and illusions of the current system: "Women's subordinate status means that, unlike men, women do not have an interest in
mystifying reality and so are likely to develop a clearer and more trust-
worthy understanding of the world" (384). Furthermore, since women's
oppression is more complete than that of other groups, a system under
which they are not oppressed will be the one most nearly free of illusions. Therefore theory that liberates them will be the most illuminating,
and the adequacy of theory can be tested by how useful it is in liberating
women.

But "women's standpoint" does not correspond in any direct way to
actual women's perceptions: it "does not refer to a perspective that is
immediately available to all and only to women. Instead, it refers to a
way of conceptualizing reality that reflects women's interests and values
and draws on women's own interpretation of their own experience"
(387). In a familiar pattern, the oppressed are to be shown their role in
history by those who have the analytical key. There will be a primary
position in such an enterprise for feminist theorists such as Jaggar herself, working co-operatively with suitably trained and appropriately
humble males.

Jaggar was, of course, wrestling with the old and serious Marxist problem of objective versus subjective interests. Even with a nod toward
drawing on "women's own interpretations of their own experience," her
formulations incorporate women into existing left-wing groups and radical feminism into Marxist feminism and allow all-women groups only as
temporary expedients. Like many liberal feminists, she equates all-wom-
en groups with political separatism and hostility to men (Richards 1982,
Midgley and Hughes 1983). As for socialist feminism, as delineated by
Jaggar it is in effect a way of appropriating radical feminism for
Marxism.

Radical feminists might well respond by rejecting the twin notions of
comprehensive theory and power for the theorists. Both are not just
leftist or Marxist but masculine ideals. Moreover, they are masculine
ideals specifically defined in contrast to and in rejection of women's daily
experience. Understanding and transformation of reality are goals analytically independent of Marxism or Marxist method. It is possible to be
aware of the complex importance of material conditions without becoming a Marxist or a socialist. And the use of the conceptual apparatus of
Marxism may be seriously misleading in the discussion of women's lives.
Jaggar faulted radical feminism for a lack of interest in the origins of
women's oppression. Here she indicated again the extent to which her
socialist feminism was Marxist rather than radical: in Marxist terms,
understanding of origins is a necessary way station for the creation of
futures. The point follows from the notion of history as progressing,

with some inevitability, toward a preordained and in principle predictable outcome.

The contrast between socialist and radical feminism can be found in a specific, classic image used by Marx: revolutionaries as the midwives of history. Apparently drawn from women's experience, the analogy is profoundly inaccurate. Uncertainty and lack of control are key elements of pregnancy as it is experienced by women, for even a midwife can know only that at some point, not much later than nine months from conception (itself a date usually known only approximately), the potential mother will no longer have a developing zygote in her body. Even the most refined technologies of mapping and monitoring will show little more about fetus than its sex, its weight, and its defects. Its paternity may well be in doubt even for the mother, a fact that expands the resulting endowment of genetic possibilities and risks, uncertain already in terms of her own legacy. It is a messy, fuzzy process but one of great promise; it is unlike the world of politics, either Marxist or non-Marxist, where options usually concern a choice between relative evils and the likelihood of a favorable outcome is low.

A radical feminist might use the processes of pregnancy and birthing as metaphors to change the nature of public life and to obliterate some of the distinctions and certainties to be found in current analyses of politics. She would not violate the experienced reality of the process by using it to express a stage in a known, predictable, and linear pattern of change. Nor would a radical feminist be willing to equate the pain and danger of childbirth with Marxist concepts of revolution and the inevitability of violent change.

Jaggar presented a fair account of the divisions most commonly imposed on contemporary feminism. They can be reduced to a Marxist/non-Marxist dichotomy, crossed by a distinction between contemporary and older theories which corresponds in a rough way to the commitment to integration or autonomy of women's groups. The four-fold division follows conventional classification of Western political theory by mainstream and leftist academic men. Radical feminism then becomes a historical development, in effect a modern perspective and a list of policy priorities, while socialist feminism refers to those relatively independent, temporarily separatist Marxist feminists who are attempting to incorporate radical-feminist insights into Marxism. The classification can be represented as follows:

	old/integrated	new/autonomous
Marxist (permanently valuable)	**Marxist feminism**	**socialist feminism**
non-Marxist (temporarily useful)	**liberal feminism**	**radical feminism**

The schema should really be three-dimensional in order to rank socialist feminism highest. It should also be dynamic in order to show that socialist feminism comes into existence after it has incorporated the useful parts of its predecessors.

This analysis is not helpful in sorting out earlier feminist groups. The two sets of belief developed by analysts of the suffrage movement coexist awkwardly with such classifications, as equal rights feminism is incorporated into liberal feminism. Marxist or socialist feminism is hard put to find representatives among the suffragists since, by and large, socialist and Marxist women rejected women's quest for the vote as a bourgeois delusion that served the interests of capitalism by dividing the working class along gender lines. Social feminism suffers an even worse fate: it is seen as the nonideological embodiment of women's apoliticism or conservatism.[21]

Jaggar has supplied the promised justification of the superiority of socialist feminism. All the feminists of the past were bound to fail, she implies, since for historical reasons they could not be "socialist"—Marxist incorporating the standpoint of women. Their apparent successes have to be written off as false consciousness, and future, fuller successes are postponed until after the development of the ultimate theory. The majority of actual feminists would dispute this view. The suggested classifications are inadequate both as description of experienced reality and as prediction of differences in mobilization and action. Jaggar's work, for all its subtlety and care, shares the fate of most efforts to classify feminism.

In fact, such classifications are both ahistorical and ethnocentric, most commonly responding to an imperfectly understood version of British and North American feminism. The categories reflect the emerging feminisms of the second wave in North America, where a new version of liberal feminism appeared shortly before a new, "liberationist" Marxist feminism (Freeman 1975). Radical feminism soon followed, a direct revulsion against leftist politics or an indirect reaction against the Marxist feminism that also produced socialist feminism. In the United States radical feminism had only a short life as anything other than cultural separatism, but its major insights were adopted by socialist as well as liberal feminists. With the exception of the small "women's rights" contingent represented by the National Woman's party, in the United States and England feminist groups representative of older versions of feminism were slow to respond to the changing situation; it was easy to relegate them and their traditions to the status of predecessors of radical feminism.

In part because European feminism developed in very different se-

---

21. Even Linda Gordon has recently suggested that "different but equal may be the gender version of separate but equal" (Gordon 1986:26).

quences, the impact of European feminist practice and theory on North American feminism has been slight.[22] The overall analysis of Marxist feminists is not closed to extracontinental influences—Jaggar cites Georg Lukács and Antonio Gramsci—but shows little responsiveness to European feminism as such. For instance, Italian feminism enters Jaggar's discussion only in a relatively brief reference to the wages-for-housework movement; English feminism is represented by Sheila Rowbotham's discussion of the difficulties of unstructured organizations. Jaggar does not deal at all with the complex issues of defining the "other" which find their most eloquent discussions in French and other Continental feminisms (Moi 1987).

This parochialism is unfortunate, since European theory has suggested modes of classification of feminism other than the fourfold schema based on American experience. Rossana Rossanda reflects Italian practice and analysis when she describes feminism as split into not four but two categories, presenting feminism with a choice to be made. She asks whether feminism intends to subvert the culture of dominated and of oppressors, to suggest different systems of relationships, or whether it wishes merely to assert a space for the feminine: "Do women see themselves engaged in putting in place a truly bisexual culture (therefore including within it the criticism of patriarchal culture), or are they engaged in legitimizing a solitary, non-communicating autonomy?" (del Re, Gadant, and Veauvy 1984:4). Unrecognizable to Jaggar's categories, these alternatives are related to them in no systematic fashion. Feminism and, by implication, women as well are presented as distinctive, not as derivative of male models.

In an environment where Marxism is part of the standard milieu of progressive politics rather than an academic and marginal mode of inquiry, it is not necessary to separate Marxist from liberal and radical feminism. Rossanda's analysis is one of many to have followed a social feminist line over time, though without identifying it as such. Historical and national specificities should not obscure what these analyses have in common, nor should the even larger variety among equity feminisms obscure a common insistence on women's resemblances to men and the necessity of integration into a male-defined society. Rossanda herself, a former member of the Central Committee of the Italian Communist party, became a prominent feminist—but not a Marxist or a socialist feminist (Rossanda 1979, Meyer 1987:153). The options she describes have institutional equivalents in the European experience, where women work actively within Leftist parties and unions as fractions or influ-

22. The term "North American" can be used for feminist theorizing since the Canadian movement has developed no significant independent theory; the practical history of the second wave there is different (Prentice et al. 1988). We do not yet have any reliable accounts of liberal or survivor feminisms even in Europe; Evans (1977) and Lovenduski (1986) are uneven in their coverage and not very reliable.

ences while simultaneously developing a separate culture in the women-only groups of the movement (Maruani 1979, Hellman 1987).

But Rossanda does more than reflect the strategic choices available in Italy. Hers is a radical feminist formulation starting with the validity of women's articulation of their own experience. By identifying two alternatives within or following from radical feminism, she makes it clear that women can articulate women's standpoint in a number of ways. Most important, she points to the continuing centrality of women's difference or specificity, which she proposes to use as "a lancet to burst open the unadmitted bias of the dominant, masculine system of knowledge" (4). She thus implies some sort of continuity, if only theoretical, with the early feminists or "womanists" whom Gordon and Berg discussed and praised—but whom they finally dismissed as limited and without relevance for present-day feminism.

CHAPTER 3

A Feminist Classification
of Feminisms

For a feminist, the most useful classification of feminisms is a simple one: social feminism and its alternate, equity feminism. Each main category has its versions, more or less clearly established; individuals may well subscribe to both. In analytic terms, however, a dichotomy is appropriate. It has the advantage of corresponding to what actual feminists thought and think, and it corresponds also to different capabilities for mobilization and for effectiveness.

The characteristic that defines social feminism is its emphasis on how women are different from men. This emphasis should not be confused with unquestioning acceptance of patriarchal definitions that include notions of impermeably separate spheres of activity. In effect, social feminists reject the most important of the characteristics ascribed to women: dependency. But they reject it by implication rather than by any form of theoretical defiance. Other "female" traits they reinterpret, some would say beyond recognition, and on them build justifications for expanding women's autonomy. This is the core of social feminist activism: the refusal to allow the exclusion from social influence not just of women as individuals but of the values and competencies associated with women. Social feminism inverts the political consequences of conservative arguments about separate spheres—a very different process from the one by which equity feminists adapt the arguments of those mainstream theories which had previously omitted women.

Social feminists note that a patriarchal society may well praise women, even value their activities and virtues highly. They agree that women have specific and valuable characteristics. But such a society ascribes those characteristics to women and only to women. Nor does it allow women a generalized social role in the exercise of their special values and competencies. Most important, women are not expected to play a part in defining either values or roles, particularly their own. Social feminists are therefore committed, whether they know it or not, to a basic transformation of patriarchal structures and values.

The alternative, equity feminism, is the simplest belief system possible for feminists. More accurately, it is a series of belief systems that classify women with whatever criteria a given society uses for classifying men. The feminist element of these belief systems consists of women's assertion of their entitlement to any roles from which they have been excluded on the grounds of gender. Such a master theory has different consequences, depending on the analysis to which it relates and the social and political context of feminist claims.

Britain and the United States, which tend to be our examples, are societies with different standards for private and public life, standards that coincide with different expectations for women and men. Equity feminists in both countries challenge the expectations imposed on women as well as the exclusion of women from public life. But they do not object to the differences expected between the two areas of life. In a society that had the same standards for private and public life but excluded women from the second realm, equity feminists would have a different, easier task. If a population expected hierarchy and violence in both home and politics, equity feminists would campaign merely for access to both domains for previously homebound women. More benignly, a collectivist, co-operative society might be enjoined to give to women the same treatment and scope of activity as it does to men. The first example might be Nazi Germany, the second the Israeli kibbutz; both have had their equity feminists, and in neither case was the argument based on natural rights. Both, incidentally, also had their social feminists (Bridenthal, Grossman, and Kaplan 1984; Blumberg 1976; Israeli 1981).

To make its arguments plausible, equity feminism has to rely heavily on the similarities of women to men, dismissing the obvious existing differences as the consequences of historical inequalities because, as individuals, women have the same capacity as men. Such an analysis has been a powerful solvent of the biological determinism that disqualifies women as a group. It can also generate sophisticated arguments for equality of treatment on the basis of the evident variability within female as well as male populations, the overlap of observed characteristics, and the small number of activities specifically related to sex-linked characteristics. In this context, also, assertions about the greater "natural" variability of males can be identified as a barrier to women's access to roles and tasks stereotyped both as more demanding and as male: this common argument implies a lower proportion of women than of men who possess talent or specialized ability (Sayers 1982).

The logic of equity feminism can be very strong even when its practical consequences are unacceptable to dominant males. All versions of equity feminism are, after all, adapted from systems already accepted. This brand of feminism has activated some of the most prominent feminist leaders in countries with the liberal Anglo-American tradition of natural rights, where political systems had often responded to similar claims made by other groups. In Britain, suffrage campaigns followed a long, gradual extension of voting privileges to politically mobilized groups of the excluded. John Stuart Mill located his influential arguments in *The Subjection of Women* in a specific national, historical tradition when he classed the rule of men over women with "all other forms of unjust authority" (1970:137). In the early twentieth century British suffragists of many kinds eventually agreed on a formulation that states the main goal of all equity suffragists: "To obtain the . . . Franchise for Women on the same terms as it is or may be granted to Men" (quoted in Rover 1967:21). In Britain only extreme radicals interpreted such a statement as meaning that all human beings, even all male human beings, had "right" to take part in government. Other equity suffragists could read the formula as encompassing exclusionary qualifications for the vote. The equivalence to male standards constituted the equity feminist goal in all areas.

In the United States the general equity arguments for the vote took a different form. There, women's suffrage campaigns responded to a long-established tradition of adult male, white governance relatively unconstrained by property differentials. Since only those persons regarded as property, as minors, or as non-nationals were barred from the vote, some of the earliest struggles of American women activists were directed toward removing these disqualifications. They started with the classification of women as property, and their campaigns to reform marriage and divorce laws should be seen in this light as well as in the more obvious contexts of personal freedom and economic independence. The reform of child custody laws had a powerful antecedent in slave women's inability to retain legal or practical access to their children. Equally, access to professional education and occupations was access to activities of which minors were incapable. The interwar interest in women's independent nationality can similarly be seen as related to the criteria for citizenship; by this time in the United States, being a noncitizen was the one remaining formal bar to full legal equality for adults, and it was also the conspicuous remaining area in which a woman's status was determined by men's decisions, in this case about migration and residence (Becker 1983).

In the two countries the consequences of removing a sex-based suffrage disqualification were expected to be different. In the United States, women would have the same access to the vote as men did—there was even some expectation that black women would find it easier to vote than black men, since physical intimidation could not be used quite as casually against them (Morgan 1972). In Britain the removal of the sex-bar provided access only to a franchise linked to property, over which women continued to have less control. The class system was not likely to be much affected by adding women's to men's votes. And men of all classes agreed, in 1918, to inflict on women an age restriction never imposed on men.

The first generations of enfranchised women were thus different in the two countries, and they differed again in France where citizenship turned on revolutionary activism. French equity feminists lost their first crucial battle when the women's revolutionary clubs were dissolved in 1793 (Rabaut 1978:66–69). After this episode, they were rarely to claim identical capacities to men. Louise Michel, the anarchist heroine of the Commune, saw herself denied the privilege of martyrdom; later French feminists disclaimed any intention of seizing power as men had done. Equity arguments justified the subjection of women to taxation and to police repression (Hause and Kenney 1981). As late as the 1930s *suffrage universel,* treasured for ignoring race and class, was compatible with a sex-bar. Under these circumstances, equity arguments contributed to women's political invisibility, and feminist demonstrations passed virtually unnoticed. After World War II a prominent politician told Louise Weiss how annoyed he had been in the interwar period by the rather mild street theater of her group "La femme nouvelle." "The right to vote overrides the right to insurrection, Madame," he "thundered" at her; he was astonished when she reminded him that Frenchwomen were not able to vote at the time when Weiss's (suffragist) group had been active (Weiss 1946:34).

The contrast between English and American equity feminism can be seen most clearly in relation to suffragist uses of expediency arguments. As a utilitarian, John Stuart Mill, the classic liberal, was prepared to take a consequentialist line, arguing that justice to women would be good for both the state and women themselves. This argument is characteristic of the whole equity aspect of British feminism. Rover (1967:29–30) points out how the leaders of the English suffragists, such as Millicent Garrett Fawcett, were untroubled by possible contradictions in the combination of justice and expediency. They linked the two by the argument that women needed the vote to protect themselves in the same way as men did; no more than men should they be expected to rely on indirect representation or protection. Like the groups of men previously enfranchised, they needed a direct role in government. Such an argument did not have to impute to women any special qualities of either worth or vulnerability. In 1912 the British Labour party finally supported woman suffrage, on the grounds that working women needed the same political tools as the rest of the working class (Rendel 1977). In the United States, in contrast, equity arguments were limited to women's entitlement and capabilities. It is precisely the assertion of (manlike) strength, the (manlike) demand for justice without concern for consequences, that Aileen Kraditor and other analysts value in the equity suffragists.

Equity arguments produced positive results for women in both Britain and the United States. By the end of the nineteenth century the political consequence of such arguments had already been significant, even for the most deprived women in the countries considered here, obtaining for them the legal capacity to earn a living and to own property, the right to divorce and to custody of children, and access to most levels of education. These were all rights men had previously acquired. In an equal rights context, the vote would presumably be used to eliminate remaining discrepancies in the enjoyment of these rights, such as restrictions on entry into certain occupations and professions and differences in wages and marital rights.

The problem was that no equity reform could help women in situations for which men's rights provided no equivalents: men had no entitlement to maternity benefits or to freedom from sexual or marital violence. The policy response, slowly installed after enfranchisement, corresponded to the armatures of the welfare state which had comprised the program of the social feminists. Since the vote was the tool, in an equity context English utilitarianism saw the vote as justified. Women's particular problems had now been subsumed into the greater number whose greater good was the test.

In contrast, American political theorists have tended to perceive consequential arguments as somehow contradictory to the purity of natural rights. In the United States, as a result, equity feminism receives approval when it adopts equal rights arguments but cannot argue for benefits to women or to society as a whole without losing ideological legitimacy. American suffragists could not use equal rights arguments to argue directly for the importance of women's (and society's) needs. But such arguments generated effective political strategies, such as the adoption of the Declaration of Independence as a model at Seneca Falls. It may well have been the equal rights arguments that were expedient when the appeal to justice was used as an argument likely to be persuasive, deployed by women whose true goal was a social feminist desire to remodel society in a feminine ideal. We may reinterpret the continuing coexistence of justice and social service arguments: the appeal to equal rights was used because, as Americans, the suffragists believed in it— and because the audience would believe in it, too. But later commentators find it hard to accept that feminists might, like other politicians, make accurate calculations of how best to achieve their goals, and they find the coincidence of ideological acceptability and genuine practical expediency simply unacceptable. Such arguments imply that the American Revolution should not have been successful; the Declaration of Independence can be used as a model, but not the Constitution.

Perhaps it is time to reexamine such judgments. After all, in the Jefferson-Hamilton debates both sides accepted slavery and patriarchy; why look to the logic of colonial democracy as a model for feminists? It may be more appropriate to look to the Constitution's pragmatic, expedient compromises if what we want is an indigenous model for American

feminists. Certainly the negotiators of the Constitution would have recognized a fellow spirit in Carrie Chapman Catt (Fowler 1986). But social
feminism was neither derived from the Constitution nor legitimated by
reference to it. The resemblance is one of style, not of content.

Equity feminism necessarily shares the characteristics of its surround-
ing society, even on an analytic level. In the United States, feminism,
defined as equal rights, seems to many observers to conflict with the
basic institution of the family. For the conservative who idealizes the
family, this is a reason to oppose feminism. But in an American context
it is possible to make the argument in the opposite direction, so that
feminism becomes a way to reform the family. Carl Degler, who does so
emphatically, describes a contradiction between "democracy, individualism, and meritocracy" in public life and a family that is hierarchical, even
authoritarian (1980:471). Feminism conflicts with the less desirable aspects of the family, for it is an extension of the more progressive features
of public life; feminism's promise is the reform of private life as public
life has been reformed. The family will be improved, Degler argues,
because reform of the family is necessary to incorporate women into
public life.

It now seems clear that the arguments of equal rights gave American
women access to the existing, flawed public systems of domination. They
also obtained for women the male entitlement to act publicly on behalf
of the patriarchal family—the right to provide economic support and to
speak for family members who were subordinate in status, which meant
for women those physically and legally dependent on them, usually for
reasons of age (Brennan and Pateman 1979). In addition, women acquired the public responsibilities that men had always had in respect to
the family—the obligation to support dependents and to enforce public
edicts including taxation, school attendance, health regulations, and military service. The positive values associated with the notion of the household in the United States, such as co-operation, consensus, and non-
violence, continued to have little impact on public life. If such values
were, nevertheless, appreciated (both as refuge and as possible source of
reform), neither equity feminism in general nor the women's vote in
particular would give those values influence on the conduct of public
life. Because Degler grounds his analysis in the ideals of public life, he is
unable to see that the undesirable family characteristics he notes are
precisely those dimensions of the family which most fully reflect American *public* life. The public ideologies he praises have been compatible in
public life with racism, significant class distinctions of status and power,
and a pervasive sexism. In the family they allow ascribed differences to
generate female economic dependency, male dominance, and physical
brutality in the treatment of women and children. Equity feminism,
based on theories about public life, can judge private life to be lacking by
comparison—but it cannot use private life to criticize the public.

Nor was it equity feminism that obtained the vote for women. In Britain the suffragettes shared with the nonmilitants an effectively social feminist ideology, most visibly in their campaigns for male adoption of female modes of sexual purity (Hume 1982, Holton 1986). In their one striking equity analysis the militants grasped the fact that in Britain other population groups, from the Chartists onward, had used force or the threat of force to back their demand for a role in politics. The Women's Social and Political Union accordingly attempted first to destroy property and then to use force in a largely symbolic fashion against political figures. Such tactics alienated not only the general public but also working-class suffragists (Liddington and Norris 1978:205). The militants had more if unintentional success with the classic anticolonial and female technique of provoking violence against themselves, producing sympathy and sometimes political support. Similar processes were to occur in British India, in Cyprus, and in the United States during the civil rights movements of the 1960s. In respect to the feminists, the appeal to the public was, deliberately or not, in terms of specifically female capabilities for silent endurance and suffering—hardly an equity appeal.

Although the martyrdom of the hunger strikers was not crucial in obtaining the vote, it certainly dramatized the situation and the dedication of the activists, and it accelerated the recruitment of women into the ranks of moderate suffragism. The experience of the hunger strikers also validated social feminist justifications of women gaining a public role through the vote. The contrast between the suffragettes and their brutal, even sadistic jailers seemed to demonstrate female differences from men as well as the admirable qualities of self-sacrifice that women could bring to public life.

Far less dramatic was the ceaseless activity of the nonmilitant, nonviolent suffragists who spent some seventy-five years demonstrating a superior version of participatory democracy, one imbued by what they would have agreed to identify as a particularly feminine tolerance and patience (Strachey 1974, Stocks 1970). Moving from procedure to content, these women also focused on a range of issues which the vote was to serve, issues they saw as derived from women's experience and neglected by the state. Theirs was a discourse in which they claimed not justice for women but social justice more widely defined, not autonomy but the chance to serve. Their arguments focused on obligation. But this obligation was not just the general human (or Christian) obligation of service; instead, they believed, it was a consequence of women's special abilities and expertise, which ought to be brought to bear on public as well as on private life.

These were the arguments also of the social feminist suffragists in the United States, where militants were less violent but nonmilitants closely resembled their British counterparts. Clearly, such arguments were not individualistic, though the individual women who presented them were implicitly claiming the right to decide their own goals. The suffragists typically claimed to speak on behalf of all women, for they believed that women as a group shared obligations. Women's special duty to do good produced rights, seen not as matching men's rights but rather as the necessary means for service. To begin with, this duty gave women entitlement to both training and opportunities to serve. "Why have women passion, intellect, moral activity—those three—and a place in society where no one of the three can be exercised?" asked Florence Nightingale in her 1859 novel fragment *Cassandra*; "Why cannot we *make use* of the noble rising heroisms of [women of] our own day, instead of leaving them to rust? They have nothing to do" (quoted in Strachey 1974:404). The necessary means were first, education, then professional training and certification, and finally the necessary freedom of action and mobility. Virginia Woolf was to make much the same arguments in *A Room of One's Own* (1928). Furthermore, women were believed to have a special responsibility for those other women who were victims in a male-dominated world. Identification of women as a group, and identification of women with that group, could consequently be very powerful (Berg 1978).

In the United States and to a lesser extent in Britain such social feminist arguments went against the grain of the natural rights tradition of public life and political change. But they were compatible with, indeed an extension of, the values understood as appropriate for the home and therefore for women. The feminists shared this appreciation and were honest in their use of the image of civic housekeeping, a metaphor that both extended their realm of legitimate activity and recognized the extent to which the household and the political system had become interdependent. Social feminism might initially seem irrelevant to politics, but it was free of any implied threat to the precious, essential qualities of either women or private life.

Equity feminism, on the other hand, was likely to become threatening if it claimed that women shared what were seen as men's specific characteristics rather than some generalized, nongendered humanity. Particularly provocative were those feminists who claimed for women the same sort of sexuality as men's, women such as Victoria Woodhull and Emma Goldman (if we may include them in the same sentence), who argued for female sexual liberation as the key element of feminism. Such women were a small minority among feminists. Their appeal to today's feminists seems to result from the changing technology of reproductive control, which makes it technically possible for women to copy men in separating sexuality from reproduction. The contrast is striking with those social feminists who, in the nineteenth century, advocated sexual abstinence and voluntary motherhood (Du Bois and Gordon 1983). There is a shared feminist feature to all these reactions to the dilemmas of women's vulnerability in relation to reproduction: an assertion of women's autonomy through control over their bodies. But it is clear that an impression of role change is extremely difficult to avoid if equal rights are claimed in respect to reproduction.

In practical terms, social feminism made it possible for women to add a political role without disrupting either their self-image or the expectations of the men around them. This is not an insignificant achievement, even though women thus added politics, as they had added paid labor, to their continuing responsibility for the household. Analysts have recognized the double shift of housework and paid labor; they have not recognized that civic housekeeping constituted a third shift. Still, this multiple shift had no theoretical inevitability. The actual adoption of tasks in the public sphere contributed also, over time, to an erosion of the barriers between public and private.

In the United States equity and social feminist arguments, which had been mutually supportive in the suffrage campaigns, came into open conflict when, in the 1920s, the surviving activists among equity suffragists moved to a vigorous support of the Equal Rights Amendment (ERA). The ERA remains the preeminent example of an equity reform. By the interwar period a significant group of women activists was strongly opposed to it (Dye 1980). The resulting conflict within the women's movement was undoubtedly damaging to feminism, though one might argue that women were demonstrating autonomy by carrying on a dispute to which the rest of society was largely indifferent. Similar antagonisms were generated by the interwar campaigns for independent nationality for women and, in the 1980s, by disputes about pornography.

Opponents of the ERA included the organized working women who logically should be the heroines of such leftist analysts as O'Neill and Kraditor. But the anti-ERA factory hands are damned by association with their social feminist supporters, who had been largely responsible for labor legislation protecting working women—legislation that was threatened by the ERA. For if women's need to protect themselves as they saw best evoked the basic feminist drive for autonomy as well as an equity argument based on similarity to men, it could also be part of a social feminist argument of a different sort. The brutal working environment of capitalism was particularly incompatible with women's maternal and domestic role. Out of that contradiction social feminists had derived arguments and practical measures that moderated working conditions, if only for women (Kenneally 1978, Scharf 1983). In its response to women's exploitation in a workplace that exploited men less, equity feminism could grasp the reality that women need freedom from constraints not imposed on men, but it could not reverse its arguments to claim that men should be treated like women and equally protected. As a result, the two sorts of feminism disagreed basically on what became a crucial symbolic policy measure related to women.[1]

Such disputes, very public and often very personal, cost the women's movement dear in terms of effort and image. Today's more consistent feminist support of the ERA has still not resolved the problem, but because of changed social conditions an equity measure once again looks to social feminists like a useful tool—while for many equity feminists it has become an obsessive goal with largely symbolic value.

The historical continuity of feminism now seems clear, but both scholars and activists have had trouble recognizing the fact. Feminists themselves have been slow to recognize their predecessors: they have rediscovered their foremothers but used them more as icons than as guides. The literature of the movement and the scanty academic commentaries draw the line sharply between first-wave and second-wave feminism for all three countries under consideration here. This divide is sharpest and least convincing for France, where historians of the movement place the dividing line at 1945, when women got the vote. The new feminism is dated in theoretical terms from 1949, with the publication of Simone de Beauvoir's *The Second Sex,* and in organizational terms with the appearance in 1968 of the Mouvement pour la libération des femmes (MLF) (Albistur and Armogathe 1977; Rabaut 1978). Until recently, historians were prepared to accept that twenty years (or only four!) were enough to separate absolutely the individuals and the beliefs animating successive stages of a whole segment of reform. Now we are beginning to see volumes on the continuing involvement of Frenchwomen with the socialist parties (Sowerwine 1978) and on the long tradition of nonsocialist feminism in France (Hause and Kenney 1984). But the familiar divisions of present feminism continue to limit attention to the past. We reclaim individuals and issues but not ideas or organizational continuities.

In the United States the women's liberation movement (WLM) tends

1. The American equity feminists associated with the National Woman's party (NWP) also demonstrated how easy it is to hold both equity and social feminist beliefs. They clearly came to accept, if only provisionally and illogically, the description of women as somehow different from men and on this basis managed to co-operate with social feminists in campaigns related to women workers. Lois Scharf (1983) is one of many to deplore their acceptance of such views, on the grounds that the "feminist advocates of economic equality for women" made a fatal error in "reinforcing the social assumptions upon which opponents of an equal rights amendment had based their position." As a result, she writes, they "confused and compromised the feminist basis for their concerns" (1983:255). This familiar criticism attributes to the ideas of social feminism the constraints imposed on feminists by the Depression and long-established expectations. Cynthia Patterson also feels that, "by placing women's values and interests on an equal footing with those of men, the NWP proposed to redefine dramatically what issues and objectives must receive political attention" (1982:593).

to be seen as the theoretically most interesting part of the new feminism, emerging directly from the New Left and the student movement. Richard Evans is one of many who, for this reason, draws a sharp line between first- and second-wave feminism: "It is the combination of socialism—though in a multitude of forms, some of them barely recognisable—and sexual liberation, that distinguishes the ideology, the beliefs and the aims of the present-day Women's Liberation movement from those of the feminists of the nineteenth century" (1977:244). For Evans, "in many respects the advocates of Women's Liberation reject the aims and beliefs of the feminists" (244); and they do so to the extent that they are not equity feminists like those he praises. Such an equity framework can rehabilitate a few individuals with the effect of partially denying novelty to the second wave: Alice Paul's militantism looks like a predecessor of the street theater of the women's liberation movement, and Jeannette Rankin becomes a heroine for having opposed in Congress the American entry into both world wars. But some of the most effective predecessors, including Stone and Catt, are presented as object lessons of the failure to produce genuine change.

In England the new feminists of the 1970s and 1980s have reclaimed Virginia Woolf as a foremother, to the surprise of the editor of her *Letters* who thought her feminism was "anachronistic" in her own lifetime, since as early as 1928 women could vote, attend universities, and enter the professions. Dismissing the arguments of *Three Guineas*, Nigel Nicolson wrote that "the Victorian patriarch and the 20th-century fascist were men of different worlds" (Woolf 1979:xv). The young women who hailed Woolf as the "mother of us all" were almost as unperceptive about her beliefs. Identifying her as an early opponent of patriarchy, capitalism, and heterosexism, they did not see her feminism as intrinsically interesting nor, by and large, did they look at its arguments or possible influence. Her feminism, unless it was socialist or lesbian, was dismissed.

We must doubt the validity of these analyses and the organizational and ideological discontinuities they imply. The suffrage movements were larger and more complex than they have been portrayed, and they were embedded in vast networks of women's organizations with often overlapping memberships. The women involved did not die out when the vote was won. The intervals in time were in fact very short—twenty years between the wars, another twenty until the first stirrings of the second wave of feminism. When Dale Spender interviewed survivors of the English suffragists in 1981, Mary Stott told her, "There's always been a women's movement in this century"; Spender had asked her what she had done during that supposed gap between the suffragists and the WLM (1983). Spender identified Hazel Hunkins Hallinan, Rebecca West, Dora Russell, Mary Stott, and Constance Rover as spanning the gap from the old to the new movement.

For the connections, we have mainly anecdotal evidence, but the anecdotes suggest a continuity that is, if logical, usually ignored.[2] In France, for instance, Cécile Brunschvicg, one of the feminist "ministresses" of the Blum government in 1936, was active in politics after the war; her ally and opponent Louise Weiss was still being consulted by *F* magazine in 1983, the year before her death. In the United States, Eleanor Roosevelt exemplifies the bridging role played by a feminist who was not primarily identified with women's organizations; she was involved in the establishment of the United Nations' Commission on Women in 1948, urged on by British women led by Emmeline Pethick-Lawrence, the suffragist who split with the Pankhursts over issues of democratic structure (Lash 1972:39–40). At the very end of her life, Mrs. Roosevelt was instrumental in the establishment of John F. Kennedy's Commission on the Status of Women and therefore an important part of the process that produced the National Organization for Women; India Edwards reports Mrs. Roosevelt's immense influence within the Democratic party, and how she herself in turn picked up the task of supporting the advancement of women (Edwards 1977).

The anecdotal evidence includes the role of the feminists' descendants and disciples: Lucy Stone's and Elizabeth Cady Stanton's daughters along with Susan B. Anthony's real and adopted "nieces" active in the early twentieth century, Carrie Chapman Catt leading the antiwar feminists until the eve of World War II, Lucretia Mott's granddaughter becoming president of the League of Women Voters in 1945. In France, four years before the summer of '68, Yvette Roudy, later France's first minister for the rights of women, encountered feminism and the feminists of the French left, including longtime activist Madeleine Kraemer-Bach, "still full of life" (1985:83). And how are we to evaluate the influence of Frances Perkins, suffragist, social activist, first American woman cabinet member? She died in 1965 after spending her last years at Cornell University's School of Industrial and Labor Relations (ILR) (Martin 1976). It seems unlikely that feminist activity at Cornell was merely coincidental; surely we can see women such as Alice Cook, a prominent feminist researcher at the ILR School, as a second generation of linkages. Perkins was actively involved in promoting the role of women in academia—logically there has to be some connection to Cornell's early involvement in women's studies, to the discrimination suit filed against Cornell by women academics including Cook, and even to the Seneca Peace Camp in which Cook also played a role.

Obviously, many less famous women also survived and retained some degree of active involvement in women's organizations. In Missoula, Montana, in 1977 a university extension course in women's history drew

---

2. As well as a body of work by American feminist historians working on the period between suffrage and the second-wave ERA campaigns (e.g., Scharf and Jensen 1983).

a "seventy-seven-year-old suffrage activist with fifty years of clippings about women" (Sands, Smith, and Thompson 1983:212). Daughters, younger relatives, and friends served as bridges. The few traceable personal links make it seem likely that the suffragists and therefore their beliefs, including those shared with older groups, had a continuing impact. If the early feminists indeed had a distinctive ideology, it would be in some way derivative of the traditions they grew out of—and it might well be influential on those who followed. The ideologies of feminism developed among the generations that produced suffragism. They need to be examined if only to counteract those analyses of feminism which have disregarded the actual content and influence of the ideas animating these earliest activists. But we must be wary of the few influential analyses of suffragists and their ideas, for those analyses shaped the current classifications of feminism. They are responsible for the illusory chasm between the two waves of women's public activism, and they have even shaped contemporary evaluations and classifications of the new, successor feminisms.

With all these caveats expressed, we can now look at social feminism as it has actually developed, embodied in actual women's groups. The simplest version of social feminism is the one known as "maternal." It sees women's distinctive qualities and duties as a simple function of biology and especially of reproduction (Gorham 1976). Having a womb becomes almost a guarantee of virtue, of finer feelings and unselfish commitment to service to one's own children or future children and thus to all of humanity. Such virtues were initially seen as complementary to male values, in the classic "separate spheres" argument that theoretically kept women and their influence confined to the home (Elshtain 1981). But the social feminists increasingly doubted a public sphere that had been left to men's untender care. Maternal virtues, even in the most simply biologistic sense, came to be seen as necessary supplements and then as correctives for public life.

The early, maternally focused social feminism was very distant from today's sociobiological theories that derive social order from male aggressivity and bonding and that portray female passivity as necessarily and permanently separate from public life. Nineteenth-century feminists encountered formidable versions of such notions (as well as silly arguments about women's propensity to faint at public meetings or to starve their wombs of blood diverted to their brains). Most serious was the claim that women were disqualified from the vote because of the necessity of force to fight wars and maintain an empire—force being the preeminent male virtue to which maternity was a bar. Mrs. Humphry Ward, a feminist who opposed suffragism, gave in her novel *Delia Blanchflower* (1914) a complex analysis of how views on violence and on proper behavior for men and women could either generate or limit activism. Women should eventually be given the vote as a means to perform appropriate public service, she concluded, but they should not deny their own nature by attempting to fight for it. Her novel is a rather repellent attack on suffragette militancy, but it voices no objection to feminist activism. Today, after the full grant of civil rights to women, such old disputes still echo in the refusal to allow women to play a role in combat—and feminist analysts such as Judith Stiehm (1976) identify combat rights as the remaining portion of women's claim to equality.

The most naive of the social feminists dealt confidently with these problems. They believed that in modern times there was no value in men's innate aggressiveness. Civilization consisted in taming such impulses, and it was now time to call on women to aid in the process. Women probably were innately pacifist, but even if they were not, they were ideally placed to appreciate and underline the ultimate argument for peace: children. Surely they could make the desirability of peace obvious to all rational human beings if they could explain it to them? The need for a political role and for continuing political action stemmed from the need for a public position, and female reproductive capacities thus became the foundation of feminism.

Some of today's feminists, building on the dialectics of Marx or of Hegel, have developed a contemporary version of maternal feminism that sees the social consequences of reproduction and reproductive technology as the moving forces of human history. Reproductive labor becomes the corrective to productive labor and women, because of their physiology, become the instruments of revolution and of human perfection (O'Brien 1981). More simply, the maternal feminists of the past, who lived in an era and a society where child-bearing was the normal experience of adult women, saw life-giving, life-enhancing, and life-preserving as intrinsically linked. The feminist peace movement, which has also experienced considerable ideological evolution, has always relied heavily on the assumption that women, who birth and nurture children, will not waste them in warfare. Canadian Nellie McClung wrote that Kaiser Wilhelm could have been prevented from starting World War I if the "blue-eyed, motherly, deep-bosomed German woman would have stood upon her feet and said, 'William—forget it!'" (McClung 1972:89). This was a suffragist argument, and for many women a compelling one.

A more sophisticated and more widely influential version of social feminism relies less on the intrinsic, biologically based nature of women and more on what a sexually segregated society has imposed on females in terms of special experience. Here social feminists join equity feminists in agreement that the potential for child-bearing need not entail child-rearing or housework. Nor need it entail tenderness or lack of aggressivity, any more than it need entail lesser education, greater poverty, or political exclusion. But where equity feminists stress the unjust consequences of differentiation, the social feminists stress what they see as the positive products of this unjust situation. Patriarchal society has produced in women, without their knowledge or consent and often against their will, certain sorts of expertise and virtue. That such qualities are devalued by men and the male public world is all the more reason why women must speak for the qualities labeled "feminine," for nurturing, cooperation, love, peace. Virginia Woolf wrote eloquently in the 1920s and 1930s of women's "civilisation," which contrasted with the barbarous entity that men have created and identified as having universal validity. In her stronger version of maternal feminism, women do not merely add to the humanizing elements of modern life; they *are* those elements. In *Three Guineas* Woolf urged women to act as an unstructured "Society of Outsiders" who would seek to achieve "freedom, equality, peace" in ways derived from "a different sex, a different tradition, a different education, and the different values that result from these differences" (1938:206). It seems clear that she saw the women's movement as an approximation to the Society of Outsiders; she had been closely associated with the social feminist Women's Co-operative Guild (Black 1983)

McClung and Woolf represent the range of first-wave social feminism. Both believed in justice and equality. But both were far more concerned with the condition of society and how women's activity could transform it. In their view, the contradiction between private and public values would disappear as family values entered politics along with women. The family, or at least its more attractive features, was for them a model for the future rather than a remnant of the past. Woolf was not naive about the exploitative aspects of the family, but she shared with all other social feminists an ideal that was domestic in nature and origin. In the postsuffrage era the successors to the franchise alliances attempted to construct social policies oriented to women's needs and values. The interwar English group, the National Union of Societies for Equal Citizenship (NUSEC), attempted under the leadership of M.P. Eleanor Rathbone to construct what they called a "new feminism":

> To the new school, the habit of continually measuring women's wants by men's achievements seems out of date, ignominious, and intolerably boring. "Here we have a world," we say, "which has been shaped by men to fit their own needs. It is, on the whole, a poor sort of world. . . . Now that we have full possession of the tools of citizenship, we intend to use them not to copy men's models but to produce our own" (Rathbone 1936:58).

In her feminist writings Virginia Woolf called for the vote and for reformed divorce laws, minimum wages, and modernization of household equipment and arrangements, as well as equal access to education and the professions. She supported NUSEC's major campaign, for a state allowance to mothers as those responsible for children, accompanied by equal pay for equal work. And McClung and Woolf, for feminist reasons, shared a principled opposition to war[3]

In addition to goals and ideals, social feminists have tended to share an insistence on women-only membership in their organizations. Theirs, after all, were women's tasks directed by women's values and experience. By the time of the suffrage victories, such preferences were already perceived as conservative by most conventional political analysts, probably because of the influence of the equity feminist arguments that strove for entrance on equal terms into male organizations. Today, the preference for all-women organization is sometimes seen as a survival of the days when women did not have access to men's groups. The implication of such a judgment, of course, is that male groups are the ones carrying on important public activities. Today, in a new (or renewed) development, it is often the most radical of feminists who opt for single-sex organizations.

In the classification of feminism I suggest here, such radical feminist groups are social feminist. They share the belief that women are intrinsically different from men in ways that society has neglected to its cost. Capitalism now enters into social feminists' analysis as one of the causes of a violent and sterile civilization. The emphasis on female functions is oriented more toward sexuality than toward reproduction, but the perspective is the same. An extreme version rejects *all* male values. Anne Tristan of the French Mouvement pour la libération des femmes writes: "To have a chance of being on the road to truth, it is sufficient to take the opposite of the values and rules of our male capitalist civilization" (quoted in Michel 1979:122).

Today the rejected values may include heterosexuality, seen as serving male purposes, but they will not include maternity, which women must redefine and reclaim. For radical feminists the situation of lesbian mothers is therefore an especially significant one. Adrienne Rich (1976) is one of those who reclaim motherhood for "woman-defined women"; Sara Ruddick (1980) one of many who argue that the experience of child-rearing generates a special sort of practical reason that is crucial for the rehabilitation of politics. In this context Sally Miller Gearhart (1982) urges a deliberate reduction of the proportion of males in the population; half of reproduction is to occur by "ovular merging," a process she insists is now almost possible technologically. This may be a deliberate parody of others' arguments, but it is nevertheless a seriously argued position. Such views should not be confused with those of the equally feminist Shulamith Firestone, who hopes to use a new technology to obliterate male-female distinctions by eliminating the need for a female role in sexuality and reproduction (1970). Firestone's emphasis on the

3. This is true even though McClung, mother of a draft-age son, came to support World War I as the war to end wars and Woolf, married to a Jewish intellectual, came to support British military opposition to Nazism.

biological causes of women's oppression has led her to be classified as a radical feminist, but hers is basically an equity argument aimed at obliterating differences between women and men. Gearhart's is a social feminist approach: "EITHER THE FUTURE IS FEMALE OR THE FUTURE IS NOT" (284). Using less apocalyptic terms, contemporary social feminists would agree.[4]

It is in France that the newest social feminism has been most explicitly articulated: the term *phallocratie* sums up a judgment of public life as male-generated, male-directed, and defective. Change is obviously imperative. But social feminists are unlikely to advocate revolution, for they see overt violence as the quintessentially male technique for social influence. The alternatives are often unclear. Annie Leclerc writes, "This stupid stinking military world is busily destroying itself."[5] She goes on: "It's over, the time of women always dragged along behind the revolutions/convolutions of men who are fighting themselves. The real revolution is coming, and we will be its heart or, as we are told, its hearth, light and heat and model for life." The female mode is laughter, fertility, female sexuality (*jouissance*), nurturance: "Someday perhaps we will create what we have put such effort into preventing: the simplest, the truest, the craziest things: the harmony of our laughter" (1974: 9, 160).

The longstanding involvement of social feminists in the peace movement continues. More recently, and distinctive of second-wave feminism, a new version of social feminism sometimes called "ecological feminism" has called on women to counteract the disastrous worldwide effects of modernization (Sauter-Bailliet 1981). This approach would have been congenial to the early social feminists, with their commitment to standards based on the domestic and the immediate. Their more analytic descendants argue explicitly for the virtues of the domestic, immediate, and small-scale. The male values of competition, aggrandizement, and aggressivity, noted by earlier feminists, are seen now to have run wild in the world system of multinational enterprises. Women are both most oppressed by the multiple dependencies and best placed to resist and replace them. Andrée Michel writes: "Feminists [should] reject the credo of societies of accumulation: competition, rivalry, worship of unlimited growth and profit, enslavement of humanity to technology and the economy, gigantism of projects, and praise of the egoism of the nation and the nuclear family" (1979:122). The analysis continues, logically, to link "the military-industrial complex and violence against women" (Michel 1985a). "Discrimination, exploitation, and violence against women are the expression of a patriarchal system where one sex domi-

4. A more moderate fantasy by a feminist linguist retains the traditional notion of women working within society as a transforming minority, in this case through the medium of a new, women-invented language. See Elgin 1984, 1987.

5. My translation. Unless indicated otherwise, all translations from French-language sources are mine.

nates the other," Michel states, as she directs the feminist reader's attention to the operations of patriarchy at the national and international levels (1985a:5). She concludes by warning women that "equality of the sexes can be imagined as submitting along with men to the acceptance of the values, models of development, concepts of 'national security' and 'defense' imposed by the military-industrial complex, that is, patriarchal power" (1985a:63–64). Equity feminism, in short, means induction into Leclerc's self-destructive "stupid stinking military world," while social feminism aims at what Jessie Bernard calls "the female world from a global perspective" (1987).

I am talking here in terms that put aside the extraordinary diversity of both equity and social feminism over place and time. It is possible, however, to see underlying consistency in general patterns of belief. This consistency in turn follows from a continuity in organizational and personal terms which tends to be overlooked. Obviously, the specific goals of both social and equity feminists exhibit great variety, and they have changed over time. The nineteenth-century feminist ideal of voluntary motherhood through abstinence has largely been replaced as a goal by free availability of abortion, equal pay for equal work has been replaced by equal pay for work of equal value (or comparable worth), Prohibition by transition houses, the vote by the ERA. The goals vary by place: polygamy and genital mutilation are greater or lesser concerns, and so are female infanticide and sexual harassment. In any given context the range of interests is wide. Yet there are some continuities within each general sort of feminism, and there have been important agreements. The issues related to pay, to reproductive control, and to political activism have drawn support across a broad spectrum of feminists, in spite of a considerable range in justifications. At a certain point most feminists agreed on the desirability of woman suffrage. Today, most tend to agree on the importance of a higher level of political participation by women.

Most present-day feminists share a considerable degree of skepticism about the likely role of women in conventional politics. More sensitive than their predecessors to the economic and psychological dimensions of public life, even equity feminists are conscious of the continuing exploitation of women in the workplace and of the continuing male domination of public life. The typical equity response is to point to the effectively minority status of women, even though the public sphere is now formally unsegregated, and to struggle to increase the numbers and the distribution of women toward parity. Social feminists are more likely to respond with an attempt to modify the male model of public life by increasing the influence of those areas of politics where men are not so dominant. Hence, in both analytic and practical terms, social feminists direct their attention to the role of women in informal or unrecognized political activities. Here women perhaps have some hope of reaching critical mass and of influencing the larger conduct of politics.

In a political context, therefore, the goals and activities of different sorts of feminists are complementary and can be mutually supportive, as successive campaigns from the suffrage to the ERA have demonstrated. Their logics continue to be very different, and so do their arguments and organizational preferences.

Equity feminism is essentially assimilationist, its goal a society in which women will not need to be treated differently from men because they will not be distinguishable from them in any way relevant to public policy. Its preferences thus are androgynous (in the sense of wishing to abolish sex roles.)[6] In contrast, social feminism is inclined to be separatist, at least in the short run. The separatist element emerges most clearly within radical lesbianism, a movement of considerable cultural vitality but no political future. Separatism also appears in feminist science fantasy, which makes clear its inadequacy for a social system.

Charlotte Perkins Gilman, who was both an equity feminist and, more important, a social feminist, presented in the early twentieth century a social feminist utopia in which there were no males at all. In *Herland* (1979), published in 1915, women can reproduce without men, and the culture they produced is wholly nurturant. Outside this geographically isolated realm of women, modern society continues a futility symbolized by the incursion of some seemingly normal young men who find themselves reduced to the typical masculine follies of rape and other physical violence. *Herland* is a stalemate, for only a biological fantasy makes it possible, and it gives no hope for brothers and sons. The same stalemate, more bitterly and brutally expressed, pervades a contemporary social feminist fantasy, *Motherlines* (Charnas 1979), where women are nomadic, barely civilized, and almost all sterile (dependent again on biological fantasy including, this time, stallions). For Charnas, the male world is postnuclear, dependent on a barbarous and literal enslavement of women, and clearly doomed. This despairing dimension of the social feminist vision has to pin its hopes on the distinctive qualities of the powerless and the isolated. Yet social feminism characteristically wishes to retain genders, even though both are to be redefined, constraints reduced,

---

6. Virginia Woolf's well-known praise of androgyny should be carefully distinguished from the androgyny envisaged by equity feminists, which involves a society with no gender divisions. Woolf was convinced that all humans had—or could have—both male and female characteristics, and she valued the influence of both. Her main concerns as a feminist were about the marginalization of women and of the female values. Women had to deal with consequences of disadvantage which included resentment and the disabling awareness of sexual identity as well as inferior education, economic insecurity, and the lack of entitlement to self-expression; men had to deal only with a narrowness resulting from their rejection of female experience and values. The androgynous mind was one able to use creatively both the male and the female elements potentially there (Woolf 1928).

options enlarged. Policy goals rely on interaction between male and female, and scientists show increasing interest in the relation of biology not just to female but also to male qualities. The distinguished sociologist and longtime feminist Alice Rossi has in recent years created considerable controversy by shifting, in effect, from a polemically effective equity feminism to what she calls a "biosocial" approach that is far closer to social feminism. She now sees physiological maternity (pregnancy and birthing) as facilitating parental relationships and their associated values, and she is convinced that there is between males and females an enduring and possibly valuable differentiation with respect to the ease with which they can be socialized into culturally desirable roles. Her recent research is on the possibly sex-specific biological and social patterns of aging among women (Rossi 1964, 1977).

The appalled feminist outcry that greeted Rossi's recent arguments indicates the commitment feminists have to an equity model and the extent of their understandable anxiety lest the admission of differences be used once again to argue for women's inferiority and exclusion (Gross et al. 1979). More perceptively, an increasing number of feminists are able, like Rossi, to analyze and praise the "female world" without neglecting its particular pathologies. Such an approach can admit the virtues as well as the pathologies of the male world. Jessie Bernard (1981) has catalogued the reality and the intellectual tradition of polarities; the female pole has been ignored in its relegation to private life. Carol Gilligan (1982) distinguishes within notions of morality to show how justice (male) and personal commitments (female) are both necessary for a satisfactory system of ethics. Mary Field Belenky and her associates (1986) are developing a model of cognitive development that allows for both intuition and rational analysis. In these cases the male version has historically been presented as a single, encompassing standard; now the female version becomes not an addition or a substitute but the basis of a transformation of relationships and values.

Social feminism is, finally, a hope and a project of social transformation. Perhaps illogically, social feminists continue to believe that feminists can be publicly active without being coopted. They are convinced that it will be possible to retain the integrity and value of the female world along with what is valuable in the now dominant male option. In policy terms, therefore, they concentrate on increasing the influence on public life of women *as women*.

Their focus is on the concept of difference, seen as both real and enabling or even empowering. Social feminists are aware that difference in the past served as an instrument of social control. Even for the conscious feminist, difference can become a mystical, lyrical justification of submission to existing social systems (Fauré 1981:84–86). Indeed, feminist separatism may be one of the more seductive forms of such political conservatism. Yet for women-only organizations, the notion of difference has in practice served to render more fluid and permeable the barriers against women's influence on public life. The gifted, the exceptional, the rebels by personality or by experience—such women identify with the powerful, imagine themselves wielding an influence they have been denied. They have the capacity to project themselves into the situation of men, and their reaction is typically indignation, energy, action, the demand for a share of privilege. Lucy Stone declared that she hoped to provoke such feelings in all women. But as Stone's own life shows, such women pay dearly for efforts to break out of the mindsets in which they were raised. Often they can do so only by identifying with men's arguments and men's situation: Lucy Stone initially was convinced she must not marry, was dissuaded only with difficulty. Later, as she attempted to reconcile male and female models of life, she lost effectiveness in a long period of nervous headaches, depression, and self-imposed exile to private life (Wheeler 1981). Few women can be expected to follow her painful path. It is easier, in part because more acceptable to others, for women to build upon their own specific experience and values.

If this work has an icon, it is probably Lucy Stone. She combined the ideologies of social and equity feminism and the two crucial activities of political action and reconstruction of the family, working for the practical redefinition of both spheres so that women could be active in both. Her life and beliefs, so often interpreted as conservative, demonstrate the complexity of the task of transforming the patriarchy.

Lucy Stone left us no theoretical work. Because most social feminists were even less theoretical than she was, we have to look at their lives for their ideology. The acceptance of social feminism as a valid category of feminism brings with it the imperative of studying women's organizations. In wider terms, the choice of women's organizations as an object of study is, for me, a response to the imperative of a feminist approach to social science.

CHAPTER 4

A Feminist Approach
to Social Science

Since feminism centers on women's claim to define their own options, feminist researchers must take especially seriously the scholar's necessary task of self-examination. The conditions of academic inquiry reinforce this need. The *female* scholar is always likely to be forced to justify her presence in a setting where women are still relatively few in numbers, their acceptance conditional on conformity with existing modes of behavior and inquiry. The *feminist* can expect serious challenge to her preferred goals and techniques; she should anticipate hostility or at best indifference. Some feminists have responded by rejecting participation in established scholarly structures, institutional or analytic, choosing instead some version of radical action-research in women's community politics. Others have opted for a self-consciously feminist scholarship that still relates to the conventional mainstream pattern. I am concerned here with a subcategory of such research, what could be called "feminist social science" or, less provocatively, "a feminist approach to social science."

"Feminist social science" sounds like an internal contradiction or at least a paradox. The very notion sounds like a political stance and might therefore be dismissed as irrelevant to the conduct of research. But the scholarly tradition to which this term can refer is, nonetheless, recognizable. Furthermore, it can be developed to give guidelines to the feminist researcher.[1]

The reader will have noted that I write of the researcher as "she." This is not a gesture against male domination of research and terminology, but an indication of the fact that, by my definitions, the feminist researcher is *necessarily* a woman (although it is possible for a man to do

1. I discuss feminist research here with special reference to political science, the field in which I work. Political science, as I understand it, overlaps with political sociology, political philosophy, and some areas of history. The general argument is applicable to all fields of social science and extensible into other areas of research; I refer also to the study of literature and to science.

74

research related to feminism). A woman who is a researcher is not, of course, bound to be a feminist, but a feminist scholar is likely to be or become a feminist researcher. In addition to the important distinction between feminism as an ideology or belief system and feminism as a social movement or political struggle, there is a third category: feminism as an analytic or academic perspective. These three aspects are necessarily related, the more so as feminism insists on the value of subjectivity and personal experience. Acceptance, for whatever reason, of feminist beliefs drastically influences a woman's perspectives and can be expected to have an impact on her analytic approach. Given the recentness of the application of feminism to scholarship and the disputes that have followed, a feminist who is also a scholar may find intellectual assimilation of her activist feminism a long, slow, and difficult process. She is likely to experience a considerable period of relative incoherence when, for instance, the relevance of feminism for a subject such as international relations is unclear. But the logic extending practice to theory is unmistakable, however difficult it may be to work through the process.

A feminist is unlikely, however, to feel that the feminist perspective is "just one more way of talking about books," as K. K. Ruthven put it. Ruthven adds, correctly, that feminist criticism "must undergo the kind of inspection made sooner or later of every type of critical discourse, each of which has its own etiology and aims, distinctive features and operational procedures, all of which can be described and assessed for the insights they yield" (1984:8). Here feminism is squarely in the world of ideas, and any number can play, with even the nonfeminist, male or female, welcome. But, Ruthven concludes complacently, "it is no more necessary to be a woman in order to analyze feminist criticism as criticism than it is to be a Marxist in order to comprehend the strategies of Marxist criticism" (1984:15). In a more accurate parallel, he need not be a worker in order to analyze Marxism. He need not be a *feminist* to analyze feminist criticism.

Feminists today are well aware of how men, even men with good intentions, can use a version of feminism as a means of maintaining dominance. Such takeovers are especially threatening to feminist researchers and theorists. Underlying Ruthven's position is the simple fact that most critics are men. In the academic environment men are also the holders of power whose domination, however moderately exercised, is necessarily challenged by feminism, however loving and conciliatory feminists may be. Ruthven's tone, offended and magisterial, is the tone of the male establishment. Feminist hackles are bound to rise at the dictum that "the female 'problematic' (the questions asked of the evidence) is too important to be left in the hands of anti-intellectual feminists" (1984:9), and at the conclusion that "even this most recent of feminisms is heavily dependent on men to articulate its position and continues to co-opt their services" (11).[2]

Far from depending on male research and male researchers, feminist scholarship starts, in general, from the recognition of sexism in research. At the simplest level, this is the realization that women are virtually absent in most accounts of human existence. Gaps must be filled, incompleteness identified and compensated for: women enter history as what was going on "meanwhile." This stage is now summed up by women's studies scholars somewhat contemptuously as "add women and stir." Because such research relies on existing methods and categories, it produces little that is qualitatively new. A comforting, related line of analysis suggests that changes in modern social science could make the incorporation of women's activities and concerns easier. For instance, political science's recognition of the political nature of social movements means that it can study the women's movement; Jo Freeman won a prestigious thesis prize on this basis in 1975, International Women's Year.

The next stage of such scholarship, perhaps the first to be genuinely feminist, shifts attention to standards and techniques, finding a more serious sexism in the failure to apply to the study of women the criteria supposedly in general use. Thus, for instance, the few volunteered remarks of foreign-born Chicago women in a 1923 survey continue to be a major basis of statements about why women refrain from using the vote. In the 1970s and 1980s analysts still retailed comments by a few of those nonvoters that a woman's place is in the home. Hardly less anachronistic than another nonvoter's observation that "woman is a flower for men to look after," such statements have helped reinforce the notion of women as apolitical (Bourque and Grossholtz 1974:256).

Though feminist in perspective and intentions, most early critiques of social science scholarship in effect ask merely for adherence to the academy's professed standards. One political scientist phrases it as follows: "Accusations of sexism—whether levelled at a field as a whole or at an individual's work—are accusations of poor scholarship. Scholars cannot make assumptions about women or ignore gender where it is relevant without violating their own canons of research" (Sapiro 1979:263–64). This attitude transforms "accusations of sexism" into relatively benign inquiries that do not question methods or goals.

Yet feminist researchers learn in practice that neither gaps nor distortions in accepted wisdom can easily be remedied with available approaches or data. In this way they acquire a deep distrust of the standards and procedures of the systems of inquiry in which they were

2. Ruthven indicates the intellectual and psychological constraints on male acceptance of feminism: "For many men, however, the feminist critique of gender is intellectually disturbing (how could men have been blind?), and, for the more sensitive, a source of shame and guilt (after such knowledge, what forgiveness?)." He also demonstrates the concrete problems as he goes on to describe feminism as "even in its mildest forms . . . accusatory, as it is meant to be; and in its most uncompromising manifestations . . . unrelentingly intimidatory" (1984:10). Wisecracks about the "*j'accuserie* of moderatism" (10) accompany a facile dismissal of feminist anxieties about male domination of the academy.

trained. As one feminist political sociologist puts it, they begin to suspect a "malevolence of method" (McCormack 1981:10). The criteria of "generality" and "objectivity" come to look like devices for maintaining male control, obstacles to truth rather than instruments for its discovery. Such reactions are encouraged by the way in which the academic establishment as a whole still ignores or repudiates the findings of feminist scholars, pushing them into the isolated if fruitful enclaves of women's studies.

In a further stage of feminist research, inquirers find themselves led to use relatively marginal sources such as oral history and participant observation. Increased sophistication in the use of such "soft" material then produces reasoned defenses of a nontraditional version of research, justifications that seek an independent rationale in terms of scientific goals. This shift represents a turn to something like social feminism's insistence on the use of methods and values outside the mainstream. Earlier stages in the development of feminist scholarship resemble equity feminism in their attempts to incorporate women into existing scholarship. In contrast, social feminism tries to transform all involved. The social feminist analysis of scholarship foresees a new mode of scholarly discourse as deriving from and supporting a new, transformed social realm.

Two sorts of feminism operate in feminist discussions of political science scholarship. The full and equal application of academic standards to the study of women continues to be part of the feminist project. At the same time, there is more fundamental criticism. Indeed, some of the earliest feminist critics backed their critique of "fudging footnotes" and distorted statistics with questions about assumptions based on the male monopoly of politics. Is it reasonable, they asked, to consider a state democratic if it denies the vote to women, as Switzerland did for so long? Do the similar votes of married men and women really mean that women are voting as their husbands order? Should adult, experienced women be seen as "immature" because they make different choices, political and otherwise, from those of the equivalent men (Bourque and Grossholtz 1974, Goot and Reid 1975)? By the 1980s such social feminist perspectives had become a significant feature of feminist critiques of social science.

In 1981, for instance, Virginia Sapiro concluded a lengthy essay on women and politics with the reassuring comment: "Political science can only benefit by expanding its view [to include women]" (713). In the same journal issue Irene Diamond and Nancy Hartsock responded with a strong statement of disagreement:

> In sum, we are not saying, as Sapiro does, that recent scholarship in women's studies can show that political science has been studying the actions of only half of humanity, and that the subject matter of political science should

be expanded. Instead, we are suggesting that the focus on the activity of only half of humanity is fundamental to what has been understood as political life for the last 2500 years. To include women's concerns, to represent women in the public life of our society might well lead to a profound redefinition of public life itself (1981:721).

Applied to the whole of social science, such comments criticize the mode of inquiry that has become enshrined as the scientific method. Catharine MacKinnon stated the most far-reaching implications: "Feminism does not see its view as subjective, partial, or undetermined but as a critique of the purported generality, disinterestedness, and universality of prior accounts. These have not been half right but have invoked the wrong whole. Feminism not only challenges masculine partiality but questions the universality imperative itself" (1982:537). Such an analysis is a powerful solvent for the pretensions of sexist theory. An interesting, sometimes important critical literature has developed in its wake (Sherman and Beck 1979; Spender 1981; Harding and Hintikka 1983; Harding 1986). But attempts to develop positive guidelines and models of procedure have been more difficult. MacKinnon, for instance, makes a convincing case for the argument that "aperspectivity is revealed as a strategy for male hegemony" (1982:537), but all she can suggest to guide alternative research is the substitution of the concept of female "desire" for male "power." She herself, as Judith Kegan Gardiner points out, retains such assumptions as a definition of female sexuality in terms of the heterosexual dyad. More important in the context of philosophy of science, she continues the "binary thinking" that lumps all female experience together as "difference" contrasted to the universality claimed by males; she makes no allowance for diversity among women or (a point not made by Gardiner) for diversity among men. Gardiner concludes ruefully that she also lacks "adequate substitute models to offer" and can recommend nothing more precise than continued attempts to conceptualize female specificity (1983:737). Sandra Harding (1986) goes a step further to praise the fluidity of analyses that are not yet committed to any single model, but under the circumstances she can hardly supply practical guidelines.

MacKinnon, as well as Gardiner and Harding, can be seen as working from a social feminist perspective in that women's values and experience provide her with criteria for judging theory. At the same time her modes of analysis are equity feminist ones that accept mainstream demands for grand theory and master concepts. She thus opts for one of the two ways in which feminists have attempted to restructure social science. The distinction corresponds roughly to the familiar philosophical contrast between deductive and inductive approaches. Feminists have tended to emphasize either language and the construction of grand theory or experience and a critique of the processes of inquiry. Both emphases can be encompassed by equity feminism; both present major problems from a social feminist perspective.

MacKinnon can be understood better when we realize that she is operating in the first, deductive mode; she is among those North American feminists strongly influenced by the emphasis that French theorists have placed on language as the repository of values and the shaper of human experience. The goal of the most influential French feminists is to purify language and ideology in order to break free of the established patriarchal ("phallologocentric") fashions of apprehending reality. The anglophone feminist's response to such efforts is likely to be divided between admiration and skepticism. In France, where the highest prestige comes from election to the editorial board of a dictionary, an assault on language seems appropriate for those who challenge the establishment, particularly as French is so deeply sexist a language. Yet the analytic modes of this deconstruction are generated and dominated by men, and not by men sympathetic to feminism. In addition, if we apply to feminist theory its own critique of conventional scholarship, asking about social consequences, we find that French feminism has been exceptionally faction-ridden and elitist. This is the country where the hegemonic, linguistically oriented group "Psych et po" actually trademarked the term "Women's Liberation Movement" (Sauter-Bailliet 1981; Kauffmann-McCall 1983; Duchen 1986).

Criticisms of linguistic analysis in terms of its origins and outcomes are, of course, made from within social feminism. In contrast, women committed to some version of North American equity feminism are unhappy with any analysis that relies on female specificity. For example, Carolyn Heilbrun, who has written approvingly of androgyny (1973), praises the French approach as "full of possibility and high intelligence," calling it a "brave undertaking" in spite of doubts that it "will eventuate in great advance for women" (1979:210). Heilbrun is less satisfied with the alternative, "American" approach, "more empirical, less theoretical," and fatally constrained by the assumption of an "irreversible" distinction between the sexes: "Womanhood must be reinvented by those who can imagine, not by those who wish to reconstruct their gender prison" (209–10). Her own position is clear: "So far, it is men who have moved upon the earth and had adventures; it is men who have told stories. But perhaps women have not told stories because there were no stories to tell. There was only the dailiness of life, the attention to food, clothing, shelter, the endless replication of motherhood" (210).[3]

3. Carolyn Heilbrun is one of the most open-minded and activist of the feminist scholars in English literature. She describes feminism as "in the intellectual as well as the political sphere . . . at the very heart of a profound revolution" (1987:222). But she has consistently underestimated the social feminist tradition in a way characteristic of equity feminists, as her published work on feminism demonstrates.

Heilbrun calls for the female appropriation of male experience and records, and for the consequent "reinvention of womanhood" as what manhood is, "a condition of risk, and variety, and discovery" (212). Her account embodies the equity version of feminist criticism which accepts existing (male) standards as a basis for changing the situation of women, through scholarship as through action. By contrast, distinctive social feminist critiques of social science, which focus on content, highlight that "dailiness of life" which Heilbrun discards as uninteresting. When anthropologists report that "women have not told stories," we should not respond that women as such lack a subject for narrative. Instead, we should distrust the account of women's lives supplied by conventional techniques of inquiry and analysis.

At the extreme, the social feminist approach concentrates on the subject or content of research and aims at an atheoretically direct examination of "the everyday world as problematic." The phrase comes from Dorothy Smith's attempt to delineate a "feminist sociology" (1987); her analysis underlines the difficulties of the approach, which I nevertheless attempt to adapt here. Smith states explicitly the feminist conviction that modes of analysis are aspects of domination and, in particular, that systems of intellectual order serve those who exercise social control. Her argument is framed in reference to sociology but applies to all social science and certainly to dimensions of the humanities:

> The implication that the actualities of the everyday world are unformed and unorganized and that the sociologist cannot enter them without a conceptual framework to select, assemble, and order them is one that we can now understand in this special relationship of a sociology constituted as part of a ruling apparatus vis-à-vis which the local and the particular, the actualities of the world which is lived, are necessarily untamed, disordered, and incoherent (89–90).

The recommended solution, a seductive one, is to go directly to "actual lived situations" (91).

Smith is surely correct that images of domestic disorder are part of the cultural control of women wherever the everyday world is seen as a female domain. The socially dominant position of the "trained" researcher plays a role in the assumption that only general principles developed elsewhere can make sense of the domestic. But this analysis attributes too much power to the investigator, who is less an imposer of order than one who may mistakenly report something not substantiated by reality. The system of control is weakened by inaccuracy, which may partly explain the emergence of feminism. Women *do* tell significant tales in spite of scholarly denials that it is possible. The feminist vision insists on the objective reality of daily life, and the more sophisticated feminist does so in full awareness of distorting simplifications of what is often fluid and ambiguous. Dominant observers are often ignorant and arrogant; their privileged position may make them misperceive reality as something tamed. But their power, though great, is inadequate to re-shape the world entirely to the pattern of their perceptions.

At the same time the aspirations of the dominated are misleading. They are tempted to read resistance into their own situation even when that situation is most often characterized merely by complexity and po-tentiality (Rupp 1981, Zimmerman 1984). The feminist researcher may well hesitate as she seeks a focal point. Smith provides guidance in an appealing form: "The determination of our worlds by relations and processes that do not appear fully in them are matters for investigation and inquiry, not for speculation." She adds, "Making the everyday world our problematic instructs us to look for the 'inner' organization generat-ing its ordinary features, its orders and disorders, its contingencies and conditions" (1987:99). She avoids the obvious traps of a naive empiricism as she recognizes the existence of structures that are not directly observ-able in everyday life and that have a wider range than the immediate activities of women. Any social science must recognize the ways in which humans attempt to make sense of the temporal and spatial aspects of their lives in the context of other times and places they have experienced or anticipate. This context must necessarily be expanded to include no-tions of connected, relating, encompassing, similar, and different lives, though such inclusiveness is in practice virtually impossible. The source of the necessary markers and definitions is the key question, and one with which all theories of induction are still struggling.

However, Smith, who seems to waive structure, in fact stipulates one. Hers is not a feminist framework, for she instructs the researcher "to look for that inner organization in the externalized and abstracted rela-tions of economic processes and of the ruling apparatus in general" (1987:99). The externalized and abstracted relations of economic pro-cesses cannot be and were not derived from women's "everyday world." Marx and his followers developed their conceptual model from careful observation of an everyday world that was characteristically male, name-ly the paid labor force under capitalism. Its components are particularly difficult to trace in operation within domestic life, as a generation of Marxist feminists can testify. Smith herself draws a far more persuasive example of induction from Kurt Vonnegut, the derivation of the nature of war from street-level experience of the bombing of Dresden, but she cites it as an argument for the ruling framework she prefers (1987:93–94).

Like so many other feminists, Smith has imposed Marxist abstractions on the specificities of women's life. Socialist feminists who emphasize the Marxist aspect of their beliefs more heavily than she does move on to praise everyday life as the locale where Marxism can best be perfected: "The women's movement has reinvented Marx's method and for that reason can be a force for revolution [and] a model for the rest of the left" (Hartsock 1979:66). Here the priority of the interests of the left over those of women is clear, and it is implicit in the priorities of analysis in Smith's account. Like the conceptual categories used to sort their experience, women are secondary. They can enter history only because they are assimilated into the systems of production defined by and in terms of men. So derivative an equity feminism can produce only limited autonomy at either the theoretical or the practical level.

Still, however illogically, Smith and other analysts do insist on the independent interest and importance of women's activities. They point in practice to the diversity that is the concrete expression of women's shared situation. Even when constrained by Marxism, feminism directs attention to life as experienced by women—in this case, to their versions of class differentiation. In addition, some Marxist feminists have suggested reconceptualizations of the household as a social unit that challenges as well as supports capitalism (Rapp 1982). Searching among women's activities for resemblances to the class struggle, some feminists have identified dimensions of consumerism as elements in proletarian resistance to the bourgeoisie (Rowbotham 1977). Attention to the everyday thus leads them to attribute value to the same differentiated activities and values that provided the starting points for the social feminists they often despise as conservative. Like social feminists, they come to see domestic activities and values as a basis of women's intervention in and transformation of the public realm.

What is closer to the family, after all, than the slogan "From each according to his ability, to each according to his need"? The feminist need only add "or her" twice, and the focus on daily activities inserts women into even conventional Marxist analysis:

> If, to paraphrase Marx, we follow the worker home from the factory, we can once again perceive a change in the *dramatis personae*. He who before followed behind as the worker, timid and holding back, with nothing to expect but a hiding, now strides in front while a third person, not specifically present in Marx's account of the transaction between capitalist and worker (both of whom are male) follows timidly behind, carrying groceries, baby, and diapers (Hartsock 1983:291).

Some Marxists, however grudgingly, are now looking at that third person.

The inductive or social feminist focus on women's activities has had even more drastic implications for non-Marxist scholarship, though again they are inadequate as a guide to research. Social science conventionally sees women's lives, on the one hand, as so trivially varied that no generalizations are appropriate and, on the other hand, as explicable by a simple reference to biology. Women's lives have been viewed as fragmented by their involvement with the contingent and the immediate, but for reasons that are constant across the lifetimes of individuals and of the species. Feminism has cast doubt on accepted accounts both of the nature of women's activities and of the reasons underlying them, most obviously in studies of the family (Thorne and Yalom 1982) but now also in areas such as political behavior (Flammang 1984). More researchers now look seriously at the activities of those who had been dismissed because believed merely to exist rather than to create or to reflect. Certainly it was inappropriate that behaviorists should have excluded such activities from their generalizations. Even the first stages of feminist scholarship transform the subject matter of research, and do so increasingly with the cumulation of reports on daily life.

At this point the optimist might see a convergence of feminist and nonfeminist perspectives. The conventional researcher has been exposed to an opening up of subject matter, and perhaps the feminist can be persuaded that some version of scientific method is irreplaceable. If a transformation of research is not imminent, perhaps it is nonetheless unavoidable in the longer run. My response is more pessimistic: the current phase of feminist critiques focuses precisely upon discussions of the likelihood and the desirability of real change and on the usefulness of feminist acceptance of some version of existing methodologies.

The feminist scholars who turned to women's experience as the basis of knowledge encountered a set of new reasons to deter them from any search for truth. They valued the everyday, so long neglected as an academic subject, and they expected to use their research findings as a basis for feminist action—for increasing their own autonomy and the autonomy of women in general. Trained as scholars, they had no trouble finding a notion of autonomy compatible with the existence of causality or the desirability of human community. As Evelyn Fox Keller noted, "the psychological sense of being able to act under one's own volition instead of under external control . . . does not mean or even suggest that one's actions are not *influenced* by others, or that one has no need of others" (1985:97). Imaginative use of the data of daily life uncovered a previously undescribed richness and complexity. If only to counter assumptions about the triviality of domesticity, these data had to be sorted into patterns. The task was easy enough; it was not twisting evidence to show that women cope, adapt, resist, influence, and respond to widely differing social structures. Women are thus demonstrably rational, even political, and admirable within the restricted sphere they have historically occupied. But in every system with a differentiated structure of authority, women turn out to be relatively disadvantaged. Always there is some division of labor based on gender, and where there is a difference in autonomy, women have less (Rosaldo 1974, 1980).

It was an impasse for the activist: feminist explanations were able to move from the biologistic to the sophisticated, but they could not offer hope for change. For instance, feminist research on violence, grounded in women's actual experience of it as a persistent dimension of everyday life, was certainly less complacent than previous discussions, but it still could not suggest how things might improve. The consequence for Susan Brownmiller was a theory that based social structure on male capability for rape (Brownmiller 1975). Such research could easily produce despair. It implied that the only hope was some violent, unprecedentedly revolutionary transformation. Yet history, especially when enriched by women's experience, seems also to show that the advocacy of drastic change has been a characteristically male mode, that revolution has not worked well when tried, and that such methods damage women even more than men.

The feminist scholar accordingly might well wish to reject the whole process of observation, generalization, theory, and policy. She could come to suspect that such methods, even if they did not coopt her, would at least disarm or mislead her. "Can we make a rigorous case for social justice when history has been unjust, and our method of empiricism ties us to past and present history?" asks Thelma McCormack (1981:5).[4] The message has not been encouraging; is it possible to trust any conclusions that may be more heartening? We are on mined ground, and injunctions to look more closely at our own and other women's experience are not adequate guidance.

To this discouragement the intellectual establishment offers its most appealing version of cooption, admitting women and their scholarly and practical significance to the Whig progression of social change. A would-be dispassionate social science, recognizing that it is value- and even bias-laden, aware also that it is a social system, can see feminism as merely the latest in the expanding, improving definitions of proper subjects and practitioners of scholarship. Emancipation advances toward the final stage of an intellectual as well as a practical liberation. Feminist critiques become the charges voiced by an excluded group—but in a setting where similar claims have already, if reluctantly, provoked a response. Should we not recognize that women are not the first on whose behalf assertions of universality and abstraction have been challenged, nor the first to react to imposed stereotypes of emotionalism and incompetence? On these grounds, some men are prepared to act as women's champions, calling on a tradition in which nonwhite, non-Western, impoverished, and otherwise "alien" men have already been not just recognized as subjects of research but assimilated into the process of inquiry (Ruthven 1984). Previous group claims have already eroded the earlier preten-

4. McCormack's answer shows the difficulty of answering the questions she poses. Peace research, her preferred model, is an established field with conventional legitimacy; its aspirations to social change, which make it attractive to McCormack, have almost entirely failed.

sions of undifferentiated universality, both in theory (hence the move to probabilism and contextuality) and in practice (hence the extension of ranges of accepted techniques, starting points, and focuses). How are women different, except in being, as so often, the last group to get in line?

This is an argument sympathetic to feminism if perhaps condescending, and it has produced a certain amount of goodwill and even progress. Yet a social feminist has to respond that women are different in this as in so many other contexts. And the implications of the difference are not trivial.

The failure of the analogy is clear from a simplified version of the nineteenth-century British and American emancipation of black slaves into the ranks of free citizens and scholars. The example, given the role of abolitionism in providing political training and theoretical analogues for some important British and American feminists, is appropriate if banal. Common to the campaigns for manumission was the crucial slogan "Am I not a man and your brother?" Brotherhood is the assertion of male autonomy, and historically it has entailed female dependence. The less common slogan "Am I not a woman and your sister?" meant only that black women were assimilated to the role of white. One of the grievances voiced by white men on behalf of black men is still the relative absence of the patriarchal family among Afro-Americans. Black nationalists in America assert that their women cannot be feminists, since female strength and independence threaten racial cohesion (Hull, Scott, and Smith 1983, Giddings 1984). Law and even science became relatively color-blind when men could identify across the boundary of race.

The male identification once made, citizenship is clearly established in principle, even though practical problems remain in a deeply racist society. But for women even the theoretical identification is impossible. Reductively and inescapably, women are defined in biological terms, and so they cannot vanish into the mass of men. In any case, men do not wish such assimilation, which would cost them control over their own women—and neither do most women, however much they deplore the control. Consequently the incorporation of minority men into scholarship, as into politics, was far easier than the incorporation of women and provides no valid precedent.

Women's claims for equal treatment represent a demand that men relinquish entitlement to define women's status. Inside as well as outside the academy, the consequence for all men would be the loss of a superior claim to knowledge and control. That perceptive observer William J. Goode has written of how "boys and grown men have always taken for granted that what they were doing was more important than what the other sex was doing," and he sees men as feeling threatened by "a loss of centrality." It is their sense of superiority as "superordinates" that feminism challenges (1982:140). Feminism, of course, denies that even the most superior of men should have authority over women. Given how little influence most humans have in this world, it is not surprising that men should cherish their gender-ascribed advantages. Nor is it surprising that women's claims become more irksome when various "inferior" castes and classes of males deny limits related to assigned characteristics. After all, the feminist demand for autonomy is fundamental in a way no previous challenge has been. It is obvious that women are to be found, however unevenly distributed, in all categories of age, physical well-being, sexual orientation, wealth, religion, even occupation. Everyone, however segregated by choice or obligation, is involved in a relationship with women: everyone had a mother, and the world as a whole is half female. Rejection of male monopoly of knowledge is the most important insubordination of all.

The feminist thus concludes that women's dependence and exclusion are different in kind from other sorts. Not only does patriarchy expect that women will each be dependent on specific individual men, but male authority is entitled to define and intervene in women's lives.[5] Feminist analysts have developed the concept of woman as "a gendered and heteronomous subject," with those two characteristics related (de Lauretis 1986:10). The conditions of women's education, nutrition, health, childbearing and rearing, sports, religion, government, dress, immortality, and sanity are still defined by groups composed of or dominated by men. The feminist will also note that sexual asymmetry, which includes women's exclusion from scholarship and from power, is the most ancient as well as the most pervasive of social structures. Present in our mythic heritage, it is a feature of all but legendary regimes and possibly a few, relatively small recorded ones.

If the scholarly establishment's stated willingness to admit women to the expansion of knowledge is welcome, more is needed. Stephen Jay Gould, a scientist as sympathetic to women as can be imagined, shows both the possibilities and the limitations of the incorporation of women into the "rise of man," in this case scientific man. Reviewing Ruth Bleier's *Science and Gender* (1984), he states succinctly the liberal (equity) justification for the equal participation of women in science: "The reason for opening science to women is not that they will do it differently and better but that good scientists are hard to find and it seems perversely absurd to place social impediments before half the human race when that half could, person for person, do the job as well as the half granted access" (1984:7). This is an argument compatible with feminism, though falling short of the assumptions of social feminism. Gould cites another argument, however, which begins to move him onto more debatable ground: "Both the content of [scientific] theories and (in a much deeper way) the

5. Colette Guillaumin makes the same points about the ubiquity of what she identifies as the female condition of "servage," but she restricts the notion by tying it to a material base of labor power (1981a, 1981b).

very character and methodology of research reflect the strong biases of patriarchy and thereby compromise good science."

But although his invocation of patriarchy implies the awareness that male rule means male ideas, Gould does not think the involvement of women in scholarship is likely to affect methodology. He is convinced, for example, that the possible revisions which Bleier sees related to female experience "are now making great headway . . . and men are doing most of the work." Gould's position is that, in spite of its defects, science as a social and intellectual system has been able to advance by its own volition, which means, of course, through the actions of its lead ers—and women are now allowed to join that liberating group. Patriarchal bias is henceforth to be recognized as a scientific flaw. But Gould will not admit that women's experience, which in practice affects science only through women, may have nonrandom characteristics that could push both methodology and theory in specific directions related to that experience. Nor does he admit that women may be uniquely placed to dispute judgments made by men: "We desperately need more women as equal companions in this effort, not because the culture of feminism grants deeper vision but because we need as many good scientists as we can get."

Paternally, he tells women scientists: "We [*sic*] must dismantle our adversary's false tools, not use them to tell more congenial (but equally speculative) stories." Women's viewpoint is thus reduced to yet another partial perspective, even if it is, somewhat illogically, one that makes women natural supporters of "methodological revisions" already undertaken by men. The gap is bridged by Gould's own definition of "good science." His perspective, unusually humanistic for a scientist, is in fact sympathetic to just those shifts of theory and methodology which could be derived from female specificity. But he retains the authority of the male practitioner, and his general argument could be used in defense of a more conventional version of "good science."[6]

A feminist approach to social science has to go beyond incorporation into the process of inquiry as it has developed under patriarchy. The individual autonomy of women researchers certainly increases as their opportunities for scholarship expand. But their autonomy as scholars is limited unless there is some way to change the overall environment of thought and of institutions which leaves male-defined limits on women. Some possibility of transformation must exist, and there must be some way of deriving it from the areas of life (and thought) which are not simply extrapolations of the existing systems of male domination.

This line of argument suggests that a feminist perspective on social science has to be a social feminist focus on what differentiates women's

6. For Gould's "science" we may read "scholarship" or at the very least "social science."

experience and values from men's. It guides scholarship to look for and at these differences as a basis for organizing principles for research. Other scholars will continue to study those areas in which men and women are alike, but with greater rigor and realism than in the past and with an awareness of the androcentric nature of most of what has been represented as generalizable. As feminist critics have now pointed out, studies of shared aspects of life should, even by the existing canons of scholarship, recognize the many areas in which male and female experience are similar. But the deliberately feminist researcher will feel that her distinctive contribution to knowledge is most likely to result from defining and examining those areas in which women's lives and values differ from men's. Through the understanding of these areas she can make the largest possible contribution to the social project of feminism: a transformed society influenced by women's experience, values, and definitions.

The content and locus of women's specificities are not easy to articulate. And the identification of an intellectual style or approach with a particular sex is as risky as any other dimension of the differentiation insisted on by social feminists. Nevertheless, we may hazard a metaphor. The notion of a feminist approach to social science can be modeled by an extended contrast between the (female) kitchen and the (male) study. The contrast is specific: not just the hurly-burly of daily life set against the life of the mind, but the ideal of the old-fashioned kitchen where women with children underfoot attend to cooking, clothing, feeding, and cleaning. The life of the mind, in turn, is symbolized by the quiet, isolated room inhabited by the solitary scholar who is undisturbed by the rest of the world and, at the extreme, indifferent to his own hunger or fatigue. Even when he does not rely on someone else, usually female, to provide for his bodily needs, he is without direct responsibility for those needs in others, deliberately detached from the variable and contingent routines of normal daily life. He personifies the noble goals of exactness and objectivity and at the same time their extension into sterility and irrelevance. His work necessarily starts and is carried on in some particular, real place, but it aims (again metaphorically) as far away as possible. By contrast, in the everyday world of women the subjective dominates, and knowledge is immediate, limited, and above all specific.

It is not obvious that understanding of society is more easily generated in the isolation of the study than in the dense social interaction of the kitchen. What the kitchen lacks, of course, is legitimacy as well as resources necessary for the pursuit and communication of knowledge. Women lack privacy, self-confidence, and independence, both intellectual and economic; this is the burden of Virginia Woolf's *A Room of One's Own* (1928). More recent feminists now argue for the values of both private and shared workspace. In *Silences* (1965), for instance, Tillie

Olsen explicitly extends Virginia Woolf's theme to point out the value of the activities that have prevented women from being "heard." The private "room"—*her* study?—would then have a new role to play, one indispensable for the completion of enterprises generated in and enriched by the life of the kitchen.

This is what a feminist perspective on the social sciences is about. The kitchen is where "all the ladders start" (W. B. Yeats, "The Circus Animals' Desertion"). But where precisely to ground the ladder and where to aim it? These issues are related to choice of subject matter, something feminists have not discussed much. Social feminism again provides suggestions.

CHAPTER 5

Choosing a Subject

Social feminism generates a feminist perspective on research which directs the researcher to the specific activities and values associated with women. It focuses attention not just on the specific, the differentiated, the domestic but on the particular dimensions of women's experience that are most directly grounded in women's activities. We expect these activities to be the ones most different from men's. The goal of such research is to produce more than a mere projection or rationalization of the limited viewpoint women have historically had. Change in the situation of women has on occasion occurred, some of it as a result of women's own initiatives, so that we can find encouraging as well as disheartening features in the differentiated female "world." Such hopeful precedents allow us safely to readmit abstraction as a basis for analysis and action. Even the conventional, male-dominated quest for a disembodied truth will benefit from these changes, as it will no longer be limited by its willful remoteness from the larger part of everyday reality.

But how are we to direct our attention amid the welter of experience we inhabit? The answer to that question is still no more than an inventory, but we can at least order it in a systematic fashion. We can imagine a schema that moves from the areas of most interest to equity feminists, those aspects of women's existence most resembling men's, toward those dimensions most unlike. This movement will at the same time, be toward those areas in which women have been most able to increase their autonomy. We should begin at the point where men and women diverge in their social existence, moving to consider the areas where they are farthest apart. As we trace this route, we move toward the more feminist of the new research on women and the area crucially important to the feminist researcher who is concerned with change in both theory and practice.

Some features of women's lives are clearly identical to men's. Although details are still disputed, at a certain level of neurological and other physical functioning all human beings exist within the same range of possibilities. Fetal development, being born and dying, the dependence of infants and of the aged and infirm, hunger and repletion, wounds and healing, disease and health—these are the same for all human beings, however society may express or evaluate them. This is true even though societies shape the basic physical dimensions of human life through differential access to nourishment, language, education, occupations, tools, and clothing. All of these resources, as we are now aware, can be and often are dichotomized along lines identified with sex. These are the definitions of gender, definitions that are more or less arbitrary, more or less completely differentiated, more or less mutually exclusive and spatially isolated. Contemporary society continues to make sharp distinctions between gender roles; it also conceptualizes those distinctions in terms of female specificity and male generality, with the latter understood as monopolizing the potential for innovation and abstraction.

Some portion of women's daily life does, however, seem connected to physical differences between women and men. Here we approach difficult issues of biological determinism, which extend today into sociobiological fantasies about genes for behavior along with the most naive extrapolations from sexuality. For example, the novelist Edna O'Brien states categorically, in response to questions about "the women's movement," that the structure of the family and of domestic life grows out of "instinct and passion," in respect to which "men and women are radically different":

> The man still has the greater authority and the greater autonomy. It's biological. The woman's fate is to receive the sperm and to retain it, but the man's is to give it and in the giving he spends himself and then subsequently withdraws. While she is in a sense being fed, he is in the opposite sense being drained, and to resuscitate himself he takes temporary flight. . . . The man may help with the dishes and so forth but his commitment is more ambiguous and he has a roving eye (Roth 1984:40).[1]

At the other, minimalist extreme are the theorists of psychological androgyny such as Sandra Bem, for whom only "anatomy and reproduction" are "undisputed biological correlates of sex." On this basis she opts for "an unambiguous genital definition of sex" (1983:611–12). She would reduce the distinctiveness of women to menstruation, pregnancy, parturition, and lactation. Since the onset and cessation of reproduction and the act of conception have male equivalents, Bem argues it is only cultural factors that make the female versions of those cases unique. Her

---

1. O'Brien does not feel that women and men are different as writers, although she shares Virginia Woolf's awareness of the special difficulties faced by women writers. But her statement epitomizes a position that differentiates all human activities on sexually defined lines.

interpretation is closely allied to an equity feminist insistence on male-female similarities. It is, paradoxically, also an interpretation likely to reduce women to machines for bearing babies (*Women's Studies International Forum* 1985).

As we learn more about hormonal and neurological processes of development, it seems more likely that at least a few irreducible biological dimensions of femaleness do exist. We continue to disagree about what other qualities can be legitimately linked to sexual differentiation: strength, endurance, aggressivity, creativity? The possibilities range, roughly, from O'Brien to Bem, and the emotional and political loading of the answers is considerable. Today's feminists find the whole question of the body—the female body—a difficult one. Its importance is indicated by Susan Brownmiller's choice of topic after her lengthy, important discussion of rape: she next worked on "femininity," defined almost entirely in physical terms (1984). Equity feminism runs the risk of adopting, in the name of equality, a distaste for the specifically female body. Social feminism for its part runs the risk of wallowing in sentimental fantasies about female reproduction and sexuality.

As the simply physical merges into what at least feels like voluntary behavior, the issue of biologically based innateness becomes frightening. Second-wave feminists are well aware how the belief in biological differentiation has constrained women and confined them to a biologically limited role and sphere. "The germinal insight of feminist thought was the discovery that 'woman' is a *social* category . . . one that has subordination at the core," writes the author of a feminist blast at the "new conservative feminism" (Stacey 1983:561). In the heyday of discussions of androgyny some feminists went so far as to argue that all examination of female biological characteristics amounted to an acceptance of the status quo and of women's inferior status.[2]

Yet if we shift perspective on such arguments, we might suggest that for women to examine the alleged consequences of their biological specificity is to assert women's autonomy, their entitlement to define themselves as they see fit. Here we find an analogy to the vaginal self-examinations promoted by women's health collectives and a link to the wider feminist current of asserting physical control and self-awareness. The intellectual consequences of such an approach can be equally significant. A distinctively modern example of a focus on women's biological distinctiveness is to be found in certain feminist notions about identity: it seems likely that the experience of pregnancy undermines the concept of the isolated individual so central to most of Western thought. Where are the boundaries between one's self and the child in one's womb? For the child, birth presumably ends perception of the overlap between self

---

2. It is in this context that Alice Rossi was attacked for her speculations about linkages between maternal biology and parent-child bonding (Gross et al. 1979).

and other, but surely it does not do so for the mother. Carol Gilligan has sparked a continuing discussion about the value of connectedness which grows out of some related speculations; it is noteworthy that her original, pathbreaking research drew examples of women's morality from the distinctively female experience of decisions about abortion (1982).

In a related way, a direct look at women's physicality casts doubt on the existentialist distinction between "immanence" and "transcendance," the first being the mundane, inferior, and effectively female involvement with existence. Simone de Beauvoir made feminist history by her eloquent exposition of women's entitlement to and capacity for transcendance, but she did not question the value of transcendance itself or comment on its practical limits and defects. Nor was she prepared to see female differences rooted in biology as a basis for formulating human goals. Instead she extended Jean-Paul Sartre's queasy responses to the animal into a clear rejection of female reproductive capacity (Seigfried 1985). An alternative, social feminist analysis that began from a positive evaluation of women's differences would infer that activities related to them ought to have validity for women and also possibly for men: everyday life might not in fact be something whose defining function is to provide support for something better.[3]

Our discussion has already moved from the narrowly biological to the social dimensions of women's lives, however, and so to areas where differences between men and women are of gender rather than of sex. Abortion as a shameful or a utilitarian rather than a simply physical event may implicate men as well as women, and social interpretations of abortion need have no significant symmetry with the condition of the fetus. The feminist approach, in this case, begins but does not conclude with an insistence on the distinctive and valuable aspects of a topic usually dismissed because of its connections with female biology. It moves on to argue for distinctiveness and value in those socially constructed dimensions of life which are associated with women.

In our particular society and intellectual tradition, the feminist perspective is likely to begin with a focus on the specific simply because the specific is what we identify as female. But attention to the specific is not enough to generate a feminist analysis; it was not a feminist who said that God is found in the details. For the feminist, it is the domestic or

3. Beauvoir remains an important figure for modern feminists. Most of us were both dazzled and illuminated by our early readings of *The Second Sex*, and we admired Beauvoir's continuing openness to new experience and new political activity (Huston 1986–87). If her chosen lifestyle now strikes us as an inadequate model, and her relationship to Sartre as one of excessive dependence, we still recognize the limits of her personal and social contexts. It is in her views of reproduction and of female sexuality that she most disappoints. Her famous abortion (with the 343 of Bobigny) had political validity as part of the campaign to reform France's archaic laws about reproduction. But the act would have greater meaning if not set theoretically in the "male" perspective that rejects any implication in pregnancy. It was no surprise to learn years later that Beauvoir was one of the Bobigny signatories who had not in fact had abortions.

female specificity that is valued. Here a major problem surfaced for feminists in, among other places, the ambivalent responses to Judy Chicago's *Dinner Party* and, even more strongly, her birthing project. Is it safe to move away from the approach epitomized by the first title of Pat Mainardi's widely read article, the assumption that "housework is shit-work"?[4] There is a risk in directing attention to the "gender prison" (Heilbrun 1979:210) and thereby seeming to praise it.

Nevertheless, a major part of feminist research has been devoted to identifying and describing the social activities most characteristically done by women. Protection is provided by a supporting theory that stresses the mutability of what is described. The most obvious example is feminist discussions of housework, whether or not conceptualized as "domestic labor." Yet as this example suggests, the cataloguing of women's distinctiveness has not produced any significant changes in the general practice of scholarship. It has had no intellectual impact except within the small community of women scholars, and it has had little effect on policy. Such documentation is equity feminist research that adds women's activities as a new set of dissimilar examples within existing analysis. It becomes social feminist research when it focuses on the contrast or relationship between female and male—and at that point it becomes capable of producing a meaningful reconceptualization.

Social activity is never truly isolated by gender, and it is now clear that the separations are not always as absolute as we once believed. For instance, among hunting peoples women may accompany the hunters to clean and carve the kill and carry it to camp (Anderson 1985). Where neither co-operation nor complementarity fits, we may do better to think of work as paired or, in other cases, shared by men and women: women gathering and men hunting, women raising foodstuffs on land men have cleared, or more complicated interactions as in the yam and cotton production reported among the Baule people in West Africa (Newman 1981:132). A social feminist perspective provides a way of untangling these complexities by suggesting that even in the case of shared activities, analysis should begin with and from the female version or dimension. The analyst of any activities that are seen as universal would also begin inquiries with the specific characteristics of the female segment.

In this way a feminist focus on production as the central human activity would generate inquiries based on the typical involvement of women in production: unpaid household labor combined with a second shift of underpaid and segregated paid labor not usually defined as productive. This double shift is rather closer to the norm. It has priority as a subject of research and, in analytical terms, at least equality as a basis for theory construction. Such an inquiry might yield a notion of the nature

4. When that article reached publication, its substitute title, "The Politics of Housework" (Mainardi 1970), responded to the fact that there is also a politics of analysis.

of the labor force like the one sketched out by Lorna Marsden (1981), who presents as modal a lifelong but varying combination of paid and unpaid labor. This perspective brings into strong relief the relatively short working day and working life of the majority of contemporary unionized male workers. The inactivity of the retired male worker we can then reformulate not as newly acquired leisure but as the continuation of an underemployment that has existed all his life.

A focus on the socially differentiated activities of women can thus have a considerable impact at a theoretical level. In political science such a perspective directs researchers' attention to the nonpartisan, issue-oriented politics where women are most typically found. The current scale of antinuclear and ecological movements in Western Europe then becomes far more easily understood and can no longer be dismissed as a temporary outbreak of cowardice and romanticism (Drath 1984).

In the process of such inquiries it will become evident that male participation in everyday domesticity has been underestimated, even overlooked. David Morgan (1981:95) notes that although the "ways in which the feminine or domestic identities become manifest in the workplace" have begun to be studied, no comparable analyses of male gender identity in the home yet exist. Nevertheless, we need to retain the recognition that it continues to be women, not men, for whom domestic life is characteristic. The home and the family are still central to female experience and self-image; the daily, repetitive activities that make possible spectacular or unique events are still carried on by women. Such activities continue to be perceived as characteristic of women and as part of their normal responsibilities even when men assist or substitute for them. In the domestic world the standard patterns are female, and men are seen as marginal or deviant, with explanation or justification expected if they begin to replicate the female role.

Not only does the understanding of daily life require us to pay attention to what women do but, even more important, we will find possibilities for change in domestic structures in what women do, not in the versions presented by the male substitute or assistant. The point seems obvious, but it needs to be made because of the frequency with which male activities and male behavior continue to be presented as not just the norm but the perceived locus of change even in the domestic realm. Thus Penney Kome, in a book about housework in Canada (subtitled *Somebody Has to Do It*), tells at fascinating length about a single father who raised a child in the cab of his truck on long-distance hauls (1982:100–102). Kome is well aware of how unusual Dan Moran's situation was. Yet Moran has far more prominence in her text than Barbara Hoar, mother of seven, whom Kome notes as insisting on children's self-sufficiency in a way very like Moran's. Hoar dealt with housework under conditions far more typical than Moran's and was not only an active community volunteer but also returned to school as a mature student (206). She is clearly

an exceptional person, but it is her liberation, not Dan Moran's, that tells
us about the possibilities for change in gender roles.

The conventional dismissal of domestic life is a long-established tradition. Kome's account approaches something newer: the validation of
domesticity because of male participation in it. Betty Friedan's well-
meaning book *The Second Stage* (1983), which correctly points to the need
for a transformation of work and family, concludes with a paean to
young husbands who are taking on a domestic role. Friedan looks to
them as the "cutting edge" of the second stage of the feminist revolution;
for her they are, in analytical terms, the source of explanations and
practically speaking the source of progress. But men are still marginal
and occasional workers in the household, and as yet they have had little
impact on the traditional assignments of responsibility or the double
shift. A Canadian Gallup poll in March 1986 was reported as about "the
general principle of husbandly *help* with the household chores" (*Toronto
Star* 1986, emphasis added); European poll data show that the more men
do housework, the less they like it, and that both men and women agree
that housework is women's responsibility (Rabier 1979:105–14). A pattern in which one parent (female) does two jobs has been replaced by a
pattern in which, at best, one (male) does half of each of two jobs, cutting
down his public obligations in order to respond to private ones, while the
other (female) assumes a full job outside but retains at least half of the
domestic labor. Indeed, she is likely to increase the intensity of her
commitment to paid labor, moving from a "job" to a career. There is no
change in the established pattern in which domestic responsibilities
dominate private life but lack impact on the conduct of public life. The
personnel have changed somewhat but not the structure. And if the
structure is to change, it will have to respond to the situation of that
majority of families where women do not have at home even the half-
time help of men. It is from the experience of these women that we can
best understand what is both possible and desirable—shorter working
days? parental leave? sabbaticals for child-rearing, seen as recycling and
educational experiences?

Studies of the new male participation in domestic labor underline the
point that gender roles are socially generated, variable, and not essentially related to sexual difference. The variability in the content of
gender roles may constitute the most encouraging evidence available
to feminist researchers. It provides the possibility, the repertoire of
change. In political science such a focus will likely direct the researcher
to the study of what is called "modernization" or "development," seen as
the most basic of all social transformations. Within this framework attention to the differentiated experience of women has a drastic impact.
Some analysts, beginning with Ester Boserup (1970), reverse the conventional, positive evaluation of modernization with the conclusion that the
change has worsened the situation of many women. Even in terms of
crude measures such as caloric intake, significant groups of women,

mainly in the more deprived sectors of the more deprived nations, are losers in the movement toward industrialization and agribusiness (Blumberg 1981).

We have now moved from women's biological specificity and their differentiated gender roles to the third dimension of the specifically female portion of life: their situation defined structurally. Here we turn to women's relative disadvantage—their situation as compared to men's. Some feminists, particularly Marxist feminists, deny the analytical comparability of privileged and deprived women. Theirs is a class analysis with a limited element of gender comparison added, in that poor women are compared to both poor and wealthy men but wealthy women are compared only to poorer men and women. Indeed, because of this emphasis privileged women tend to be attacked rather than studied, as Anette Goldberg points out in a discussion of feminism in Brazil (1986). The feminist insistence upon context, and particularly upon perceived or experienced context, is rejected, as is any legitimacy in the notion of gender as a defining category.

Clearly, women in dominant or advantaged groups may have practical advantages over everyone in disadvantaged groups. Within groups, women even benefit in ways men do not, largely for biological reasons. Women tend to live longer than comparable men once obstetrically related disorders become amenable to medical intervention. But arguments about upper-class women cannot adduce any further intraclass advantages for women, however privileged. It is difficult, for instance, to argue that slaughtered men among defeated populations suffer a worse fate than women who are raped and enslaved along with their children.

On the extreme outer rim of society, men and women both suffer as members of specific classes or castes. Nevertheless, within both powerful and powerless groups women have fewer benefits and lesser impact on the distribution of benefits. The worst oppressed creatures in existence are those women whose situation combines sexism with other forms of oppression. In 1983 the United Nations identified "especially vulnerable and underprivileged groups of women" as including

> rural and urban poor women; women in areas affected by armed conflicts, foreign intervention and international threats to peace; elderly women; young women; abused women; destitute women; women victims of trafficking and women in involuntary prostitution; women deprived of their traditional means of livelihood; women who are sole supporters of families; physically handicapped and mentally handicapped women; women in detention; migrant women; refugee or displaced women; minority women; and indigenous women (Forward Looking Strategies: para.41, in United Nations 1985).

No woman should feel confident she will never be in any of these categories in the course of her life. If she escapes catastrophe, she can be certain that, compared to men as fortunate or unfortunate as she is, she will have less access to the basic resources that affect chances in and style of life, resources such as nutrition, shelter, education, and occupations. At the United Nations conference for women in 1980, one antifeminist slogan was current: "To talk feminism to a woman who has no water, no food, and no home is nonsense." As Dale Spender (1980) pointed out, the core of the quotation was women's lack of homes, food, water. Why do they lack them? she asked, and her answer focused on the lesser power that explained the lesser resources—and to which feminism was the response.

Lesser power comprises the relational dimension of women's socially defined experiences. The gap between the sexes is measured in terms of entitlement that is assumed to have general human validity. Nothing in either biological or social differences implies that women ought to be poorer, worse fed, paid less, more often illiterate or otherwise less educated than men. In many cases these differences, intrinsically and practically disadvantageous, are masked or compensated for by social arrangements, so that the underlying reality of inequality may become visible only when social structures have changed, most often as a result of modernization. The Arab rejection of women's working for pay does not look like a handicap as long as a network of male kin adequately supports even single women. The contrary Soviet assumption that all women will work for pay as well as bear children in support of demographic reconstruction seems equally undiscriminatory—as long as a pool of older women is available to provide childcare (Youssef 1974, Jancar 1981). In both cases women have been constrained by limits that do not apply to men; Arab men always had a range of ways to work for pay or not, for Soviet men the burdens of children were minimal. A discrepancy of options, and therefore of resources, produced a difference of results that at the best did not disadvantage women but at the worst disadvantaged them a great deal.

In such cases a nonfeminist analysis will be reluctant to attribute women's situation to their gender and to a structure of disadvantage; instead it will attribute their situation to external causes. One common explanation for the plight of Arab women is the Western erosion of Islamic values, while Soviet analysts see the as-yet-incomplete eradication of class as the cause of the as-yet-incomplete socialization of child care. Both "explanations" assume that women's situation can be explained without recourse to sex or gender. They are transformed when we bring women's relative disadvantage into the analysis.

The debates at the first and second conferences for the UN Decade for Women (1975 and 1980) demonstrate how structural discrimination against women is rejected as a subject worth attention. Underdevelopment, war, and socially sanctioned prejudice against women were identified as making women poorer and less powerless than men (Black 1981).

In the face of contrary evidence, the conferences explicitly denied that women in modernized, peaceful, and legally egalitarian societies suffered any disadvantage.[5] As far as we can tell, the experience of most women is not conscious persecution, any more than the attitude of most men is of active hostility to women. Even wife-beaters and rapists, who represent an active daily aggression that is sex-linked, seem to respond to the structurally caused powerlessness of women rather than to hatred of them. At the same time, in every society we know women have less of those resources which are the basis for influence and for personal well-being.

By the time the documents of the UN's third conference on women were being drawn up, women's relative disadvantage had attracted a degree of official recognition: "[development] should be conducive to providing women, particularly those who are poor or destitute, with the necessary means for increasingly claiming, achieving, enjoying and utilizing equality of opportunity" (Forward Looking Strategies: para. 12 in United Nations 1985). A more strongly feminist analysis would add that, for structural, gender-linked reasons, *all* women lack this equality of opportunity. The issue is resources and differential access to them for members of different genders. The disadvantage is relative and has meaning only within a comparison.

This kind of analysis has its own problem: it is likely to produce an image of woman as victim. Albert Camus (1972) writes eloquently about the choice between the *bourreau* and the *victime*. The sane response is, first, sooner the victim than the torturer and, second, this relationship is intolerable. For the feminist, the trap here is a double one: to praise the qualities of the victim, thus accepting male justifications of inequality or, conversely, to seek to emulate rather than eliminate the torturer. But to attempt to document and understand the world from the victim's point of view, what Elise Boulding (1976) calls the "underside of history," is an assertion of female autonomy. Such research is likely to lead to major reinterpretations, as when Joan Kelly-Gadol cast in doubt the notion of "the" Renaissance by asking about its impact on the lives of women (1977). She concluded that women in fact lagged behind men at that point in history because men gained in ways that had no relevance for women and to which women's access was actually reduced.

Feminist research that focuses on the relative status of women is the research that can look for the deeper structures that explain daily life. This is the most important meaning of "the personal is the political": the experience of individual women is part of a larger structure of subordination which can be thought of as superimposed over the structures of

5. Certainly underdevelopment and war lower the levels of existence for all human beings. Certainly women and children suffer more. And certainly, also, explicit prejudice against women seems to explain some of the more flagrant refusals to consider women's preferences. But these are in large part manifestations of more basic structural problems.

class and caste.[6] This particular structure is one to which men's relationship is by definition different from women's. It may be less intractable than biologically based differences. It is also more pervasively influential in the patriarchal system in which we all exist.

Finally, in one additional way women's lives differ from men's—in their attempts to resist masculine control. Here is a feature of women's experience which men logically cannot share. It is not to be confused with the ways in which individual women or groups of women have participated in various historical struggles against oppression based on class or caste. Feminist historians have demonstrated the existence of feminine forms of "resistance and revolution" (Rowbotham 1977). For example, the bread riots that initiated both the French and the Russian revolutions have precedents that derive such civil disorder from traditional patterns of female authority. Similarly, the role of women in guerrilla warfare and the Resistance is beginning to be made known (Rossiter 1985). Such activities, however, even if rooted in tradition, belong in a different category of women's activities, the gender-differentiated version of shared social patterns. Understanding such experience—making it first visible and then comprehensible—is important. But it contributes to female autonomy only indirectly, by illuminating the context within which claims must be made and change occur. The possible confusion is great, especially in the context of women's union activism, as Margaret Maruani makes clear in her careful discussion of the difference between "women on strike" and "women's strikes" and their differing impact on an emerging "feminine identity" (1979:78). What the self-identified group then does in the interest of its own autonomy is something different.

Here we move to the direct attack by women on male privilege as such. Here it is no longer a question of women's modes of coping with the overwhelming male reality, nor of their adaptation to control. Instead, the researcher now looks directly at attempts to reduce that control, whether done knowingly or not. And as she focuses more directly on successful attempts, she is in both logical and practical terms as far away as it is possible to be from those areas of existence which women share with men. Paradoxically, of course, she is also directing her attention to the closest and most intense interaction possible between women and men, the interaction that is most generative of awareness of difference and also most likely to produce a shared future reality. Equity arguments cease to be relevant, and analogies weaken. By her very focus of attention, she has performed a feminist act, insisting on the maximum of self-definition, on the most extreme possibility for identifying her topic

6. I use the word "caste" to refer to any ascribed and unchangeable group characteristic. Today the common label is "race" or "ethnicity"; it also includes religious identification in those contexts where religion corresponds to structures of domination.

of research and her aspirations for social change. She can also expect the maximum of hostility from the men of goodwill who have shown such great sympathy for her desire for equality.

In sum, the feminist social scientist who wishes her research to assert and extend women's autonomy (beginning with her own) has four possible areas of concentration: biologically based specificities of women's experience, gender roles with a focus on the female, women's relative disadvantages, and women's resistance to male domination. Discussions of how to choose among these possibilities for research must handle the usual considerations of leverage, relevance, manageability, and access. The relevant choices are made more complex by a number of factors: the image of women as nonrational (which may drive the researcher to either abjure or overemphasize the established canons of procedure), the image of women as ineffectual (which may set a premium on demonstration of success and of power but also suggests that these are masculine ideals to be discarded), and the scarcity of data, especially in those areas where women's experience diverges most from men's. A self-consciously feminist researcher is likely also to see herself as part of a social or political movement, which makes her research decisions the more momentous. If she can avoid pomposity and self-importance, she will still have major problems. Yet feminism itself suggests some guidelines.

No one claims that all research topics are of equal interest and importance. A feminist researcher is certainly entitled to give priority to topics related to women and women's autonomy. The goal of self-determination justifies her choice. Further, she is entitled to identify and value those of her own characteristics which relate her to feminist inquiry and ease her access to data and understanding. It is proper, and it is likely to be profitable, to generate research directly from whatever unique mix of experiences and situations she has acquired. There is no reason to value the "objectivity" of a researcher who states that she studied Canadian suffragism because the war prevented her doing an English topic and Canadian naval policy had already been examined (Cleverdon, quoted in Cook 1974:vii). Again, the two guidelines of effectiveness and autonomy reinforce the basic but much-neglected scientific obligation on a researcher to identify her or his relevant characteristics—characteristics that may be a source of bias but primarily serve as guides and as bases of understanding.

In the introduction to her important collection of articles on second-wave feminism, Elizabeth Sarah (1982) conducts an anxious self-examination: are we not following "malestream" history, which focuses on "movements and revolutions"? (520) are we not identifying as effective those "movements" which resemble the ones we are ourselves involved in? She concludes: "That we are prompted to excavate our feminist past by our participation in the feminist present is perfectly valid as long as

we acknowledge the extent to which our current experiences and preoccupations influence what we look for" (521). Like many other feminist
researchers, I believe we may be more positive. We should value the
directions in which our experiences send us and the perspectives they
can give.

Unfortunately, dicta like these may be encouraging but they are
vague. And it is all too easy to slip into validations of research because it
increases women's resistance to male domination or, in the context of
research, their resistance to accepted modes of inquiry. The growth of
women's active involvement in research, especially antiestablishment research, is undeniably a demonstration of autonomy, as is the vast proliferation of other feminist activities and institutions. The mere existence
of deliberately feminist research can easily come to seem a sufficient
criterion, especially for researchers acutely conscious of the practical
male monopoly over positions of scholarly authority. For example, Jill
Vickers, who published an early (1974) indictment of women's limited
role in the Canadian academy, ends an article on feminist research by
praising its productivity. Its "political" value lies in the mere fact of its
being a challenge (1982:44). Again, if it is enough to be feminist and
productive, how to choose?

How are we even to select among the definitions of feminism used to
justify research simply because it is feminist? Hilda Scott (1976) defines
"feminist" as embodying "a view of women as a distinct sociological
group for which there are established patterns of behavior, special legal
and legislative restrictions, and customarily defined roles" (370). This
interpretation produces the conclusion that "women are simply another
group whose rights have been restricted systematically by the powerful
within a particular society" (371). Such views, of course, are specifically
denied by the theories I have identified as social feminism. Given this
disagreement, why not simply select the interpretation that is the most
empowering for women at a given time?

The answer, for feminists as for everyone, must turn on notions about
reality. Necessarily underlying the whole of the feminist argument is an
acute awareness of the importance of causality. The consequences of
actions are most directly obvious in the domestic realm, in the world of
conception, not of ideas but of children. Certainly the female involvement in reproduction can be seen as directing attention to consequences
in a way men can more easily avoid. Take Annie Leclerc's suggestion
that female *jouissance* should include an appreciation of menstruation.
We may or may not be persuaded by her statement that happiness includes "feeling the tender, warm blood flowing from myself once a
month" (1974:39). The idea is more likely to commend itself to women
who can be certain that menstruation means, on the one hand, that
fertilization has not occurred and, on the other, that fertilization is possi-

ble. This knowledge, rather than merely a feminist assertion of will, is what can turn menstruation into a blessing from the "curse" it was labeled when it looked like a magically symbolic wound. Belief in the possibility of change is necessary if change is to be sought through deliberate, conscious action. But it is important to recognize also when change is unlikely, when power is low, and when strategies of adaptation and manipulation are rational. If history shows anything, it shows that lies and self-deception have been inadequate tools for control and worse ones for liberation. And it shows that the more we know of specifics, the easier it is to choose among alternatives.

In the collection of essays including Hilda Scott's piece, Berenice Carroll (1976) provides guidance for researchers in her analysis of the choice between two influential and incompatible views of women's role in history: Simone de Beauvoir's vision of women as victims to men and biology, and Mary Beard's claim that women have been an unrecognized "force in history." These contradictory interpretations result from two different research strategies, two different modes of analysis. By Vickers's and Smith's criteria both are equally valuable, for the two opposing, inconsistent myths of subjection and of hidden power became in the hands of Beauvoir and Beard effective tools for research and for mobilization.

But Carroll is able to show how each of the accounts can be criticized in respect to data and interpretation, in part because other scholars have followed up lines of inquiry initiated by Beauvoir and Beard. As a result, she also suggests an analytical rethinking of the central notions of power and powerlessness to focus on capacity rather than control. Such a redefinition finds a place for the approaches of both writers.[7] Carroll has moved from a critique of research to an examination of competing assumptions about reality—an observable reality that includes human experience and can serve as a basis for criticizing theory. As a feminist, she adds the crucial insistence that women are a distinctive and significant part of humanity. Finally, she asserts that focus on women and their experience enables, indeed obliges the researcher to reformulate both description and analysis. The apparent contradiction between Beauvoir and Beard can be transcended as more detail is gathered about what actually happened to women and about how to think about them. Consequences matter, but they depend on information. Feminism directs attention to the importance of information and particularly to the importance of information about women.

This context makes it reasonably obvious how to justify a focus on all-women organizations and particularly on those which are actively feminist. Here are both the issues and the groups farthest removed from

7. Here, interestingly, she picks up on the sophisticated notions of power used not by those who study women but by those who have studied international and bureaucratic politics.

male experience. For precisely such reasons all-women organizations have been overlooked or dismissed in analyses of social movements and social change. We therefore have relatively untouched areas of research available, undistorted by mainstream analyses other than the initial assignment of irrelevance. We are beginning to perceive, even if not entirely understand, the role such groups play in producing change for women. Additional study can help provide both the necessary, mounting substratum of data and the crucial possibilities of reinterpretation and selection. The key is the desire for autonomy and the belief that knowledge can accelerate it; the choice, that which is most distinctive about women's experience and at the same time most relevant to changing it.

Society does not change spontaneously. No dominant group has ever voluntarily given up its monopoly power to make decisions, however benignly motivated. Why should we expect men to act differently when they have to deal with women? Women's organizations have been the means and the location of the movement to bring both women and women's issues to the public agenda. They are therefore a logical focus of attention for the feminist researcher.

Within the category of women's organizations, the social feminist groups are the farthest of all from either mainstream or male situations and therefore the embodiment of the most extreme form of a feminism based on difference. I note again that *all* feminism necessarily has built into it some assumption about difference, in the awareness of exclusion and of lesser autonomy; this is the core of Zillah Eisenstein's (1981) argument that even the most moderate liberal feminism (equity feminism in my terminology) implies the existence of a "sexual class system." *All* feminism necessarily is a concern more of women than of men and therefore in the last resort dependent on the efforts of women. Again, it is important to remember the argument about self-determination being logically a result of one's own efforts.

But equity arguments and equity organizations are more likely to focus on specific perceived impediments to equality. Consequently their actions are likely to be more episodic. Equity feminists were most likely to see the vote as a final achievement, a point at which to stop. Lady Rhondda, formerly a suffragette, sums up the characteristic equity feminist viewpoint. She notes the relief with which, "when, at last, in 1928, the vote came on equal terms, one felt free to drop the business" of "fighting for equal political freedom for women and men" (1933: 299, 298).[8] The goal of an equity feminist group is to eliminate the need for its own existence. By contrast, social feminists are more likely to see the need for the continuation of women-only groups, as fosterers and prop-

8. It should be noted that, with the employment issues of the 1930s, she found a new set of equity concerns and was much involved with the Six Points Group.

agators of female values. As we look at the past few centuries and the resistance to feminism we see around us today, we may well ask which perception is more accurate.

I argue that the embodiment of social feminism in activist women's organizations is the most radical step toward social change that feminism has produced. This organizational step gave social feminism its potential impact through its potential transformation of public life. It meant women in public life, and for reasons not part of public rhetoric. As a result, social feminism meant more than a change of personnel (already started by what women were doing). It implied a change in agendas and values, including a blurring of the distinction between public and private because of an incursion into the public of the private (both private persons and private concerns). We can reverse the axiom of the women's movement: social feminism made the political personal and used that claim to move into the political. In this claim lies the possible recuperation of public life through the family. From it comes the insistence of today's feminists that males must become part of the private and accept the private values—or, better, that the distinction of realms should not have the meanings it has had for our dichotomized society.

I add my conviction that the further feminist researchers move away from the experience women share with men, the more powerful will be their contributions to knowledge about reality. In this way they will enable themselves to have the maximum impact in terms of significant added data and possibilities for reformulations of theoretical understanding. They will be acting on their feminism in a variety of ways: asserting autonomy by selecting topics marginal to accepted male canons of research and relatively difficult for direct understanding by men, extending self-determination by increased knowledge and understanding of the areas in which women are characteristically involved, and enhancing the possibilities of feminist action as a result of this knowledge. Such a research strategy is persuasive because it is the consequence of what seems logical to me, that women's resistance to men is the women's activity most remote from any experience that men may have. Men are oppressed by men and very rarely by women, but not because of their gender; if they are treated as women and accordingly oppressed, they may possibly share sympathetically in what gender-based oppression means (though in fact they do not seem to do so) (Frye 1983). But men can never organize against male privilege, for when they do so, they use male privilege for the purpose. The clearest example here is John Stuart Mill, M.P., arguing for votes for women. Few men are as sensitive to the contradiction as Mill, who felt that men should not take part in any woman suffrage organization (Strachey 1978:111–12).

These are my own reasons for working on feminism as it manifests itself in ideology and in organized groups. But, to a degree I distrust, my

own situation and training coincides with what I find most usefully remote from male (researched) experience. I am not sure if I should be
reassured by the extent to which I have moved to this position while my
activism was within a feminist group; certainly that experience gave no
nourishment to illusions about the degree of influence that women's
organizations may wield. I have no way of knowing to what extent I am
involved in an elaborate rationalization of a line of inquiry into which I
fell without premeditation. But even if it becomes necessary to rethink
the categories I set out as increasingly remote from male experience, I
think it is possible to argue for focusing feminist research within the
whole cluster of subject matters I have been discussing. For each feminist researcher, some combination of her own experience and training
will direct her to one or another of these categories and direct her
choices within them. All are needed. Other feminist researchers, who
have not had any direct involvement with activism as such, are likely to
find that the combination of their experience and training directs their
own research to an area closer to what they share with men.

A central message of feminism is to value the usefulness of whatever
capabilities and experience the active individual possesses. Conventional
canons of inquiry correctly warn against the possible biases of inquiry
grounded in one's own situation; they say too little about the potentialities of one's own experience. That experience is surely most useful in
directing attention to subjects that have not been recognized as of general interest and in illuminating those subjects.

PART II

THE WOMEN'S
CO-OPERATIVE GUILD

The Women's Co-operative Guild (WCG) has begun in the last few years to acquire a modest visibility as a first-wave feminist organization.[1] Its longevity is a major part of its interest; it may now be in decline, but this group, founded in 1883, obviously did not die in 1920. Marxist and socialist feminists in particular find the WCG appealing because of the class basis of its political affiliations. Although they regret that its members seem to be the wives of the labor aristocracy, they note that the WCG has always had an explicit commitment to working-class identity, to the Labour party (through the Co-operative party), and to the ending of capitalism.[2] In addition, the Guild was a pioneer on many of the issues central to the women's movement today, including equality in the workplace and reproductive freedom.[3] It was actively suffragist and supported the efforts of women to serve in public office. Finally, its unswerving pacifism is congenial to the contemporary women's movement, which is also more inclined than earlier feminism to value the Guild's stubborn insistence on remaining a single-sex organization.

The feminist historians who have recently rediscovered the Guild have therefore been delighted at the degree to which it is a *women*'s and a *feminist* organization. They have tended to underestimate the degree to which it is *co-operative*. At the same time the Guild's own histories have tended to underestimate the group's feminism and have interpreted it in terms of more general social change (Gaffin and Thoms 1983).

In fact, feminism and co-operation interacted to produce over a hundred years of activism. The ideology of the English consumer co-opera-

1. The first name of the group (The Women's League for the Spread of Co-operation) was changed in 1884 to the Women's Co-operative Guild. The title since 1963 is the Co-operative Women's Guild. I use the name by which the group is best known.
2. Gaffin and Thoms 1983:19–20. Many guildswomen, including early presidents, had been in the paid labor force before marriage (Davies 1914:22, 27–28, 61–62). See the appreciations of the Guild expressed by Sheila Rowbotham (1977), Jill Liddington and Jill Norris (1978), and Jane Lewis (1980).
3. Jean Gaffin (1977) was the first to point out this pioneering role.

tive movement proved to be exceptionally supportive of an effective social feminism. The co-operative movement provided an invaluable organizational context for a rapidly growing women's auxiliary. As the Guild matured, however, it came increasingly into conflict with its parent group, a conflict resolved in favor of the guildswomen's emotional and ideological commitment to co-operation. In the process feminism lost out, and the Guild declined decisively in both membership and importance. Today, more than a century after its founding, the Guild is little more than a memory.

The peculiar character of the WCG and both its strengths and its weaknesses are an essential part of its close relationship over time to the organized consumer co-operative movement. Chapters 6 and 7 look at how the Guild's history links with the ideology and structure of the co-operative movement. But the Guild's beliefs must also be understood as growing out of social feminism. In particular, its pacifism, compatible with the ideology of the co-operative movement, is part of a clearly established and continuing feminist tradition and is discussed in Chapter 8. This history illuminates some of the advantages and disadvantages of associating social feminism with conventional political structures and, in this case, with a slightly less conventional ideology.

I shall not directly examine the more remarkable episodes of the Guild's feminist action. These include an impressive involvement in attempts to reform divorce legislation (costing the Guild four years of Co-operative Union subsidy during World War I), the earliest commitment to access to contraception and abortion of any mass membership women's organization in Britain, a strong suffragist effort, campaigns for women workers within the co-operative movement, and important activities for maternal welfare and rights. Instead, I focus on how this was a *co-operative* women's group, what its goals were, how it reacted to and related with its parent movement. My purpose is to show how the movement affected its very activist auxiliary.

CHAPTER 6

Feminism and the
Co-operative Movement

The Women's Co-operative Guild is an authentically feminist group whose goals have always included the needs of its women members as defined by themselves. The WCG also had a clear notion of the solidarity of women as a group. Guild leaders were convinced they spoke for all economically dependent woman in the home, the women who were the majority. In 1927 Catherine Webb, a Guild and co-operative activist, summed up in the group's history its significance: "The emergence of the married working woman from national obscurity into a position of national importance" (10). Employing a recognizably social feminist rhetoric, the Guild took pride in its work for "national reform in [our] lives as mothers and housewives" (WCG 1958:14).

Yet the WCG's feminism is of a particular sort. It is clearly social feminism and it is also a feminism explicitly positioned within both the ideology and the structure of the English consumer co-operative movement. As Webb explains, "married women in the home had existed apart, voiceless and unseen. . . . The married woman first emerged and joined hands with her sisters *as a co-operator*" (11).

When the Guild listed its own achievements in 1958, the first section was headed "Co-operative Work." In this useful and characteristic self-analysis the co-operative movement came first not just in placing but explicitly in priority: "The Guild organizes Co-operative women and its first aim is the progress of Co-operation" (1958:9). The Guild cites proudly a series of campaigns or projects whose meaning is obscure for those who do not know the co-operative movement: "the special need for capital" for the movement, the extension of co-operation into poor neighborhoods, co-operative education, the Co-operative party, and "relations with labour" (1958:10–12).[1] Under the same heading, "Co-operative Work," also appears a cluster of activities related to the working

1. This last category concerns alliances with the trade-union movement, including mutual support in strikes and propaganda intended to persuade trade unionists' wives to shop in co-operative retail stores.

conditions of women employees of the co-operative stores and other services, as well as the Guild's campaigns on behalf of these women for first a minimum wage and then equal pay for equal work. The final item in the same section is "the training of women to take their places in the work of the movement" (1958:13).

The 1958 report makes no references to the Guild's early support of contraception and abortion, which seems so significant from the perspective of today's women's movement. And although a second section, "National Work," focuses on issues more familiar to students of social feminism, the list is still somewhat unusual, combining campaigns about public health and housing, divorce law reform, woman suffrage, "international brotherhood [*sic*] and opposition to militarism," "cost of living," and "[women's] representation on public bodies" (1958:17–18).[2] Obviously the Guild does not classify its own activities as an explicitly feminist analyst would. Issues related to employment of women in the paid labor force and to their political action (in the sense of influence and position within a social movement and its political party) are not grouped with other concerns about women's political role and the consequences of their situation in the larger patriarchal structure. Instead, the orientation is to the co-operative movement, and classifications are based on whether the action discussed takes place inside or outside the movement.

At the same time, the issues with which the Guild has characteristically been concerned under the rubrics of both co-operation and national welfare are issues of particular concern to women. About them the guildswomen claimed a particular expertise not just as co-operators but as women. For example, "open membership," a key concern of the more democratic and idealistic co-operators, was also crucial for women; it allowed several persons in the same family to join a co-operative society as individuals and was therefore central to women's eligibility to participate in the governance of the movement. Similarly, in the continuing dispute about the relative merit of high dividends and low prices, the guildswomen drew on movement traditions, of course, but they also drew on their own direct experience and preferences as the persons who made household purchases. In this case they unsuccessfully argued for lower prices that would immediately benefit less prosperous families.

The complex impact of co-operation dates from the Guild's founding. The existence of a women's branch followed logically from the ideology of the English co-operative movement, which in turn had its origins in Christian socialism and in Owenite theories of social co-operation (Cole 1944, Backstrom 1974). These beliefs contributed to the movement an initial missionary fervor and the utopian goal of the creation of the "Co-

2. Specifically, the list includes campaigns about health of school children, the Insurance Act and maternity benefits (1913 and 1917–18), national maternity services, and a National Health Service.

operative Commonwealth," a New Jerusalem where "production for use" would be the guiding principle. There, public life would be demo-cratically controlled by users—by the workers in their capacity as con-sumers. Community ownership of production would be an essential ele-ment of the Co-operative Commonwealth, but the key would be a system of self-government that would eliminate the individualism, class conflict, and orientation toward profit characteristic of capitalism (Woolf 1921:67–71). All of society would be run like a giant co-operative union.

The philosophy has produced a wide range of co-operative organiza-tions, among them the agricultural distribution co-operatives wide-spread in many countries. In England, after a considerable struggle within the movement, retail trading societies became the characteristic form of organization. By the last quarter of the nineteenth century it was clear that English co-operators would be purchasing rather than produc-ing the bulk of the goods sold by the retail societies. Even at this time it was evident the movement would not be using income from the stores to carry on direct social action. The organized co-operators came increas-ingly to focus on the prosperity of their stores and themselves. When the Co-operative party was established as a political arm for the movement after World War I, it was in response to disadvantages felt by co-opera-tive stores during wartime (Carbery 1969:17–18). The vision of the Co-operative Commonwealth receded. Although co-operators were to be disappointed by the actual practice of a Labour government, their re-sponse even to national politics became increasingly instrumental and pragmatic.

But the movement's ideology was well designed to handle a postpone-ment of utopia. It had always made a clear distinction between short- and long-term goals and was clear about how progress would be made toward the latter. In the short run, those who believed in the ideal future could work toward it by improving their own situation and simultane-ously giving an example to others. The working class would themselves become owners and managers of the retail stores they patronized as consumers. They would thus provide a first, small model of the ideal society, lacking separate classes and therefore lacking class hostilities and not needing class warfare. The capitalistic profit motive could be elimi-nated by keeping the return on capital at a modest level and returning it to owners/workers/consumers in the form of dividends, not on shares but on purchases. In this microcosm of the Co-operative Common-wealth, decisions would be made openly, democratically, and jointly by all elements of production and consumption, and neither workers nor consumers would be exploited. Trade unions, organizing the workers, would be indispensable partners and could be encouraged to push work-ing conditions toward the co-operative ideal even in nonco-operative establishments. On the larger scene, the unified co-operative movement would use the leverage of its purchasing power and group cohesion to affect conditions nation- and worldwide. And since everyone was a consumer, all would eventually come to recognize their interest in a universal system of co-operation.

One knowledgeable source gives a wry summary of the Co-operative Movement in Britain: "The Rochdale pioneers discovered in 1844 a formula which effectively combined the ideal of human brotherhood with a natural desire to obtain cheap groceries. Their formula was dividend on purchase, and the outcome of their successful synthesis was an expansive and enduring consumers' co-operative movement" (Stocks 1970: 55). This account accurately identifies *two* key elements, one practical and one ideological. For the committed co-operator, the desired future society was an inducement for membership and participation in a co-operative establishment. Those less devoted could obtain the immediate benefits by participation, the dividend and also the advantages provided by clean stores and high-quality goods. This practical element could not stand alone, however. To begin with, co-op groceries were cheaper only in the long run since prices tended to be somewhat higher than in other retail stores, and the "divi," as the dividend was affectionately nicknamed, was available only on a quarterly or semiannual basis, so that it represented a form of savings rather than an immediate discount. Nor did the co-op stores give credit. In addition, even when co-op stores were at their most plentiful, purchasers often had to go considerable distances to reach them. The propagandists of the movement pointed out that higher costs in part reflected greater attention to sanitary conditions and the working conditions of employees (higher pay and shorter hours, for instance). But some sort of commitment to "human brotherhood" and to a model of a better future was necessary if such arguments were to have much impact even for the economic class that could afford to choose a morally appealing version of consumerism.

Women's role followed logically from the premises of co-operation. The Co-operative Commonwealth was a nonsexist ideal, for in it women would take part in the productive as well as the consuming dimensions of life. Accounts of the co-operative future do not discuss whether women will in fact participate in the paid labor force, but they are very clear about women's future equality. By implication, the movement believes that women should have an equal involvement with men in running the retail stores. The first co-operative society, the Rochdale Pioneers, had women members (Reeves 1944, Holyoake 1900: 86).

What was more important, however, was that women made the household's retail purchases. In Britain, working-class women have generally controlled the outlay of the (male) paycheck. At the least, they controlled routine household expenses. If any saving was possible out of such expenses, women traditionally handled it. The most desperately poor families have always had little choice about where to make purchases; if not in the clutches of a company store, they have had to seek credit where they can get it. But if a working-class family could afford for the wife to stay at home, that wife had considerable discretion in outlays.[3] These families were the logical constituency for co-operation (Black 1915). A producers' co-operative movement would have involved women only indirectly and in terms of future possibilities; consumers' co-operation focusing on the retail store, initially and mainly a retail grocery store, depended on women's support. And strictly utilitarian motives were not enough to get housewives to join and be loyal to co-op stores. Consumer co-operation therefore needed to recruit women to the cause, not just to the stores. This was obviously women's work. It was less obvious that the recruitment of women entailed establishment of an auxiliary with only women members and with women in charge.

The foundation of the Guild thus grew out of co-operative necessities—the need to have women patronize the stores and, to that end, the need to have them committed to the movement's principles. It also grew out of the existing structure and power elite of the movement. Many important guildswomen, including founding member Mary Lawrenson and Catherine Webb, their historian, were part of established co-operative families. The daughters of Samuel Bamford, Abraham Greenwood, G. J. Holyoake, and Charles Shufflebotham were all active and influential in the Guild; they bore names of great significance for the co-operative movement (Gaffin 1977:114, 116; Gaffin and Thoms 1983:6–7).[4] Kathleen Kempton, who ran the Guild after World War II, is another who was "practically born into the co-operative movement" (Stott 1978:134). The founders were also part of the wider networks of Christian socialism that embraced Toynbee House and other parts of the settlement movement. These overlapping connections account at least in part for the involvement of Margaret Llewelyn Davies, the second, crucially important general secretary.[5]

Most important of all, the individual shapers of the Guild had powerful roles within the co-operative movement itself. Mary Lawrenson, the first general secretary of the WCG, had worked closely with the legendary E. V. Neale, the single most important figure in English co-operation in the nineteenth century.[6] The co-operative activities of the Guild's founders and early organizers precede and extend beyond their

3. Wives working for pay may lose some degree of control over male pay packets, but the income of such working wives typically goes directly to household expenditures (Lewis 1984).

4. Greenwood was one of the original Rochdale Pioneers (Gaffin 1977:114).

5. For Rosalind Nash, Arthur Dyke Acland seems to have been one of the important links (Brown 1928:166), and for Davies the connection was probably her father and her brothers (Davis n.d., Nash n.d.).

6. As secretary of the Co-operative Union, Neale arranged for the WCG's first subsidy from the union, £10 granted in 1886. Lawrenson, who had been Neale's secretary, was on the Management Board of Woolwich Society and one of the very few women ever elected to the Central Board of the Co-operative Union (Brown 1928:99).

role in the women's group. The Women's Co-operative Guild was not co-operation's first auxiliary. The first guild supporting the co-operative movement preceded the WCG by five years; from 1878 to 1895 a mixed-membership group, The Guild of Co-operators, had the role of "advocating and advising the formation of new societies" (Brown 1928:88).[7] In the Guild of Co-operators both male and female members gave lectures promoting co-operation and traveled to attend meetings and conferences; the WCG initially abjured such aggressive behavior on the part of its members but later adopted it. Among those active in this first auxiliary were A. H. Dyke Acland and his wife Alice, Mary Lawrenson, and Mr. and Mrs. Benjamin Jones, as well as Margaret Llewelyn Davies. All were significant figures in co-operation as well as important for the Women's Co-operative Guild: Mrs. Acland and Mrs. Lawrenson founded the Guild, Miss Davies was its general secretary for more than twenty years, and Mrs. Ben Jones was among its most important early presidents.

The Guild's founders deliberately promoted an account that disregards the personal role of the Guild's founders in the wider co-operative movement and their autonomous activities in other organizations. In fact, we know little about the founders of the Guild, although their husbands' lives are relatively well-recorded and make the co-operative connections clear. Mrs. (later Lady) Alice Acland traveled with and assisted her husband. The *Dictionary of National Biography* (1922:30) reminds us that Arthur Dyke Acland, later Sir Arthur, was a man of rather more national distinction than historians of the Guild usually note, a member of parliament from 1885 to 1895 and minister of education under Gladstone. He was "the founder of the Co-operative and Labour Travelling scholarships" (Brown 1928:82). He presided over the Union Congress in 1891 and coauthored, with Ben Jones, the movement's first authoritative public history and statement of principles, *Working Men Co-operators* (1884).[8]

It is no accident that the Guild first appeared and flourished in London during the membership drive there; one reliable source links the WCG decision to allow public speaking to the Guild for Co-operation's invitation to participate in its campaign for "the spread of co-operation around London" (Brown 1928:89). Only when Davies had to accompany her clergyman father to Kirkby Lonsdale in Westmoreland (in 1889) did the WCG began to make progress in the north. Davies attributed difficulties to northern conservatism, which may well be true—but certainly the Guild did well in the north once she moved there, and while giving some credit to Davies's superb skills as an organizer, we may also note that northern connections were ready to be tapped, beginning with the

7. W. H. Brown, the historian of London co-operation, describes the group as "the energising force [for co-operation] in London and the South of England" (1928:88, 80).

8. This volume was superseded in 1914 by Catherine Webb's *Industrial Co-operation: The Story of a Peaceful Revolution.*

Ben Joneses. For his part, Ben Jones was a major figure in the co-operative movement, a leader of the northern co-operators who finally set the movement on its retail- and trade-oriented course (Saville and Bellamy 1972). His wife remains a shadowy figure, although we know she was one of a significant number of guildswomen who had been in the paid labor force before marriage. Davies notes that she had been a millworker and lists her with the better-known Sarah Reddish (Liddington and Norris 1978, Liddington 1984) as "working always for the united causes of women and labour" (1904:23, 32). Her influence was great, and she was remembered with affection after her early death at the age of forty-four; the Guild set up a Convalescent Fund in her name (Gaffin and Thoms 1983 Appen. I:261–63). All accounts of the early Guild note that it was Mrs. Ben Jones who insisted that guildswomen should put aside their self-imposed limitations, particularly those barring public speaking from the platform.

We do not know the details of how the Women's Co-operative Guild was planned and set up. At the coming-of-age celebration of the Guild in 1904 an aged Mary Lawrenson charmingly told the Co-operative Union Congress that she "well remembered the first meeting of the guild, when Mr. Acland came to Woolwich to speak on brotherhood, the while Mrs. Acland and she conferred on sisterhood. Thus the guild was born" (Co-operative Union 1905:422). Even that preliminary discussion between Mary Lawrenson and Alice Acland is seldom mentioned. All is supposed to have begun when Alice Acland floated the idea in her "Women's Corner" column in the *Co-operative News* of February 1883 and Lawrenson replied.[9] The resulting correspondence and the response of women relatives of co-operators are generally portrayed as having created the Guild. The demure and self-effacing first name of the WCG, from 1883 to 1885, was the Women's League for the Spread of Co-operation. But Davies (1904:32) cites a marvelous exhortation by Mrs. Ben Jones, catching what feels like an authentic presence and tone:

> She welcomed the prospect of women becoming members of [co-operative society management] Committees. . . . It did good that women should take part in everything, and the Guild, as an association of women, should take up all subjects with which women were concerned. . . . Many men could not understand a balance sheet, and it was a thing which women could learn. They should remember that at least they could not make greater blunders than men had done.

It is the statement of a woman already well-established in the world of co-operation. It is also the statement of a feminist.

9. Margaret Llewelyn Davies, who surely knew better, gives this version in the earliest Guild history (1904), and it is picked up by other researchers such as Barbara Blaszak (1981) and even Jean Gaffin and David Thoms, although they note the importance of the "personal contacts" of Mrs. Acland "and others" (1983:3).

Instead of presenting a public image of the competence and standing they had within the movement, however, the early leaders of the Guild played a typically female role of modesty and inexperience. Certainly they did not present themselves as feminists, for reasons that seem obvious. When Alice Acland suggested in print the foundation of a Women's League for the Spread of Co-operation, she was "bombarded with criticism." Acland carried on with her project, but she produced for the new Guild the slogan "Study to be quiet and do your own business," and she publicly deprecated women "imitating or competing with men, pushing themselves into positions which have hitherto been held by men, speaking on platforms, or thrusting themselves on to Management Committees, where they would be liable to be laughing stocks and stumbling blocks" (Davies 1904:11). Within the decade the Guild was making major efforts in all the areas that Acland had gone to such pains to reassure men about, but the policy served to allay initial hostility and also reluctance on the part of potential members. A social feminist insistence on domestic style and virtues served characteristic purposes of empowerment and protection.

The co-operative movement was fortunate to tap the services of women to organize women, pulling them in through family connections to co-operation and to a wider philanthropic and educational tradition. The movement was even more fortunate in the extraordinary caliber of its early women leaders and their thorough commitment to the movement in both its ideological and its institutional dimensions. The early founders understandably accepted the co-operative movement as a framework for activism. They were convinced and experienced co-operators, and at the time of the founding of the Guild many such women represented their local societies at the Union Congress; Catherine Webb was one of the very few women to become a member of the Central Board of the Co-operative Union (Gaffin 1977:117). Their expectation was that as women became more educated in general and about co-operation in particular, and more active in the central part of the movement, qualified women would come to take an appropriate share of seats in the bodies that made movement policy. It is surprising, however, that the women who founded the Guild were strong feminists. When the Guild was set up, in 1883, it had four stated objectives. Predictably, three of them are related, in general terms, to knowledge and support of co-operation. What is unexpected is the group's fourth goal: "To improve the condition of women all over the country" (Webb 1927:21). This statement is on its face so unlikely that it is easily overlooked.[10] From the start, the extraordinarily broad scope of the Guild's concern thus extended beyond co-operative women, working-class women, or even mar-

10. Gaffin and Thoms (1983:43) list only the goals related to co-operation.

ried women. Women who were co-operative activists and also feminists were enthusiastic about the idea of a women-only group within co-operation, and they saw such a group as more than merely a movement auxiliary.

The priority the Guild's founders gave to broadly defined women's issues was unusual for the social democratic movements that consumer co-operation most resembles. In the belief systems of such groups, it is a feature of the future socialist state that equality will be possible between men and women. But for most, the ending of capitalism is primary, and women are important only as recruits for millenarianism. Women's own articulation of interests gains a hearing only when it seems to be a condition for getting women to work for the movement. Co-operation seems to be something different, so that the Guild at any rate is able to see women's needs as integral to co-operation's. Perhaps the Guild existed only because its early founders had just such a perception.

One possible explanation comes from a crucial element of the nature of co-operation as a creed: the way in which it was simultaneously a utopian program for the future and a way of life for the present. The life of the co-operator was at the same time a way to bring closer the Co-operative Commonwealth and a microcosm intended to have demonstration effects. For a movement that did not believe in revolution, or in change by legislation, the role of such examples was crucial. Because in the Co-operative Commonwealth men and women would participate as equals, that equality and its results had to be present also in the here and now. Co-operative principles gave a double reason for the elimination of sexism within the movement: not just the practical need for women's participation—especially important for the practical conduct of consumer co-operation—but also the ideological need to demonstrate equality. Neither part of this rationale was available to women in most other political and social movements.

But why did the Guild take on from the start the goal of improving women's condition in the larger society? Part of the answer may be the guildswomen's awareness that all married women shared the crucial function of management of consumption. This perception combined naturally with the social feminist view of all women as potentially or actually sharing the married state and the maternal role. The founders of the Guild were aware how much the specific and concrete disadvantages of women, especially of married women, were consequences of public policy; in this sense they knew that the personal was political, not individual but shared. Their major publicity campaigns, embodied in the volumes *Maternity* (Davies 1915) and *Life as We Have Known It* (Davies 1931), used individual testimony by members to make precisely that point.

The group used familiar social feminist arguments to derive public duties from domestic ones, arguments that were particularly striking in the case of peace work; they thus followed the social feminist route outward from the home—and also from the movement. But it is important to note that the WCG called for woman suffrage and for changes in public policy from the earliest days of the organization. For its founders, social feminist ideas helped set the goals of the Guild rather than their Guild experience leading them to a notion of women's obligation and entitlement to public service. Later members of the Guild were, in many cases, to come to feminism through the organization, as they developed feminist ideas by extrapolation from co-operative ideology. But the founders initially inserted an independent feminist tradition.

Further research may turn up the details of how the founders of the WCG derived their feminism from their specific experience and environment. Davies, for instance, was the niece of Emily Davies, a major figure in English feminism. I merely note their beliefs and turn to what happened when the Guild insisted on the intimate connection between co-operation and feminism. This connection was unacceptable to many male co-operators.

The interaction of co-operative and feminist principles for the WCG is clear in the group's own statements of goals and objectives. The Guild repeatedly articulated its goals, for this was a self-conscious organization. Over the years it carried out several major reorganizations, and at each point it restated intentions. In addition, the group's commitment to orderly, formal constitutional procedures included a deliberate role as instructor to its members, who usually had no previous organizational experience. Consequently, handbooks, statements of principle, and training manuals were issued frequently. In these respects the WCG was typical of both traditional women's groups and workingmen's organizations, the two sorts of social structure whose purposes it combined. Members of such groups tend to be painfully aware of their relative lack of formal education and of the likelihood of their being dismissed as amateurs. The need for impeccable form and explicitness of intention and structure is particularly compelling for women involved in any sort of public organization. As cultured a woman as Margaret Llewelyn Davies was far less credible in her philanthropic enterprises than, for instance, her brothers and would have been so even if she had completed her university course (Nash n.d.). Even today the women involved in women's voluntary associations are likely to be less well-educated in a formal sense than their male relatives, although none will now lack secondary education; among earlier Guild members were many who had not even attended school (Nash 1904).

The goals of the Women's Co-operative Guild have shown great consistency over a century of existence. They have also, inevitably, changed considerably, and the main changes have concerned the degree of prominence given to feminist goals. Initially, the feminist aspiration to improve the situation of all women was the last of four goals, following the goal "to spread the advantages of Co-operation" and to increase interest in and appreciation of co-operation among those already committed to it.[11] By 1920 the Guild's statement of objectives had incorporated both marital and, by implication, class dimensions. It also attempted to relate co-operative and feminist dimensions. A booklet published by the Guild restated the objectives as follows: "(1) To promote Co-operation in every possible way and to help women to take their full share in every side of the work of the movement; (2) to express the views and needs of married women and to get the reforms they require in their own lives and their homes, in their towns and in the State" (WCG 1920). This is slightly more limited than the initial fourth objective, but feminism, though never identified by name, remains as important as co-operation. When the connection between women and co-operation is spelled out explicitly, the feminist dimension becomes even stronger: "Co-operation is mainly a married women's movement, because at the bottom it depends on their purchasing power. Therefore it is through Co-operation that married women are best able to organize and to take their part in the Labour movement and as citizens." Although co-operation is clearly a good in itself—the overriding goal of the group—it is also of instrumental value, because it is the basis of organization and influence for married women. Thanks to their involvement, such women express their own particular point of view, work for their own objective interests as defined by themselves, and take part not just in the movement but in the larger labor movement and even in political life beyond Leftist politics. Nor are women restricted to being the support staff who sustain the co-operative system by loyal purchase. Their equal participation in "every side of the work of the movement" has become a stated objective.

In 1926 new Model Branch rules were issued. The object of the Guild is now described as "to promote a new social order in which co-operation shall replace capitalism and women shall have equal opportunity with men. . . . For this purpose," the text continued, "it seeks to organise women for the study and practice of (1) co-operation and other methods of social reform; (2) improved conditions of domestic life; (3) and, with this object in view, to work with and support the Co-operative Party" (WCG 1926). Again, women's equality (not this time limited as within the movement) receives the same prominence as co-operation. Concern for conditions of "domestic life" is prominent, a central case of women's own specific interests. However, the Co-operative party, very much a public structure, is deemed necessary for women's interests, and women's in-

11. Point 2 was "to stimulate among those who know its advantages a greater interest in the principles of Co-operation." Point 3 was "to stir up and keep alive in ourselves, in our neighbours, and especially in the rising generation, a more earnest appreciation of the value of Co-operation to ourselves, to our children, and to the nation" (quoted in Gaffin and Thoms 1983:43).

volvement in the party has become a central tenet of faith. It seems clear that co-operative women do not expect equality to be an automatic consequence of the replacement of capitalism by co-operation. Furthermore, they do not restrict their efforts at reform to efforts to bring about co-operation.

Two years later the "emancipation" of women, a customary formulation for women's groups, acquires an explicit, independent significance in Guild statements. It is, of course, valued because it will double the number of citizens able to share in "hastening forward a new stage in the realisation of the Co-operative Commonwealth." This statement comes from the Guild's welcome to the completed enfranchisement of British women, voiced in its 1928–29 report (WCG 1929). In the same report the Guild emphasizes its pioneering suffragism and claims a continuing superiority to the many newer women's groups now competing with it. "The Guild," it asserts, "not only voices the co-operative woman's point of view, but it can still claim to be the most representative organisation of the married working woman in the home, and as such still commands attention and respect, for the women in the home are still the largest section of women in the country" (WCG 1929). Such statements represent the Guild's most extensive feminist claims. The term "married working woman" is always somewhat ambiguous; sometimes it means married working-class woman, sometimes it expands, as here, to mean all housewives—all women who work at domestic labor in the home. In the 1929–30 report we can see the clearest possible statement of the Guild's resulting social feminism: "The simple housewifely virtues have in them the seed of all that is great for mankind. The woman with the basket is still the greatest symbol of the power that rocks the cradle of the world to be" (WCG 1930). All these women have potential political power in at least two ways: by their purchases and action within the co-operative movement, but also by direct involvement in more conventional politics outside the movement on its and their own behalf.

Conventional politics mainly meant action through the Co-operative party. The Guild's ties to the movement's party have deep roots. Guildswomen had been among those co-operators most enthusiastic about the movement's creating a political arm after World War I, and the Guild has always supplied the bulk of the female majority of party members (Carbery 1969:61). The WCG was unique among the co-operative auxiliaries in insisting that only members of the Co-operative (or, later, Labour) party could be officers (WCG 1930, Groombridge 1960).[12] However, in the interwar period the Guild's commitment to the party was qualified by a remarkable additional clause saying that the party would be supported provided that the policy of the Co-operative

12. In addition to the Women's Co-operative Guild, the English co-operative movement had a mixed guild, a men's guild, and one for young people (Gaffin and Thomas 1983:194). Only the WCG was very successful.

party was not inconsistent with the policy of the Guild as declared by the Guild Congress.

Here we see reflected another important dimension of Guild history, the insistence on policy independence. The earliest episode was a skirmish over the Guild's endorsement, just before World War I, of a liberal policy concerning divorce; this stance cost it four years of Co-operative Union subsidy.[13] Conflicts with other sectors of the co-operative movement typically occurred in relation to what were clearly women's issues, although the movement did endorse woman suffrage. We have to assume that the Catholic co-operators who objected to divorce policies objected also when in 1924 the Guild endorsed access to contraception and when in 1934 it did the same for therapeutic abortions. By the eve of war, peace became a woman-identified topic on which the Guild was prepared to override Co-operative party policy. This time the cost was considerable: for several years guildswomen were barred from lists of possible candidates for constituency adoption (WCG 1943).

In general, the Guild's documents from the 1930s show a tendency to reduce co-operation to an instrumental value, in part because they are designed for potential rather than actual members. The annual reports and the objects of concern of the Guild suggest that co-operation did in fact become only one of a number of objectives for the Guild. One instance is a simple little booklet, "The ABC of the Women's Co-operative Guild," published in 1931 and apparently intended for wide distribution. For the objectives of the Guild, readers are given the words on the membership card, which describe the group as "a self-governing organisation of women, who work through Co-operation for the welfare of the people, seeking freedom for their own progress and the equal fellowship of men and women in the Home, the Store, the Workshop, and the State" (WCG 1934). The Guild clearly did not accept the standard view that full enfranchisement, accomplished in 1928, was sufficient for women's liberation.

Another small publication, undated but evidently from the later 1930s because it refers to a membership of over sixty thousand, also looks like a recruiting device. "Would You Like to Know?" lists aims that downplay co-operation as such and emphasize the Guild's pacifism: to prevent war by building a real league of peoples; to assist in obtaining better conditions for workers; to keep down prices; to secure the return of women to co-operative boards, local authorities, and Parliament; and to arouse the public to an active interest in all women's questions. The mention of

13. Gaffin and Thoms give the best account of this dispute, which began with Guild representatives testifying before the Royal Commission on Divorce Law Reform established in 1909; their views were explicitly attacked in the Minority Report. The WCG was the only workingwomen's group to make a presentation to the Royal Commission (1983:48–51). Flanagan (1969:81) mistakenly writes that the union merely "threatened to withhold the grant."

lower prices is of some interest, since the context makes it clear that the reference is not to the WCG's continuing campaign for lower prices in co-op stores but rather to the reduction of retail prices in general. The point is not the familiar one that lower store prices (rather than higher dividends) would draw in new members. Instead, guildswomen believe that the cost of living is itself an issue, a problem that cannot be solved within the co-operative movement. As their other concerns suggest, they are far from seeing the movement as the solution to women's problems.

The 1930s were the days of the Guild's greatest expansion and hopes for influence. The WCG helped to found an International Co-operative Women's Guild and developed an increasingly aggressive pacifism. By 1939 it had eighty-seven thousand members and the energy to found a magazine of its own. All of this lasted less than a year; World War II put an end to illusions of progress. Unrelentingly pacifist, the Guild started the war out of step with its movement, its political party and, roughly speaking, its country. After the war a decline began that it never managed to check. In response, guildswomen reversed direction, without noticing it, to privilege co-operation even in areas where it had no direct relationship to feminism. This choice had its own ironies. Co-operation also declined in the postwar era, and in its decline it continued to evolve away from the ideologies and structures that had helped the Women's Co-operative Guild flourish. But the Guild could not cut free from the memories and habits of the golden years when co-operation and feminism had seemed mutually supportive.

CHAPTER 7

Women Co-operators,
Not Women Co-operating

The Guild's strong identification with the co-operative movement cannot be overstated. Underlying it was a notion of the movement that justified the central role the Guild attributed to itself and to its members. A major segment of the concrete activities on which the movement depended had to be carried on by women, since men, given the conditions of industrial life, literally could not do the purchasing. Guildswomen thus carried on, in their daily activities, the essential tasks of constructing the world of the future. As Margaret Llewelyn Davies put it in 1921: "In providing for the well-being of her family the co-operative woman is inevitably acting in a way which leads to the establishment of a juster order in her own country, to the foundation of a world-wide Co-operative Commonwealth, and to the longed-for advent of universal peace" (1921:12). A. Honora Enfield, general secretary first of the English WCG and then for many years of the International Co-operative Women's Guild, articulated women's mission even more dramatically: "Scrubbing, washing, cooking, take on a new meaning, when it is Co-op soap that is used and Co-op food that is cooked. . . . Every purchase is a fresh stone in the building up of the Co-operative Commonwealth" (n.d.:4).

More immediately, women were the ones with practical knowledge about the actual conduct of business in the stores. Logically, they should be the shareholders and the managers, the more so because store management was clearly analogous to household management. The claim of the average working man to understand store management was the dubious one. Davies spoke for the Guild members when she wrote: "Co-operation might justly be called a women's movement. Co-operators as consumers, and trade unionists as producers or workers, may be regarded as forming two halves of the same circle. And if a *man* be taken as the type of a worker, a *woman* would certainly represent a body of consumers or purchasers" (1904:65).

The Guild's notion of movement structure corresponded to their conception of the distribution of functions and goals within the movement.

123

Co-operation was the overarching purpose, and management of the stores and the societies themselves was central. But women had a privileged perspective as consumers and lacked only the necessary education to have a claim, almost a superior claim, to be on the Management Committees and the larger structures into which these fed. Women's own organizations therefore had to be a major part of the self-governing structure of the movement as a whole. In addition, the Education Committees started early in the twentieth century were of special concern to women; the Guild had been central in getting them started. Women needed education even more than men did, and in any case they needed a special sort of education fitted to their situation. If Management Committees were to have women members, women must be recruited and trained as co-operators by the Guild and the Education Committees. Davies put it categorically in her 1904 history of the Guild: "The Guild considers that no Society is complete in its machinery for carrying out the ideals [of co-operation] . . . unless it possesses what have been termed 'the three wheels,' i.e. a Management Committee, an Educational Committee, and a branch of the Guild" (73). All of which adds up to an amazing set of claims on behalf of women and amounts to saying, with Davies, that co-operation is a women's movement. In this model, after all, women have exclusive access to one sector of the movement and a superior claim to participation in the other two. The Women's Guilds were necessarily women-only groups that, in the co-operative tradition, must be allowed to govern themselves and choose their own topics of concern. Finally, the WCG ought to be subsidized by the rest of the movement because it was essential to bring more women into Co-operation.

The Guild's notion of the national institutional structure of the co-operative movement corresponded to its ideas about the proper structure for the individual society. The "three wheels" of the individual groups were seen as generating the three larger wheels of the overall movement. Each sort of committee—Management, Education, Guild— was federated into a set of parallel districts. Nationally, representatives of constituent units in each sector held regular meetings to elect national officers and executives and to make policy decisions that were then communicated to lower levels. Representatives of all sectors met at the Union Congress to make policy decisions that applied to the movement as a whole. These decisions were to be communicated downward through each sector and fed into public life through the Co-operative party. In such a structure women would play a major role, and the Guild would be a women's section in its strongest possible version. This pattern allowed for the important annual congresses of the Guilds. It might also allow for a formal role for Guild representatives in the annual Union Congress and on the Central Executive that acted for the Union Congress between sessions.

The Guild did not see the structure as enabling the movement as a whole to control the activities of its components. The Guild repeatedly made it clear it would not take orders about where to direct its attention. Movement commitment to democratic self-government would keep the flow of authority upward, and the Guilds would have great freedom to act in support of both co-operation and the interests of women. The 1982 version of the movement's official document, "An Outline of the Co-operative Union," confirms that this understanding of the way power affects the co-operative societies is correct: "The Co-operative Union has no power to compel societies to conform to national policy but can only use moral persuasion " (Co-operative Union 1982:7)

However, this same official document shows clearly just how far the Guild has been from acquiring the position it wanted within the movement. It defines the societies as the groups that manage the individual stores, and their Management Committees are the centrally important bodies. The Women's Guild does not appear separately on the organigram of the movement, nor do its congresses. Instead, a small box headed "Co-operative Auxiliaries" is linked to the Education Committee of the Central Executive; in it "Guilds," including the Men's and Mixed Guilds as well as the older-established, much larger Women's Guilds, are combined with the children's "Woodcraft Folk" and the "Youth Movement." Together, all auxiliaries have one representative on each sectional Education Council, as well as two places on the Education Executive and two on the Co-operative Party Executive. They have no direct connection with the Congress or with the Central Executive.

Obviously the Guild's interest in the ancillary elements of co-operative societies is not shared universally. In fact, by no means all societies ever had more than the Management Committees required to actually run the stores. There were few women on the Management Committees, even fewer on the governing boards of higher levels. The Guild's annual reports regularly note the difficulty women have in getting access to any of the significant governing bodies, and the notion of reserved seats for women accordingly surfaces from time to time, but never with success.[1] The Education Committees are not equal in standing to the Management Committees, and the Guilds are obviously even less important.

What is missing from the Guild version of the co-operative movement is the Co-operative Wholesale Society (CWS). This is the big business part of the movement, set up in 1863 to meet the trading needs of the retail societies; it thus antedated the WCG by two decades.[2] The CWS is now to a substantial degree a manufacturer for the retail societies, but its

1. In 1920–21 a proposal for a paid Union executive committee of five members is noted as likely to block women, and it was suggested that some of the societies might propose a reserved seat for women; in 1936, when Mrs. Cottrell, a guildswoman, left the Co-operative Wholesale Society Board, the Guild went so far as to ask for four reserved seats for women on the Union's board (but in 1948 they reversed their stand on the issue) (WCG A.R.1921, 1937, 1949).
2. The North of England Wholesale Industrial and Provident Society Ltd. became the CWS in 1872.

main activities have been as wholesale purchaser and distributor for them; in more recent years it has moved into insurance, banking, agricultural production, hotel and travel management, and overseas trade. It has always had a major, explicit representation on the Union Executive and sectional boards and at the Union Congresses.

The Guild's disregard of the CWS may have a historical explanation. WCG leaders originally favored more producer activity and involved themselves with efforts to set up co-operative workshops for women. Mary Lawrenson and some others supported E. V. Neale in his unsuccessful attempts to direct the English movement toward producers' co-operation (Backstrom 1974). The WCG did not formally give up its own commitment to producer co-operatives until after 1888, when Llewelyn Davies along with Rosalind Nash made a tour of inquiry to profit-sharing workshops and factories on behalf of the CWS. In 1891 the Guild accepted the argument that "it is more to the advantage of the worker to have good wages and shorter hours than the doubtful chance of a share in the profits" (Webb 1927:81). A hankering after producer co-operatives lingered on, however, particularly for women workers.[3]

More significant than sentimental regrets, even after the WCG acquiesced in the wholesale function of the CWS, is that the Guild seems not to have grasped the implications for women. The victory of the CWS meant, in fact, the victory of that business- and profit-oriented element of the movement in which women had the least claim to expertise. It was difficult to extrapolate household experience to the wholesale trade. Women's values directed the Guild, in this context, to arguments against using commercial viability as a criterion for movement policy—arguments that had less and less appeal. Possibly the co-operative movement's change in orientation was initially masked for the Guild by the influential presence of the much-loved and respected Mrs. Ben Jones, member of the Guild's first Central Committee and Guild president from 1886 to 1891; her husband, the leader of the pro-CWS group, also supported the founding of the Guild. By 1905 the pattern of the future was reasonably clear, and it showed itself in the rejection of a Guild pilot project that combined rather too much settlement house activity and philosophy in a proposed model for extending co-operation into poorer neighborhoods and strata of the working class. The Coronation Street project did not actually lose money, but it was too close to "good works" for the developing movement. The Management Board of the Sunderland Society finally voted to withdraw support from arrangements that included attention to the nonretail problems of the poor (Davies 1899, Webb 1927:88).[4]

3. It resurfaces in the 1985 sessions on women in the co-operative movement, reported by Cope and Gaffin (1985:5).
4. Margaret Llewelyn Davies presented to the movement in 1899 a paper, "Co-operation in Poor Neighbourhoods," which was followed in 1902 by a Guild survey of the

Women have been very little involved in the governance of the co-operative movement and particularly in the CWS. Eva Dodds, the woman invited to preside over the Co-operative Union Congress in International Women's Year, was the second woman to become a director of the CWS; she was not a guildswoman.[5] The Guild did support the protracted struggle to get Dodds onto the CWS Board of Directors, an effort criticized by the Labour newspaper, the *Daily Herald*, as a "feminist campaign" showing that women were "more interested in the advance of feminist politics and women's interests than in the improvement of co-operative administration and trading   a gloomy prospect" (December 9). This was in 1957.

Over the years the English consumer co-operative movement has moved steadily away from the original model of the small, local group focused on a retail store run by an ideologically committed co-operative membership. The retail stores now give purchasers National Dividend Stamps, like other stores' trading stamps, thereby eliminating the necessity for co-operative commitment—membership is no longer a prerequisite for rebate, and there is no longer a delay in receiving the dividend. Customers have no reason to feel any involvement with the well-being of the store, nor indeed any involvement with a particular store at all, since stamps from any store can be put in any savings book. The consolidations of retail societies have in any case destroyed the intimate early connection with an individual society. Society numbers increased in the earlier years of the movement, but they have decreased since World War II, largely in response to increased competition from the new supermarkets. In recent years the policy is actively to reduce the number of societies, with twenty-five the goal in 1987 (Co-operative Union 1987:2). These will necessarily be regional and very large, with a Board of Governors that bears little resemblance to the original Management Committees. In addition, the co-op stores now give credit. And the arguments for membership and members' participation are, at the most, those in favor of consumer activism and of democratic participation. Co-operation as a means of transforming society seems to have vanished.

The current nature of the movement is clear in the "Co-operative principles as established by the Rochdale Pioneers and as reformulated by the 23rd Congress of the International Co-operative Alliance," published in 1982:

---

financial constraints that prevented poor families from becoming co-operators. From 1902 to 1904 Coronation Street had resident women social workers (amateurs including Davies) who arranged classes and entertainments for children and adults. It also had provisions for selling small quantities of cooked food, provided assistance through loans, and lowered membership fees and prices (incidentally lowering dividends as well) (Gaffin and Thoms 1983:62–66).

5. Dodds was the second woman to be granted such an honor. Margaret Llewelyn Davies had been the first, upon her retirement as general secretary of the Guild. Nora Willis, Guild president, was the third in the Guild's centenary year.

1. Open membership.
2. Democratic control (one man, one vote).
3. Payment of limited interest on capital.
4. The economic result arising out of the operations of a society to be distributed to members in proportion to their trade with the society.
5. Provision of education for members, officers, employees and the general public.
6. Co-operation among co-operators nationally and internationally (International Co-operative Alliance 1982:1).

The payment of dividends on purchases rather than shares, as well as the emphasis on education and on co-operation at both the national and the international levels—these are principles central to the movement, and ones the Guild worked for steadily. But their meaning has changed, as has the meaning of more specific measures. Neither "democratic control" nor "open membership," previously implying the entitlement of women to be members, means much when only those trained in the management of big business will be involved in running the stores. This is a document aimed at "the general public," not just at co-operators. In 1982 the document lists the following "advantages which the Co-operative Movement offers ordinary men and women": it "mobilises the strength of consumers; trains them in the arts of democracy; secures collective action without losing sight of the importance of the individual member; creates pride in owning and directing a successful business; distributes rewards according to personal loyalty; and offers an easy way of saving" (1982:2). The image of the Co-operative Commonwealth is now remote, as is the feeling of a select group (self-selected, under conditions of open membership) with a mandate for social change. There is no longer a vision of the New Jerusalem. Certainly there is no significant role for women. Ironically, they have attained a form of equality as consumers now that consumption has become a purely economic function.

The Women's Co-operative Guild had developed from the co-operative movement's ideals a structure and a rationale that gave priority and a political role to women. But both structurally and conceptually the movement moved in directions that denied the validity of such claims. By the time of the Guild's centenary it was clear that, for the movement, the WCG had no claim to a role in policy making, women had no special claim to participation, and any feminist assertion based on the specificities of women would have to look beyond co-operation for support. In the postwar years the WCG facilitated this development by its commitment to the movement, its refusal to jettison co-operation for any form of separatist or feminist action.

　　The group had always shown concern for differentiation from other women's groups. Generally speaking, the WCG was unenthusiastic about coalition efforts although it was prepared, up to a certain point, to work in groups coordinating the efforts of working-class women. Its suffrage efforts focused on the People's Suffrage Federation, a coalition of Labour and Liberal suffragists in which Margaret Llewelyn Davies was central (Black 1983). In the interests of female trade unionism the WCG worked with the Women's Trade Union League at a very early date and joined the league in founding the Women's Industrial Council; Margaret Bondfield, Britain's first woman Cabinet minister, was an important link in this connection. The Guild was proud to be appointed to the governmental body, the Standing Joint Committee of Women's Organisations, when it was founded in 1916, and is still represented on the committee's successor, the Standing Joint Committee of Working Women's Organisations (Gaffin and Thoms 1983:59–60; Rendel 1977; Soldon 1978:78, 89). But after World War I it refused to join with the first successor to nonmilitant suffragism, the National Union of Societies for Equal Citizenship, in a protest against dismissal of married women and instead passed its own separate resolution (WCG 1921).

Even with women's groups in the labor movement the Guild always had significant disagreements in areas where ideological differences produced different preferences about strategy. If the Guild felt it had a mandate to speak for and to all working women—and especially all married working women—it also felt it possessed the single set of correct doctrines necessary to serve the cause of such women. Central among these doctrines was a fierce commitment to the ideas of co-operation. Neither Fabian nor Marxist socialism was an effective substitute. Although guildswomen had been active early supporters of the entry of the co-operative movement into electoral politics, the WCG disapproved of the effective merger of the Co-operative into the Labour party, whose insistence upon the importance of nationalization disappointed the Guild. Enthusiastic about the Bolshevik Revolution, the group supported the subsequent regime because of non-Marxist and not wholly accurate notions about the role of co-operatives in the Soviet Union. Later, in spite of endorsement in 1939 of a United Front policy, the WCG became fiercely hostile to the British Communist party and was the only co-operative auxiliary to bar members of that party from representing the group (Carbery 1969, Groombridge 1960). The women's branches and agents of the Labour or Communist party were often regarded with suspicion, as competitors or as dupes.

For women's organizations that were not working-class, the distrust was greater, even when such groups shared the Guild's social feminist concerns. "Some of [the other women's organizations] receive heavy grants from public funds, others are strongly supported by leisured women of the well-to-do classes," the WCG Central Committee told members in a postwar flyer entitled "A New Approach to Guild Education." The committee noted with concern that "many women co-operators to-day are finding activity in non-co-operative women's organisations [and] . . . in some cases Education Committees and Management Boards are even providing meeting rooms, or other facilities, for such non-co-operative bodies" (n.d.). Mixed-sex groups, with the exception of the coalitions related to peace and to international organization, were not seen as relevant. Middle-class women as such do not seem to have provoked any hostility. Co-operators did not believe in any inherent conflict of interest based on class and, after all, the heroines of the Guild were Alice Acland and Margaret Llewelyn Davies. But middle-class women's organizations looked as though they could seduce working-class women away from co-operation and political action. The Townswomen's Guilds that became active in the 1930s were a particular threat, for they had been deliberately designed by successors to the suffrage movement to appeal to the relatively uneducated among newly enfranchised women. The Townswomen's Guilds grew in membership throughout the interwar period and experienced a boom just when, after the war, the Guild began its decline. Run by middle-class volunteers and paid experts, they drew on a Morris-related tradition of crafts and popular entertainment. The WCG feared these new organizations and, to a very limited extent, were influenced by them; the historian of the Townswomen's Guilds sees the WCG as providing an example, and in more than just the name (Stott 1978). The Townswomen's Guilds had a nonpartisan orientation very remote from the WCG's fierce commitment to co-operation.

Such distinctions and inhibitions are clear in the prize-winning entry in a contest in the Guild's short-lived magazine *The Guildswoman.* The use in 1939 of the topic "Are the Guilds Devoting Too Much Time to Activities That Are Not under Co-operative Control?" immediately says something about the tensions in the WCG's relationship to the co-operative movement. In this last year of peace the Guild was at its impressive peak membership of over eighty-seven thousand and actively involved in resistance to war and rearmament in a way that had alienated the co-operative movement and angered other women's groups. Refusing to join in efforts to organize evacuation of children from the cities, the beginning of the Women's Voluntary Services structure, the Guild merely set up a register for reception of possible evacuated co-operative children (Ganley n.d.).

The winner of the *Guildswoman* competition suggests opposition even among WCG members to the wide range of reform activities in which the Guild was involved. The prize essay, "The Guilds and Their True Purpose," lists inappropriate topics for meetings: "Eugenics, cremation, birth control, mental hospitals, air raid precautions, milk demonstrations, cookery talks, Left Book Club, modern authors, Indian workers' problems" (*Guildswoman* 1939:99). The essayist considers pacifist activities inappropriate, as is concern for conditions in the home and for

issues relating to public health, including those connected with reproductive freedom (eugenics was one of the forces behind the legitimation of contraception and abortion). Labor issues not related to co-operation are ruled out, as is concern with the empire; nor is the Guild to
become involved with any organizations other than the League of Nations Union.[6] The writer uses the narrowest possible definition of areas
relevant to co-operation, and she clearly does so in reference to the wide
range of other groups seen as more properly involved with these other
concerns. For her, "Co-operative Control" seems to mean movement
control rather than Guild control. The point of view presented here was
common in the co-operative movement as a whole, though often resisted
in the Guild; it rings oddly in a journal almost entirely devoted to war
resistance at a time when the co-operative movement and Co-operative
party had, however reluctantly, decided to support the war effort.

WCG separatism continued into the era of the second-wave women's
movement, with the organization reluctant to be associated closely even
with organizations sharing major goals. In 1975 the Guild experienced
International Women's Year in isolation, featuring a National Service of
Dedication at Westminster Abbey. In 1980 the WCG was not listed
among the large and varied group of women's organizations associated
with Women's Action Day.[7] Only on peace issues has the Guild been
willing to associate with other women's groups. But the Guild does not
seem to have played any role in the new movement of feminist antiwar
protest, and it has had no involvement with the Greenham Common
peace camp.

To an uninvolved feminist observer it seems obvious that such separatism has helped keep the WCG's appeal limited and its membership
restricted. But many in the Guild would disagree; in the 1980s older
members, some of them active public figures such as M.P. Joyce Butler,
apparently continued to feel that the Guild's main importance was the
linkage it provided between women and co-operation (Gaffin and
Thoms 1983:250). This, the primary rationale for the founding of the
Guild, had become stronger in the years after World War II.

In 1943 the Guild tried to outline its goals for the postwar era. "Woman of Tomorrow" looked ahead to "an efficient virile community of
earnest women." Such language was fairly common in a period when
even feminists lacked today's sensitivity to sexism in language (indeed,
lacked that concept). What is surprising, coming from the Guild, is appeals to women veterans and businesswomen, along with a new emphasis
on social and cultural activities. The goal of the group was now to have

6. The writer opposes Guild involvement with militant workers' conferences, the Labour hospital, the Union for Democratic Control, and private organizations arranging
outings for poor children (*Guildswoman* 1939:99).

7. The National Joint Committee of Working Women's Associations, to which the Guild
belongs, did make a late endorsement.

"every Guild branch an up-to-date local community offering attractive facilities for enjoyable social intercourse among people with mutual cultural interests and also a chance to serve in the wider field of public affairs." Co-operation had disappeared. Self-development had become central and public service secondary—almost an afterthought. Concerned with the competition from other women's groups, the Guild briefly reacted by becoming more like them.

More characteristic and less trendy, another internal document, "A New Approach to Guild Education," probably issued in 1948, stresses the Guild's history of commitment to adult education. Furthermore, this is education for co-operation: "The aim of adult education should be to make a more self-reliant citizen, socially conscious and . . . Co-operators should, moreover, seek to establish a well-informed membership of active Co-operators who will apply the principles of Co-operation not only to trade, but also to the wider problems of civic life." New activities may attempt to draw in younger women, but only to "continue to educate them in Co-operation and citizenship for the common good." In a period when women's groups were not very feminist, the Guild sought differentiation in terms of co-operation and not in terms of feminism. The loss of distinctive educative/co-operative characteristics was feared more than loss of members.

In 1949 the Guild's recruitment document, relatively glossy in Guild terms (which tend toward the drab and businesslike), was entitled "The Woman of To-day Steps Out." It describes the Guild as an organization that "caters for women of all ages, and organises activities to fit them for the many duties of citizenship." It makes a clear attempt to expand and make more attractive the actual activities of members. "The Women's Co-operative Guild," the reader is told, "is now desirous that Co-operative women shall touch upon many things other than the political and social matters that have hitherto been almost the sole activities of bodies that work for the advancement of women." But still we assume that a Guild member is previously a co-operative woman; it was impossible to join the Guild without first joining a co-operative society, and since the 1920s Guilds had been expected to affiliate with the Co-operative party or at least the Labour party.

Attempts at new activities and images did not have any substantial effect. Guild membership continued to decline and to age. For the Guild, the 1960s did not mean a feminist revival. Instead, it meant reacting to the Groombridge Report. This study of co-operative auxiliaries, commissioned by the Co-operative Union, produced a remarkably favorable assessment of the Guilds, at least as compared to the other auxiliaries. But Brian Groombridge seems to have been unaware of the feminist antecedents of the group; he praised the Guild as representing grass roots consumerism within the co-operative movement. The Guild then set up its own Modernisation Committee, which essentially agreed with Groombridge. Accordingly, in 1963 the WCG reconstituted itself as the Co-operative Women's Guild, and adopted the set of objectives it still lives by. These objectives are worth examining, for they show how the Guild finally reconciled its often contradictory goals. Above all, they show how, as feminism began to reemerge into public view, the Guild rejected it.

The first objective is "to promote through the expansion of Co-operation such conditions of life as will ensure for all people equal opportunities for full and free development." *Women's* equality has ceased to be paramount or even explicitly identified. When women appear in the second objective, they do so only instrumentally: "To educate women in the principles and practice of Co-operation in order that they can play a full part in the control of the Co-operative Movement and, through active membership and participation, whenever practical, encourage and support the establishment of Co-operative forms of organisation." The impetus to extend Co-operation is obviously weak, and the emphasis is on women's influence within the movement—at a time when very few co-operators have any influence at all.

The third objective focuses on public and political action: "To work for improvement in the status of women and to encourage and prepare women to take part in local, national, and international affairs." The weak formula "take part" is a retreat from earlier statements about increasing the representation of women on local authorities and in Parliament. "Encourage and prepare" is also somewhat anachronistic, echoing anxieties about the interest and competence of newly enfranchised women. Earlier Guilds had less uncertainty about women's willingness and abilities in relation to public office; they had been outraged when, for instance, the Co-operative party failed to nominate any women candidates in the first election after the full enfranchisement of English women (WCG 1928).

The fourth goal, "To work for the objective of world peace," is again a vague, unspecific liberal commitment without any indication that women or women's groups have a specific vocation or role to play or that co-operation is relevant.

Finally, the fifth objective is an astonishing departure from tradition: "To provide social, cultural and recreational activities through which members may live a full and interesting life." Previous guildswomen had never thought of "a full and interesting life" as being a goal in itself. Like other social feminists, they stressed service and obligation, even self-sacrifice. Guildswomen now, it appears, are persons with leisure to fill, a great change from the past. It is an even greater change to retreat from educational to "social, cultural, and recreational" activities to fill up what leisure time there is.

This final objective is emphasized in the Service of Dedication central to the Guild's celebration of International Women's Year (WCG:1975).

In the program for this service, held in Westminster Abbey, the Guild is described as: "one of the oldest women's organisations in existence. Its objects are to encourage and educate women to play a full part in the Co-operative Movement and in local, national and international affairs. It strives, through a wide variety of educational, social, cultural, and recreational activities to enable each of its members to have a full, interesting and useful life." The co-operative movement has regained explicit prominence in the Guild's statement of objectives. But the notions of women's distinctive situation or of any need for equality have vanished. Each branch works on a National Theme and raises money "for a nationally agreed charitable project." "A full, interesting and useful life" has taken the place of the ambition for a feminist transformation of society; the same banal goal is featured in a 1980 training manual.

In 1978–79 the Guild did take "Women's Rights" as its branch program theme. But it did so as part of the National Co-operative Joint Auxiliaries Council (in cooperation with Education Department of the Co-operative Union), and the discussion guide was drawn up by the National Council of Civil Liberties. The theme title—not a social feminist one—should be noted. The contents make no mention whatsoever of any past role of the WCG in relation to the topics discussed, which include equal pay, reproductive freedom, maternity and other social security provisions, and issues of income and taxation. The document is entirely on the current state of the law in Britain, and on the need for further legal change.

The Guild knew what *its* movement was and was tempted by no other. Nor did the organization any longer aspire to change either co-operation or the larger society. Feminism, defined as women's rights, was something other groups did and told it about. And the Guild was now involved with charitable endeavors like those which had first motivated middle-class women in the late eighteenth and early nineteenth centuries. In its earliest years the Guild had been far more politically organized and aware than it was a century later.

In 1963 the Guild carried out what will likely be its last reorganization, and became the Co-operative Women's Guild. The name change reflected what the Guild had become over its hundred years. It had ended up the auxiliary the movement expected, in the process virtually ceasing to be feminist. The founders of the Guild described themselves as founding a women's support group for the co-operative movement, and the Guild has always been described as a women's auxiliary. In fact, it is probably something closer to a women's section in its ambitions. Both structures have an antiquated flavor today. Certainly women's auxiliaries—*ladies'* auxiliaries—are something no contemporary feminist would now set up, even though women's groups as such have acquired a new approval even from some thoroughly assimilationist equity feminists.[8] Set up for male-defined purposes within a hierarchy established and controlled by men, women's auxiliaries have historically been the groups that make coffee, not policy. They seem to represent the inequalities and the lack of autonomy to which feminism reacts. "Groups that help"—the very terminology is unacceptable today.

A women's section of a political movement differs, at least analytically, because its members' function is not to help the party but to represent a portion of the potential constituency. That represented group may be seen mainly as a source of service or support, but sometimes it may also be recognized as having particular perspectives and subjective or even objective needs. For somewhat similar reasons, even a modern political party may also have a youth section that is parallel in structure and function to the women's section. The main group still, of course, is (adult) men, and any other section is secondary. Although representation of an auxiliary in the group's policy making is unlikely, special interest sections may have formal status, with women or youth members being elected or coopted to make up a designated fraction of a governing body. The British Labour party makes such arrangements to have women on its governing body; the Co-operative party and co-operative movement do not.[9] Modern feminists are likely to be unenthusiastic about the existence of a women's section, even with representation in policy-making bodies. They have found the situation presents an intolerable conflict for the women involved, who cannot maintain credibility within the larger group if they push hard on the issues of special concern to women or with their own constituency if they yield to the overall strategic search for influence or power in the state. Ghettoization and absorption seem to be the two alternatives, and plenty of case material shows the problems. The experience of socialist and communist women is well-known (Sowerwine 1978). At the same time evidence shows that under favorable circumstances women's sectors of political groups may serve the development of a feminist consciousness and activity of some significance (Manderson 1977).

More often, the experience of women's sections, as of women's auxiliaries, shows how the argument based on female distinctiveness may become a trap. It is fatal to allow these differences, as defined by men and

8. This new approval usually takes the form of willingness to accept women's groups as strictly temporary expedients; for example, Mary Midgley and Judith Hughes remark that women "are not being silly in preferring to operate on their own" (1983:23). Midgley and Hughes in general lay considerable emphasis on co-operation between men and women in the cause of feminism; one of their major complaints is that modern feminists are unaware of the role of men in the achievements of the women's movement. One of their criticisms of radical feminism is what they see as a tendency to separatism.

9. The women's representatives are not necessarily drawn from the women's commission or section. The friction between party- or movement-loyal women on the governing body and more feminist or women-oriented women on the commission may be considerable. The analytical point here, however, is the possible recognition of women as an interest or constituency, something a women's auxiliary leaves untouched.

consenting women, to exclude women from policy access or authority in public matters and from the policy making of a political movement. When the women's group is defined as an auxiliary, it is bound to be shut out from any such access. Even so, the movement may still be able to use the auxiliary to recruit women to act as supporters—as volunteers and voters. They will be expected to support the movement-related activities of their men, whether literally to fight and die, as in independence struggles, or simply to devote to the movement time and resources that otherwise would be expended on the family unit. This is the role of the activist's or the politician's wife, a role seldom carried out by the husband of the female activist or politician (Werner and Bachtold 1974). Creation of an auxiliary means a group effort in such directions. It may also include raising money, sometimes in amazingly large quantities (Mitchinson 1979).

The co-operative movement needed somewhat more from its women's auxiliary. The Guild was recruiting not merely auxiliary or supporting party members but crucial elements of the movement. Under those circumstances it was hard to keep the Guild from trying to assume a policy role in the movement as representative of those it had recruited. And it was bound to encourage its members to take a more active role in movement management. The logic of the case it had to make as recruiter entailed such activities.

Apparently the movement thought it was setting up a normal auxiliary, a support and recruitment device with no autonomy or policy implications. This arrangement was basically incompatible with an ideology that makes women's role central and a practice that made their assistance indispensable. Davies justified the separate women's guilds in a way that made them far more than an auxiliary:

> As all who work in any democratic movement find out, the special circumstances of women's lives, and the effects of these circumstances, together with the fact that men are in possession, and not without prejudice as regards women's place and work, make it essential, if men and women are to come together on terms of real equality and comradeship, and if the women's point of view is to be properly expressed, that women should for some time yet have special organisations of their own (1921:7).

Women's special circumstances, men's power and prejudices, and women's point of view—these are not the circumstances that define humble helpers. But the movement as a whole saw no need for a stronger structure, a women's branch or section. Nor were the men who actually ran the movement prepared to recognize in structure or in practice any equal, let alone superior claim that women *as such* might have to make policy. Acting with some plausibility, they proceeded to set up men's and mixed guilds as additional recruitment auxiliaries. None did very well.

At the same time the movement was unable to prevent the activist leaders of the Guild from taking advantage of the facilities provided by the movement. Anyone who has tried to set up a voluntary organization will appreciate the enormous value of ongoing mailing lists and newsletters, not to mention models for manuals, forms, and other publications. The co-operative movement supplied an accessible constituency of potential members served by a professionally staffed newspaper and the rest of a good communications network. When female relatives of co-operators comprised a group of women who were aged and declining in numbers, they limited the Guild's potential; initially, and for a good long time, they were an invaluable resource. In addition, even though the WCG could not tap the central decision-making structure of the movement as a whole, it could certainly imitate it. The movement provided an appropriate organizational model, consisting of self-governing small groups organized on a local basis around immediate issues, federated in sections, pouring resolutions into a central committee and congress, circulating information and educational material. Most valuable of all, however, was the legitimation of Guild activity by the ideology of the movement. As long as women were studying co-operation and trying to acquire more women for co-operation, even the surliest husband could not effectively object to their meetings.

There were built-in limitations, and women encountered obstacles as soon as they attempted to put into practice the ideology's further implications that women should also help run the stores and the movement as a whole. Over time a tendency developed to specialize in the tasks involved in store management and the related political management of the societies. These tended to become men's tasks to the extent they were carried on after hours. The women were disregarded, and if a family had only one co-op member, it would be the husband. Some societies even had rules enforcing this condition, though the movement as a whole set no such restrictions. Under law the dividend, a result of the household expenditures that came out of the husband's pay, was legally the husband's property even if the wife bought the share (presumably with "his" money in any case). Hired managers and full-time or virtually full-time professional co-operative directors tended to take over—and they were nearly all men. After the establishment of the Co-operative party, external political activities were carried on by full-time professionals, and very few women were to be found among the Co-operative party's members of Parliament. Even tasks that seemed appropriate to women tended to be handed over to movement groups other than the Guild. Both in 1920 and in 1928 disputes arose about the campaigns and the educational material that were to teach newly enfranchised women voters about co-operation; the Guild was refused permission to carry on these activities and in turn rejected the material prepared by the Central Education Executive (WCG 1921, 1928).

The ideology of the movement meant, further, that Guild activism could be called illegitimate if it seemed to harm the movement or interfere with women's devotion to their stores. This was, of course, the complaint against the prewar Guild involvement with the issue of divorce. The voice of Mr. Burns of Salford, speaking in 1914, echoes down through the history of the Guild: "People who believed in co-operation, if they were wise, would work for co-operation only. If they introduced subjects about which all people differed, they could not possibly push co-operation." And it is seconded by Mr. Greening: "They must satisfy themselves that the co-operative movement alone was sufficient for them. There were outside organisations to carry on the questions in regard to both politics and religion" (Co-op Union 1915:12, 14). The women of the WCG protested in vain for over fifty years that women's issues were central to co-operation. In the end, out of devotion to their own view of what co-operation was or could be, they accepted the constraints of the movement.

No one could mistake the early leaders of the Guild for members of an auxiliary, whatever their groups were called. Their own independent stature and their involvement in the movement as individuals masked the extent to which their demands challenged the whole structure of consumer co-operation as it developed in Britain. Their access to decision making was personal and informal, justified not by their arguments but by their own lives. And they served the movement well, as energizers and as consciences. But their influence, which was considerable, barely touched the political structures within which they worked. Both they and their followers were misled about how little real impact was possible inside co-operation for the Guilds and for women as a group. Ironically, the resulting political role for women *outside* the movement was their real legacy. It is sad that their devotion to co-operation limited what their group could do. But the feminism that was interwoven into their co-operation did significant things for their fellow members of the Guild and, as they had hoped in 1883, did indeed help improve the condition of women.

The Guild maintains its central interest in co-operation, though the co-operative movement is even less like its ideal now than it was in the past. In earlier years, however, the WCG's feminism was reinforced by and also served to reinforce its co-operative views. Now the old social feminism is gone. In 1985 the reporters on a series of workshops on women in the co-operative movement found that "the women present fell into the two standard categories: those who thought that a woman's place was outside the home, and that her children should take second place at all times to her career or her public life, and those who believed that at least while a woman had small children, they should come first" (Cope and Gaffin 1985:2). Those in the first group, whose views certainly do not correspond to those of the founders and most of the active guildswomen over the years, wanted to "bring the Guild up to date" and bring in young women by convincing them "that the Guild was a kind of umbrella organisation which could accommodate those whose principal objectives were full employment, peace . . . or almost any other worthy cause, with the improvement of conditions for women as a kind of corollary to the rest." They were equity feminists, who were likely to have trouble inside co-operation. The second group "saw the Guild primarily as a help and protection to women, especially working class women." They were "not interested in the Guild as a political force, but as a source of practical assistance" (Cope and Gaffin 1985:2–3). Theirs was social feminism, if a limited and curiously old-fashioned sort. For both groups of members, women's issues had become either secondary or unpolitical, and this development is most striking in those most like the WCG's typical adherents.

Too feminist to devote all their energies to the service of the changing co-operative movement but too committed to co-operation to leave the movement as it became an inappropriate vehicle for feminism, the women of the postwar Guild finally opted for co-operation as the group's distinctive characteristic. The WCG was bound to be dragged down by the movement's decline. By the time of its centenary in 1983, the WCG's membership was smaller than it had been in 1900 (Gaffin and Thoms 1983:268). Its main legacy to women was the lessons of its past struggles. Of these, one of the happier memories was the experience of feminist pacifism.

CHAPTER 8

"The Mothers' International":
Feminist Pacifism

It is hard to imagine members of the Women's Co-operative Guild, of whatever era, reading England's radical feminist magazine *Spare Rib*, let alone liking it. Yet in 1984 *Spare Rib* celebrated the Guild in an article entitled "'She goes on and on, you can't kill the spirit!' Women's Involvement in Older Peace Movements" (May 1984a).[1] But on the next page another piece, "Why Peace and Not Feminism?" expressed a familiar anxiety about social feminism and about women's association with peace: "This difference between the interests of men and of women drew very heavily on women's child-bearing role and for this reason poses some problems for feminism which has set out to win equality for women and to minimise the effect of biological differences on the choices women have in their lives" (*Spare Rib* 1984b:26) The specific context for this concern was the women's peace camp at Greenham Common, which has produced much ambivalence among English feminists. But the concern is a more general one—the standard criticism of social feminism as conservative and constraining because it encourages an emphasis on what is different about women. The old dispute between equity and social feminism continues, as the Guild exemplifies the way in which social feminism, in particular, is drawn toward international involvement. Here again, being part of the co-operative movement was both a help and a hindrance.

Strictly speaking, equity feminists should eschew any particular role for women or women's groups internationally. Yet they also have found it necessary to involve themselves in a range of feminist efforts that have a more-than-national dimension. On the national level the battle for equal participation in public life eventually encounters institutions re-

1. The Women's International League for Peace and Freedom (WILPF), a slightly younger and much more Leftist group (Bussey and Tims 1965; Berry 1977), was also praised as the article marveled at both the social feminist and the equity feminist versions of pacifism.

lated to foreign policy, which are only slightly more welcoming to women than the church. At some fairly advanced stage in activism the diplomatic corps and the army are bound to become targets of affirmative action, on the basis of the injustice of excluding any particular group of citizens from employment. But the relevant considerations have nothing to do with international politics or with women as a group, and it was for different reasons that equity feminists became involved in international connections with activist women in other countries.

On the simplest level there was a need for information. The tactics and successes or failures of women in other countries could supply examples, encouragement, or warning. Lacking legitimacy in domestic politics, activist women looked across national boundaries for mutual support, both as individuals and as part of international networks of women's organizations. In a related development, the nineteenth century had seen the burgeoning of international functional agencies and associations. Those agencies, as well as such interwar international organizations as the League of Nations and its active International Labor Bureau, provided international focuses for the shared concerns of women's groups in different countries (Walters 1952).

All feminists found international dimensions in some issues, particularly in the question of the citizenship of married women which absorbed so much of the energy of the American National Woman's party in the interwar period. International treaties, often negotiated through international organizations, attempted to impose standards in such areas as equal pay and working conditions. The League Charter specified equality in hiring (as the result of the efforts of a coalition of women's groups at the time of the Versailles Settlement) (Whittick 1979); it thus provided a model for national policy and a leverage point for local activists. Equity feminists also found themselves involved in the campaigns to get women included in national delegations to the many international assemblies and conferences. After 1945 the interdependence of nation states and the development of some rudimentary social and legal community on the international level brought segments of every sort of equity feminism into some relation to international politics. By this time the universal international organization was ready to establish a Commission on the Status of Women. Equity feminists were of course involved in attempts to develop a United Nations convention barring all forms of discrimination against women. The European Community, for its part, followed the International Labor Organization in a series of directives and conventions binding member states to end certain sorts of discrimination against women; these requirements have been enforced with some success by the European Court. Equity feminist international nongovernmental organizations included the many federated associations of professional women as well as groups such as Open Door International, formed to work for equality in employment in all nations. In principle, none of this activity had any special linkage with specific characteristics attributed to women. In practice, many of these group activities tended to acquire additional, social feminist rationales.

A similar but significantly different process brought social feminists into the international system. For them, the key element was women's own international nongovernmental organizations. International social feminist networks shared the equity feminists' needs to consult and coordinate efforts, as well as the drive toward contact and mutual support by similar groups in different nations. They also reacted as lobbyists to the existence of international organizations made up of governmental representatives. But the logic of their ideology drove them one step further, to an advocacy of peace and even of pacifism. This was an intrinsically international goal, even though it had a national dimension in the attempt to restrain warmaking in individual nations. Peace was in fact the main focus of the international women's movement in the interwar period. More recently, women's groups have been concerned internationally with the processes of development. In both cases, the logic of involvement is the social feminist analysis of women's experience as a basis for the reconstruction of society.

The history of women's international organization has not yet been studied systematically. It is clear, however, that a network of travel and correspondence had established extensive connections among European and North American women by the middle of the nineteenth century. In 1840 Lucretia Mott and the young Elizabeth Cady Stanton had their mythologized meeting at the World Anti-Slavery Conference in London. The contact they maintained was one of many friendships among activist women who lived far apart but formed networks that extended internationally (Bacon 1980).[2] By the last decades of the nineteenth century the numerous large international conferences already included some whose subject was the situation of women, and organizations that linked the proliferating national women's groups began to appear. They developed a series of characteristic international projects and concerns, the most important of which was peace.

In 1888 Americans set up the first great international league of women's organizations, the International Council of Women (ICW). The ICW's general goal was summed up in the Golden Rule, and its diverse membership precluded much focused common activity, but the organization's specific tasks, beyond a general improvement of the situation of women, included equal political rights and, importantly, peace and disarmament. Suffragism was considered too divisive to allow suffrage groups to join the ICW, so in 1904 a second international organization

2. The travels and correspondence of women such as Anna Jameson, Frederika Bremer, and Margaret Fuller indicate the connections among women interested in the situation of women, as does the rapid diffusion of the work of such theorists as Mary Wollstonecraft and John Stuart Mill (Sebo 1976; Hurwitz 1977; Evans 1977).

of women's groups, the International Woman Suffrage Alliance (IWSA), was started, again by Americans, to "stimulate and assist national women's associations to obtain the franchise for women" (Whittick 1979:30). The year 1910 saw the beginning of the International Union of Catholic Women's Leagues, a group reported in 1936 to have 33 million women as members in 723 member organizations including 52 national leagues (Boy 1936:81). Closely supervised by the church, the international union concerned itself mainly with issues of social policy, emphasizing the battle against "immorality"; in 1932 it managed to prevent the League of Nations from endorsing contraception (Boy 1936:82). But the group also supported the great international peace campaigns of the 1930s. In 1915 another group mainly of American women founded the Women's International League for Peace and Freedom (WILPF). And 1921 saw the start of an international women's organization even less well-known that those already mentioned: the International Co-operative Women's Guild (ICWG), founded chiefly as a result of efforts by the English Guild. All of these groups are still in existence, although the ICWG became a committee of the International Co-operative Union in 1963.

These are only a few of the vast number of international women's organizations active in the interwar period.[3] Since the Women's Decade of the United Nations, so many more organizations have developed that a catalogue, let alone a classification, is impossible. In the only study of the subject, Magdelaine Boy produced in 1936 a classification of international women's groups that identified some, including the ICW, as essentially "feminist" and others, including WILPF, as "pacifist."[4] Boy thought these organizations invaluable because they served to coordinate the League of Nations' social action and to influence public opinion (155–56). Here she seems to be responding mainly to their role as early versions of the functional nongovernmental organizations now so widespread and, by and large, so much appreciated. The strictly feminist groups she optimistically thought were on the point of putting themselves out of business; "some of the pacifist leagues" she dismissed as based on "more or less nebulous fantasies." But she praised what she called the "feminine international" as able to "adapt itself to new social

3. In 1923 the League of Nations' annual *Handbook of International Organisations* indexed the following under "feminism": the International Council of Women, the International Federation of University Women, the International Woman Suffrage Alliance, the Women's International League for Peace and Freedom, the Office Central de documentation féminine, the International Union of Catholic Women's Leagues, and the Swiss Union mondiale de la femme pour la paix internationale. By 1938 twenty-six organizations were listed.

4. "Professional" included the ICWG as well as the many associations of women doctors and lawyers; "confessional" included the World YWCA and the International Union of Catholic groups; "altruistic" was a smaller category made up essentially of groups whose only concern was the issues, important for the period, of prostitution and the trade in women and children. In "unions of associations," the final category, all the groups mentioned above reappear (Boy 1936:155–56).

conditions, to pursue action both civic and social, to train women for it" (56). And she saw it as the forerunner of a new international social order, thereby repeating with precision the social feminist view of an international role. "Civic and social" was of course the formula used by the French Union féminine civique et sociale, very active by this time nationally and also internationally through its overseas branches and Catholic linkages.

Boy was accurate in seeing a logically limited future, both nationally and internationally, for what she called feminists and I call equity feminists. In practice, however, such feminists continued to be active outside their national borders simply because disadvantaged women, including exiles and those without access to their own national politics or media, turned for help to experienced activists in other countries. But equity feminists expected change within each existing belief system and political unit, so their focus for action tended to be national.

Yet even equity feminism, however illogically, has been concerned with the international suffering of women and children. In the interwar period attention focused on what was then called the "white slave trade," traffic in women and children, along with international drug networks. Social feminist arguments were not necessary to justify concern, for women's disproportionate suffering could be taken as indicating discrimination. In particular, opposition to prostitution and its criminal affiliates could be understood as a consequence of the advocacy of a single moral standard for both sexes. Such approaches fitted comfortably into existing ideological systems. After World War II, equity feminists used the same arguments to justify attention to problems related to women refugees and migrant workers and, later, to women involved in the offshore operations of multinational enterprises, women displaced by modernization, and the female majority of illiterates.

Even on the key issue of peace, certain groups of equity feminists tended to become involved, following the development of the master theories that their feminism extended. For example, a liberal version of equity feminism would include a commitment to international organization or development but include women proportionately, as actors and beneficiaries. Most often what happened, as it had in the suffrage movement, was the coexistence of the two sorts of feminism, sometimes within the same individual and, more important, within the same organization. Internationally, the prime example of the interaction of different sorts of feminism was the International Woman Suffrage Alliance. The IWSA itself, ostensibly organized only for suffragism, began passing resolutions on peace and in support of a League of Nations as early as 1913 (Whittick 1979:301). After the departure of the group's first president, Carrie Chapman Catt, in 1923, the balance in the organization shifted toward social feminism. At its 1926 meeting the organization established new commissions on peace, women police, and family endowment (mothers' allowance). Incoming president Marjorie Corbett Ashby defended the changes: "The demand for equal responsibilities must not wait for the granting of equal political rights or for equal education. . . . The woman's movement seeks to deepen woman's sense of responsibility and to widen her sphere of activity from the home to the city, from the city to the nation. . . . The League of Nations permits us to complete the circle and work beyond our own frontiers for the peace and welfare of the whole world."

Without apparent irony (she was an ardent Liberal and a parliamentary candidate for the party) she stated that "as soon as women are voters the political party machines can be trusted to undertake their political education with zeal as remarkable as it is tardy." Women's groups would continue to be needed, however, for they "must show the woman voter how she in turn can educate her party in all those social reforms which add to the health and happiness of the race" (quoted in Whittick 1979: 93).

Some members of what was thenceforth called the International Alliance of Women (IAW)[5] recognized what was happening and objected. One early and devoted member, Nina Boyle, wrote indignantly to the *IWS News* in 1928 that "our Alliance has finally struck its flag to the two most dangerous rivals and foes of feminism—peace and the social reformers." This would be the complaint of *Spare Rib* almost sixty years later, though Boyle hardly shared *Spare Rib*'s ideological preferences. She wrote that she supported feminism but also "imperialism" and felt it was dishonorable as well as inappropriate to drag peace into the IAW: "I do not wish to belong to a pacifist organisation" (Whittick 1979:97–98). This was equity feminism incarnate in an imperialist version.

The historian of the IAW, a great admirer of Marjorie Corbett Ashby, attempted an equity feminist defense of the organization's international involvements: "By engaging in activities beyond the immediate objects of the Alliance women can demonstrate their abilities [and thus] demonstrate to men their right to full citizenship." He added, "That peace and disarmament were among the chief concerns of mankind in the early thirties, was sufficient justification for all women's organisations to participate as fully as possible in the furtherance of such activities" (Whittick 1979:100, 107). This was not the argument Ashby was making. Nor would the members who remained in the IAW have accepted the description of their activities as following from "the chief concerns of mankind"; as feminists they insisted on designating their own concerns, and they gave higher priority to peace, they believed, than "mankind" did. This was the social feminist justification of efforts to increase the public role of women.

For social feminists, the arguments for women's special aptitude and

5. The full title of the group at this point was the International Alliance of Women for Suffrage and Equal Citizenship, which changed again in 1945 to International Alliance of Women–Equal Rights–Equal Responsibilities (Whittick 1979:95, 100). From 1926 on the group is usually referred to as the International Alliance of Women.

responsibility in relation to peace were the familiar ones: women as nonviolent, whether by biology or by training, and the family as model, with its processes of conciliation and nonviolence. Ulla Olin made the argument in sophisticated form at a 1975 seminar preceding the first United Nations Conference on Women. The context now was development policy rather than simply peace; the international model should be the institution that "shelters, protects, and nurtures *all* its members; it is also a place of constant competition and rivalry, with compromises and sharing as its basic ingredients in resolution of conflicts; it demands sacrifices and gives rewards." The institution she had in mind was the somewhat idealized family of social feminism. With the family as starting point "there would seem to be scope for much needed social innovation, in which women would have an opportunity to contribute their share *as women*" (Olin 1976:128).

Olin was not able, however, to spell out what women would do to transform the international system. In general, even social feminists have found it difficult to generate distinctive international actions based on women's specific qualities or experience. It is difficult to argue that the world is already just a larger household, on the pattern of municipal housekeeping. What we see instead, in the persistent feminist images of the "family of man" and the sisterhood of women, are attempts to make public, international relationships more like private, family ones. The preferred policies amount to attempts to bring together individuals and particularly individual women and children so they may communicate informally. Women's peace groups tend therefore to favor the learning of foreign or international languages; the Women's Co-operative Guild supported Esperanto. They attempt to establish new branches of their own or similar groups overseas, just as the Guild promoted the development of other national guilds and finally the International Co-operative Women's Guild. Finally, they travel and exchange visits with other women's groups, as the WCG did after World War II whenever guildswomen could afford the time and the money.[6]

All such activities aimed to increase international understanding, especially among women. A logical extension was to inform group members, who were assumed to be relatively ignorant, about world events they probably would not follow in the nonfeminist press. Such educational activity, intended to produce peacefulness out of familiarity and mutual understanding, could be seen by feminists as part of an indirect and long-term strategy to produce peace. Furthermore, only with the

6. The other groups discussed in this book carried on similar activities; the Union féminine civique et sociale had branches overseas and a strong interest in conditions in the French empire; the League of Women Voters has at least one expatriate branch and a very wide range of activities through its Overseas Development Fund. But though both have always been strongly internationalist, they are not pacifist or centered on peace activism in the way the Guild is.

support of an educated wider public opinion could women's peace petitions have any effect on their own governments or on international organizations.

But apart from access to their members or women in general, and apart from the imagery of internationally shared maternity and family experience, such educational activities were no different from those of all progressive internationalist pressure groups. Women's organizations did manage to argue distinctively against expenditure on armaments: not only were such programs fueling the arms race but they were taking funds away from the essential social services on which social feminists concentrated their domestic attention. In Canada and the United States early women legislators Agnes Macphail and Jeannette Rankin used this feminist logic to justify their votes against armaments and against war. These were difficult arguments to make in times when armaments were perceived as defensive; Macphail and Rankin were both defeated in wartime elections, partly at least because of their social feminist pacifism. At best such an analysis provided a different gloss on the opposition to arms articulated by other peace groups. For most women, the expression of these views—by petition, meetings, and other forms of protest—was bound to be in combination with other, nonfeminist groups. Any distinctive role for women in such educational and pressure activities was unlikely to be publicly visible. Nor was it obvious why women or especially feminists should play any special role in opposition to war. Most social feminist efforts were either ignored or ridiculed.

In 1980, for example, a well-reviewed book on pacifism in Britain entirely omitted mention of the WCG and puzzled over the presence in the peace movement of many former suffragists. The author could see no "logical" connection (Ceadel 1980:84), and he discussed feminism only in a passage on the "left-wing idiosyncracies" associated with pacifism in the 1930s. Here he explicitly followed George Orwell's account in *The Road to Wigan Pier*, grouping feminism with temperance as one of the illogical and impractical preferences of pacifists. "Other causes [in addition to feminism] attracting equally committed, but less wide-spread support" from pacifists included Esperanto and the Woodcraft Folk, identified as "a left-wing, William Morris–inspired alternative to the 'militaristic' Boy Scouts." The author finally attributed the presence of individual and influential feminists in mixed-sex pacifist groups to their various personal and sexual situations.[7]

Such an analysis dismisses any ideological connection between femi-

---

7. Examples given include Vera Brittain's unusual commuting marriage and Maude Royden's "platonic triangular intimacy" with the Hudson Shaws (Ceadel 1980:93). Ceadel documents just how male-dominated, even sexist, most pacifist organizations were in interwar Britain. His interpretation also contradicts evidence he himself cites (see especially Brittain 1975 and her account of the reasons she wrote her very popular tract against war, *Testament of Youth*).

nism and pacifism in a way typical of academic discussions of feminist pacifism. The description of the Woodcraft Folk as one more freaky marginal structure is characteristic. The Woodcraft Folk were in fact the co-operative, coeducational youth group that was intended to replace both boys' and girls' groups, "to show children the values of peace and cooperation rather than war and confrontation." In 1987 this "national youth organisation in its 62nd year" was reported to have 18,000 members in just over 550 groups across Britain (Neville 1987). Enthusiastically supported by the WCG, the Woodcraft Folk represented the one distinctive role women as women were able to find for themselves in pacifism. As mothers and potential mothers they could direct themselves to issues related to child-rearing and socialization, especially the demilitarization of influences on children. Many women's peace groups were critical of existing youth organizations, and all opposed state support of military cadet groups for young people. The model for both Boy and Girl Scouts and Girl Guides was the native scouts of the Boer War, and the structure, drills, uniforms, and paraphernalia remain military. The implied attitudes about the link of gender roles and male support of violence appear in the recurrent disputes about the status and even the name of the girls' group: in Britain it had the appropriately deferential title "Guides," and the U.S. adoption of the more forthrightly competitive "Girl Scouts" nearly entailed a law suit from the established Boy Scouts of America. Only very recently have boys included in their activities the domestic training that was always part of the badge structure for the girls. Pacifist endorsement of the Woodcraft Folk therefore extended opposition to war into crucially important areas of socialization—those which had promoted militarism along with a segregation of women that meant subordination.

Similarly, many women's groups, and most conspicuously in 1930s' England, the WCG actively campaigned against the sale of war toys and games, the availability of war films to children, and the attendance of children at any sort of military or patriotic ceremony. They were particularly strongly opposed to the use for such purposes of school facilities or hours (implying compulsory attendance and formal legitimation). The annual Armistice Day commemoration eventually prompted the imaginative production, beginning in 1933, of a white "peace poppy." It seems to have had some success, particularly after it began to be worn along with rather than as a substitute for the regular red flower; in this way it was possible for wearers to continue to show respect for the victims of World War I while indicating objection to armament for a possible second. Eighty-five thousand peace poppies were sold in 1938 (Gaffin and Thoms 1983:110–11). Substitute "peace plays" also proliferated but tended to be less successful, as were suggestions to abolish Armistice Day altogether in favor of a national Peace Day.

Still, though such activities were authentically feminist in origin, they remained at best indirect and likely to be slow in their effects. A further difficulty lay in social feminism's crucial arguments about the differential effects of gender or at least of experience. Logically, social feminism could rely only on the concerted action of women. In *Three Guineas* Virginia Woolf traced the implications: a refusal on the part of women to accept any status or honors in a society organized on militaristic and patriarchal principles (1938). In the second wave of feminism such arguments were to lead to lesbian separatism. In a more interventionist fashion, social feminists could try to direct their policy efforts specifically at mobilizing women to use against war any influence they had as women. But, as Woolf also pointed out, women had little economic or political power, and women's groups represented in any case only a small fraction of the population. This is perhaps why they tended to concentrate their efforts on general campaigns to change opinion. The Guild participated in many of these campaigns, in spite of its hesitations about collaborating with other organizations.

What was lacking in all these efforts, moreover, was something specifically feminist that could tap the structural causes of war, something that was truly international rather than merely related to the existence of an internationally distributed population of women. The WCG was exceptional, and exceptionally fortunate, in that consumer co-operation, as it developed in England, provided a genuinely international as well as feminist rationale for women's peace action.

For co-operators, international war was caused by conflicts among states over resources, the same way class warfare occurred domestically. At both levels, violence could be prevented by the functional separation of individuals into workers, employers, or owners—and consumers. Their interests would then be shared rather than opposed, and the resulting increased prosperity would ease any temporary, transitional tensions. Under these conditions, human beings would stop settling disputes by force, just as they would give up competition and the profit motive (Woolf 1921). Women, who were rarely owners and usually only temporarily workers, had a major role in the process as the preeminent consumers. As such, they could operate simultaneously at the national and the international levels without neglecting their families.

To repeat Margaret Llewelyn Davies's statement, emphasizing the international dimension, "In providing for the well-being of her family the co-operative woman is inevitably acting in a way which leads to the establishment of a juster order in her own country, to the formation of a world-wide Co-operative Commonwealth, and to the longed-for advent of universal peace" (1921:12). Patronizing and supporting the co-operative stores became a mission for world transformation and peace. And it was a task carried out primarily by women, in the conduct of women's normal activities.

For members of the Guild, their more organized co-operative activities developed naturally into a strong awareness of women's—and co-operation's—international potential. Virginia Woolf outlined the process in her writings about the Guild:

> As membership grew and twenty or thirty women made a practice of meeting weekly, that one house [where they met] became a street of houses; and if you have a street of houses you must have stores and drains and post-boxes; and at last the street becomes a town, and a town brings in questions of education and finance and the relation of one town to another town. And then the town becomes a country; it becomes England; it becomes Germany and America; and so from debating questions of butter and bacon, working women at their weekly meetings come to consider the relations of one great nation to another. . . . [They were] asking not only for baths and wages and electric lights, but also for co-operative industry and adult suffrage and the taxation of land values and divorce law reform. It was thus that they were to ask, as the years went by, for peace and disarmament and the sisterhood of nations (L. Woolf 1967:IV, 146).

A second version of this passage, revised to appear with a collection of guildswomen's memoirs, omits the chain of expanding interests and the appealing vision of the "sisterhood of nations." The final international demands are now less sentimental, more focused on the co-operative movement: "Thus in a year or two they were to demand peace and disarmament and the spread of Co-operative principles not only among the working people of Great Britain, but among the nations of the world" (Davies 1931:xxxvi). But as co-operation meant a nonconfrontational and nonsexist world order, this is the core of social feminism.

If their domestic tasks in support of co-operation were not sufficiently satisfying, co-operative women also had a specific international task; it grew naturally out of their activities in the Guild, as domestic concerns expanded to include international ones. In 1921 they took the obvious step of founding their own international nongovernmental organization, the International Co-operative Women's Guild—with its own program and its own song, "The Mothers' International." By 1915 women's co-operative guilds already existed in Austria, Holland, and Switzerland as well as in England, and that year they issued a joint resolution supporting co-operative principles. Under English leadership they now banded together (*Labour Woman* 1941). Their beliefs were straightforward:

> There is no class to whom the cause of Peace can make a stronger appeal than to International Co-operative Guildswomen, for war casts its dread shadow in a special way on the lives of wives and mothers. Nor is there any class whose ideals can more effectively undermine the causes of war. For the brotherhood of nations is the religion of Co-operators, and under an Inter-

national Co-operative system of trade and industry the material interests of
nations are no longer in conflict, but the resources of the globe are pooled
and divided in the interests of all (Davies n.d.:1).

The connections among the concerns and activities of the ICWG are
complex, with co-operation always central but peace (therefore) constantly an issue. The point can be seen with particular clarity in the
report of its Third Triennial Meeting, held at Stockholm in 1927.

The first day of this ICWG meeting saw discussion of the co-operative
movement's recurrent dilemma: "Low Prices or High Dividends?" This
question related to another, how to increase membership in the movement, with the English Guild as always in favor of lower prices. The
second day was devoted to "The Family Wash," a major problem for
working-class women (Strasser 1982). The third day dealt with the topic
"Food Purity and Food Values," recommending that international scientific laboratories be set up to monitor quality, possible adulteration, and
prices of foodstuffs. Conference resolutions supported disarmament efforts, noting that women should be involved in the various international
negotiations on the issue. They also included a protest against the execution of "Zacco [sic] and Vanzetti" as well as a call for each nation to
establish a governmentally appointed committee of housewives, indus-
trialists, and technicians to work with the ICWG to lighten the burden of
domestic labor (*Women's Leader* 1927).[8]

The ICWG meetings thus combined standard Leftist interests of the
time with the international activities and projects common to peace
groups. Most of the conference was nevertheless devoted to women's
issues, and to a particularly domestic and concrete version of them. An
expansion of women's role in public life was urged, along with expansion of public agencies and policies directly related to women's interests.
In this unusual combination a unique role was played by the specific
concerns of the co-operative movement, to which fully one-third of the
conference's time was devoted.

A 1944 ICWG document spells out the connections. "In the past none
have tried harder than Guildswomen to be peacemakers" begins a section that describes the co-operator's international task as "to increase co-
operative influence and deal with all current world problems from the
co-operative angle." Guildswomen, being women as well as co-operators,
have a specific assignment, a sort of mission to other women: "By becoming active co-operators, by striving to make their co-operative organizations of all types strong and efficient, yet ever true to their great social
purpose and ideals, women everywhere can win the world they want for

8. Resolutions demanded total universal disarmament and deplored the breakdown of
the Washington Naval Conference and the failure of the League of Nations' Preparatory
Commission on Disarmament. In addition, an International Economic Conference was
recommended and, in Geneva, a Committee for the Rationalization of Industry.

themselves, their loved ones, and mankind. To convince them of this is the most momentous, most inspiring task of the International Guild" (ICWG 1944: 6). As the English Guild instructed its speakers to say in 1957: "To work for the strengthening of [the Co-operative] Movement is to work for peace and prosperity" (WCG 1957). Peace and prosperity were inextricably both domestic and international. The practical injunction laid on women was therefore to strengthen co-operation both nationally and internationally—a far more specific and concrete task than any other feminist pacifists had.

Less obvious, however, was what the guildswomen interpreted as a corollary: the strengthening of the guilds themselves and particularly the International Co-operative Women's Guild as an agent of international action. It was all too easy for them to perceive co-operation as merely instrumental. The movement gave them a specific series of tasks along with organizing structures and funding, both nationally and internationally. But the movement also saw the Women's Guilds as simply one element in a series of auxiliaries. The WCG's commitment to pacifism was to produce the most direct of the resulting confrontations.

The 1930s were the heyday of the Guild's independent activities, the peak of membership and self-confidence. Although the Guild maintained an emphasis on support of co-operation, it was increasingly involved in direct pressure activities relating to public policy. In 1938 it clashed with the co-operative movement over the support of British participation in the coming world war. The Guild refused to abrogate its absolute opposition to war, although the Co-operative party, now part of the Labour party, had moved with Labour to support collective security. "The Co-op women as usual are magnificent," Virginia Woolf wrote to Margaret Llewelyn Davies. "I had seen the resolution—they beat the Labour Party hollow" (Woolf 1984:250).[9] The text is strong: "This congress of co-operative women, being opposed to war at all times, . . . [reaffirms] an absolute pacifist policy, and refuses to take part in war or preparation for war between the workers of the world, and asks for a disarmament conference for all nations" (WCG 1939).

The next year's report shows no retreat: "Recent European events have shown the tremendous need for Guild Pacifist principles to be put into practice in every country. . . . This time there is no doubt in the minds of working class people everywhere the war is nothing but a waste of effort, time, and money" (WCG 1940). The Military Training Bill is protested, and apparently the peace poppy is still being produced—thirteen thousand are sold. Even resolutions drawn up in May 1940

9. Gaffin and Thoms call the 897 to 623 vote at the Guild Congress a close one, which it was not; in June of 1938, just after the May Crisis in Czechoslovakia had seen France and Britain threatening armed response to any coup in the Sudetenland, the decision was remarkable (Gaffin and Thoms 1983:115).

continue to insist that "no good results are ever secured by war," to call on the government to explore all avenues for ending hostilities, and to ask for a permanent Ministry of Peace, with 50 percent of its members women (WCG 1941).

The Guild continued these protests, although they also became much involved in voluntary war-support activities. One was a vast and successful project for feeding those sheltering from raids in the deep tunnels of the London Underground. In addition, the Guild was much concerned that the war should be conducted in as progressive a fashion as possible: an advance statement of peace aims should be prepared, and plans should be made for a peace conference that would not be as vindictive as the last one; democratic principles for the postwar world should be put in place in dependent territories such as India; the rights of conscientious objectors should be recognised by the co-operative and labor movements as well as by the government; women should be treated equitably, with equal pay for equal work and with equal compensation for injuries suffered in the bombings. But there was no doubt of a continuing if not unanimous opposition to the war. Resolutions in 1942 included the statement that "war is futile and can only end in misery and privation of the entire world" (WCG 1943). Even the deep-shelter feeding project came in for criticism from members. "The Guild did this feeding of troops in the deep shelters," recalled one member, who was confused about exactly whom these efforts had served, "but I wouldn't take part in it. It caused a family row because my mother-in-law was the District Secretary . . . but I refused to do it because I said it was part of the war effort and it caused a big hullabaloo" (Salt, Schweizer, and Wilson 1983:41).[10]

The annual report for 1942–43 gives some indications of the difficulties produced for the Guild by its pacifism. There were problems with the Co-operative party, which refused to include two guildswomen on its list of possible parliamentary candidates to be submitted to local selection committees. These women were both members of the Guild Central Committee and had been nominated by it; the reason given for their rejection was the "Peace Issue." The Guild felt, with some justification, that the party was suppressing minority views for fear of seeming to endorse them. Any selection committee would be free, after all, to make whatever judgment it wished (WCG 1943). Mrs. Ganley, who was elected to the presidency of the London Co-operative Society in July 1942, may have been one of the two possible candidates but does not mention the episode in her manuscript history. She does report, however, that 1942

10. The member already quoted added that "I refused to do it but [General Secretary] Cicely Cook got the OBE for it—but everyone said she didn't deserve it—the OBE should have gone to my mother-in-law which it should if you look at it in that way—because she did all the work and Cicely Cook didn't have anything to do with it, other than saying the Guildswomen would do it" (Salt, Schweizer, and Wilson 1983:41).

saw the formation of a Joint Auxiliaries Council, which it seems reasonable to interpret as yet another attempt to control the unruly Guild. There is no record of why the Co-operative party changed its views about the Guild, but in 1943 it included Mrs. Hutchinson and Mrs. Ridealgh of the Guild on its panel. The 1945 election saw three guildswomen, including Mrs. Ganley and Mrs. Ridealgh but not Mrs. Hutchinson, elected to Parliament along with twenty other Co-operative party representatives (Ganley n.d., Gaffin and Thoms 1983:156).

The Guild never recovered after the war. Its feminist élan declined, though it praised the Beveridge Report for "recognition of the housewife as a member of society and eligible for benefits in her own right." In 1944 it got the Co-operative party to approve efforts at legislation to gain for the "married working woman" equality within the household and especially in regard to savings (in one notorious case a husband had gone to court to obtain his wife's savings). And in 1947 it obtained party support for equal pay—but not for opposition to civil defense (WCG 1945, 1948). By 1981 there were only 578 WCG branches, a figure not significantly higher than the 521 in existence in 1899–1900 (Gaffin and Thoms 1983:268). Support for the Committee for Nuclear Disarmament and similar campaigns was strong, but the group's reputation for exceptional pacifism faded, in part because of its association with mixed-sex organizations. In 1963 the English Guild was outvoted, and the ICWG became a committee of the International Co-operative Alliance. In that same year the English group changed its own name to the Co-operative Women's Guild (CWG).

When the second wave of feminism appeared in Britain, the Guild had virtually no basis for affinity with it. It was a movement growing out of left-Labour politics close to communism which the Guild had come to distrust (Rowbotham, Segal, and Wainwright 1979); the WCG was the only auxiliary to bar Communists from holding office. In 1983 Mary Stott noted sadly how Establishment the Guild had become and that it was now praised only for its glorious history: "one of Britain's first women's organisations." Stott lamented the decline of the Guild, which she linked to the decline and disappearance of the movement's retail shops. And she described its character—in the old days but not, by implication, in the present—as "radical, feminist, and working-class." What would "some of the pioneers" have thought of a centenary ceremony at Westminster Abbey featuring the queen? "Pacifists to a woman [they] might well have preferred to mark the centenary by a mass turn-out at Greenham Common" (Stott 1983).

Within the co-operative movement, the guildswomen were sparsely represented at the time of their centenary: two each on the CWS Board and the Union's Central Executive, six on the Education Executive, two on the National Executive of the Co-operative party, three on the

Union's parliamentary committee, and nine on sectional boards (Gaffin and Thoms 1983). Less than ever were they inclined to make feminist claims, even within their own movement. In 1983 the president of the Guild, who had headed a Co-operative Union Working Party on Women in 1972, was unwilling to support any sort of affirmative action (Willis 1983:44–45).

By the second decade of second-wave feminism, co-operation, feminism, and pacifism no longer worked together. Co-operation meant nothing special for either women or peace, for the Co-operative Commonwealth could no longer be hopefully anticipated. The Co-operative party, from which so much had been expected, was so effectively a part of the Labour party that few were aware it had ever had a separate identity. The Labour party itself, once office became possible, had shown the contingency of its commitments to peace and social change and above all had demonstrated a commitment to nationalization that lacked appeal for co-operators. But the co-operative movement took no stand against it. Pacifism had become the property of middle-class radicals. The feminists among them probably stirred in the aging and respectable working-class women of the Guild much the reaction the violence of the suffragettes had produced so many years before.

Academic analysis has not been kind to feminist pacifism. Such beliefs are most easily classified with religious-based opposition to war, an easy association given women's greater religiosity (Ceadel 1980). They are then assimilated into other supposedly absolutist and unrealistic beliefs that have led to women being dismissed as apolitical. One much-cited study used as a public affairs index the interest of young children in war news (Greenstein 1965); in 1982 two respected political scientists interpreted the slightly lesser inclination on the part of women elites to favor overseas intervention as a result of ingrained, nonrational devotion to hearth and home (Holsti and Rosenau 1982). As a basis for activism, pacifism has been interpreted as part of a failure to engage in the mainstream of social and political activity; pacifists are labeled marginal to social change. At best such groups are likely to appear ineffectual, having so obviously failed to influence war. When Jeffrey Berry (1977) seriously studied WILPF as a pressure group, he reluctantly concluded that it was amateurish and essentially irrelevant to mainstream politics. If Women Strike for Peace and Canada's Voice of Women attract political attention, it is to identify them as red-inspired and red-controlled. This interpretation dates from the 1930s, when WILPF's socialism was believed to explain an otherwise inexplicable feminist pacifism as inspired by the Second International (Lemons 1974). In such cases women are seen as dupes, perhaps one stage above simple deficiency because of nature or socialization. The interpretation denies the possibility of any autonomous feminist political responses.

Naturally enough, there are equity feminist responses to such a reading of the connection of women to nonviolence. Some argue that women's pacifism is part of a false consciousness that has supported their exclusion from meaningful political power (Stiehm 1981). This inversion of the standard interpretation argues that pacifism prevents women from authoritatively using force. A complete "cross-over" of women's and men's work and, with it, equality thus becomes impossible. Lillian Robinson (1979) argues with some ferocity for a more direct, uninstrumental takeover of any power needed. Women must prepare themselves to fight—literally—alongside other progressive forces working to transform the world. Less belligerently, Betty Friedan (1982) praises among new, "second stage" women the female graduates of the military academies.

Typically associated with such arguments are hopes that women can use military involvement to subvert war or the patriarchy. The University of Maryland's European Division, which offers academic programs on U.S. Army and Air Force bases to active-duty and civilian personnel and their spouses and children, has a Women's Studies Program with that intention, as well as workshops "to counter sexist assumptions about women." Both seem to be consequences of the presence of women in the armed forces. But Tobe Levin and Janet Miller-Goeder report that prejudice, though driven underground, continues. Because they feel the intrinsic violence of the military is impervious to feminism, Levin and Miller-Goeder describe themselves pessimistically as "struggling to project a utopian vision within a hostile setting" (1984:13, 15). The same ambivalence recurs in feminist reactions to a unisex draft or women in combat. Even equity feminists have some difficulty with this particular claim for equal treatment; the issue helped defeat the Equal Rights Amendment and was one of the first problems to emerge as the Canadian government attempted in the 1980s to bring legislation in line with the equality provisions of the new Charter of Rights.

Equity feminism thus follows mainstream thinkers, liberal and socialist alike. For them, war is a basic feature of current international politics, and the ending of war as a goal is distinctly secondary to desired political and economic changes. Peace, like women's equality, is anticipated as a result of structural changes for which women's specific experience or perspective has no particular relevance. Furthermore, war or at least violence is usually seen as an inevitable part of major structural change. Whether the opposing groups are classes or genders, or both, those with power are expected to resist change. The only thing special about women's struggle is that women must contend not just with powerlessness but also with the internalized belief that power is inappropriate to them.

Here we have shifted from war to violence and power, social tools that women are expected to abjure. The equity feminist is likely to claim all three; the social feminist will typically find nonviolent power adequate.

In effect, social feminists reject the notion that social change requires violent conflict. They believe that neither class nor gender hostility is inevitable. The model is the family, where order is maintained without the use of capital punishment or, today, corporal punishment. This underlying belief explains the WCG's eagerness to promote the non-violent policy tool of the (co-operative) political party; it also explains guildwomen's opposition to corporal punishment in schools and to the birching of young offenders. Also, in larger terms, it explains their opposition to international war.

The necessary improvements in international politics cannot be extrapolated from the family or from domestic politics. An international police force would not relate to its constituency as a national one would, for instance, and even arbitration changes the weight of problems of enforcement when it is international. Yet it is changes in the family that give support to the belief that basic human institutions can change without the confrontations that are part of the Western political tradition. Within the family, however disproportionate the advantages, all adults clearly have a degree of shared interest in reaching some accommodation. This is the logic all social feminists applied to national and international affairs, but the model of the family had few concrete suggestions to offer about institutional arrangements.

The co-operative movement supplied for its social feminist members something feminists have often, and rightly, been criticized for lacking: an economic and political explanation of the structural bases of violence and inequality. Furthermore, the movement provided a collaborative model of social change, which included prescriptions for a feminine task. Finally, it offered an institutional model for a reformed world order. The original organizational preferences of the movement were those with which women's groups felt most comfortable: small decision-making groups that were egalitarian and nonsexist. Profoundly pragmatic and secular, it was compatible with a nonreligious and activist pacifism.

This was the *theory* of English consumer co-operation, which energized co-operative women in a way that astonished even themselves. The *practice* of co-operation turned out to be different. Even in days of relative prosperity, the movement became increasingly hierarchical and commercial-minded, male-dominated and oriented toward profit (anathema to the early movement). It became less utopian and also less successful even as a retail network. And it drew its auxiliary with it, away from any distinctive pacifism and away from feminism. To the extent that the Guild retained its initial beliefs, it became increasingly marginalized in and by the movement to which loyalty bound it. In 1984, with Guild membership and activities at levels lower than before World War I, a mimeographed Guild *Newsletter* sent to all branches noted reproachfully that "the Guild Rule on Society membership is not being adhered to in some areas." The only campaign mentioned was the despatch of postcards to M.P.s in a "health service campaign" (CWG 1984).

Four years later the CWG released a report on "carers," persons who look after "elderly or chronically sick" dependants in the home. Its recommendations called for providing information, training, and support for these women. In the report's preface the organization is described as "an education auxillary [*sic*] of the Co-operative Movement." Its "proud history of campaigning for women" is represented by maternity benefits. Peace work including the peace poppy is also cited, but only two postwar activities are mentioned: a campaign with Oxfam to collect money for wells in Botswana and a campaign "along with many other organisations" to retain doorstep delivery of milk. Feminist ambitions to influence public life remain in only a dim echo: "The Guild encourages women to play a fuller part in local, national, and international affairs." It also nominates women to the Public Appointments Committee (Webb, Paskin, and King 1987:2, 1).

The Guild in its earlier years was often described as a "ginger group" for the co-operative movement. In retrospect, we can see it had little effect on the movement as a whole. The movement, in spite of its ideals, rejected any primacy for community service, as it was to reject significant attention to women's concerns or to pacifism. Co-operation as such was expected to provide the transition to the Co-operative Commonwealth. A self-sustaining, self-governing commercial enterprise was the necessary and sufficient means. The conventional tools of pressure and partisan politics were adopted to protect the movement.[11] Rules such as cleanliness and no credit were maintained for commercial reasons, not as exemplars of the future good. Fair treatment of employees mainly resulted from an effective union. Equal treatment of women, as employees or as Society members, was of strictly secondary importance. Well after World War II the Guild was complaining that some Societies still did not admit women as members. Only with difficulty did the Guild achieve a living wage, not an equal wage, for women employees, and the Guild never gained adequate representation of women among the decision makers of the movement.

Most Guild members probably accepted most of what happened and settled for socializing and good works. The reminiscences of older members show how important the first function must have been in the earlier period, when money, time, and inexpensive entertainment were scarce for married working-class women. Even in 1960 the Groombridge Report noted (disapprovingly) the extent to which the Guilds functioned as social groups.

11. The initial decision to organize a Co-operative party was self-protective, in large part a response to rejection of the requests of co-operative employees for exemption from military service during World War I (Carbery 1969).

It is possible to argue that the main impact on the Guild of increased commercial emphasis came from the reduction in the number of societies and the overall drop in co-op membership; the first took away meeting spaces, and the second had a corresponding effect on potential members for the Guilds. A decline in movement profitability also reduced the level of funding available for auxiliaries. That is, the Guild rose or fell with the movement, so all we need discover are the causes of the decline of the movement. Such an analysis makes the decline of the Guild secondary; the Guild, like its parent movement, suffered from the transformation of the working class and the effective competition of highly capitalized chains of retail stores and supermarkets. For the women's auxiliaries, equivalent problems relate to the higher level of education and workforce participation of women who in an earlier generation would have been guildswomen. Like the whole movement, the Guilds were outfoxed by the institutions of the new capitalist era.

This analysis, offered by many of those interviewed for the Guild's centenary history, effectively denies that the Guild had any autonomy. It implies strongly that the Guild never had a chance of influence within the movement. Also, it discounts any role for the co-operative ideology, for movement and auxiliary alike. As usual, women activists are portrayed as apolitical and nonanalytical. Such a characterization hardly seems to fit the WCG, however exceptional the Guild's feminism and pacifism may seem to the uninformed analyst.

What might the consequences have been for consumer co-operation in England if the Guild had succeeded in making the co-operative movement into the pacifist and feminist organization it had the potential for being? Our assessment of that imagined possibility has to depend on how we assess the actual history of the co-operative movement. Are we to consider the political side—the Co-operative party—a success? Does the earlier expansion of the retail stores make up for their more recent, seemingly irrevocable decline? Did the Guild itself necessarily have a limited audience—the uneducated, married working women of the prewar and interwar working class? Or could co-operative men and women really have built together something closer to the Co-operative Commonwealth?

A Guild more integrated into the co-operative movement, potentially more influential internally, might not have acted as boldly as the Guild actually did in its relatively marginal position. Which would we then choose? A more radical, more feminist, more pacifist co-operative movement that still would have remained less radical, feminist, and pacifist than the Guild in its heyday? Or the divergence that actually occurred and was effective for a period of the Guild's history? There can be no doubt what the founders of the Guild would have preferred. Ironically, their inherited commitment to the co-operative movement seems to have prevented the Guild, when disagreements became irreconcilable, from taking the ideals of the movement as a justification for leaving it.

PART III

L'UNION FÉMININE
CIVIQUE ET SOCIALE

The Union féminine civique et sociale (UFCS), founded in 1925, is frequently mentioned as one of the few French women's organizations with political influence.[1] Matteï Dogan and Jacques Narbonne suggested in 1955 that about four hundred fifty members of municipal councils were UFCS members, and they noted the "interesting" case of Privas (Ardèche), where thanks to UFCS efforts female electoral turnout surpassed male (Dogan and Narbonne 1956:130; Duverger 1955:19, 36, 38).[2] Andrée Michel and Geneviève Texier identified the UFCS as "the best-known women's pressure group" (1964:II, 89). The movement, as its members call it, has been involved for over sixty years in lobbying and publicity campaigns related to women's working conditions, disarmament, mothers' allowance, and women's civil status (Offen 1987). It has included members of the National Assembly as well as representatives on national planning commission and councils, and the group provides a continuing, significant "apprenticeship for social responsibilities" for some ten thousand members (Poujol 1975:6).[3] Commentators note par-

1. I have translated all French sources, and I have italicized words or phrases in French as they would be treated in English. I have usually retained French titles of organizations and publications.

2. UFCS representatives are noted on national planning commissions on the family, the reform of the Civil Code, and the various segments of the national economic plans (Michel and Texier 1964 II;101), as well as a range of governmental councils related to scholarships, regulation of publications, social security, and consumers (Dogan and Narbonne 1955:131).

3. In 1975 a sympathetic account reported 8,000 paid-up members and influence on 200,000 more (Michy 1975:55). A UFCS document put 1975–76 membership at 14,000 and contacts at 350,000 (UFCS 1977). In 1983 the movement claimed 10,000 members, of whom 3,000 were *militantes* or active members, plus 500 regular volunteers; it believed it reached a "public" of about 300,000 people a year (Fiche descriptive; letter from Evelyne Usé, secretary to the national board, 21 September 1983). I was told that most members renew only every other year, so paid-up memberships understate the numbers involved—but the difference is mainly in the consumers' clubs, which are relatively recent and less relevant to the elements of the movement discussed here. Membership has certainly dropped in recent years, as it has with all such volunteer groups; the Union recorded 15,000 members in February 1939 (*LFVS*).

ticularly the role of the movement in training and supporting women in municipal government.

But the UFCS has not received from political and feminist analysts the approval one might expect. It is virtually never seen as part of the women's movement. The group nearly always appears in the context of an indictment of the manipulative and reactionary influence of Catholicism on women.[4] Only Jean Rabaut has praised the organization, as the first-wave women's group most successful in adapting to the post-1968 feminist revival (1978:356–57). But even Rabaut, who noted approvingly the group's "very strong publicity efforts about the new rights of women" and its commitment to upgrading and return to the paid labor force, quoted with disapproval a UFCS statement that if "work [for pay] can be a means of advancement, it is not advancement itself." He also took issue with a passage in which a mother tells her daughter it is all right to be married or single, worker or housewife; what matters is "to accept yourself as a woman, equal to a man but different from 'him'" (357).

This is, of course, social feminism, and Rabaut's hesitancy is part of a standard reaction. Feminist analysts emphasize the same links and stress that the Union is part of social or separate-spheres feminism. All see the group as primarily and continuingly Catholic.[5] We may wonder about this insistence on labeling the UFCS as Catholic and as (therefore) manipulative of women at a time when neither is true, if it ever was. Our queries are worthwhile because the answers relate to the group's social feminism. The experience of the UFCS demonstrates how a feminist group can grow beyond the constraining ideology and organizational structures within which it first appears. Unlike the Women's Co-operative Guild, the UFCS was able to leave its parent body and ideology to move toward a stronger feminism.

Consumer co-operation, I argued, initially provided an ideology and an environment supportive of social feminism and therefore supportive of the Women's Co-operative Guild. Catholicism, I shall suggest, also can

4. Dogan and Narbonne discussed the UFCS explicitly as an example of an organization controlled by the church (1955:128–31), and it is central to Michel and Texier's indictment of the Catholic church's continuing malevolent influence on the status of women (1964 II:87–89). More recent accounts, drawing mainly on Michel and Texier, make the same judgment. Gisèle Charzat also queries the group's association with the church (1975:81). In their history of French feminism Maïté Albistur and Daniel Armogathe give the UFCS a paragraph under the heading "apolitical associations" (groups without affiliation to a political party) but, again, cite and reject its claims of independence (1977:449).

5. Rabaut is the only commentator to recognize changes in the group and to identify its explicit submission to the church with its prewar beginnings; even he explains postwar changes as "reflecting . . . that of part of the Catholic world" (1978:281, 357). Michel and Texier lay heaviest emphasis on the religious connection: for them, separate-spheres or social feminism is in the case of the UFCS a simple application of Catholic doctrines and therefore both restrictive of women and subservient to the church. Jane Jenson (1987:70) seems unaware of the continued existence of the group (though she cites Rabaut on Catholic feminism in the first wave).

be compatible with social feminism. In Chapter 9, I look at the origins of the UFCS and why it has provoked continuing hostility from feminist writers. The reasons are to be found in the historic relationship of the French women's movement, both first- and second-wave, to leftist parties and to trade unions. Chapter 10 deals with how the UFCS handled women's relation to the paid labor force and to political choices, and Chapter 11 recounts the way in which the movement dealt with the issue of its feminist identity and came to approve contraception and abortion. Finally, Chapter 12 analyzes the UFCS in relation to the actual participation of women in politics, especially as elected municipal officers; it shows how the movement promoted and supported an active political role for women.

CHAPTER 9

Social Catholicism
and Social Feminism

The Union féminine civique et sociale was founded by and for Catholics. In 1925 woman suffrage seemed imminent in France, and the UFCS was consciously designed to recruit future female voters to defend the church's views of the proper role of women as well as the church itself. The group's first publication stated the UFCS rationale: "If the Frenchwoman votes tomorrow, she must, by her vote, serve the country by protecting the family." This meant: "The Frenchwoman cannot ignore the great social problems. She must, henceforth, prepare herself to seek the solution to them in the civic arena. . . . The Union féminine civique et sociale applies in the civic arena, soon to be opened to women, its program, which is that of the social Catholics, and it works in close collaboration with them" (*Circulaire* September 1925).[1] The reference to Catholicism is explicit, and reliance on the teachings of the church was constant in the early years of the UFCS. As a result, the UFCS could not avoid condemnation by progressive analysts and, especially, feminists.

In the Third Republic the secular/confessional division was the central issue of public policy, encompassing and envenomed by the Dreyfus Affair (Bosworth 1962, Rémond 1959). In the interwar period a number of policy preferences placed the UFCS squarely on the confessional side. Most conspicuous was support of the *écoles libres,* the religious "free" schools, a clear resistance to republican efforts to produce a new generation of citizens as a bulwark for democracy. The UFCS's trade-union associations were not with the class-based unions of the Communist Confédération générale des travailleurs (CGT) but with the independent women's unions and then with the Catholic Confédération française des travailleurs chrétiens (CFTC) with which these unions affiliated. These commitments placed the Union squarely on the side of those attempting to reinsert religious influence into public life. From the republican per-

---

1. The UFCS's *Bulletin périodique* or *Circulaire* became *La femme dans la vie sociale* in April 1927 (Women in society—cited hereafter as *LFVS*) and, in 1966, *Dialoguer.*

spective, women such as the members of the UFCS, whether dupes or believers, were organized for reactionary purposes. They were on the wrong side of a battle of good against evil.

In a more specifically feminist context, the UFCS in the interwar years supported the family vote and the juridical concept of male head of household. It also supported mothers' allowances, as a means of getting mothers out of the workforce, and founded two international organizations with this goal. Hostile to abortion, contraception, and divorce, it continued even after the war to oppose contraception and abortion, to be against the construction of crèches, and to be unenthusiastic about mothers of young children participating in the paid labor force. After women finally acquired the vote, the UFCS, though it did not direct them to vote for the Christian Democratic Mouvement républicain populaire (MRP), certainly urged them not to vote for Marxists. The memory of this history has colored the present image of the organization and has survived changes in affiliation and policies.

The group's early stance on reproductive freedom is the most important clue to its image for French feminists, for reasons central to the history of French feminism.[2] In both waves the major elements of feminism grew out of Leftist politics in a special mixture of devotion and repudiation. Woman suffrage in France was opposed by the conservative parties of right and center-right, and so was most change in the status of women. But the left did not simply support the rights of women. The peculiar history of French socialist and communist parties subordinated feminism to the perceived needs of the leftist parties, even by socialists or communists who were themselves feminists (Picq 1986). The fear of internal schisms combined with the fear that church-dominated women voters would threaten the Republic, which was at least secular if not particularly progressive—so that under the Third Republic these parties paid only lip service to changes in the situation of women, particularly the vote (Sowerwine 1982). Between the Left and the Right were the independent suffragist groups, so-called neutral feminist groups such as the Ligue française pour le droit des femmes and the older Union française pour le suffrage des femmes. But in this political context "neutral" merely meant secular or non-Catholic, and these groups tended to be fairly closely linked with the Radicals, the party just to the right of the Socialists. Though independent in structure, their organizations had clear partisan commitments in ideological and often also in personal terms. The Radicals themselves, moreover, were antisuffragist and only marginally responsive to other feminist demands.

In the Popular Front government of 1936, the high point of leftist

2. For instance, Gisèle Charzat, who notes that the group has a contradictory image—seen by the left as "rightist at heart" and by conservatives as "a breeding-ground for the left"—takes disapproving (if inaccurate) note in 1972 of the absence of any discussion "whatsoever" of contraception (81, 82).

influence in interwar France, three women were appointed under ministers, charmingly called *ministresses*. As Alain Decaux comments drily, "we can measure the importance of this victory if we recall that these women-ministers were not yet voters" (1972 II:1011). The nominee of the Radicals was Cécile Brunschvicg, active in the National Council of Women, head of the Union française pour le suffrage des femmes, and personally connected closely with the party.[3] Neither of the two other ministresses had any feminist connections, and the women in the 1936 government initiated no action on behalf of that symbolic feminist goal, the vote, let alone on reproductive issues.[4] Yet their parties were the only apparent alternative to a reactionary, church-backed autocracy of the sort that was to reemerge so repellently and easily under Pétain. Certainly no feminist would expect gains for women after the defeat of democracy, however patriarchal that democracy had been.

The relationship between French feminists and the parties of the Left therefore continued to be difficult, marked by the memories of repeated desertions. Michel and Texier observe bitterly that "each time [the parties of the Left] have to act on their responsibilities in respect to a claim dear to women, they evade it" (Michel and Texier 1964 I:193). At the same time the general policy position of the parties left of center remains the standard for French feminism. As the Socialists' minister for women's rights, Yvette Roudy, put it relatively recently, "feminism is a force of the Left" because the Left necessarily has to be opposed to inequality (1985:118). The practical result was that, for feminists, two initiatives emerged as separate from the leftist agenda: the insistence on the necessity for autonomous feminist organizations, and the assertion of women's reproductive rights. The UFCS started on the wrong side in regards to each of these issues.

Autonomous feminism and reproductive freedom are crucially connected in France because birth control is the only area in which, before the appearance of second-wave feminism, French women acted without partisan support. In the battle for civic equality the parties of the Left had given at least theoretical though not concrete support, thus effectively throttling any independent feminist action on behalf of suffrage. All parties, however, were natalist in the interwar period and supported, for differing reasons, the brutal 1920 legislation on abortion. Even "family planning" was officially endorsed by no established political grouping or public figure until 1961, when the Socialists presented a proposal for abrogating the 1920 law (Rabaut 1978:327). This was followed in 1965

3. Louise Weiss underlines Brunschvicg's connections with the Radicals (Weiss 1945:12–14), which she stressed again in an interview in May 1975; Albert Brimo identifies Brunschvicg as "radical-socialist" (1975:107). Enfranchised, she became active in the Radical party after World War II, voting "with public enthusiasm" for them in 1945 (Hause and Kenney 1984:281).

4. The other two were Irène Joliot-Curie and Suzanne Lacore; Joliot-Curie was assigned to *Recherche scientifique*, Lacore to *L'enfant*, and Brunschvicg to *Education nationale* (Weiss 1946:191–93).

by statements by the Socialists' presidential candidate, François Mitterrand, supporting contraception (Halimi 1981:105–7, Roudy 1985:84–85). It is understandable that Choisir (Choice), an offshoot of the family planning movement, had become a feminist political party by the 1970s and then moved to support Mitterrand's successful presidential candidature in 1981.

The Catholics, early opponents of the anticlerical Third Republic, were and continue to be the group most actively opposed to birth control. On this crucial question for French feminism, therefore, the UFCS was on the side not just of men and male politics but of their most reactionary segment. In the interwar period, furthermore, the church was cited with pride by the UFCS as justification for its whole range of policies—even those it shared with non-Catholic feminists. No wonder the UFCS was interpreted as a Catholic-controlled group whose opposition to birth control continued into the 1960s; the UFCS's political influence was interpreted as reactionary both in general and in more specifically feminist terms.

Yet if we return to the UFCS's early statements of principle, the references to *social* Catholicism, though usually ignored, are also important. They indicate a context in which even the most hierarchical of the Christian churches permitted laymen—including laywomen—considerable scope for initiatives. In this space Catholic feminism could develop. The clergymen involved with the 1925 founding of the UFCS were among the more liberal of the French Catholic hierarchy; the future Cardinal Verdier drafted the statement of principles. These men were associated with the tradition of Catholic activism which, following the encyclical "Rerum Novarum" (1891) and inspired by such figures as Alfred de Mun, focused lay efforts of social reform on the "condition of the people" (Fogarty 1957; Rollet 1960:95–96; Corlieu 1970).

The UFCS was designed not just to compete with secular feminism but also to give special attention to women of the working classes, particularly married ones—the first of many resemblances to the English Women's Co-operative Guild. The founders tried, in the words of the historian of French social Catholicism, to place the group "between a traditional view that confined [women's] horizon too narrowly to the home and a sectarian feminism that isolated them in the name of emancipation by breaking the natural and sacred bonds of the family." He sums up their central principle as "an absolute fidelity to the better understood mission of wife and mother . . . [which includes] the accomplishment of civic and social duties necessary to the common good" (Rollet 1960:194). This is not an apostolic mission, unless anti-Catholicism sees conversion as the major task of even lay Catholic groups. Nor is there any explicit political role, whether pro- or antirepublican. At the same time, this principle clearly indicates a social feminist expansion into the public realm.

Historians of social Catholicism agree in placing the UFCS not within

Catholic Action, where the laity worked under close supervision of the church to form consciences and prepare for action rather than acting, but within Christian Democracy. Social scientists such as Dogan and Narbonne, as well as Michel and Texier, barely distinguish the UFCS from the women's Catholic Action groups that retained large followings and influence well into the postwar period. But the historian Michael Fogarty describes the group as "associated with" and "under the guidance of" the hierarchy, an organization in which "the laity take over entirely and act on their own initiative and responsibility, though within the normal framework of the beliefs, rules, and practices of the church" (Fogarty 1957:283, 284). Fogarty sums up Christian Democracy as

> the movement of those laymen, engaged on their own responsibility in the solution of political, economical, and social problems in the light of Christian principles, who conclude from these principles and from practical experience that in the modern world democracy is normally best: that government, in the State, the firm, the local community or the family, should not merely be of and for the people, but also by them.

He notes that "Christian Democracy is the movement of those who, having regard to the Christian revelation, . . . conclude that conditions in the modern world call for the widespread use of such techniques as political democracy, joint responsibility in industry, or the withering away of the patriarchal family" (5). This formulation, published in 1957, explicitly allows room for feminism within Catholicism.

The UFCS for its part certainly praised even the patriarchal family well into the postwar period, when its ideology began to catch up with its feminist practice. Otherwise, Fogarty's is an accurate description of the activities of the formidable founder, Andrée Butillard, who ran the organization for thirty years until her death in 1955. For her, there was obviously no distinction between faith and works. Some of her reported remarks catch this: "Don't get drowned in detail; it isn't our goal . . . and the Lord would not bless it." Her advice to a working woman whom she was coaching for a public presentation: "Accept in advance the possible humiliation, offer it for the cause, say a good *Veni Sancte,* and get on with it" (Rollet 1960:176, 53). Although she took her religious commitment seriously, she had no problem with considerable independence and a movement away from explicit reference to the wishes of the church. Her associates describe her as "a saint" but also as "a revolutionary," and her organization was always in some tension with the church she followed with such fidelity. "Oh," said a member of one group she addressed, "you are a socialist, that's easy to understand" (Rollet 1960:94).

Beyond the disputed issue of independence, we may note that not every analyst finds social Catholicism necessarily benighted in terms either of general social policy or of particular policies related to women.

Although most analysts have interpreted women's tendency to vote for Christian Democratic parties as conservatism (Mossuz-Lavau and Sineau 1983), Matteï Dogan, in contrast, states that "the Christian parties are not parties of the Right in the classic sense. Often, because of their Christian notions and their electoral base, they are more responsive to the claims of disadvantaged social groups and more open to social change than radical, liberal, or other parties that take pride in being leftist" (1956:165). This passage may suggest another reason why he and Narbonne (1955) gave so much space to the UFCS.

The distinguished Catholic philosopher J. M. Cameron notes that the social Catholics of the interwar period were able to combine "an untroubled adherence to Catholic dogma with a radical critique of bourgeois society . . . [thus accompanying] social radicalism with dogmatic orthodoxy" (Cameron 1981).[5] He comments on how this combination puzzles and annoys the current generation of liberal Catholics, theologically more radical but in terms of social policy less so.

In a more directly feminist context Maria Lourdes de Pintasilgo shows that, even in the present generation, Catholicism can combine with a radical version of feminism. A respected Portuguese public figure, formerly minister of social affairs, ambassador to the United Nations, and briefly prime minister, she is a longtime activist in an international organization of Christian women, Le Graal. For her also, feminism is compatible with a continuing Catholic identification and indeed brings with it a strong commitment to purify the church. She is aware of male control even of terms of definition: "All of us—men and women—are submerged in a unilateral culture which was formed solely by one part of humanity" (1980:43). Feminism challenges the values of this society: progress, accumulation, industrialization. It is therefore "a revolutionary perspective which [has] as a point of departure the concrete situation of women [and] opens on a completely different, unplanned future" (81). Central to change is the response of women to the activities of multinational corporations, for which they are the crucial labor source and whose failures they can evaluate on the basis of women's particular concern for social conditions (84). This is the position voiced by feminists such as Andrée Michel, but as Pintasilgo demonstrates, a continued commitment to Catholicism can coexist with a focus on world structure and women's shared oppression. Social feminism can operate within the confines of the church's structures.

We may compare the views of Cécile de Corlieu, a feminist activist and also a would-be reformer within the Catholic church, one of the interwar generation. She was convinced that in the absence of major doctrinal as well as structural change in the church, suffragist and other feminist

---

5. This note is an obituary article discussing Dorothy Day, founder of the Catholic Worker movement in the United States.

activities had to be carried on elsewhere. Corlieu accordingly turned to the National Council of Women (Corlieu 1959). From her radical Catholic perspective, the UFCS appeared fatally constrained by its church connections and particularly its commitment to church doctrine.[6] In her condemnation she included any reliance on arguments of difference, which were doubly suspect because of their placement in a Catholic context. Corlieu was Michel's main informant in respect to the UFCS, and Michel in turn was the main source for postwar analyses of the movement.[7]

For Michel, Catholic doctrines were contrasted with *personnalisme,* best translated as "individualism," an equity feminism based on Jacobin doctrines of human rights.[8] In the 1970s she modified her beliefs so that *personnalisme* could include appreciation of women's values. On this basis she was able to incorporate into feminism both the condemnation of militarism and the rejection of communist and capitalist expansionism (Michel 1977, 1978, 1985). The result, as I have noted earlier, was clearly continuous with the basic ideas of social feminism. But Michel continues to single out Catholicism as treating women in an "instrumental" fashion—even though she notes that this attitude is more properly associated with patriarchy and is found in fascism and the regimes of Eastern Europe as well as in developed capitalist countries (1979:97).

This background helps us understand why Michel so influentially attacked the pre-1960s' UFCS and praised among feminists of the interwar period the leaders of the National Council of Women of France (CNFF). Such praise seems inexplicable otherwise, because the lowest-common-denominator national councils of women are usually regarded as conservative. But during the Third Republic the CNFF was the only group of women activists without an overriding commitment to one of the existing political forces (Michel 1979:80–81).[9] The diverse membership of the councils of women necessitated an openness to divergences of analysis that was quite foreign to the French political scene. The cooperation of French feminists of varying perspectives, without reference to partisan links or mainstream political interests, is interpreted by Michel as a shared commitment to the individuality of women. That the most virulent of the anti-individualists, the Catholics, refused to join and

6. For instance, her personal rejection of the 1932 encyclical "Casti Connubii" meant that UFCS citation of it damned the group as an unthinking tool of the church (1970:27).

7. Andrée Michel has now reevaluated the UFCS on the basis of my research; virtually no material was previously available about movement activities in the 1960s through the 1980s.

8. Michel was kind enough to introduce me to Corlieu, who reiterated her analysis. Officials at the UFCS told me that Albistur and Armogathe disregarded information they supplied about the movement, preferring to rely on Michel and Texier (inaccurately even in terms of that source; the founder appears as Andrée Burillard).

9. Even Louise Weiss, who did find the CNFF conservative, nevertheless agreed that it was uniquely free of partisan linkages (Weiss 1946:40–41).

would co-operate on no more than a limited basis only reinforces the analysis.

The national councils of women are usually disparaged precisely because they united social rather than equity feminists, seeing women's rights such as suffrage as "expedient" for social causes rather than as goals in themselves (Strong-Boag 1976). Founded in 1888 as an international umbrella group, the International Council of Women (ICW) linked through its national councils "associations of women in the trades, professions and arts as well as those advocating political rights [and] women workers along all lines of social, intellectual, moral or civic prog ress and reform [as well as] literary clubs, art and temperance unions, labor leagues, missionary and industrial associations" (International Council of Women 1966:12).[10] Women's rights and status as such were hardly a central concern of these diverse organizations, but they did share a focus on women and on goals articulated by women for themselves. The social changes they pursued were ones they had selected and defined, and they developed together an agenda for feminism that can provide criteria for classifying other feminist groups. A similar process occurred at and below the national levels, showing that even social feminist groups like most of the components of the councils of women can contribute to the increased autonomy of women as individuals. Most analysts are unable to reach such a conclusion, however, and they find it doubly difficult if the social feminist group has Catholic links or origins.

Michel in effect identified—misidentified— the councils of women as inspired by equity feminism in a natural rights tradition. In contrast, she sees the UFCS following a Catholic tradition of treating women as merely instrumental and domestic in nature. That is to say, if hers was an accurate description, the UFCS also would be equity feminist, but Catholic equity feminist and therefore in a tradition that in France cannot be dissociated from reactionary policies and groups.

In fact, both the UFCS and the councils of women were essentially social feminist groups, using the specificity of women not to limit women, as the Catholic tradition did, but to expand their autonomy. In the UFCS, the Catholic elements became less important over time—except as far as their reputation has been concerned. There are many indications of a deliberate distancing from the church in the period when other Christian Democratic organizations were secularizing themselves. In 1945, in the postwar revision of its key public document *La femme au service du pays*, the movement replaced references to Catholicism and the church by a vaguer "Christianity," and documentation of the 1950s shows no confessionalism (Butillard 1942, 1945). In 1968 the UFCS's

10. Some individual woman suffrage associations belonged to the ICW until the International Woman Suffrage Alliance was founded in 1904.

revitalized journal, *Dialoguer*, traced the process of secularization and pointed with pride to consistency of social policy shown throughout the changes recorded (*Dialoguer* February–March 1968). The UFCS was thus at least theoretically capable of some independence. To the foreign observer there is no obvious reason why such a group could not be effectively feminist, progressive, even radical. But in France it was loaded with history and with an inherited ideology that remained social feminist even when it ceased to be unambiguously Catholic.

In contrast, when second-wave feminist groups in France eventually developed arguments similar to those of the earlier Catholic social feminists, they were able to do so without links to older traditions or policies. In ideological terms, Leftist beliefs made it possible after 1968 for the new feminists to move back to an appreciation of women's differences. The insistence that capitalism was the culprit legitimized the view that patriarchy antedated and underpinned relations of production, forcing even anticapitalist political groupings of men into antifeminist behavior. Analogies between capitalism and patriarchy eased the transition: both were structural, both were material, both were historical, both can be transcended by efforts of the main victims but for the benefit of all. The values and the social institutions of these victims can then become the basis of a critique and a possible transcendence of the existing structures of domination. The content of the resulting belief system was often very close to far older social feminist beliefs about the value of women's experience—but the institutional and ideological origins were, in French terms, free of the taint of Catholicism and reaction.

Today, feminists who study the councils of women usually have trouble with the groups' social feminism, but they find their policies astonishingly progressive. And it is worth noting that the UFCS supported in the interwar period virtually all the substantive policies of the ICW; the list of reactionary policies given earlier by no means exhausts the UFCS's policy preferences at this time. The ICW advocated:

1. equal pay and access to work for women (including women's right rather than privilege or obligation to participate in the paid labor force);
2. protective labor legislation applicable as appropriate to both sexes, but giving priority to state support of maternity and enforced by inspection;
3. abolition of the double standard of morality, of state-supported or state-regulated prostitution, and of the international trade in women and children;
4. the vote and all accompanying civil rights for women, including independent nationality;
5. improvement of the situation of workers in the home, including both housewives and domestics;
6. international arbitration, peace, and international organization (with equal participation by women);

7. consultation of appropriate women's organizations in relation to policy affecting women and children; and
8. an international convention on equal rights of the sexes (based on ICW 1966).

The last item does not appear in the UFCS's records, and the Union would probably not have approved it, but they actively supported the remaining goals, with special attention to the vote and to women's paid labor.[11]

Today, we would want to add to the ICW list a bundle of issues related to reproduction, sexuality, and violence against women. In the interwar period both the ICW (and the UFCS) either evaded such issues or took stands not acceptable today. These issues have now joined the list of criteria for feminism. On them, we find substantial changes over time in the UFCS's position. But the underlying social feminist arguments remain constant.

Here is the nub of the criticism of the UFCS. Beyond its identification with what were, in French feminist terms, reactionary groups and policies, the UFCS is criticized precisely because of its quality of social feminism, its insistence on difference. Implicit in the doctrine of difference is an analysis along gender lines that is acceptable neither to equity feminism nor to mainstream political analysis.

The only way to rehabilitate the UFCS and, along with it, social feminism, is to look at the history of the movement. I do so in relation to the crucial areas of paid labor, reproduction, and political participation. To introduce this discussion, I look briefly at the problem of evaluating women's and specifically Catholic women's unions in France (and women's role in them). This issue is a microcosm of the wider problem. The French women's unions were often founded by lay Catholics and joined the Catholic federation, the CFTC (now the Confédération française démocratique du travail or CFDT). More important, the crossclass nature of both women's and Catholic unions, as well as their origins, contributes to labeling of the groups as reactionary in French political and feminist analysis. The assessment of such unions is particularly relevant to the UFCS because of its relationship to the Catholic women's unions.

Given the sex-based segregation of work, the organization of women into single-sex unions is less a conscious rejection of the role of class in producing social change than an indication of the nature of the workplace. For example, in Jeannette Laot's account of the creation of a CFTC union of women in the state tobacco factories in 1949, neither

11. Though it is a moot point whether at this time the Union saw work as a "right" for anyone, it certainly backed women's entitlement to work (point 1).

feminism nor gender solidarity plays a role. She and her young women coworkers were devout Catholics. They found the established socialist Force ouvrière (FO) union that had split from the CGT insufficiently militant, but the CGT alternative did not allow the mass of the workers to participate in policy formation. Both unions were also explicitly anticlerical (1981:36).

Laot, hardly a typical woman worker, became an influential tradeunion feminist. Starting as a member of the relatively progressive anticonfessional minority in her union's national federation, the CFTC, and then of the federation's women's commission, she became the first woman member of the federation's executive. She recounts how this formerly Catholic organization became the first French union federation to call for abrogation of the abortion law of 1920 (1977:87); it agreed in 1973 to allow Laot, by then a member of the executive, to serve as vice president of the pro-abortion Mouvement pour la libération de l'avortement et la contraception (MLAC)(Maruani 1979:61–62). In general, the group moved quickly and strongly to support its women members in the period of the second wave of feminism (Rabaut 1978:372–73). In this it resembles the UFCS. Both groups epitomize a working-class feminism that grew out of social Catholic organization of women workers.

A foreign observer finds these links reasonable enough. But in France the notions of women's unions and working-class feminism are problematic, even without Catholic origins. Laot was unusual in that apparently neither she nor her union of women encountered overt hostility from male fellow-workers and union members. Women's unions, especially those organized as such, have been ill-received by the main union movement and by their analysts. As early as 1910 the CGT formally opposed women's unions on the ground that "sex warfare" was being substituted for "class warfare" (Rabaut 1978:232). The presence of any form of feminism was doubly suspect. One typical analyst sums it up: "In France the word feminism has always had a middle-class connotation, so much so that it always seems necessary to choose between sex solidarity and class solidarity" (Zylberberg-Hocquard 1981:9). Of "working-class feminism," Margaret Maruani writes, "this expression seems to contain a paradox or a contradiction, so much has history taught us that the two terms can be antagonistic" (1979:258). Only tentatively is she prepared to suggest that "feminism is a plural [term]" with a multitude of possible currents and versions (1979:248). This is the intellectual context in which the UFCS is judged in France.

In this sort of analysis, middle-class feminist attempts to organize working-class women may well be read as meaning not just that class identity is secondary for women but that feminists' class identification is with the owner class through its women. Such an interpretation is reinforced when social feminist ideology echoes the corporatist mode with its suggestion that women's unions could adopt a nonconfrontational stance in relation to the bourgeois males who are the employers. If the provenance of such an ideology is, in addition, Catholic in a country where Catholicism is understood as the enemy of basic democratic liberties, then women's unions, however organized, are likely to be interpreted in a particularly hostile fashion.

Marie-Claire Zylberberg-Hocquard epitomizes this response. She sees the goals of the Catholic women's unions as double: to continue the passivity of the working-class woman by maintaining her in an "infantile" state, and to use her as a means of "rechristianization of the working class" (1981:157, 202–5). That the UFCS was feminist made even stronger the conservative implications of its association with the CFTC. "Dialogue seems impossible between the class warfare unions and Christian unions, and it is not women who will be able to mediate," she writes; "in wishing to replace the solidarity of workers by the solidarity of women [feminism] would contribute to prolonging the exploitation of men by men, and in that way the exploitation of women" (220). And she singles out for special condemnation both the Catholic feminism of Marie Maugeret and the activities of Catholic organizers of women's unions (97, 156–57). This was the tradition in which, unabashedly, the UFCS's founder and the group itself were active.

The only way to handle such accusations is to examine the women's unions with which the social Catholics and particularly the UFCS were involved. The difficulty is the usual one, that little is yet known about either women's unions or the system of Catholic unions that were associated with social Catholicism. The latter tend to be dismissed as confessional, the former as appurtenances of them.[12] The Catholic unions appeared in response to the encyclical "Rerum Novarum" as an essential part of social Catholicism. They are commonly referred to as *mixte*, not in reference to gender but in reference to class, because they included employers, at least in the sense that employers sat on their councils which negotiated wages and benefits on a continuing collaborative basis. The earliest were founded within a year or two of the crucial encyclical.

The organization of Catholic women workers began with the activities of Marie-Louise de Rochebillard among the women textile workers of Lyons, in about 1899. The organized workers were hardly passive: an earlier, very militant women's union among the silkworkers (*ovalistes*) was founded in 1869 after a bitter strike; it affiliated with the First

---

12. Hause and Kenney (1984) are almost alone in examining seriously these and other forms of Catholic feminism in France, but their study stops in the year 1922. In a brief passage they give Marie-Louise de Rochebillard major credit for "a Catholic women's labor movement" (62). With the aid of Marie-Louise Danguy's volume (1946—she was secretary general of the CFTC), a brief discussion in Madeleine Guilbert's authoritative but Left-oriented study of women in the early years of French trade unions (1966), some hostile references by Zylberberg-Hocquard (1981), the biography of Andrée Butillard (Rollet 1960), the autobiography of Jeannette Laot (1981), and the invaluable analysis by Margaret Maruani (1979), it is possible to piece together a little more information.

International (Azuzias and Houel 1982). And women organized pro-
ducer-cooperatives in Lyons even earlier, after the Revolution of 1848
(Strumingher 1979:107–8). In Paris, a few years before the turn of the
century, Marguerite Durand, founder and publisher of the feminist
journal *La Fronde*, organized nonconfessional unions for florists, secre-
tary-typists, and typographers (Rabaut 1978: 231–32). By 1902 the
Catholic "rue de l'Abbaye" unions in Paris included those for women
officeworkers and "free school" teachers (Danguy 1946:3).

Rabaut, who is sympathetic to feminism but critical of its practitioners,
gives a fuller account than most of the women's unions but classes them
together, jeering at Durand's involvement and dismissing all as "of a
collaborative type, that is to say under religious control or maternalist in
orientation" (231).[13] Rabaut shares the view of the CGT and of most of
the analysts of unionism: in Zylberberg-Hocquard's words (1981:194),
women's unions "condemn themselves to powerlessness and cut themselves off from the workers' movement." This model of unionization sees
unions as the major locus of structural change and is relatively uncon-
cerned with specific concrete gains for individual groups of workers. In
addition, structural change is defined in terms of class oppositions.

In this interpretive context we must place Rochebillard's successful
efforts to organize dressmakers and officeworkers as well as women
workers in the silk industry. Ironically, she was accused by employers of
setting workers against employers (Rollet 1960:34). Other, similar
unions developed in the first decade of the twentieth century, grouping
textile workers, seamstresses, and glovemakers. The pattern was different from that of normal unionization, for it had a strong educational
element. Members were provided additional training in their own occupations: these were to be craft unions. They were also trained in further
skills, including those necessary for running a union which would carry
on continuing negotiation of work conditions and remuneration with
the employer: this was a corporatist model and did not expect confrontation. Training in household activities and religious instruction was also
provided. Especially for younger workers, there were classes in the basic
skills, such as mathematics and French, in which middle-class young
women were routinely trained, including finer needlework and music.

Since this mixed bag of services presumably responded in some degree to demand, it is both brutal and condescending to object to the
provision of embroidery or music classes. More positively, an adequate
level of basic literacy and numeracy was essential for any political activity
or impact; advanced training in one's own crafts was necessary for advancement and improved pay. Although housekeeping and religion cer-

13. An important conflict with the (male) typographers organized in a CGT union is
summed up as the women involved having finally acted as scabs, although Rabaut does
describe with some sympathy how would-be women members had been treated by the
typographers' union.

tainly sound traditional enough, the first should be evaluated in the context of the routine double day of these working women, and so perhaps should the second. In addition, various support services were provided, such as sanitariums for ailing or recuperating workers.

The goal of these women's unions, as articulated by Rochebillard, was to form a Catholic working-class elite that could serve as leaders of its own class, though within a model that was both sex-segregated and nonconfrontational. Sex segregation was, of course, the situation of women's work; nonconfrontation was consistent with the ideals of social feminism. It was not the intention of these unions to force women out of the paid labor force, though they thought of it as a distinct second best for women with children. As a very young woman, Andrée Butillard worked with Rochebillard and was impressed by her ideas but not by her realization of them; Rochebillard was not good at following through. In Paris, Butillard took on the task of organizing women outworkers, mainly seamstresses. She had come to share Rochebillard's fierce opposition to the middlemen who handed out work assignments; in removing this exploitative layer of intermediaries, she became involved in obtaining work contracts for unionized women. She retained the key elements of Rochebillard's scheme: Catholic commitment, mixed unions in which employers and employed co-operated but employees had their own organizations and representatives, sex-segregated unions so that even the organizers were women, an emphasis on education and on development of leaders from among the workers, a strong motivation to change social arrangements and toward active initiatives to produce change.

The UFCS, aimed primarily at women in the home, was to maintain all these elements but focus them on political rather than economic change. The family was the context of the unions and of the UFCS. But from the very beginning both implicitly evaluated women as rational creatures who made choices in response to the conditions of their lives. To change their choices, it was necessary to teach and organize them how to change those conditions.

The impact of the women's unions is not easy to judge. Certainly they were more numerous than their virtual absence from labor history would suggest: 10 percent of all unions were women's unions in 1900, including 15.3 percent of unionized women; in 1911 the figures were 17 percent and 24.9 percent respectively (Guilbert 1968:38), and by 1914 women made up 16 percent of the members of *mixte* unions (the Catholic or independent ones, including the women's unions).[14] The Catholic women's unions included the unions of outworkers started by Butillard and were joined by women's unions in state industries such as the refineries, the post office, and the manufacture of matches and tobacco prod-

14. In 1914 women comprised only 8.7 percent of the "class unions" but 36 percent of the paid labor force (Rabaut 1979:234); approximately 50 percent of adult women were working for pay (Maruani 1985:16).

ucts (e.g. Jeannette Laot's union) as well of those of women teachers in the Catholic schools. All but the union of Catholic preschool teachers had apparently joined the CFTC by the beginning of World War II; all fused with the corresponding male unions at the Liberation (Danguy 1946, Rabaut 1978, Maruani 1979:343, CFDT-Information 1979:78–79). These unions produced specific gains for women workers, beginning with a minimum salary for outworkers in 1913 and a reduction of work hours for refinery workers from ten to eight in 1918.[15] Issues related to pay, length of working day and week, working conditions, and benefits; in the 1930s these unions were fighting with some success for maternity leave, sick leave, and regulation of work in basements and at switchboards and calculators. Clearly, gains were made for women workers in industries that the class-oriented unions rarely attempted to organize, that is, industries where all the workers were women.

Even Zylberberg-Hocquard reluctantly praises the actions of these women's unions; she gives credit to feminism. Noting the specific gains made for women workers, she admits that "the action of the feminist movement could contribute to the improvement of the situation of working women; we have many examples" (1981:194). But, she goes on to say, this sort of activity "did not call in question the social organization of work" (194). It could not, she thinks, precisely because it was organized around gender rather than class. And gender, in her view, corresponds to no significant structure of work or of change. More generally, critics of the collaborative model of unions assume this domestic-derived model is inappropriate for producing industrial change. Co-operation is interpreted as collaboration or cooption, and only confrontation and, ultimately, revolution can produce significant social transformations.

Women might well respond that the other model has obviously not worked for them. Only recently has a more careful analysis begun in France, with Maruani's suggestion that the proportion and role of women in a union may have profound and even positive implications for the conduct of strikes and the nature of unions in general. She suggests that the formerly Catholic CFDT unions, especially those with a large membership of women, have tended to be more influential in this respect (1979). On a more directly feminist level, which Maruani includes in her discussion, the question is what the participants gained in terms of their ideology and self-image. Zylberberg-Hocquard, who sees the women's unions as at best a "goad" for the workers' movement, nevertheless concedes that "they taught the women workers about the route to unioniza-

15. Also a 48-hour week and indexation of future raises to cost of living. In 1919 a nine-day paid vacation and a 48-hour week was obtained for dressmakers, a pay raise for perfume workers. Three weeks of strike in 1923 won the dressmakers indexed wages with minimum salary, overtime, unemployment payments, apprentice courses during working hours, and a permanent mixed commission. The post office union, founded in 1920, got equal pay for women workers in 1927 (Rabaut 1978: 240–41; Danguy 1966:3, 5, 6; Michel 1979:84).

tion, they grouped them, they compelled them to have interests other than those of the family. They contributed to making social beings out of women" (1981:220, 157). Under feminist impetus (apparently including even Catholic feminism) women learned to "take their fate into their own hands" (156). For her, this development was flawed because feminist analysis teaches women how to "improve their own lives without touching the structure of society" (156). But this is another way of stating the belief that unions which are not class-oriented lack the potential for social change. In France radical feminists have only recently responded that gender is also the basis of a structure of domination: "The first power was that exercised by men over women, and it will be without doubt the last to survive. It is illusory to attack the others if you leave that one intact in the family and in the trade unions and political organizations" (Le Garrec 1976:178).

Laot points out that even the best of unions is still unable to accommodate the specific conditions of most women's lives as workers; she was effective because she was single and devoted her whole life to her work and her union activities. Even the most successful of the women's unions made only small inroads on women's inequality in the workplace. But this is not an argument against a nonconfrontational, gender-oriented organization of working women in the current, patriarchal world. It suggests instead that the problems of working women and possibly of women in general are the result of factors which are at best only partly accessible through the relations of the workplace. A confrontational class analysis at that point turns to revolution. But another possible response is to turn to direct political action, as Andrée Butillard did with the UFCS.

The UFCS was from the start particularly aware of and responsive to those of its members who belonged to the working class. To help its less-educated members the UFCS produced a supplementary, less technical newspaper that included short fictional accounts demonstrating, for instance, the disastrous impact of venereal disease. Beginning publication at the end of 1929, *Notre Journal* seems to have remained independent until 1952, when it combined with *La femme dans la vie sociale* but maintained a more popular tone. It was aimed at the married working-class women not in the labor force who, for a period beginning in 1930, were organized as Groupes d'action populaire (GAP) (*Notre Journal* March 1930). The UFCS insisted on the importance of its working-class members; a knowledgeable staff member, previously a volunteer and a close associate of Andrée Butillard, told me that in the postwar period the movement's leaders felt that one of their major missions was to represent the working-class woman, and particularly the married one, who had no voice in public policy. In the GAPs the emphasis was strongly on parish-pump politics growing out of the needs of the particular *quartier*.

After women had gained the vote, a political role was represented for the working-class reader by the fictional Maria Espéridoux, who came to the municipal council through concern about the water supply in her quarter and "immoral" movies (*Notre Journal* January 1948). In contrast, members of the more numerous Groupes d'action sociale (formalized only in 1932; LFVS March 1935) were expected to be somewhat more educated and capable of handling abstract arguments. They were to be the organizers, the researchers, and the ones who went on delegations. Because of the insistence on forming a working-class elite, the class differences among activists were downplayed. In any case the distinctions among section types lapsed after the war, when the need to make concessions to an uneducated working-class membership declined as women of all classes became better educated.

The UFCS's views about the nature of workplace and domestically based activism—and about their similarities—are set out clearly in its pamphlet on civic action, *Madame Jourdain: Citoyenne sans le savoir* (Caron and Doneaud 1963). Unless married, adult women are in the workforce and self-supporting. It is made clear that the working woman must be active in her union and must also participate directly in civic activities if she can. The woman in the home has similar responsibilities. To quote the back cover of the pamphlet: "Participation in civic and social life is not reserved for specialists; it can and must be the activity of all women who simply become aware of their involvement in the human universe. It is the business of women not to complain about their situation any more but to seize the numerous possibilities offered to them for participating in the construction of society."

Zylberberg-Hocquard noted that for women to organize and speak up about their conditions of work was to "ruin totally the image society has of them" and to challenge all the basic structures of society (1981:8). She thus, by implication, noted the potentially radical impact of such women's organizations as the women's unions and the UFCS, which was their successor and collaborator. The UFCS, as we shall see, endorsed and worked for changes in society which analysts such as Zylberberg-Hocquard said such a group could not even envision.

CHAPTER 10

Women's Work and Politics

The early UFCS developed its own positions concerning women's paid labor and their involvement in politics in relation to the situation of the Catholic church. The church is at present enduring a phase of reactionary response to all elements of innovation. In particular, Pope John Paul II and the factions he represents have attempted to reverse movements, among laity and clergy alike, that favor major shifts in policy regarding women. What was orthodoxy a generation or two ago has become, after Vatican II, reaction. In the interwar period, by contrast, no significant support of feminism existed within the church. Social Catholicism, important though it was, remained a marginal movement.

In both today's reasserted Catholic conservatism and that of the interwar period, the UFCS sides with change in the situation of women. Woman suffrage, although officially endorsed by the pope, was not generally favored by Catholics in 1925, at the time of the founding of the group. Nor was paid labor or unionization for women, even for the unmarried or those in "women's occupations". Committed to these causes, the UFCS was far from an ideal model even for those Catholics who admitted that women might extend domestic responsibilities beyond the home. Even more important, the UFCS was disapproved of by orthodox coreligionists because of its independence. On the whole, Catholics did not favor lay activism; women's action, feminist action, was worse, especially in co-operation with other feminist groups, as in the 1930s' campaign to change the French Civil Code to give women separate legal identity. As a result, although the UFCS's rationale and goals were based on Catholic doctrine and a definition of women as wives and mothers, Union interpretations were considered inappropriate and, in the context of a secular state, outright dangerous.

The anticlerical Left and center-Left feared that women were under the priests' thumbs, but the Catholic Right doubted it and was convinced that such a politically oriented group was likely to decrease whatever control existed. The very process of implementing the church's goals was likely to change women, the more so as the UFCS put considerable energy into promoting not just issues (though these were the justifications) but political participation itself. Like the Women's Co-operative Guild, the UFCS started out with a clear list of goals that required women's political activism; like the WCG, it was bound to enable members to be political on behalf of other goals or, more often, to modify initial goals in response to their experience. The process of change is evident in two crucial areas, paid labor and political activism.

In the interwar period the UFCS campaigned against the participation of mothers in the paid labor force, starting from orthodox assumptions about the primacy of maternal duties and the self-expression and service that would grow from them. The Union's earliest publication, a *circulaire*, (September 1925) outlined the movement's first major project, which was to investigate "women's work": "Examining primarily mothers in the industrial labor force, the Union will orient all its social and economic effort toward the return of the mother to the home, where another, more womanly task awaits her."

During this campaign, members of the group came to understand the reality of the conditions under which women worked.[1] UFCS policies accordingly included not just a mothers' allowance that would enable women to have a choice but also equal pay for equal work. More radical than the WCG's demand for a fair wage, this policy rejected the suggestion that women earn only a "secondary salary" (*salaire d'appoint*) or are able to live on less than men.

In addition, the group actively opposed efforts during the Depression to force women out of the labor force, signing a public declaration to that effect along with other Catholic organizations. In this statement, issued in January 1936, the UFCS asserted that wives worked to supplement inadequate family incomes and unmarried women worked because they needed to in order to survive. The right to work came from the right to survival, which also entailed equal pay for women workers. The signatories therefore opposed any legal barrier to women's working for pay, as well as recent laws cutting women's sections in the public service and lowering women's salaries. They also objected to attempts to blame women for unemployment. The next month the UFCS stated its disagreement with the feminist Open Door International (well-known for its efforts to equalize women's access to paid labor), on the grounds that in its attempts to make women equivalent to men Open Door was opposing all protective legislation, including maternity leave and mothers' allowance (*LFVS* February 1936). Here is the familiar clash of equity and social feminism.

1. In 1933, 1937, and 1947, UFCS organized three major international conferences on the theme of the return of the mother to the home, which in turn generated two international nongovernmental organizations still active, the Mouvement mondial des mères and the Ligue de la mère au foyer.

The issue of mothers' allowance was always important for the UFCS, which interpreted the payment as the *allocation* for the mother at home. The Union objected to its designation as part of a "family wage" (*salaire unique*), which masked the purpose of enabling mothers to stay home to care for their children as it was assumed they would prefer to do. We may compare the campaign for family allowances in England in the interwar period, when the "new feminists" argued that women should be given a social payment for child-rearing services because of their special situation. English feminists also saw equal pay for equal work as the complement to mothers' allowance. They differed from the UFCS, however, in seeking economic and psychological independence for married women; the UFCS never accepted independence as a goal (Lewis 1975; 1980:169–70).

The UFCS was aware of the scale, significance, and practical contribution of women's work. As early as January 1927 women's paid labor and payment of taxes were cited by *La femme dans la vie sociale* as reasons for their needing the vote and as a demonstration of their ability to handle public life. In May 1947 *Notre Journal*, the section of the UFCS newspaper directed at working-class women, told members firmly there was no contradiction between "women's right to work and the mother's right to devote herself to her home." Furthermore, women were entitled to "equal pay for equal work." A decade later a professional statistician wrote in *La femme dans la vie sociale* about the conflict between "what we agree to call 'the maternal vocation' and the choice of a profession." Astonishingly, she discussed the "sacrifice" to the home of "the autonomy acquired through the profession," as well as the difficulty a single woman might have in finding an adequate emotional life. She concluded by recommending for both single and married women "a profession chosen because of real aptitudes" (*LFVS* June–July 1957).[2]

By the early 1960s, a time when the group was becoming notorious because of its opposition to the expansion of crèches, the UFCS's views about working women were more complex than analysts have realized. A municipal councillor, for instance, wrote about the double shift growing from women's continued responsibility for the household and noted that women's work in the paid labor force was characterized by low pay as well as being tedious, repetitive, and unproductive. It did not correspond by and large to womanly interests and aptitudes, but it represented security for young girls and a supplement to an inadequate family income for young mothers at a time when men's pay and family allowances were low (*LFVS* December 1965). The point about "womanly aptitudes" may be jarring today, but we can reinterpret it in terms of a meaningful job. We probably cannot accept the assumptions that women

2. This was recommended as "a factor of balance" (*equilibre*), which implies psychological benefits in combining public with domestic roles.

should retain responsibility for home and children, that the existence of crèches might tempt them away, or that young women ought to be trained for household instead of workplace responsibilities. But we may well agree that as long as family income remains low, young mothers are bound to work and should have decent work conditions.

The UFCS's reported opposition to crèches is baffling in this context, for obviously the movement does not simply subscribe to the classic accusations that working women rob their children and rob themselves of satisfactions they are entitled to.[3] One would expect it to want better facilities for the unavoidable necessity of childcare. In fact, the policy of the movement always supported short-term childcare for nonworking mothers and also daycare for older children; only facilities for infant care had been opposed.[4]

The movement's attitude to childcare was summed up in two sentences in a 1961 *Dossier*: "After all, it is basically abnormal for a child to be deprived of its mother's care and presence from a very early age. Infant daycare seems to us to have to be considered only as a palliative to a difficult family situation" (UFCS 1961). This attitude is the basis of public daycare policy in both Britain and North America (Ruggie 1981); it is unacceptable to equity feminists. In response to the obvious needs of working mothers the UFCS was nevertheless arguing by 1968 that a variety of childcare services was necessary (*LFVS* February–March). By 1973 the whole range of support services was demanded for working women, including canteens for prepared food and homemaker teams for times of sickness and the unavoidable absence of mothers (UFCS 1973). The movement noted, however, the heavy cost of state-supplied facilities and parents' lack of control over them; it interpreted positively the use of family arrangements, locally organized, for childcare. This policy has unfortunate echoes in the present period of reactionary "privatization" of social services, but Yvette Roudy, the Socialist minister for women's rights, made the same populist criticisms of state-run crèches in her memoirs published in 1985 (1985:194).

The UFCS's opposition to crèches was not, of course, the main reason for feminist criticism of the movement's policies about childcare. Instead, feminists focused on the assumption that it was preferable for women to be in the household—an assumption that was in fact virtually absent from the movement's statements. Even in very early days the occasional remark that women ought to be in the home and men in public life was regularly followed by the robust reminder that women were in fact performing valuable functions in the world. The general formula was the *mother* in the home (*la mère au foyer*). In the absence of

3. This argument is rare but is indeed made, as for instance in the little narrative in *Notre Feuille* of February 1946, "Mon gosse est à moi" (My kid belongs to me).
4. The terminology is important here: *crèche* in France means daycare for infants, but a *garderie* takes older children.

contraception, of course, this phrase usually meant the married woman at home, at least for some considerable period.

The UFCS analysis of the situation of the working woman evolved over time. She always had a right to work. Economic security, not to be confused with independence, was recognized as important, particularly given the possibility of widowhood or spinsterhood; the situation of the many widows of World War I was a constant concern. As early as 1933 a careful distinction was drawn between those women who are in the paid labor force because they must work for pay but who would prefer not to—the majority, it was assumed—and the smaller elite with satisfying and relatively skilled jobs, even in the "liberal professions" where their "gifts" were effective (*LFVS* December). Certain sorts of work were seen as satisfying and socially valuable, and from an early period jobs were described and working women interviewed. The reported occupations changed over the years, from infant school teacher to professor, from clerk to businesswoman to workers in microtechnology and the non-traditional skilled trades.

By 1968 the situation was explicitly described in terms of free choice. Conditions affecting the reasonable decision not just to work but even to return to work included the husband's occupation (i.e., income), the health and character of children, working conditions, and available support from the family and the state. The quality of the work available was also relevant. Although the UFCS suggested that volunteer work, as in the Union itself, might be equally worthwhile, it stated unequivocally that the individual woman was entitled to decide and should not be made to feel guilty for her choice (*Dialoguer* February–March). In addition, women were entitled to support: "Society must become aware of the fact that women must not be the only ones burdened by the handicap which maternity is in the workplace." The UFCS was getting into position to opt for free choice in the even more contentious area of maternity itself. In the same issue of its revitalized journal it accepted contraception, though with the explicit exclusion of intrauterine devices because they were in effect abortifacients.

But the movement had gone even further. In this same issue, six months before the upheavals of '68, it insisted that men, not just a generalized, impersonal "society," must accept responsibility for children. When there are young children in the house, part-time work should be an option for men as well as for women, with everyone recognizing that women's salaries are no more "supplementary" than men's. Finally, the Union renewed the appeal for the possibility of good, non-alienating jobs for everyone, women and men alike.

In 1971 an internal document entitled "Motherhood: A Specific Function" finally settled policy on the problem of infant care. It compared the mother to a working man, each performing a socially valuable function and therefore entitled to support services, retraining, and benefits. The contradiction between women working and their having children was not acceptable and, even though the child had the right to be raised at least through the first months of its life by its mother, she for her part was "free to choose the way of life which best suits her household and her child." The child in turn had a right to "collective services" such as crèches and to other forms of childcare such as infant schools. The argument stopped just short of wages for housework, precisely because it focused not on caring for houses but on caring for children (1971b). Two years later, a *Dossier* on crèches stated categorically the need for more facilities, at a price accessible to all. All that remained of earlier emphases was the insistence that a variety of services must be available to meet the needs and preferences of mothers, who should be able to choose, for instance, between home and public childcare (2 February). Eventually the movement praised a 1976 government report for "making possible the symmetry of parental functions" and therefore moving toward the recognition of "the social equivalence of masculine and feminine roles" (UFCS 1976).[5] Old social feminist—and Catholic—beliefs about complementarity and value of the domestic role for women had become an argument for the sharing of parental obligations, and the UFCS regretted that a proposed twenty-four-month maternity leave would not be available to fathers as well. Because of its high estimation of the tasks carried on within the family, the UFCS had first permitted and then obligated men to share them.

By this time the family as described by the UFCS had undergone major transformations. It was no longer hierarchical. The woman had now acquired the right not just to support herself and the family as necessary but to have a socially useful and personally satisfying paid job under decent working conditions. Her claim to political activity, both conventional and volunteer, was long established. And now her "companion"—the term increasingly used—had acquired domestic responsibilities, or at least responsibilities in relation to children. Consistently with the movement's emphasis on group rather than individual decisions, the UFCS continued to focus on the family or, more often now, the couple. The family remained the key unit of society, and reproduction remained the key shared project of the family.

This is not the model of the Mouvement pour la libération des femmes. It is clearly still social feminism; traditional values and especially the family are still central. Nor has paid labor as such become an element of emancipation. But in terms of the family, the UFCS had experienced an extraordinary evolution.

If we are to understand the UFCS, we must move away from that focus on paid labor which grows out of Marxist feminism. The UFCS's

5. This response was to the "Projects for Women" prepared by Françoise Giroud, secretary of state for women (*Secretaire d'Etat à la condition féminine*); the UFCS had been invited to comment.

origins were in the organization of working women, and the movement retained a central concern for the situation of working women, but its main clientele was a somewhat different group. Active members of the UFCS, as of all voluntary women's organizations, were necessarily women who were not in the paid labor force. Many, if not the majority, had jobs before marriage—the young Mme. Jourdain, a typical member, had worked as a cashier until a difficult first pregnancy (Caron and Doneaud 1963:76–77).[6] They were probably rather better off than the members of the WCG and more likely to belong to the so-called labor aristocracy or the very lowest middle class (petty bourgeoisie) rather than the mass of workers; Mme. Jourdain had worked in a butcher's shop, not a large establishment. Consequently, though their organization's attitudes toward unions, labor force participation, and childcare services are significant in characterizing the group within feminism, the core of the UFCS's beliefs is to be found in its views about the role of the woman who works only in the home. Here we might expect the Catholic origins of the group to make the group docile, conservative, and unadaptive. Instead, the UFCS developed for the housewife an active and innovative practical role in politics.

Traditional separate-spheres arguments relegated women to the home, and politics is in theory, as it is preeminently in practice, the sphere of men. As late as 1978 approximately one-third of the population in North America and Europe, female and male alike, was prepared to agree that women did not belong in politics (Rabier 1979, Black 1980). Women's low participation rate in partisan politics is often explained by their acceptance of such a judgment, and even their increasing level of voting tends to be identified as "social" rather than political (Sapiro 1983). The UFCS never accepted such a sequestration of women. Even in the years before enfranchisement (a period of twenty years following the founding of the Union) the movement encouraged women to seize all available means of participating in political decisions. The slogan "Influential because competent" urged members to develop "*competent, informed* commitments" that would combine "guiding principles" with their own "indispensable social capability." These phrases, including the emphases, appear in the group's first publication, and Andrée Butillard followed them with a typical statement indicating the ambitions of the group and the vigor and initiative expected:

> We wish to carry out a large social task, to seek to penetrate all milieux, to protect the threatened French family, to correct the deviancies of society, in short, to PREVAIL.

6. France has had very high female workforce participation in this century, even though the level dropped steadily with the decline of the agricultural sector in which so many women were employed. Certainly unmarried women in the working class and, increasingly, in the middle class, are likely to be in paid employment. Since 1960 women, including those married and with children, have poured into the tertiary sector in France as in other countries (Maruani 1985:15–17; Maruani 1986).

> For this it is necessary to LIVE.
> Only the living, only those who act can PREVAIL.
> Therefore, *intense life*: RECRUITMENT, ACTION (*Circulaire* September 1925).

For unenfranchised women, neither voting nor candidacy was yet possible—but everything else was. French suffragists took civic action seriously; the long delay in enfranchisement may have made them more adept than other feminists in the use of techniques other than the vote to obtain social change.

In January 1926, within six months of the founding of the UFCS, the predictable praise of the wife-and-mother and of the family vote as a counterbalance to individualism and selfishness was accompanied by a brisk admonition about the "duty to vote." Women who owned their own businesses or were involved in trade, who owned rural properties or who were workers or employers, could participate in policy-making groups such as Conseils de Prud'hommes, Chambres de Commerce, Tribunaux de Commerce, and Chambres d'Agriculture. For this purpose all UFCS members were told to get a practical, simple, and comprehensive manual for mayors and municipal councillors (ten francs from Librairie C. Dalloz). The Prud'hommes were particularly important, for they sent representatives to the governmental commissions on cost of living, on working women, and on children, as well as to the Superior Council of Labor. In 1929 Mme. Daniel, a UFCS member, won a "feminine election" to the Prud'hommes, representing a Union of Homeworkers (*LFVS* December 1929); Maria Bardot, an official of a dressmakers' union, also became a UFCS heroine when she won in the same Prud'hommes election (Caron and Doneaud 1963:78). All sorts of available public pressure were discussed and recommended.

The arguments defending this activity drew on women's situation and values, but the movement was alert to the possible pitfalls in any identification of a role or an area for women. Asserting its feminine identity, the UFCS opted very early for feminization of titles, and in its statutes the incumbents are referred to as the *présidente*, the *vice présidente*, and the *déleguée*; the current text, approved in 1969, continues the practice. Nevertheless, the movement resisted the establishment of a special electoral system for women, predicting that it would be fraudulent (*LFVS* June 1936), and it understood very well the limited role and implications of the 1936 government appointment of three *ministresses*. The UFCS noted the appointments did not even mean that the interests of women and the family were put ahead of party interests.

The one feminist struggle always clearly identified as political was the vote—regardless of how its use might later be evaluated. And the UFCS had started with a commitment to votes for women. However, the organization wanted the franchise also to reflect the interests of the family. As late as 1945 the movement was calling for some version of a "family vote" to be added along with woman suffrage to the existing manhood suffrage.[7] This policy has also provoked considerable criticism from feminists. Here the UFCS arguments for woman and family suffrage are crucial. In 1926 the movement justified woman suffrage as enabling women to speak on their own behalf, representing their positions and their specific values; at this point the family vote would help balance that of unmarried persons. The group was convinced that other suffrage societies were being too "individualistic" in their demand simply to add women to the electorate (*Circulaire* January, September 1926). In 1927, the Union argued, the women's vote followed from the larger role women were playing in public life, whereas the family vote was a social necessity that would represent "the basic social unit" (*Circulaire* January, March). In 1928, the search for the family vote must never put woman suffrage at risk, and the slogan should be "family vote united with women's vote" (*LFVS* November). A woman voted as mother and potential mother; she, and the family, were forces for peace (*LFVS* February 1929). In 1935 the family vote had the natalist form of an extra vote for families with three or more children; it was not clear who would use it (*LFVS* July–August). But by 1939, in what was presumably the full flow of conservatism, the demand was for an extra vote each for mothers and fathers of large families (*LFVS* February).

When Frenchwomen were finally enfranchised in 1945, the UFCS made its last request for the family vote, now to take the form of an additional vote for each "legitimate" mother or father.[8] In the same issue of *La femme dans la vie sociale* as the program including the family vote, however, a long article on the new franchise made no reference to a bonus for parenthood. The UFCS pointed out that suffrage was now, finally, entitled to be called *universel*. But only under conditions of social justice, including decent pay and working conditions for both male and female workers, would the vote help improve institutions, develop harmony, and so on. And only then would it be possible to have "true equality in rights and duties" (*LFVS* February 1945). The UFCS therefore had a double task: "to form and organize women for the coming election and, not less important, to press for social reforms able to put Frenchmen and Frenchwomen in a position to carry out their civic duties better." All of which suggests that the logic of the family vote was a strengthening of the impact of domestic on public life—something social feminists favor. The interwar UFCS, of course, would have denied that domestic considerations could conflict with the interests of women.

7. Corlieu (1937) implies that at one stage the UFCS abandoned the demand for woman suffrage in favor of a family vote wielded by the male head of household on behalf of women and children combined; she is mistaken.
8. The distinction between legitimate and illegitimate, whether family or child, was important for the UFCS, which was unhappy when so-called adulterine children were given the possibility of recognition by their parents.

The demand for the family vote must be understood in terms of the significance of the vote itself for French feminism. The potential value of the vote was perceived as great, but it did not become the obsessive goal it was elsewhere. Possibly as a result, French suffragists did not have the unreasonable expectations about enfranchisement found in other countries. Indignation about the UFCS's family vote proposal stems in part from equity feminist assumptions about the symbolic importance of woman suffrage itself, views few French feminists have held. French equity feminists tended to be socialists or Communists, who were unlikely to value the goal, or else they were committed to the antisuffrage republican parties.

The hostile feminist response to the family vote also stemmed, more importantly, from objections to the UFCS's view of the family as essentially a benign environment and one that should influence the state. This social feminist perception is one most French feminists would vehemently reject. In the UFCS, however, the demand for representation of family concerns persisted. It reappeared in different form in the movement's response to the referendum on the constitutional draft of 1946, a flyer in which the argument for voting "no" included the proposal to add a second legislative chamber representing "family, local, and professional organizations." The same flyer called for "legitimate freedom for individuals, families, schools" and social justice "for individuals and families" (poster reproduced on back of *LFVS* April–May 1946).[9] This is moderate corporatism in the social Catholic tradition, with a strong commitment to social justice and social change.[10] It is not obvious that a corporatism including representation of family interests would necessarily disadvantage women. The key points are the role of the woman in the family, the access she has to public life, and the extent to which she herself can define both; and the UFCS was committed to all of these.

It was in the political context that the UFCS showed most clearly the paradox of social feminism: insistence that the domestic role is superior combined with insistence on a constantly expanding degree of civic action derived from that same role. The unmarried, childless Butillard had experienced no practical or theoretical conflict between domesticity

9. "Legitimate freedom . . . for schools" refers to the Catholic school system, as does the call for "fraternal tolerance"; Catholic arguments appear also in the call for "moral recovery," but there is no explicit reference to Christianity as in the earlier General Program of Policies in February 1945.

10. Corlieu noted that a formula giving extra family votes to mothers as well as fathers of exceptionally large families fitted the model adopted by the National Council of Women of France from the English National Union of Women's Suffrage Societies: that women get the rights men have. She disliked it nevertheless because it supported the importance of the family—and in her view, to see the family as a social unit rather than a mere aggregate of individuals is a major source of oppression of women, reducing them from persons to instruments. She was correct in seeing here a contradiction of the radical individualism she personally supported (Corlieu 1937).

and political action designed to enhance domesticity; her way of contributing to the family was to construct profamily organizations to aid actual
and potential mothers. For the members of the group she founded,
however, the contradiction was potentially serious. The ethic of the
movement had a continuous insistence on commitment at a very high
level. Both study and action groups must be headed by members, who
must be from the same milieu as other members, and these groups were
expected to be as active as possible. Even when the major goal of the
group was to "give back to the home she who is its guardian and its
queen," the task required substantial amounts of attention and time
(*Circulaire* January 1926).

A member calling herself Rolande gave voice in 1985 to costs that
must have been felt throughout the history of the Union. To pay for
volunteer work, she explained, special saving was necessary. The family
initially opposed it, and outsiders criticized the involvement that for five
years took three quarters of her time. Even more problematic, she
worked her way to "autonomy" in her family as a result of this volunteerism, and she ended up with a full-time job. "You are either responsible
for yourself or not," she stated firmly, and she attributed to the movement the possibility she had found to "go all the way" (*Dialoguer* March–
April). The UFCS has frequently been praised for giving women precisely this experience, this increase in competence and self-esteem. But
women who were active in the process were hardly centered on home
and children in any simple or traditional sense.

The extent of expected involvement is suggested in the group's
statutes:

> [The UFCS] has the goal of permanently grouping individuals who wish to
> study social, civic, cultural, family, and economic problems together, partic-
> ularly those affecting consumers and users at all ages, all aspects of [these
> problems] including administrative, financial, and juridical, at all levels in-
> cluding local, national, or international, and to attempt to contribute to their
> solution by all the legal means they dispose of (UFCS 1969).

An equally comprehensive list of methods follows, ranging from intern-
ships and study sessions, publications, briefs, lectures, and commissions
of inquiry, to conferences at the national, European, and international
level.[11] The basic assumptions are that "each person is capable of individual progress" in a group context and that each "must not only speak
out, but also act and be responsible." These last statements come from a
1977 *Dossier* explaining the UFCS, which notes cheerfully that such ac-

---

11. Also included are support for adult education; local, regional, and national committees; collaboration with other organizations at all levels; and "organization of any sort of
initiatives and services to improve the life and development of the Association [by] aiding
members and their families."

tion may produce challenge to the whole social system. Finally, and here the message to the housewife shows the full scope of its demands, "more specifically, the UFCS seeks the advancement of the greatest possible number of women, by giving them the possibility of knowing themselves, of daring, of becoming aware of their individual and collective responsibilities in society."

Obviously more than a merely passive or marginal commitment is required. In 1959 the movement achieved official recognition of one of its most important dimensions and was certified as an organization of "mass education," thus gaining status and certain specific legal advantages in France. But educational goals were always linked to action, and to something more active than good citizenship through normal channels. Especially before emancipation there was the paradox that most such activities were available to women only in their nonfamilial capacities, and they could hardly be expected to use them to discard the very activities that give them a political claim. Mothers who so choose should be enabled to stay home, but they would not include the UFCS's (female) champions of motherhood.

In the interwar period the problem was serenely ignored or explained by a vision of a better future world in which mothers would not have to be in the paid labor force. Later the potentialities of varied roles for women won a more positive endorsement. The UFCS decided that what it had seen as feminine tasks were simply human ones, so that men must have domestic obligations to counterbalance the civic duties of women. By 1985 the UFCS, which in the 1930s had fought other feminist groups to maintain the formal authority of the male head of household, approved a proposed reform of family law calling for "complete equality of powers of companions [*conjoints*] in managing and disposing of common possessions." The measure was reported under the heading "Capable Women," and the article stated firmly that shared parental authority over children was the goal (*Dialoguer* March–April). The UFCS now stated that politics was the way to improve women's situation, with parties the reluctantly endorsed central element of politics.

But it had taken the UFCS a long time to recognize just how political its activities were and that women needed to play a full role. Discussions tended to focus on the goals of political participation, and there was a reluctance to accept office-holding or partisanship. Initially, some version of the vote was expected momentarily, and by January 1927 an ambitious political program had been outlined: battle against "social scourges," defense of the family, the organization of national defense so as to prevent war, freedom of religion and education (the "free school" issue), freedom for unions, and the right to pass on inheritances. Opposition to divorce joined the list in May, and in June, paid vacations for all women workers as well as the right of women to serve on juries. In 1928, with elections coming up, housing policy and family allowances were added. And by April 1935 a survey of members showed an impressive list of goals that Frenchwomen would pursue "if they could vote," backed up by a justification that was pure social feminism: "Women make and remake the home. Will they be allowed to remake the nation?" (*LFVS* April 1935).[12]

The logic of these goals was quite technical and demanding. The UFCS presented it to its members in small working groups, in lectures, increasingly in special publications, and through sophisticated discussions in its journal. Bridging the intellectual gap from household to city, writers also interspersed throughout Union publications a series of fables or stories where personifications of various sorts of women or actual examples make the arguments more vivid. Thus in November 1927 "a woman farmer" told about the problems of rural life and rural depopulation, and in December 1927 "Mlle. Souris, trade unionist," made the case for cross-class unions. In May 1928 the results of a survey of members about election issues was presented in little dialogues, with a nurse speaking about the perils of tuberculosis and syphilis and a "mother of a family" about the need to censor pornographic publications and movies.

The UFCS continued to use the personification of political lessons as a pedagogical technique. Its most striking example was a small, rather attractive book published by the Catholic publisher Fleurus, *Mme. Jourdain, Citoyenne sans le savoir* (Caron and Doneaud 1963). Mme. Jourdain represented the young mother who was in principle the main object of the UFCS's attentions. Mme. Dubois, a neighbor, stood for the UFCS's active local volunteers; Mme. Martin was the typical municipal councillor, mother of two adolescents, occasionally assisting her husband as cashier in his shop; and Mlle. Gilberte was the unmarried trade unionist. This rather charming work was remembered with affection years later by municipal councillors interviewed in 1975 (Guérin: 34).

The reader cannot help but be struck by the amount of work expected of activists in all these texts and the moral force with which civic action is recommended, as well as the recounted impact on those women involved. Mme. Martin's story told how she was relegated to "women's work" in the council, found it interesting and important, but was driven by her social concerns to learn about the masculine mysteries of the municipal budget (Caron and Doneaud 1963:47–48). The goal is quasi-professional, and beginning in the 1950s the UFCS moved into both skills-training and assertiveness courses for a wider membership. The resemblance to the Women's Co-operative Guild is again obvious.

12. Specific projects comprised the following: fight against immorality (pornography and prostitution), respect of parents' rights (free schools), fight against slums, protection of battered and abused children, the return of the mother to the home, women's vote, family vote, fight against the (economic) crisis, reform of the Civil Code (in respect to women), reform of voting procedures (preference for proportional representation), protection of small farmers, and "mutual understanding of peoples."

All UFCS members needed help to handle the demands posed by the movement itself, let alone the wider public sphere into which it pushed them. The movement therefore relied heavily on specific programs of training, first in the Ecole normale sociale that Butillard had organized before she turned to the UFCS, then in series of courses, more and more of them by correspondence. In 1927 "civic and social talks [*causeries*]" were organized, the first description stated, less to educate the members than to stimulate them to self-education (*LFVS* January). Internally, *Dossiers* of information were developed and, for external use, workbooks on civic education (Cahiers d'education civique), incorporating extensive research and references. Volunteer and then paid *animatrices* were educated to run training sessions, some of them related explicitly to politics; in the postwar period the paid professionals tended to train the amateurs.[13]

In politics the focus was municipal. This was true also of the Mouvement républicain populaire, with which the UFCS had close links in the early postwar period, but the movement's interest in municipal politics predates the MRP. A Women of the World series started in 1926 with a discussion of Belgium, where Catholic women had used the municipal franchise to purify politics: "It is not necessary to be in parliament to carry on vigorous social and civic activity" (*Circulaire* April). As early as 1937 a series of articles entitled "Dans ma commune—les voies publiques" dealt with how to get improved municipal services (*LFVS* December). And well before enfranchisement it was possible for women to be significantly involved in municipal decision making. Under an 1894 law, women could be designated "experts" and placed on commissions on hospitals, schools, and so forth, and apparently UFCS members carried out these duties (Renard 1965:23). They could also be coopted directly onto municipal councils. In April 1938 the UFCS reported one-hundred coopted women councillors in fifty towns, attending meetings though unable to vote. A 1968 assessment by the movement singled out women's interwar participation in municipal government as the most important preparation for their using the vote (*Dialoguer* February–March 1968).

After World War II, it became possible to be more authoritatively involved. The UFCS organized in 1944 a day's study session bringing together women municipal councillors (*LFVS* April); a similar meeting took place in 1948. In 1950 an international three-day session brought in participants from Germany, Austria, Belgium, the Saar, and the Netherlands, as well as the League of Women Voters of the United States (*LFVS* December). Correspondence courses on municipal affairs started in 1952, and *La femme dans la vie sociale* acquired a municipal page (eventually subsumed into a section on Europe and no longer in existence). Two years later a course in municipal adminstration was added for

13. The term *animatrice* is untranslatable, so much so that English-language groups now use it; "facilitator" is probably the best equivalent, but these women often carry on quite formal training sessions.

women actually in office (*LFVS* March 1954); by 1956 it had become a "Feminine Civic College" with sessions both in Paris (on "Civic Training") and by correspondence (on "Municipal Training") (*LFVS* December 1956).

The initial message of civic action growing directly out of family and local concerns necessarily changed as the movement expanded its activities. What was described in the UFCS slogan as "competence" came to be supplemented with the notion of a more technical expertise. In 1961 a municipal councillor told the UFCS "Good sense is not enough" and went on to explain the specific skills an elected official had to acquire; these were, as we would expect, mainly budgetary and financial (*LFVS* Special Issue 1961).

Yet the UFCS tended to be skittish about recognizing how political its activities were. The leaders of the group were acutely aware of women's hesitancy about politics. When the UFCS assessed its activities in 1935, after a decade of activism, President Marie de Tailhandier questioned why "civic" was part of the movement's name. Apparently at this time even civic action was seen as inappropriate for women, and politics was remote and disliked. She therefore described the UFCS in homely metaphors. The movement started with women saying "that the machine runs badly. Let's each bring our drop of oil to make it work better." They then moved on to realize that extensive civic action would be necessary: "We see that certain social improvements can be obtained only through appeal to the law or by modifying it and by going to those who make the laws: the government, the parliament." This is more than just civic, she explained; it is political activity, even though it does not operate through the parties.

In the same issue of *La femme dans la vie sociale* Eve Baudouin, later to be one of the UFCS's prized Resistance fighters, described the group as "avant-garde." Even in very early days the UFCS protested against "fiscal injustices" such as the inadequate pensions of widows and situations where abandoned wives had to go to court to get support allowances. The successes she listed included many that any observer would identify as political, such as family allowances (to assist women who leave the workforce), maternity leaves in state industries, and state aid to battered children. On invitation the UFCS had sent suggestions to the Senate's Reform Commission, and it had helped produce legislation on the family home and weekly rest days.[14] The methods she enumerated went well beyond mere civic action, for they included the use of publicity, delega-

14. Other successes, also clearly political, included censorship of movies; women supervisors for playgrounds, washrooms, and cloakrooms in coed schools (the UFCS supported coeducation but wanted women teachers and feared "immorality" in mixed playing and dressing); helping to keep private organizations free of tax on apprentices; working for and to some extent getting provisions favoring the mother in the home; opposing and helping to stop a proposal to end procedures terminating liquor licenses for reasons of immorality (related to prostitution?). Efforts to obtain the family vote have the same quality.

tions to the government and to deputies of all parties, and service on public bodies where possible (*LFVS* February–March). But Baudouin never used the word "political." Lacking the vote, the movement did not have to face hard questions about its relationship to electoral politics and to political parties.

With the vote once acquired, the situation changed. The movement's postwar views can be derived from a series of political statements beginning with a "General Political Program" presented to the newly enfranchised women of France in February 1945 (*LFVS*). In this two-page document the first four sections were headed "for women," "for woman workers," "for mothers," and "for the family." For every woman the UFCS claimed "legislation and social practices [*moeurs*] which recognize both her personal dignity and her own particular role in the family and in public life." A footnote clarified the implications for equality of treatment: "Why are there two different legislative measures about conjugal infidelity, about disposing of property, etc. . . . ? Why do the matrimonial regimes in practice continue to keep married women in the situation of minors? Why is an unmarried woman supporting relatives unable to get credit for them in relation to taxes and social service payment?" The only measures that would appear offensive to individualist feminist critics were to be found under the heading related to mothers and families: they involved enough money coming into the household so the mother could stay at home, and a distinction between "legitimate" family and children and those "outside of marriage."[15]

In February 1945 Andrée Butillard was still very much in command of the movement, as she would be until her death in 1955; she emphasized both the religious rationale and the activist dimensions of the movement's position, in a statement of principles that appeared conspicuously in the middle of the General Program over her signature. In a text that twice affirmed the "Christian" commitment of the UFCS, she stated a theme to be picked up again in the constitutional flyer: opposition to "all fascisms: those of the Right and those of the Left."

This General Program provided the outlines of UFCS policy for the next few years. It included, for working women, better pay and pensions and equal pay for equal work, unions "fitting their aspirations," and protective legislation covering morality and outwork as well as the more usual areas.[16] Mothers were to get recognition and support, and the situation of widows was to be improved. Government action should facilitate housing and acquisition of property for both working men and working women, as well as improving provision of education (including

15. This last concern, common in traditional women's groups, is fueled by the insecurities of the dependent wife; its hostility to the children of such liaisons is repugnant and not really compensated for by the UFCS's willingness to provide support for unwed mothers.

16. Maternity leave is not mentioned, however.

free and private schools). Action, mainly educational, must be taken against "social scourges," among them alcoholism, prostitution, slums, tuberculosis, venereal diseases, and cancer. "As economical housekeepers" (and social feminists) the UFCS urged measures to favor savings and regulate provision of credit, plus a series of rather vague hopes for reconstruction and a more precise list of measures to promote electoral justice. These last included compulsory voting and proportional representation, the family vote (for the last time), more women appointed to boards and commissions, and generally improved election proceedings. The UFCS also called for a "colonial policy compatible with the civilizing mission of France": a response to "legitimate aspirations" of colonial populations should tighten the links of empire. Finally, "for a durable peace" France must maintain the (antifascist) alliance and set up a system of juridically organized security based on an international peace force. The position relied on arguments that were, as Dogan and Narbonne noted of UFCS opposition to the earlier constitutional draft, more "specifically political than . . . . Christian" (1955:130).

UFCS policy in regard to political parties was established at enfranchisement. The UFCS expected women to pay attention to politics and to be active. But even though eight of the MRP's nine women members in the first legislative assembly of the Fourth Republic were UFCS members, the movement did not expect women to become the sort of unquestioning party members typical of France's highly ideological party system (Dogan and Narbonne 1955:130). As early as January 1945 members were warned in *Notre Journal* to beware of the attempts of candidates to win their commitment to a party or a party grouping and urged to think instead of the common good, of France as a house that must be set in order for the sake of the children. It was impossible to support the Communists, but given that, support should still be limited to particular measures (*Notre Journal* Annexe, mid-October 1946). At the same time Butillard explicitly attacked communism, mentioning Lenin and Kollontai; the objection, as the reference to Kollontai suggests, was to the supposed abolition of the family in the Soviet Union. The UFCS equated the Communist party with the Soviet Union and rejected it on that ground (*LFVS* September–October 1946).

For the next national election, the first for the Fourth Republic and for women, the UFCS carefully sorted parties into "spiritual" and "materialist," with the first group described as run by Christians and committed to families and public liberty, including the right to free schools; the second was run by atheists. But distinctions were drawn even among the materialist parties, and criteria other than spirituality were used to evaluate all parties: the Communist party was dictatorial and totalitarian as well as committed to the destruction of the family and to collectivization; the Socialists were Marxists and "statist" but not under Soviet control; the MRP had women representatives in the Constituent Assembly;

the relatively unmaterialist PRL was reactionary; the RGR was conservative as well as atheist (*Notre Journal* November 1946). These points were made in the publication aimed at less-educated members of the UFCS, and the message was clear: vote MRP. But a political argument reinforced the religiously oriented one: "To save our civilization it is necessary to vote for the party which is capable of being stronger than the Communist party." Many MRP voters moved to the Socialists once the MRP was no longer available (Mossuz-Lavau and Sineau 1985).

Instructions for the new women voters were detailed. Parties were judged first on the nature of their directors and general programs, then on program commitments to women and in relation to the policy preferences of the UFCS. One criterion was support for women's political participation, even at the highest elected levels. Of the second Constituent assembly, in 1946, the UFCS complained that too few women appeared on the electoral lists and not high enough: even though it would be "ridiculous" to have a parliament with a female majority (since "a political vocation" is rare in women), qualified women "bring to political life a healthier and more disinterested climate, more human and more fraternal [*sic*]" (*LFVS* September–October 1946).

The same criteria were also applied to unions and to women's groups. Goals were often shared, but the UFCS insisted on separate action because of the differing values and political preferences of the activists. When the Union des femmes de France, identified with the Communist party, invited the UFCS to an International Congress of Women in 1945, the invitation was refused. All women had shared in the Resistance (the UFCS was understandably proud of its martyrs), all now faced common obstacles, but only "rarely" could they work together (*LFVS* September 1945). Two years later, on the occasion of voting for social security administrators, the UFCS used the same distinctions between totalitarian bureaucratization and the rights of families to sort out the lists presented by different union federations. The movement conceded, however, the possible good faith and even "spirituality" of some French Communists: "They are close to us in a desire for better justice, a wish to respect social and family liberties." Yet they represented only a small minority in a Marxist-inspired majority "under the influence of a wind coming . . . from the East" (*Notre Journal* Supplement March 1947).

The movement's attitude toward communism thus showed a certain sophistication that increased over the years. The central criteria were always specific policies. Toward the end of 1948 (*LFVS* December) the UFCS noted that despite their atheist belief that perfection is possible here on earth and all means are permitted to that end, some Communists recognized the necessity of getting the working class out of its current miserable conditions, of ending certain unjustifiable privileges, and of aspiring for justice and fraternity. Communists, it was noted drily, often shared such beliefs in spite of their doctrines. In 1950 the

UFCS went against its own principled commitment to private property to defend squatters who moved into vacant housing (*LFVS* March). That year a document titled "Five Points" was sent to all the parties, and women were urged to vote on the basis of party responses (*LFVS* November).

The Five Points of 1950 were prefaced by the wish for a larger representation of women in the legislature, compulsory voting, and decent electoral campaigns without defamation, violence, and intimidation. A larger place for women in the machinery of public life would make these goals possible. The demands had been voiced as soon as women were enfranchised. The Five Points themselves were familiar, oriented toward the situation of the family and a concern for international peace; the situation of working women did not receive attention this time, alcoholism had gained prominence, and the European Community appeared as it had in the study programs of the organization itself (*LFVS* November 1950).[17]

The UFCS now faced directly the question of whether women should join political parties. Five years after women received the vote, this was only the second election in which women would participate. They were told they should join parties, especially if they were interested in national office. If they selected a party, it should be in terms of the Five Points (*LFVS* May 1951). Since "free" schools were included in the Five Points, of course, the anticlerical parties were ruled out. In practice, those UFCS members interested in public office were likely to be active at the municipal level, where political orientations were clearly understood but party labels were most often avoided.

Election succeeded election, and the UFCS became more politically experienced. The 1951 election was the last in which it voiced opposition to atheism and materialism, this time on the grounds that the church had condemned "rationalism and liberalism." Even during this election UFCS voters were supposed to act independently. They were advised to avoid *panachage* (moving candidates from one list to another) and instructed instead simply to drop individual candidates from a party list, since the lists meant something about commitments (*Notre Journal* June 1951). In this year interest in municipal politics produced a regular municipal page in the journal, as well as the important correspondence courses in municipal politics.

By the time of plans for the next election, late in 1955, the UFCS had articulated preferences on housing, immorality (including prostitution), family policy (including economic and fiscal implications), alcoholism,

17. The Five Points were 1) a guaranteed basic standard of living so that mothers can stay home if they want, with special measures for unmarried women and widows and aid to the gifted young; 2) housing policy; 3) the battle against alcoholism; 4) "the moral health of the country" (a reference again to social scourges); 5) peace both social and international, beginning with European unity.

European unity, colonial self-determination and aid to the Third World, disarmament and an international police force, and reforms to produce stable parliamentary majorities and a greater degree of decentralization in France (*LFVS* November–December 1955). These positions were backed up by a knowledgeable critique of the achievements and non-achievements of the retiring Assembly and a discussion of the political parties which concluded that the only remaining ideological distinction was in terms of attitudes toward national sovereignty—willingness or unwillingness to submit France's policies to another's priorities. At the same time, parties were criticized for letting a commitment to national sovereignty override responses to legitimate demands such as those from the developing countries. The UFCS preferred a flexibility that would support the federation of Europe and a variety of overseas connections. Eurocommunism would now presumably be acceptable—but only in terms of specific deputies' commitments on key issues. The UFCS now recognized that all parties would henceforth support secular schools; although there is some anxious speculation that state education could mean a war against religion, free schools cease to be an issue. The final admonition was to "be demanding and realistic."

Although UFCS members had been cautioned that "politics is the art of the possible," they were disappointed with the outcome of the 1955 election, for the Communists did well, and fewer women were successful than in the previous election (*LFVS* January–February 1956). Proud of its achievements over thirty years of pressure group activity, the movement continued politically active.[18] By 1968 we find in the renovated *Dialoguer* a more sophisticated perspective on women's role in politics (February–March).[19] The UFCS president, Geneviève Delarhenal, posed directly the question of whether the group was committed to "institutional" or to "political" action. After the usual evasiveness about the political, she finally stated that the UFCS *is* political if by politics we mean living together in harmony and participating in society at the service of all. Hers is a view of society that needs no class organizations and particularly no political parties. The same point is made by the forms of UFCS action she identifies as political: preparation and submission of amendments to projects of law (for example, in respect to re-

18. In 1955 the UFCS took pride in its role in producing the following: enlargement of the rights of married women, including measures against men who have abandoned their families and failed to support them; mothers' allowance; moving allowance for the poor moving to a smaller dwelling; lower income tax for unmarried woman with dependents; nomination of a mother to a commission (of the Ministry of Justice) which regulates children's publications; barring unaccompanied children from cafés; gas and electricity rebates to widows with two children or other families with three; influence on time-payment organizations; measures to build apartments designated for widows, the ailing, and large families; and the antialcoholism campaign (Special Issue).

19. The 1968 summary and review of the organization preceded the events of that turbulent summer and are best interpreted as the UFCS's self-examination at the completion of deconfessionalization.

gimes for matrimonial property), communications to ministers for and against specific measures, deputations to ministers suggesting desirable measures, and participation in official appointed bodies. It is the same list Tailhandier had given in 1935, though the range of issues has widened. In the same issue of *Dialoguer*, discussing the title of the journal, the secretary-general enunciates a view of the voluntary group as representing its members directly to the government, attempting to take a general rather than a selfish view of policy. The president had made the same point, giving as an example the demand for part-time work for everyone, men as well as women. The UFCS clearly preferred group to individual activity. It was more comfortable with pressure-group and appointive than with partisan and electoral politics.

The logical next question, as Delarhenal points out, is why the group should be made up of women. The answer is not entirely clear. The UFCS president questions whether women should be considered a "social group" now they are "integrated, like men, into each socioprofessional category." Part of the answer, an implicit denial that integration is so very complete, is to be found in the small proportion of women among those represented at "official consultations" of the nation—which presumably includes parliament, since this comment ends with the observation that women are, after all, more than half of the electorate. Therefore, "since we believe that women have something original and indispensable to say, the UFCS serves to transmit it." Furthermore, since "dialogue" covers the range from approval to challenge, women need training, "which our movement feels itself particularly good at supplying for women." Women's lack of direct representation in the halls of power justifies their having a voice of their own, along with the training necessary to deal with the powerful.

Although the assertion of difference has receded, it is still present. The complementarity of male-female aptitudes is central and, it is noted, is more difficult in public or professional than in domestic life: "she" often wishes to play man, and "he" is likely to want to "restrict her to the so-called feminine tasks." It is hard for women to find their place in a period when there is talk of liberation. Then an extraordinary passage denies the whole notion of spheres of activity: "But the essential certainly doesn't consist in delimiting places, but in learning to 'be' oneself. For perhaps there isn't any feminine or masculine domain, but simply ways to 'be' that are characteristic of women and others that are characteristic of men."[20] What is the meaning of "ways to 'be' oneself"? roles, education and training, habits, innate characteristics? The answers do not seem to matter; the practical implication, we are told, is that men and women will perform shared tasks but keep their different personal qualities for mutual enrichment. Then children will be educated by fa-

20. This is one of the passages Rabaut so dislikes.

thers as well as mothers, and tasks such as building the city and economic development will not be exclusively masculine. The UFCS then abjures any desire to demand women's rights or to compete with men for the places they have. The movement has "nothing feminist about it," and if it is "feminine" it is so only because of "pedagogical necessity."

The UFCS, in short, was not an equity feminist group. As late as 1968 it refused to admit it was feminist at all. But the movement's interest in politics did not diminish. The anxiety about the Communists receded; ecological and consumerist concerns were added to established areas of interest. The status of women and the situation of women in other countries became more prominent, in a logical extension of prewar activities; the UFCS had several branches in Algeria and one in Madagascar and had shown concern for the situation of women in the French colonial empire (Rollet 1960:138–41). Areas of interest were retained even as emphases shifted. Family policy was always central, even when the couple replaced the large family as the focus of attention. In the political era affected by feminism, UFCS politics also came to include a more active commitment to the cause of women and an astonishing support of reproductive freedom.

Underneath these changes was a continuing insistence on the special roles of women, their value, their obligations, and their capability to act rationally on their own behalf. In 1925 the UFCS had adopted the slogan "Influential because competent," and the main task of the organization was to provide the possibilities for becoming influential. As the movement passed its sixtieth anniversary and moved further into the 1980s, task and slogan alike survived.

The biggest changes were, of course, in the period immediately after secularization, which was also the period of the revitalization of French feminism. It was during these years that the UFCS best showed its adaptability—when it came to approve first contraception and then abortion.

CHAPTER 11

Feminism and Reproduction

The UFCS's first meeting was in a women's restaurant, an impeccable symbol of its commitment to women and to the autonomy of women.[1] In its early years the movement had no hesitation in describing itself as feminist. Later, in the period of second- wave feminism, it was more reluctant to claim the title, but it retained the commitments.

The UFCS retained also an insistence on the distinctiveness of its own ideology and activities. At the time of its founding the movement asserted that it shared some but not all goals with existing feminist organizations. At this stage the objection was to the "neutral" feminists' "egalitarianism" and especially "individualism"—their version of the secular republicanism of their time. The UFCS contrasted to this position the Catholic image of an ordered, hierarchical society structured by religious edicts and authority. The assertion that women should define for themselves a place in no way inferior to men's was shared with other feminists, however. This view, while compatible with a nonpatriarchal republicanism, was irreconcilable with church expectations for laymen, let alone laywomen. The movement also shared with other feminists the belief that, for whatever reason, women have a distinctive situation and perspective related to their domestic role; this is the basis of women's obligation to participate in and improve public life.

As early as July 1926 the UFCS newspaper was telling readers that the neutral suffrage leagues were "inadequate" or incomplete, a relatively mild condemnation. In 1929, after the leaders of Catholic women's groups including the UFCS had attended the Women's Estates-General convened by the International Council of Women, Andrée Butillard analyzed what she called "Good and Bad Feminism" (*LFVS* March). Legitimate feminism, the UFCS's, stressed the unique personality of women, who were involved more with detail and less with synthesis, were less logical, more intuitive, and more emotional but also more tenacious.

---

1. Restaurant féminin Stanislas (*Circulaire* September 1925).

God's plan "made men and women equal in nature but different, complementary one to the other in the family and in society." The legitimate version of feminism could co-operate though not affiliate with bad feminism. In 1934, when the UFCS compared the two great international leagues of feminist organizations, the International Council of Women and the much larger International Union of Catholic Women's Leagues to which the Union belonged, it granted the ICW a "humanitarian philosophy" and "an open mind, daring solutions, a generous effort." There was considerable agreement between the two leagues, especially on issues connected with children, even though the ICW could not deal with the spiritual dimension of life (*LFVS* September–October 1934).

Throughout the 1930s the UFCS praised the actions of particular feminist groups or individuals.[2] Butillard's epitaph for Cécile Brunschvicg makes the bases of collaboration and evaluation explicit: "Morally chief of French feminism, Mme. Brunschwicg [*sic*] had an agnostic orientation that 'La femme dans la vie sociale' sometimes had to combat." For instance, she was wrong in her opposition to the man remaining the head of the family under the revised Civil Code in 1938 and in her view that the mother at home was in a dependent situation with limited horizons. But she was logical and had a will for peace. Butillard praised her in these terms: "That modesty, which so easily could have become humility, is admirable. She achieved the best-known profile of the women of our time and, without being Christian, sought, as well as she could, to serve" (*LFVS* November 1946). Brunschvicg was praised again in 1948 for her "moral authority" and for her mode of rigorous argument, which had a significant effect in "reducing the sexual prejudices of an irrational and old-fashioned masculinism" (*LFVS* September).

Modesty, humility, service—these quintessential womanly virtues are apparently incompatible with the public sphere, yet Butillard presented them as the proper attitudes for public activity in the service of women and the family. It should be recalled that Brunschvicg had been as actively engaged in mainstream politics as was possible for a woman of her generation; she was a member of the Popular Front government in 1936 and involved with the Radical party after enfranchisement. Feminine virtues and interests had taken her a long way. After deconfessionalization, the UFCS would no longer have to say that such women were almost Christian (that is, Catholic).

In the years that followed the war and the enfranchisement of Frenchwomen, feminism as a recognized movement was in eclipse, and the

2. For instance, the mock election organized by Femme nouvelle (Louise Weiss's group) was a good idea, and so was its justification of politics as municipal housekeeping (but offices and polling stations should not have been set up in cafés) (*LFVS* June 1935); the ICW meeting in Istanbul did not attack women's domestic role (*LFVS* February 1936); Maria Vérone was right to attack the proposed pseudo-college to "elect" women as municipal councillors (*LFVS* June 1936); she is honest and unstinting in her efforts, even if we do not always agree with her (*LFVS* June 1938).

UFCS had no need to define its own position in comparison with other organized groups of women. But in 1960 it nevertheless prepared a formal statement, "The Advancement of Women." Significantly, it was the first of the mimeographed "Documentary Files of Social and Civic Action" (later the "Workbooks on Civic Action"). This document deplored the tendency to see women functionally, merely as part of the family, and cited Hitler and the Marxists as the worst offenders. In deliberate contrast, the UFCS described itself as stressing freedom of choice, something women had in principle but in practice found limited by the inadequate financial resources of families. Both pay and family allowances were insufficient, and there were other problems: at home, women had not learned the value of development of children, and at work they had not learned the value of "development of competence in the service of the group." Being at home, according to the UFCS, need not be impoverishing for a woman open to the world; being at work should not be needed for either personal or economic influence. The ideal was an alert and active presence in the home, followed by unpaid social and political activity when children are older. There was a sophisticated discussion of why women avoid political participation: they think it is "dirty" and inefficient, they cannot see connections between politics and their daily problems, their husbands do not encourage or help their participation, the parties block their entry. And to the fear that politics would "virilize" women by replacing their "basic vocation" of wife and mother, the UFCS responded that this outcome was indeed a danger but on the whole women would bring their "maternal" qualities —intuition and the sense of the concrete—into public life.

There was no mention of feminism. Nevertheless, the movement's position was summarized in a statement that describes core beliefs of social feminism:

> It is, to sum it up, the duty of women, not an easy task, on the one hand never to forget that the family is the foundation of all society (what families are worth is what the state is worth), on the other hand to know how to move out of the "cloister" of the family (or to accept being deprived of it), bringing to the outside world the natural qualities that balance at home the masculine abilities (January–February 1960).

In 1965 the UFCS was prepared to take on both Betty Friedan and Simone de Beauvoir, as well as the Marxists who had just discovered women's home-related needs. The movement thought the Marxists "opportunistic." Friedan overlooked the value of domestic work, and Beauvoir had illusions about possibilities of freedom. The same journal issue noted that for "some" women their daily activity could acquire civic dimensions and thereby become a means of "development" (*Dialoguer* March–April).

When women's liberation emerged after 1968 the UFCS did not identify with the rebellious young women involved in insurrection. Its specific public response to the May Days was embodied in resolutions entirely lacking in feminist content.[3] In fact the feminist dimensions of the 1968 revolt were slow to appear, and the French liberationists' first visible public act was in 1970, when a wreath was presented publicly in August to the "wife of the unknown soldier" (Léger 1982). November 1970 saw another, vast Women's Estates-General at Versailles (Decaux 1972 II:1091–94). In *Dialoguer* the question of feminism was not raised until 1978. In the meantime the journal and its readers continued to struggle with defining and extending the role of women.

In 1969, in a special summary issue of *Dialoguer*, a survey of members on the subject of work reported agreement that conditions were bad. In addition to adjustment in the business world, such as more flexibility in working hours and support services including daycare of all sorts, working mothers needed "evolution" in husbands' roles so that they would take on responsibility for maintenance of the household and for children's education. Some respondents even claimed it was better for children when the mother worked, because the father was then more involved with them. The section of study groups called "Family" (not yet "Women") was still focusing on family allowances and saying that pre-school children had a right to have their mothers at home. But it insisted also that each mother should have a real choice between staying home and working. This is a familiar position with familiar inconsistencies; it has at least the twin virtues of recognizing the burden created under current double-shift conditions and of leaving the necessary decision to each individual woman (*Dialoguer* September–October).

In 1970 the UFCS wrote to Premier Jacques Chaban-Delmas, responding to his appeal that women help build a new society. Why so few women in the study and consultation groups, they asked, and in particular, why was the UFCS barred from the commissions on housing, cities, and social equipment? The premier was then lectured on social policy, but issues relating to the status or situation of women were not singled out (*Dialoguer* March–April). Two journal issues later appeared an important response to apparently substantial protest from members who felt the UFCS had gone beyond "women's business." The UFCS, they said, should not be concerned with fiscal and tax policies and politics. The answer was an indignant list of rhetorical questions, culminating in whether "women's work" should be limited to health care, family budgeting, and the education of children—or should the movement recognize

3. The three resolutions were: endorsement of the need to improve society, a commitment to justice and solidarity entailing concrete reforms related to the cost of living and employment, and support of democratic participation especially by the young and workers (women not mentioned). In addition, a letter to the minister of information urged more objectivity and decentralization in the national radio system (*Dialoguer* June–July 1968).

that national policies on revenue and education shape all these? Should couples discuss only strictly family problems—or should they examine social and economic questions together?[4] Our practice adds up, said the author sharply, to a refusal to accept domains limited to women and to men. We know that democracy needs the participation of all. "We bring our women's point of view to the development of social policy" (*Dialoguer* May–June 1970). These are precisely the issues that the Women's Cooperative Guild had faced, but without the added constraint of an englobing organization.

As the second wave of feminism became more influential, the heritage of suffragism and social activism continued to be celebrated. The fiftieth anniversary issue of *Dialoguer* (February–March 1975) even featured a picture of French suffragists with a banner calling for the vote. It was "certainly not the UFCS," I was told by an elderly member; the movement did not engage in such activities, and the picture is probably of members of La femme nouvelle.

By 1978 the UFCS could no longer avoid the issue of its own feminism. The study groups on women, which had been meeting since the year before, now prepared a workbook of civic action on the subject of women and feminism. In this workbook the Christian feminism that the UFCS had previously claimed was relegated to a "traditional" strand among women's movements. But the authors were evasive about where to place their own group. The other two ideologies of women's organizations were classified as "feminism" based on the ideas of Simone de Beauvoir and "humanism." The latter, equity feminism in the equal rights tradition, dealt with woman "principally as a human being," and the authors were not prepared to recognize it as feminism. Nor were traditionalists accepted within a typically French description of feminism as something engaged in public action "since the intellectual revolution of 1968." "Revolutionary or radical" feminism wanted "above all to change the ideologies and structures of society"; it consisted of a "doctrine with the goal of the extension of the role of women in society [and] collective action growing from women's awareness of their alienation, with the goal of improving their condition" ("alienation," it will be noted, not "oppression") (5).

In addition, the notion of a historical as well as contemporary "reform-

---

4. The other questions were: Should we just accept that women are incompetent—or list the qualifications of the UFCS's leadership and the serious studies our Commission on Work has prepared? Should those of us who are on the planning commissions of the Plan (the UFCS was represented on Social Action and Consumers) simply accept our colleagues' ideas—or should we give them the UFCS's suggestions? Should we agree that wives of wealthy businessmen are happy just spending their husbands' money—or should we say that they can save the extra money they will soon need for medical insurance? Should we say that those on minimum wage should be happy their children get scholarships for their education—or should we state that they would be glad to exchange such good fortune for a better standard of living?

ist feminism" was included, described as "the feminism of struggle for progressive improvement of the situation of women without challenging the social institutions as such, with advances and retreats" (5). It is here the UFCS seems to belong, but the movement was not discussed under that rubric. Instead it appeared as one item in a subsection of an annotated list of women's movements, grouped with the National Council of Women of France, the Ligue française pour le droit des femmes, and Jeunes Femmes. These groups were identified as "Movements with Global Objectives (generally pluralist, without excluding a certain political dimension)" (30). The contrast was with movements associated with political parties, such as the Communist Union des femmes de France, and new political but nonpartisan movements such as Choisir and the "radical" feminist movements of women's liberation. Significantly, the UFCS was not placed, as it so often is, among groups "for the defense of the family" or the "confessional groups" including Action Catholique.[5]

It is also significant that the UFCS's offshoots, the Mouvement mondial des mères and the Ligue pour la mère au foyer, which have remained essentially unchanged since they were founded by Andrée Butillard, were used as examples of traditional groups. The account of these groups was detailed and on the whole sympathetic, ending with the following statement: "In response to the terms 'advancement,' 'rationalization,' 'social support services,' 'sharing of tasks,' and 'financial independence,' they refuse to move forward into an entirely different conception of existence, and they reply: 'generosity,' 'self-forgetfulness,' 'special relationships,' 'respect for life,' 'conjugal love,' 'moral responsibility,' 'vocation,' and 'destiny'" (28). The UFCS had by now accepted all the terms in the first list while struggling to hold onto the ones in the second.

The authors of the workbook on women and feminism backed away from definitions that might make their own group less than feminist. To the question "In this presentation of diverse expressions of feminism, where does the UFCS place itself?" they answered that, in effect, one must look at what the UFCS actually did. It was "concerned to assist women to act as free and responsible individuals, in a society which up to now has not accepted women's claims." The UFCS had established its sections on women to work out "how to experience and express our solidarity with women of differing opinions." Within the movement, on the basis of "the daily preoccupations of women," small groups, self-knowledge, personal development, and the theme of women's autonomy and dependence generated demands to be made to the state. The personal is the political, though that phrase is not used, and this model closely resembles that of the consciousness-raising groups of women's liberation.

5. Other listed categories of women's groups include professional associations of women and support-system groups.

At this point the most self-consciously feminist segment of the UFCS, the Section on Women, now proceeded, as the conclusion to the workbook, to define the movement's policy goals as whatever was necessary for "a real liberty for women in their personal life." It included shorter working hours for all so that work, household tasks, social life, and leisure could be shared. Continuing education should make it possible for women to be "equal to men in all professional training" and training and retraining should be made available for those women who wished to join or rejoin the paid labor force. Quality collective support services should include infant and childcare facilities (specifying crèches), as well as preventive physical and psychological health services. At the very end, in large letters, the UFCS demanded "IN GENERAL THE DISAPPEARANCE OF ALL DISCRIMINATION AGAINST WOMEN" (29).

A comprehensive list of UFCS demands would have been much longer. But although the role of the explicitly feminist and relatively new UFCS study groups on women was exaggerated by the workbook's authors, who were members, the workbook did provide an accurate description of the operation and effect of the small groups making up the UFCS. They captured the attention given to education along with the strong underlying emphasis on the lives of women as the source of their actions and their demands on the state. Only our current definitions of feminism, particularly the French versions, produce doubts that what they were describing was feminism.

Continuing devaluation of the UFCS by feminists reflects, at base, the present assessment of social feminism—and the workbook account makes very clear how squarely the UFCS belongs within that category. In addition, it is likely that the thorny issue of reproductive rights still presents difficulties for a general recognition that the UFCS was and is feminist. The issue was particularly salient for second-wave feminism in France.

The history of second-wave feminism is even more difficult to untangle in France than in other countries, in part because France is generally believed to have produced prototypes of both the organization and the theory of the new period of feminism. The Mouvement de libération des femmes (MLF) groups emerging from 1968 and focusing on the beliefs of Simone de Beauvoir are usually identified as initiating the new era. Yet this is a misleading account or, rather, a mythologized one (Duchen 1986, 1987). Although *The Second Sex* (1949) was one of the landmark volumes of the women's movement, its author was not then a feminist and at that time had no ties with organizations concerned with the situation of women. Beauvoir's work seems to have influenced French feminists only indirectly, as returned to them after two decades by American feminists such as Betty Friedan. This is the view suggested by the translator of *The Feminine Mystique*, Yvette Roudy (1985:113–14). Roudy points out that two new strands of feminism developed in France after 1968, one based on established institutions such as unions and political parties, the other, the MLF, independent and hostile to such established institutions. Neither had connections, either in doctrine or in organization, with any part of the first wave.

In addition, however, Roudy gives a rather unexpected account of her own induction into feminism, an account that casts doubt on the usual version of the beginnings of the MLF. In 1964 she was working on *La femme mystifiée*, getting a "jolt" as she recognized around her the same "problem that has no name" (1985:76–77). Other books that much impressed her at the time, as she translated them, were Eleanor Roosevelt's autobiography and Elizabeth Janeway's *Man's World, Woman's Place*. All three books are very different from Beauvoir in both analysis and impact; Eleanor Roosevelt was the only social feminist among the authors, but all grounded their analysis in women's experience of domesticity. Roudy attributes to these books her own willingness to accompany Colette Audry to the Mouvement démocratique féminin (MDF) (1985:83–84). At the MDF Roudy met Marie-Thérèse Yquem, Simone Menez, and, most significant, Marcelle Kraemer-Bach, who had impressed Louise Weiss more than thirty years earlier when Kraemer-Bach was vice president of Cécile Brunschvicg's Union française pour le suffrage des femmes (Weiss 1946:12). Roudy says, furthermore, that from the MDF she moved into François Mitterrand's first presidential campaign in 1965. She adds, "Contrary to many women who have since entered politics, I myself came to active politics by way of feminism" (1985:85).[6] The MDF and Roudy herself played a significant role in Mitterrand's decision to support legalization of contraception in his 1965 campaign (Rabaut 1978:327).

Roudy's memoirs do not discuss the development of second-wave feminism in any detail; I cite them here as another reminder of the continuities of feminism and also as a first corrective to existing accounts of the development of feminism in France. Roudy herself identifies the MDF as merely one of numerous *groupuscules* of the noncommunist Left that appeared in the 1960s. But she mentions at least one more feminist group like it. In fact, even before 1968 "a new breath of life" revivified French feminism in new organizations and invigorated older ones (Albistur and Armogathe 1977:447). But most French analysts perceived all pre-MLF groups as accepting the values of existing society and therefore doomed to failure. This seems a harsh judgment of socialist feminist groups such as the MDF; it includes the usual rejection of older social feminist groups.

Such an emphasis on the structures and theories of 1968 amounts to

6. Other sources simply describe the MDF as affiliated with the French Socialists in a way that implies primacy for the partisan element; Albistur and Armogathe, for instance, identify it this way, along with the Club Louise Michel, also founded in 1964 (Rabaut 1978:327; Albistur and Armogathe 1977:448).

yet another denial of the possibility that feminism might autonomously develop its own organizations and critiques. It also ignores the history hinted at by the experience of Yvette Roudy. The attention paid to Beauvoir is particularly unfortunate. Although her writings were radical in impact, she was nevertheless an equity feminist applying the phenomenology of Sartre, who indeed suggested this application to her. Similarly, the MLF was initially formed to apply to the situation of women the beliefs of the radical student Left from which it emerged.

Reproductive issues, in France as elsewhere, moved feminists away from a simple application of existing theories. More generally, the second wave in France emphasized issues of reproduction because the area was salient for women but not for male radicals. It was also the area where older groups joined the new ones in both analysis and activity. I first encountered the UFCS in 1974, in conservative, provincial Aix-en-Provence, as part of a coalition of women's organizations urging approval of the Veil law reforming the legislation on abortion. Earlier, abortion had produced the most dramatic public acts of the post-'68 movement.

Even in the context of reproductive rights, however, an account that begins with 1968 is incomplete. The previous legalization of contraception by the Neuwirth law of 1967 was a significant turning point. It in turn is inseparable from the Mouvement français pour le planning familial and Dr. Lagroua Weill-Hallé's group Maternité heureuse, founded in 1955; and there are even earlier connections with Dr. Jean Dalsace who was active in the interwar years (Rabaut 1978:319–20).[7] Jeunes Femmes was also active in family planning campaigns in the immediate postwar period (Delhaye and Dunand 1969).[8] If the new feminism is not seen as beginning with the groups of 1968, however, it is most commonly identified with a movement for reproductive rights dramatically initiated with the 1971 declaration by 343 prominent women who had (or said they had) undergone abortions and followed by the Bobigny trial of the next year.

The declaration of 1971 initiated dramatic and ultimately effective public activity related to abortion. Choisir was founded in 1972, the Mouvement de libération de l'avortement et de la contraception (MLAC) the next year; branches of the MLAC were soon carrying out (illegal) abortions (Manceaux 1974). Analysis focusing on reproductive rights makes the first major triumphs of the revived women's movement the Veil law and the legislation providing for reimbursement of contraceptives by the state health service, both passed in 1975. Out of Choisir came

7. Jean Rabaut, who accepts reproductive rights as a central issue and calls his chapter on postwar feminism "From woman suffrage to birth control" (1978:305), breaks this period in 1967 with the Neuwirth law.

8. Jeunes Femmes is a small Protestant group that has not been much studied but seems to be a descendant of the neutral feminist groups of the interwar period (Michy 1975).

the Common Program for Women and feminist involvement in the electoral campaigns of 1981, when Choisir and the MLF, otherwise decidedly at odds by this time, both endorsed François Mitterrand for president. They thus chose association with a particular partisan option instead of the post-1968 hostility to all mainstream politics or the older feminist pattern of reluctant, merely instrumental involvement.

How Choisir decided upon partisan alignment is worth examining, for its logic is very close to that of the UFCS. After Choisir split with the MLF and decided to participate in the Bobigny trial, it then moved to a nonpartisan participation in politics.[9] This change is made clear in the text justifying the group's *Common Program for Women* developed for election purposes and published in 1978, when Choisir was preparing to reorganize as a political party presenting candidates. The logic of an election manifesto for a "party" that had no chance of electoral success lay precisely in women's alienation from the parties that ought to attract them. Aware that the Socialist party was better than the others on reproductive (and other) issues, the Common Program nevertheless quoted Mitterrand's condescending, paternalistic remarks in 1977 about women and feminism and Gisèle Halimi's angry response (Halimi 1978:42–43).[10]

Drawn toward socialism, the organization articulated the reaction to political parties of even Leftist and politically active Frenchwomen. This is their judgment on the programs of the Left: "Women, sorry, we forgot, are additional points, appendixes or annexes to programs" (Halimi 1978:40).[11] The Common Program forecast dire results stemming from parties' and men's disregard of the problems and participation of women: "The future will only hobble along if it is constructed merely with men's hands and women's waiting." Its response was a social or radical feminist one: "The substance of this future, we women carry it in each of us. It is as diverse as it is homogeneous. This fertile and unique difference makes women's struggles primary in contrast to struggles in general. . . . And, starting with our own experience, calculated or chanted, we must build" (1978:20). This lyrical outburst still produced a program of action: "Not to leave electoral games in the hands of men, of par-

9. Albistur and Armogathe, who do not much like Choisir, classify the group as "parapolitical." Writing for publication in 1977, they described it—inaccurately even then—as having a "precise and limited" goal: the abrogation of the restrictive 1920 law on reproduction (448).

10. Me Halimi was a well-known radical lawyer who had made her public reputation in legal resistance to the conduct of the Algerian war; Andrée Michel was one of many feminist academics and other public figures associated with Choisir.

11. Michel and Texier are even harsher in judging the parties of the left: "An opportunist and short-sighted policy, not concerned about women's emancipation, this has always been the attitude of the French left in respect to the women problem" (1964 I:192–93). They add that the other parties are no better: "The few rights that they enjoy in society, Frenchwomen owe only to their own struggles and as a result they owe *absolutely nothing* to political parties" (1964 I:200).

ties . . . but to make use of this antisexist book, which is therefore political" (1978:21).[12]

Political systems being what they are, such an approach is bound eventually to mean attempts to work through the existing parties. Choisir's candidates got 1.5 percent of the votes cast in the 1978 election, not enough for leverage even in a system of proportional representation (which France did not have)(Rabaut 1978:376).[13] Choisir eventually found that, however reluctantly, it must use its program as a basis of choosing among the existing political parties. Referring to the presidential choice of 1969, the Common Program described the choice between Pompidou and Poher as "plague or cholera" (Halimi 1978:16); we may infer that in 1981 Mitterrand was more like cowpox. The women of Choisir, who would have been Communists or Socialists if they had not become feminists, thus turned to the parties of their original choice once those parties responded (minimally) to their concerns. "The message of the left—like that of the words of Christ—is about justice, dignity, and universalism," wrote Halimi. "Socialism with a masculine face is only perverted socialism," she concluded; "with our women's voice and at the side of our companions, the *just ones*, we will continue to construct History" (Halimi 1981:12, 13, 14). The UFCS, especially in its Christian days, would have agreed, even though the group would not have looked to socialism for the "just ones."

In fact, the UFCS's agenda of issues, as well as its rhetoric, resembled Choisir's; by 1978 its goals were similar in specific details, though the UFCS never centered its public policy in the same way on reproductive rights. The two groups also shared the same relationship to a political party—with the difference that the party sharing the UFCS's general perspective existed only at the very beginning of the postwar period.

After Liberation, the Mouvement républicain populaire (MRP) was the party closest to UFCS members' general preferences. It was the party they had most contacts with, the one through which they were politically active, and the one that supported measures they favored. But the UFCS's evolution toward partisan commitment was barely started when the MRP dissolved. Having lost the party that might have fitted their needs, the UFCS members continued to see their partisan commitment as limited and instrumental.

Yvette Roudy was appointed minister for the rights of women under

12. The Common Program used historical evidence, tables of statistics, and personal testimony to support recommendations on politics, family, work, the legal system, sexuality, media, education, women and the arts, and peace. It concluded with proposed texts for legislation revising family property law, forming a public fund to guarantee support payments, changing regulations related to the forty-hour week, and affecting equal pay, sexual discrimination in the workplace, women's names, abortion, sexism in the media, composition of juries, women's and feminist organizations, parental authority, parental leave, and abolition of the death penalty.

13. Other feminist groups had agreed to ask women to protest by abstaining or spoiling ballots.

Mitterrand; it was in an MRP government, had one ever occurred, that a UFCS member might have been given some official responsibility for women. Indeed, Marie-Madeleine Dienisch held positions as a junior minister in centrist governments including the MRP; she was a member of the UFCS (Irving 1973:151; Charlot 1980:186; *LFVS* December 1946); she also served in the second Messmer government (Brimo 1975:108). Michel and Texier comment disapprovingly on UFCS access to positions on public commissions and boards—because they saw this access, for stand-ins for the church, as used to deny rights to women. From the UFCS perspective, however, this was precisely the way to forward policies important, even crucial to women and articulated by women themselves within a women's organization. Here also the demise of the MRP served to limit the movement's access.

At the same time the UFCS may have gained some advantage in their loss of an obvious partisan linkage. Socialist feminists such as Roudy point with pride to the movement of the Socialists, under their influence, to a far more progressive position in relation to women's issues. They hoped, and were sometimes able, to move the party some distance toward a not-entirely-logical commitment to social feminism, as well as to the far easier equity feminist extensions of socialism. It seems nevertheless unlikely that feminism made any major impact on the party overall. Nor is there evidence that the UFCS managed to affect the MRP stance on women's or other issues (though there are references in the literature to the women being the more progressive element in the party) (Duverger 1955:104). But neither did the party provide the disillusionment or the subsequent reconciliation that the Socialists did. The MRP never had a dominant position in government, and by the time women's issues began to reach the agenda of French politics—probably best dated sometime after the 1968 upheavals —it had vanished. The experience of Italian feminists with their Christian Democratic party is informative. In Italy, Socialists and Communists were slow to come around, but eventually supported women's right to reproductive freedom. The Catholic party, by contrast, remained just that, unequivocally opposed to abortion (Beckwith 1987). The UFCS, which did not need to appeal to a putative anti-abortion Catholic electorate, was able to work its way toward a more liberal position. The loss of the MRP gave it both nonpartisanship and the freedom to evolve in areas particularly sensitive for organizations with a Catholic origin.

For the UFCS reproductive issues were particularly difficult to handle because of the uncompromising position of the Catholic church and the long affiliation of both organization and surviving militants. As late as 1956 the group was still almost hysterically opposed to contraception; a woman doctor wrote that the use of birth control encouraged homosexuality (*LFVS* April). But in 1961 the UFCS discussed and basically approved contraception for social reasons—housing and income—as well as the health of the mother (although rhythm was the only method sanctioned). In the same year an internal *Dossier* discussed and rejected abortion (*LFVS* April–May; UFCS 1961a). But though in 1968 the approval of contraception explicitly excluded the IUD as an abortifacient, the 1973 Civic Education Workbook "Women in France" accepted contraception without any quibbling about methods (*Dialoguer* February–March 1968; UFCS 1973b). And ten years later *Dialoguer* reported with approval a play prepared at Lille for the sexual education of adolescents aged thirteen and over. Its two protagonists, described as "lucid and responsible in their love," each use a contraceptive, singing together "two ways are better than one, one is better than none." The article did not suggest they were married. In the same journal issue the Lyons branch of the UFCS reported on a training course on women and contraception and entitled their report "Women's New Power" (*LFVS* December 1983–January 1984).

Abortion, as might be expected, was a more difficult problem, capable of producing major difficulties within the movement as late as 1980. It was discussed and rejected in both 1967 and 1968, though without public statements (UFCS 1971). In 1970 *Dialoguer* faced the issue with three substantial articles focusing on the "conflict of responsibilities" involved: we favor individual choice free from external rules but feel that law should enlighten individuals and give them both social and economic aid; we are still working out a policy (November–December). In 1971 the movement found, unsurprisingly, that the majority of members polled were convinced that life began at conception and that abortion was therefore the destruction of a life. Members would not discard this position, which underlies the organization's insistence that abortion must not be seen as either trivial or beneficial. At the same time the UFCS inherited from its earliest days both a strong commitment to treating women as independent moral agents and a continuing reluctance to allow the state a role in decisions about domestic life. Both views flow from the earlier situation of a Catholic women's group in an anticlerical state, where an assertion of a woman's judgment was an assertion of a Catholic judgment. They can also be seen as intrinsic to the feminist insistence on women's claim to autonomy. Later, such views would be expanded in the context of second-wave feminism.

The UFCS entered the abortion debate with a preference for prevention. The key 1971 document, an internal *Dossier* entitled "Choices in Relation to the Right to Life," was a sophisticated discussion of the options available to those who cannot take a completely restrictive or a completely permissive view. The relevant general principles were derived from the philosophical position of the organization: the "rights and responsibilities of the human person" included the right to life but also the right to liberties of thought, conscience, religion, and expression, along with the responsibility to inform oneself about important major questions affecting human beings. In addition, it was crucial to decide, for such questions, whether the problem was private and individual or collective, and how the different social levels were related

Following these guidelines, the first UFCS initiative on abortion was co-operation with other family and adult education associations to promote positive measures that would reduce the likelihood of abortion. These began with education, including sexual education of children and adults, medical measures including pre- and postnatal care and immunization against German measles, and provision of appropriate social support services for pregnant women.[14] The Dossier noted with regret the small likelihood of producing in France any great interest in the adoption of unwanted children. Clearly, at the time of this 1971 document the UFCS was still at the stage of circulating information to members and stalling.

By December 1972 (the date of another internal document, "Notes about the Legislation on Abortion") it became necessary to adopt a formal position both internally and for public use. The adopted position avoided any explicit statement about when life begins.[15] Instead, it focused on allowing women to make an informed, free choice, with the notation that social conditions currently constrain many women to see abortion as neither evil nor an attack on life. The UFCS therefore opposed various suggested laws that would have enumerated acceptable reasons for abortion, on the grounds they would remove individual responsibility. At the same time collective responsibility should not be abdicated as it had been in the 1920 law, which paid no attention to the social causes of abortion. The law must be changed so it can be effective. It must attack the roots of abortion, by providing education not just about contraception but also about sexuality and by favoring an attitude of responsibility as well as making it possible for those seeking abortion to make an "informed decision" about the causes and consequences of their act. That said, it was necessary to "respect the individual in her decision, for this final choice belongs to herself—and this without condemnation by society." The role of doctors was never discussed; the "couple" appeared as an element the next year, in the workbook "Women in France."

The UFCS supported the Veil law, eventually passed in 1974 with support of the opposition, which provided abortion on demand during the first ten weeks of pregnancy with substantial provisions for information about options. Under this legislation, doctors had to be consulted

14. These are continuing interests of the UFCS: early in 1975 *Dialoguer* reported that the president of the UFCS, as a member of the Conseil supérieur de l'education, was involved with the development of courses on sex education (December 1974–January 1975).

15. The Civic Education Workbook for 1973, "Women in France," is evasive on this point also.

but decisional power was left to women as individuals, an allocation of responsibility that the movement approved. However, as the *Dialoguer* of March–April 1973 shows, many members had objected strenuously to the position taken by the UFCS.

Odile Courtot, the vice president in charge of the issue of reproduction, spelled out the process of consultation and the rationale for the final adoption of policy; she had apparently been accused of imposing her own views on an uninformed council. She personally opposed abortion, she explained carefully, but freedom of choice and respect for others' views were crucial. The discussion in *Dialoguer* brought out details of the UFCS position not mentioned in the press releases. Although "the couple," not just the pregnant woman, was to be given information about abortion, the woman was to make the decision, without consent of the commissions the UFCS envisaged to provide this information and without any doctor's approval. Housing policy was part of a "right-to-life" package, since housing conditions often affect the decision about having children.[16] A year later the woman's right to choose was underlined: the law "must leave to the woman alone the final decision to abort or not abort, by assuring her of conditions that respect her health and her dignity" (*Dialoguer* December 1974–January 1975).

In 1979, when the extension and renewal of the Veil law was being discussed, a Civic Education Workbook, "The Juridical Status of Women," included a discussion of abortion. It summed up the position of the UFCS, noting that it preceded the vote of the 1974 Veil law:

> [The UFCS] reaffirms the right of each person to have or not to have a child and to demand the means to make this choice possible.
>
> While hoping that the responsibility for procreation will be assumed by men as much as by women [the UFCS] recognizes that women should have the liberty to have or not to have children, which implies:
> a) the right to sexual and contraceptive information;
> b) the real resources necessary either for taking a pregnancy to term or for abortion;
> c) initiating the means for giving children their place in society.

The UFCS outlined three possible positions regarding abortion and proceeded to place itself consciously in the middle category. Unlike the interwar UFCS and probably also the postwar group until the middle 1960s, it was not aligned with traditionalists who wished to return to the 1920 legislation, backed by further prochildren and profamily measures. But neither did the UFCS wish to align with the "partisans of a total liberalization of abortion." This latter position the workbook at-

16. This 1973 account also mentions in passing that the controversial press release which provoked members' protests had been drawn up in response to urgent requests for statements on the part of two women's magazines—an indication of the significance attributed to the UFCS's views on this issue.

tributed to the MLAC and also to the mainstream Family Planning (though the document noted that even these groups did not regard abortion as a routine or satisfactory method of contraception).

The 1979 workbook summed up the middle position which the UFCS accepted as follows: "Abortion is a serious act, an intervention against what could become a human life, but one cannot say that all those who carry out—or undergo—an abortion commit a serious fault." The statement no longer referred to life beginning at conception; the next sentence said that abortion was not infanticide. Christians, said the UFCS, ought to be able to accept such a position, and to agree with "movements . . . which expect that society will really let persons fully assume their own responsibility."

In 1979 the executive called for an even bolder policy that would extend unrestricted abortion to the first twelve weeks of pregnancy (after which the law provided a procedure for more restricted therapeutic abortions), along with public funding for the operation. The statement also urged that conscientious refusal by doctors and nurses to carry out abortions should be individual rather than in terms of whole hospital sections, a way in which the medical establishment had been sabotaging the Veil law. Headed "In the name of the right to take responsibility the UFCS takes a position," this program was presented as a report on the "consensus" arrived at by some fifty UFCS study groups including more than a thousand members (*Dialoguer* September–October 1979). But at the end of the year the "Report of Activities, 1979–80" merely noted "the necessity for a law that permits women the recourse to abortion under conditions of safety and respect."[17]

This general position on abortion was a remarkable change for the movement, even if it was one that fitted well into a continuing commitment to greater autonomy for women. However, this progress, or what seems like progress from a feminist perspective, was not accepted as such by all members of the UFCS. The 1979 reports of the study groups showed significant disagreement: twenty-seven had wanted to preserve the Veil law unaltered in order to keep abortion from becoming routine and "banal," while twenty-three had wanted a far more radical liberalization. The first group must have included those UFCS members who still felt that life begins at fertilization—and who wrote indignantly about an editorial in the previous *Dialoguer* where Marie-Laure Roland-Gosselin had defended the Veil law in a lyrical paean to motherhood. As a number of them pointed out, the same issue of *Dialoguer* had included a

17. The role of the legislator was "to support people's taking responsibility." To this was linked a position of "welcome to life, co-responsibility of the couple, and the availability of contraception." There is a positive side to the policy: "Real sharing of responsibility, rights, and tasks between men and women; economic and fiscal policies taking account of the real costs of families; environmental and housing policy corresponding to the needs of family and children, [and] effective administration of the Neuwirth law on contraception" (UFCS 1980).

favorable account of the Marseilles UFCS's involvement with a local coalition put together by the organization Family Planning to support abrogation of the 1920 law and reinstatement of a strengthened Veil law. For some this position seemed hypocritical. For many the UFCS was in this context acting in an unacceptable way to support unacceptable doctrines (*Dialoguer* September–October 1979). This issue forced members to face the implications of deconfessionalization and the potential conflicts between their commitment to the church and their beliefs in the nature of lay organizations. Even in the 1970s many early UFCS activists were still among the leaders and, still more, among the members. Some found it painful to move away from the specific doctrines of the church and even more painful to abandon the practice of uniform and unquestioned formal policies.

A parallel case of the impact of feminists within a social Catholic organization can be seen in the Confédération française des travailleurs chrétiens (CFTC) as it secularized and became the Confédération française démocratique du travail (CFDT). Our main source is the memoirs of Jeannette Laot. Laot was a practicing Catholic, too poor to go to any but state schools but ideologically bound not to affiliate with a Marxist and anticlerical union such as the local of the Communist Confédération générale du travail (CGT). Representative of an all-women tobacco workers' union affiliated with the CFTC, Laot became associated with the "minority stream" interested, after 1945, in reducing the union's dependence on the MRP (by preventing leaders from holding positions simultaneously in both organizations), in deconfessionalizing the union, and generally in producing some union alternative to the too-bourgeois though socialist Force ouvrière (FO) and the militantly Leninist CGT (Laot 1981:42). Laot recounts how she came to join the Women's Commission of the CFDT, established in 1945 when the women's unions were fused with the men's (CFDT-Information 1979:79). Although working originally in an all-women environment and organizing an all-women union in that workplace, she had taken for granted the equality of women in the union and had no interest in being their special representative. Her membership on the commission was part of an attempt at minority influence on a group majoritarian in orientation. Other members of the Women's Commission by and large favored retaining links with the MRP and the church and therefore were conservative in union terms. But in feminist terms they had a radicalizing effect on Laot because they made her aware how little influence women or women's problems had in the unions (56–61). By 1963 the Women's Commission was able to stage a public seminar for women union members to which they brought feminists including Colette Audry. The events of 1968 did not produce a more strongly feminist current in the union, but they also failed to provoke the hostility to the MLF seen in the CGT. And after the declaration of the 343 in 1971, Laot took the issue of abortion to the Executive Committee of which she was the only woman member. The CFDT became the first union organization to call for abrogation of the law of 1920 and produced in 1972, after difficult discussions, an impressive *Dossier on Contraception and Abortion.*

Laot, an old warrior in the union wars, said the campaign on behalf of women was the most painful she ever engaged in. She also felt that it completed the process of deconfessionalization in the CFDT, and she quotes an older woman militant to that effect: "Jeannette, the battle you are engaged in is a great deal harder than the battle of the [free] school, and it is one that will really make the CFDT into a lay organization respectful of personal convictions" (87).

The MRP did not last long enough for the UFCS to fight parallel battles within the party. This was a reflection of the party's incapacity to adapt and survive. Instead, the UFCS worked through the combined issues of deconfessionalization and active support of feminism within its own ranks. And there also the struggle focused on the issues of reproductive rights—as it must in an organization that was French *and* feminist *and* had started Catholic.

A comparison of CFDT and UFCS policies on abortion shows the constraints of union organization. As Laot makes obvious, in the CFDT questions of reproduction cut across the customary division of majority versus minority, for even the break with the church had left virtually unchanged the role of women within the federation. The alliance of union women across different ideological categories was necessary to produce action on reproductive issues.

The edginess felt by the CFDT bureau, even after long discussion, is reflected in their 1972 formulation of policy about reproductive rights. They put the question in context by stating that the issue of contraception is "an integral part of the condition of workers," even though the point is not usually realized. However, a union should not pronounce for or against the use of contraception or abortion, on the grounds that "it is not up to us to substitute ourselves for the persons concerned [in order to] choose, to decide in their place." Religion, ethics, particular situations will determine the choice. A union's responsibility is to act in accordance with a key principle: that society should provide "the conditions of information, the means permitting a free and responsible personal choice." The language is remarkably close to that of the UFCS, as is the insistence that abortion is an "anomaly," a social evil, not an acceptable form of contraception. The echoes or coincidences of perspective continue. Those involved are not to be condemned; instead the social causes for such actions are to be eliminated. In the CFDT's analysis, these causes include the repressive nature of class society. To the UFCS's list of social measures (contraception, education, social support) the union therefore adds changes in legislation, attitudes, and social structures so that women and especially mothers "can choose freely their form of activity and their integration into society." In 1976 the CFDT added the demand that abortion should be covered by social security, to provide for all "the preconditions of a voluntary and conscious procreation" (Laot 1981:219–21). The union had managed to transcend its Catholic origins, though not without difficulty.

For the UFCS the abortion debate was even harder, for it brought to the surface a profound disagreement about the conduct as well as the content of the UFCS. Putting aside abortion policy, what could be interpreted as an admirable adaptation to second-wave feminism seemed to a significant segment of UFCS members the result of manipulation by an unrepresentative group of feminist leaders. The disagreement crystalized around the issue of abortion, which provokes deeply rooted, strongly held, and divisive reactions even in groups without a Catholic tradition. In addition, however, the disagreement represented choices about political activism.

CHAPTER 12

Volunteerism or Politics?

When Frenchwomen finally got the vote, the passage of UFCS members into mainstream politics seemed likely to be straightforward. Five UFCS members participated as MRP representatives at the Fourth Republic's first Constituent Assembly.[1] Eight women made up 7 percent of the MRP representatives, a percentage topped only by the seventeen Communist women who made up 11 percent of their party in the assembly (*LFVS* September 1945; Dogan and Narbonne 1955:153; Michel and Texier 1964 I:183). These women were of a parliamentary cohort that Dogan and Narbonne describe as "specializing fairly specifically in the traditional tasks of the housewife." With an edge of disapproval, Dogan and Narbonne add "they still work like women: they do not work specially for women. They are more feminine than feminist" (1955:165). The UFCS would have had no trouble with this description, which included the women deputies from the Leftist parties.

La femme dans la vie sociale outlined the background of the UFCS women deputies: three, including Peyroles who was also a lawyer and a mother, had been municipal councillors (September 1945). The pattern of involvement in politics ran from UFCS to municipal office, activism in and through the MRP, and finally national office. Certainly the literature comments repeatedly about the role of women members of the MRP, which had the largest membership percentage of women in the 1940s and 1950s. Duverger estimates women membership at 25 percent in 1951, and he adds that according to his informant, "women delegates at the [MRP] party congresses and in the party committees incline more to the Left than the men do" (1955: 104, 105).

1. They were: Marie-Madeleine Dienisch, Solange Lamblin, Germaine Peyroles, Renée Prevert, and Marie Texier-Lahoulle. Peyroles and Dienisch were to have moderately significant political careers. Rabaut describes Peyroles as "one of the outstanding" women deputies (1978:305); she stayed in office until 1951 and had another year in Parliament in 1954–55. Dienisch was one of the few women to hold any Cabinet office in France until very recently (Charlot 1980:189; Brimo 1975:108) and is described by Irving (1973:243) as a "leading" member of the MRP.

But by 1958 the MRP had only two women, including Dienisch, in its small parliamentary contingent and was on its way to extinction. Although the party initially had a major role in postwar governments, it declined rapidly with the growth of Gaullism, and by 1967 it no longer existed (Noonan 1970; Irving 1973; Charlot 1978). The logical channel of advancement for politically ambitious UFCS members in the postwar period had disappeared entirely by the time they might be expected to be seeking it in larger numbers. The attitudes and choices of the UFCS therefore become more diffuse, because Union members could only briefly enjoy any privileged access to partisan influence and national office. As a result the movement retained its pressure group activities and developed a nonpartisan role as a "launching-pad," very much like the one now recognized in the American League of Women Voters. Unlike the League the UFCS did not think of itself as apolitical, but it also experienced tensions between partisan and nonpartisan activities and between versions of feminism and feminist politics. By the end of the 1970s these strains had produced open confrontation. Disagreements within the UFCS crystalized around the difficult issues of feminism and abortion. Those who objected couched their disagreement in terms of models of procedure, opposing public statements on feminist issues. Pressure politics and public education remained priorities for the movement, but actual participation in decision making now became central.

The disputes within the UFCS were triggered by responses to increased opportunities to participate in the formation of policy. Some members now wished to focus on nonelectoral politics, but to make them both more public and more feminist, while others yearned for earlier times when education had been stressed, complemented by small-scale local projects. A third group, not as prominent, was interested in participating directly in electoral politics. Those actually involved in municipal or other mainstream politics were likely to disagree with the new, young feminists who rejected existing organizational structures and also with those who wished to restrict women to self-education and indirect influence. Elected politicians demonstrated the greatest impact of the UFCS and the greatest degree of its evolution. Because they came to politics out of women's concerns and activities and through a woman's group, their participation had major implications for the possibility that women, by their participation, might effect some transformation of politics.

But for most members, who were not interested in elective office, questions about the political role of women had to be fought out within the movement. In 1973, when the problem first emerged in the pages of *Dialoguer*, it was ostensibly in response to the vice president's not having consulted sufficiently before issuing a press release on abortion (March–April). By 1975 the attack had become generalized. A response stated defensively, evidently after repeated criticisms, that since the UFCS was often asked to make public statements on issues, the national executive had to take a stand on behalf of the movement. Their criteria were the following: Does the issue obviously fit the UFCS's goals ("respect of the individual, essential liberties, democratic life")? Do we know enough, and can we control our statement? Who else will be signing a statement? How do we balance the need for a speedy response against our obligation for consultation? How can we keep our response balanced? To illustrate the results of such considerations they listed the public statements made in the previous two months. Of these, the most controversial in content was a protest with a publications group about the image of women in media and against the climate of defamation and violence against women that is related to racism.[2] This was an outright attack on sexism, and one that has since provoked considerable notice and hostility in France; it clearly identified the UFCS as feminist and activist. One can guess that, in general, the content as well as the fact of public statements was causing trouble.

Topics wax and wane in the UFCS, as in all such groups, in response to the interests of activists as well as to the fashions of the day. After 1968 some younger, outspokenly feminist members made an effort to mobilize the institutional and ideological resources of the UFCS in the service of the women's movement. The old section Women and Family, which had become merely Family and then faded away from lack of membership interest, was revived as Women-News (*Femmes-Actualités*) and then, by May 1978, Women. In that year the members of that section were the most active members of the UFCS's governing national executive. They included Marie-Laure Roland-Gosselin, the person most clearly identified with this tendency and a public militant on the abortion issue.

In the February–March issue of *Dialoguer* the journal was described explicitly as the internal organ of a pressure group: the UFCS was an activist organization of women. A National Assembly focusing on pressure group activity was organized. And a semipoetic meditation signed by Roland-Gosselin and one other councillor praised "multiple feminisms." This formulation is unusual in the context of French second-wave feminism, which tends to identify as feminist only those groups growing out of the student left of 1968; it seems likely that readers would perceive the article as affirming allegiance to the MLF and its successors.

That was issue 57; an undated special issue, no. 60 (1978–79), pushed harder to identify the UFCS as feminist or at least as focused on women. Entitled "Myself as a Woman," the special issue contrasted the helpless-

2. The other public statements were a denunciation of conditions in Spain, issued in the company of an established grouping of youth and adult education organizations and an International Women's Year coalition; a telegram to the president about the release of Françoise Claustre, issued with other women's groups; objection to the *Express* serialization of the pornographic novel *L'histoire d'O*; expression to the government of (solicited) opinion on the "Plan de Relance."

ness of the isolated individual woman with the resources of women together and concluded, "Let us fight for our rights as women, in solidarity."[3] The layout was stylish, the photographs elegant, and this issue was printed on glazed paper; the language was militant. It was a recruiting document that identified the UFCS as a "women's movement" as well as "a movement of continuing education, [and] a movement of consumers which brings together women of diverse tendencies and permits them to act together for greater justice and solidarity." The front page showed pictures of "Myself as a Woman," the back spoke of "we women" as "little groups of women and teams all across France [getting together] to reflect and act locally." In retrospect, one can imagine the effect on the long-time, middle-class member who joined the UFCS for good works and self-education or even on the middle-aged community activist who had worked her way into municipal politics.

In March–April 1980 *Dialoguer* seemed to be continuing on its explicitly feminist course. A front-page story asked if feminism was outmoded and used case histories and readers' letters to show it was not.[4] There were also letters from divorced, abandoned, and battered women and an article about a new series of UFCS courses on automobile maintenance. A full page was devoted to UFCS members' participation in a women's collective that was agitating for the establishment of a community center for sexual education and family planning, and an article on "the husband, the wife, and taxes" discussed "the financial dependence of women in the couple." The St. Maur section reported its decision not to participate in a group of "S.O.S. emergency help to mothers" that entailed unremunerated home care of infants for periods of up to forty-eight hours: the state should provide such services and pay caregivers. Moreover, providing such services keeps women out of the employment market, sidetracks them from action-oriented groups such as the UFCS, and "maintains masculine status." Such projects, the reader was told, undercut efforts at sharing tasks and mutual support within the couple. All very feminist.

But there were some danger signs. In the article about the health-care collective some UFCS members expressed concern over the "politically engaged" feminism of others who "want to exercise power . . . to shake up the masculine system, demedicalize information, even certain medical acts . . . to attack the power of doctors, to make their own ideology succeed . . . to challenge regulations and even law." And a "very urgent" message in large print on the front page announced that the national executive of the UFCS had decided at its May meetings to cancel the

3. "Luttons pour nos droits nous femmes solidaires."
4. The examples were: a post office employee does not allow a young woman to sign for a postal savings book for her son; shopkeepers chide women customers for being too assertive; a woman manager moves to a small town in the north with her husband and is told it is absurd for a woman to look for work at the executive level.

national Committee and General Assembly scheduled, as usual, for the next June: "The fundamental questions that are posed today for the life of the movement [the UFCS] justify this decision." Local and regional meetings would allow all members "to discuss the arguments and propositions that the Council is going to address to them personally."

The next issue of *Dialoguer*, another special one, showed what was going on. The UFCS, like all voluntary organizations, had problems with decline of membership and with decreasing participation; also, government support for such groups might be decreased. At the same time, certain regional sections had been reluctant to support initiatives of the national council. Under these circumstances the yearly council effort to define priorities had apparently turned into an attempt to galvanize this aging organization into something explicitly activist and feminist. As part of this effort, normal consultative procedures had been canceled while the council sent a letter to all members proposing a redefinition of the UFCS and asking for responses from groups and sections. This letter set the council's suggestions in the context of threat to the movement, starting with assertions that: "The power of association is threatened. All associations are threatened. Association itself is threatened. Our asso-ciation is threatened" (UFCS May 16, 1980). The more overtly femi-nist tone of *Dialoguer* had also, apparently, been part of the attempt at reformulation, intended to make the movement more attractive and more dynamic.

After a month of intense discussion about one hundred sixty comments had been received from groups, and about as many individual members also sent in responses. A carefully picked team (including dele-gates of sections or regions, members of sections, animatrices, and coun-cillors) concluded that responses were clearly divided between the origi-nal—feminist and activist—proposal and a position opposed to it. A complex, decentralized system of voting on the two alternatives was set up. The journal issue printed the resulting motions, along with alterna-tive definitions of key terms such as pluralism, militantism, and femi-nism, as well as the relationship between training and action. The im-plications of the competing positions were drawn out honestly, backed by what look like representative letters from partisans on both sides.

The contrast was clear, and it is one familiar to the student of women's organizations. On one hand was an activist, even aggressive militantism that saw the united action of women as a basis for remaking society, that wished to focus on initiatives producing change, that would rely on hired and appropriately paid staff members to replace less expert volunteers, and that saw working women as a crucial target. Popular education would still be central, but it would enable women to act collectively, to get them "ready to work to transform society." This was the council's pro-gram, formulated as option A. It was probably supported by younger, more recent members of the UFCS. For them, "pluralism" was likely to delay or even inhibit action, and majority decisions of council must be allowed to direct "militancy." They saw the UFCS as feminist and were proud of it; for them, feminism was political, and they were happy it was so. Andrée Butillard would, I think, have recognized them as fellow-spirits, however much she might have disagreed with specifics of their feminism.

The opposing, option B supporters seem to have been older members who would have preferred to leave politics and social reconstruction to other movements (the MLF, for instance, or political parties); the UFCS should get women ready to join such other groups but should not act like them. Political interventions? only at the local level or if all members agree. Volunteerism should be relied on. The UFCS was "feminine," that is, a women's group but not a feminist one. Any earlier notion of a moderate feminism was now forgotten, and feminism was interpreted as man-hating, confrontational, alienating, hostile to the family. Supporters of option B stressed the domestic role of women along with the family context.

The tension between education and action, staff and volunteers, the desire to be apolitical and to serve as a launching-pad rather than to intervene directly—these are struggles within the League of Women Voters as well. They emerged in the Guild only in its days of decline, in part because commitment to the co-operative movement disarmed even the strongest feminists. Distinctive in the UFCS is the identification of feminism as a political and even a partisan alternative. Within French politics, feminism as articulated by the supporters of option A could not look nonaligned, let alone claim to be apolitical. It had to be interpreted as leftist, bringing with it a whole history of anticlericalism. Paradoxically enough, the French feminist tradition also incorporated a deep distrust of the whole paraphernalia of mainstream and particularly partisan political structures.

Of those UFCS members who voted on the choice between options A and B, about 54 percent opted for B, the older pattern. The reaction of the council was to resign en masse, protesting that they had simply attempted to "dynamize" the movement "by proposing that the members accentuate the associative power, that they carry out vigorous national actions, and that they develop the power of women." They had had no intention of renouncing the traditional pluralism of the UFCS in developing global action and national positions (*Dialoguer* November–December 1980). This statement was disingenuous, for the options had significant content; at issue was not just procedure but also goals.

Nevertheless, if the newly elected president abjured the rhetoric of her predecessors, she did not entirely abandon their positions. In her first statement in *Dialoguer* she stressed the centrality of education for the organization: "Our originality . . . is founded in large part on the training provided by the movement." But she continued, in a way recognizably activist and feminist, "education has no meaning if it does not lead to action, action starting from where we live, there where we are, in our own time." Such action, she warned, means change, destruction of established habits, "an enlargement in our way of seeing, a change in our way of life." The movement was not interested in power for women but in participating, in a way complementary to all forces of progress, in areas such as domestic and international poverty, ignorance, the plight of the young, jobs, housing, quality of life. The UFCS did not struggle for "a narrow egalitarianism with the other sex—we have our own richness" (January–March 1981).

This is a traditional social feminism. In 1981 it selected as priority projects the preparations for the presidential elections (members were asked to rank a list of ten topics), a survey of women's purchasing habits (option A had focused on consumer action rather than education and put consumerism low on its list of priorities), and a "White Book" describing women's lives in their own words. Yet this familiar mixture of goals and activities is far from abandoning the changes that have occurred since the 1960s. The White Book was described as intended to give a voice to those who are still unheard, so that they may "speak, describe, denounce" (*Dialoguer* September–October).[5] Alongside more conventional projects related to local history, children's out-of-school activities, and hospitalization of infants, UFCS sections were involved with drugs and drug abuse, genital mutilation, transition houses, and the rights of single women. The new council, many members of which stress the importance of women working not just for themselves but for a better world for all, included at least one reelected councillor who had supported option A on the old council and another who identified herself as a feminist. Option A partisans seem to have been more active in the movement, and option B supporters, having made their point, had no desire to take over the activities necessary to the running of the movement.

To evaluate the impact of this dramatic episode, it is useful to look at the next issue of *Dialoguer* (April–May 1981), once again in the more expensive magazine format. The theme was "Innovate or Vanish," and an editorial defined the goal of the restructured journal: the search to contact and interact with women who are not members. This is an option B preference, but it is also thoroughly compatible with feminism. Inside, the ranking of suggested themes to be presented to the presidential candidates put "human rights"—in French, the "rights of man"—at the head of the list and "women" almost at the bottom. Respondents' comments made it clear they considered all the areas connected; they also rejected any special consideration for women. A typical comment was that "all is connected: Education, News, Quality of Life, Health, Stan-

5. Staff members told me this was a more innovative project than it appears to the outsider; it had been proposed in 1976 but never got under way.

dard of living, Women's problems, Employment." For instance, the right to work was described as "an essential right of men, women, the young." Finally, the last comment quoted was one that asserted, "Women, who are human beings in every respect, don't have to be considered in relation to their specific problems in an electoral program: their problems are found in all the others." This looks like equity feminism, rather surprising in the UFCS. But it can also be seen as an assertion that women are not problems but problem solvers. Certainly other reported activities bear out the latter interpretation. In a similar vein, Margaret Maruani reported that union women she talked with at the CFDT were reluctant to articulate any "women's problems" and more inclined to stress the ways in which "they could bring something" to working-class struggles (1979:99); they focused on their positive contributions rather than their difficulties.

The UFCS, it seems, was continuing its feminist activity. As the same issue of *Dialoguer* reported, the project to gather women's testimony had produced in Lyons under UFCS auspices what was first a consciousness-raising group and then a women's center. A short play used in the preprofessional courses was reprinted; it lamented the tendency of participants to be "misogynist," to think of women as secondary earners, and to stereotype jobs. "If each of us is ready for personal advancement," it asked, "why is there so much hesitation about the collective development of women?" And the Tours section wrote about involvement with a rape case. They wanted the UFCS to change its statutes to include "the battle against sexual violence" as one of its goals so that they could bring charges in rape cases. Topics and attitudes suggest that, after all, the UFCS had managed to travel into the second wave of feminism.

At the same time the movement had become a resource and support for women who wished to move into the more conventional political arena of partisan politics. Alongside the militant feminists and the volunteers or *bénévoles* were a substantial number of politically active women. Unfortunately, we have no way to look directly at the opinions of UFCS members holding or desiring elected office.[6] But a certain amount of material is available about the political role and opinions of the large mass of members and, more specifically, about the many who became active in municipal politics.

The earliest relevant example is to be found in the 1965 special issue of *La femme dans la vie sociale* marking the movement's fortieth anniversary. Three anonymous and archetypal members were interviewed on the topic "Why did we come to the UFCS?" The three were an active member from a working-class milieu in Brittany, a municipal councillor who was also the mother of a large family, and "a young mother" from Paris.

6. I could not even be certain I had identified all the UFCS deputies, and it proved virtually impossible to get information about them. Politicians at the municipal or volunteer level rarely appear in any sort of literature.

The working woman had previous organizational experience in a work-ing-class family organization but preferred the UFCS and found that being in a women-only group made her more rather than less effective; she had become active as an organizer, speaker, and demonstrator. The councillor relied on the UFCS for necessary information and had found-ed a new UFCS section locally to train other housewives and also to provide a support and consultative group through which she might find out housewives' views. The young mother saw the UFCS mainly as edu-cational, justified it as helping her educate her children, but would, thanks to the UFCS, move into civic involvement as her children left her more free time. The general message was that in 1965 the woman activ-ist, even when elected to office, had not yet moved out of the designated female sphere of activities. But she was preparing to. The UFCS's con-tinuing educational and recruitment role showed no signs of abating.

Three years later another group of members identified by category was described under the heading "They Are the UFCS." The article included accounts of four women who were not individualized but were used to represent what the UFCS would like its members to be and what it would like them to find in the movement: a housewife, a lawyer, a teacher of home economics, and the mother of a large family.[7] The fifth woman was the most interesting. A municipal councillor, formerly a trade unionist, she commented: "At the UFCS I learned about politics and got ready for politics," moving to it through "civic action." At the UFCS she learned to use but not be ensnared by a political party. She noted that her own interest was in the economic consequences of the Fifth National Plan and that her movement training enabled her to be active in the municipal council on this issue (*Dialoguer* February–March 1968). Her interests represented, we may note, a significant extension of the domestic.

Feminine interests, feminine situation, feminine organization, politi-cal consequences—by this time the process was clear and its goal recog-nized. In 1973 the movement denied apoliticism: "Let us remember that we remain outside of the battle of political parties. We have no aspira-tions to take over power. . . . But to identify ourselves as 'apolitical' would be dishonest, would be to condemn ourselves to inactivity" (*Dia-loguer* February–March). Two years later there was a careful examina-tion of the relationship of women to partisanship. An article on politics and coherence recommended against choosing or accepting a party be-cause of the "social group" it corresponded to, that is, religious or class identity. The author remarked in passing that "a Catholic could today

7. The housewife, obviously middle-class, described the group as "a movement where you become adult," and the woman lawyer spoke of the "concern to act competently." The teacher of home economics was from a rural school and said she had "found the common good preferred to the individual [in the UFCS]," while the mother of a large family stressed that "the UFCS is open to all social classes."

find moral comfort in belonging to a party either of 'the Left' or 'the Right,'" and there is no need to underline the importance of such a statement coming from a group that began in social Catholicism. Women were told to make the effort to inform themselves on the programs of all the parties and to mistrust the information the parties themselves offered. But finally, however reluctantly, they would have to choose. On the facing page an article examined the question of party membership under the title "Political Parties and Feminism," accompanied by rather surprising feminist cartoons: a male party speaker boring a group of women by economistic mystification, a group of male listeners envisaging a female orator nude, a woman trying to squeeze her way to a place at a male-surrounded conference table. The conclusion was: go to it, from *civisme* to *politique,* and our movement will give you the means to do it effectively (*Dialoguer* April–May 1975).

A major focus was the municipal level. The previous election had doubled the number of women councillors; the goal in 1975 was 50 percent women. A UFCS announcement headed "Objective: the Mairie" announced new *Dossiers* and courses for that purpose (*Dialoguer* April–May). This, the fiftieth anniversary issue, was unmistakably feminist in its description of the impact of the movement on its members: "After a certain number of meetings in a group, in training sessions, a woman becomes aware that she exists in herself and not in relation to others. She stops blaming herself, detaches herself from the image of a woman made only to be an effective mother, an admirable wife." The back page, about sexism and stereotyping in advertising, reproduced a sadistic advertisement showing a woman in bondage.

In the same year another set of personifications of membership summarized the UFCS's self-image. Members were described as having a remarkable range of ways of life, the result of "thoughtful choice"; they were contrasted with those other women who are passive and fearful, relating to the world only through their husbands. Interestingly (and realistically), six out of seven prototype members were presented as in or having had experience with the paid labor force. The seventh was a grandmother who now wanted a free life and therefore would not commit herself to permanent childcare responsibilities; there was no suggestion she ought to be considered selfish or unfeminine. Only one of those in the paid labor force was there unwillingly, the young wife of an unemployed worker engaged in a retraining program; she had selected ill-paid knitting work because it could be done at home and combined with care of her three small children. Women like her had always made up the bulk of the UFCS membership, along with those like the next example, a relatively prosperous woman who had worked for six years before marriage and four children. In a more modern pattern another member, aged fifty-two, had returned to part-time work after a UFCS retraining course. An older woman, almost sixty, had been introduced to the movement by her daughter; she was now an organizer for Golden Age groups at the UFCS. Yet another member combined care of her three small children with volunteer work, the latter substituting for and preferable to the part-time job she had had before. All of these patterns are reasonably easy to accommodate within earlier expectations of the UFCS; they are current adaptations of older models. The seventh representative member, however, is different. Mother of two, she had always worked for pay. Her husband made a good income—they could always afford live-in help—and she worked because she wanted to. She was also, of course, active with the UFCS.

To French feminists, the emphases in this list on part-time work, volunteerism, and relatively large families damn the UFCS as reactionary or at best conservative. To social feminists, of course, such emphases are perfectly acceptable to the extent they can be seen as compatible with or deriving from women's autonomy. Crucial is an insistence on women's own choices, as well as the acceptance of a variety of possible relationships between home, paid labor, and civic action. On all these fronts UFCS views continued to become more feminist.

In 1976 the UFCS launched a concerted but still unsuccessful campaign to increase the number of women in municipal government from 20,000 to 100,000. On the *Dialoguer* front page announcing the campaign, a cartoon showed a city council committee of five men seated around the table. The chairman was saying, "Well, gentlemen, the problem is simple. You are pregnant and you are working. Do you want a communal crèche or not?" (*Dialoguer* February–March). A large drawing on the same page showed a young woman and a small child holding up a sign asking why the number of women in municipal office should not be doubled. A loaded shopping basket was sitting nearby as she announced, "Civic life is everyday life."[8] Surely the the Women's Co-operative Guild's symbol, the Woman with a Basket, broods over this perfect statement of social feminism's views about politics.

The same remarkable issue of *Dialoguer* included the results of a poll on "the social status of the mother" answered by 760 persons; the illustration was a bearded young man, wearing a wedding ring, holding and feeding a small infant. Just under half of those responding thought the most important part of a family policy would be "measures favoring a better sharing of responsibilities between men and women," including attitude change, shorter working hours for all, and parental leave. The author of the report compared it to views expressed by Simone Veil, the much respected minister of health, and noted rather snippily that Veil seemed to think that only mothers had to reconcile work and home responsibilities. By contrast, the members of the UFCS, "women who have reflected on the question and who are experiencing the situation,"

8. "La vie de la commune c'est la vie de tous les jours."

favored a redistribution of tasks. They were also, in increasing numbers, involved in actual political office.

In the December 1983–January 1984 *Dialoguer* "Anne" was typical of these municipal officials. A real individual, she came to the municipal council in Rennes from the UFCS, consumers' affairs, and—something new—the women's center in Rennes.[9] The UFCS had given her the specialized training she needed, and she was moving from single-issue advocacy to larger questions of general policy and party politics (nonparty herself, she had been invited to stand for office on the slate of the unified Left). Apparently she did not see herself as a feminist. Equally clearly, she brought specific social feminist priorities and perspectives with her. She was prepared to see herself as political and to deal with political parties and with political structures. And so, by this time, was that majority of the UFCS membership which was not involved in elected office.

But what perceptions—what ideology—can explain this adaptation by the UFCS? I have traced the Union's movement into second-wave feminism and politicization through the movement's publications. My interpretations are validated by four surveys that touch more directly on the political perceptions of UFCS members. Three of these surveys questioned women active in volunteer groups or municipal politics; the fourth, conducted by the UFCS in 1983, asked the movement's members about feminism and politics (Renard 1965:100–140; Guérin 1975; Gros 1971; *Dialoguer* October–November 1983).[10] The four groups of women were similar: urban, lower-middle-class, mostly married, and mostly with children. The clubwomen tended to be in the mid-forties; the municipal officers were a bit younger (43 percent of Gros's sample were under forty) and had slightly fewer children than the clubwomen, who had average or above-average numbers of children. The elected officials also had slightly more professional experience, though none of the differences looks significant. It seems reasonable to treat all as a group and to extrapolate from them to the UFCS.

Let us start with the study by Brigitte Gros of women elected to municipal office in a Paris suburb (les Yvelines) in 1970. These women were, like the others, community activists with wide organizational memberships. Predictably, they did not identify themselves as feminists. Nevertheless, some 30 percent felt that the events of May 1968 had facilitated their entry into politics. They seem unaffected by the MLF; 86 percent of the group denied any such connection. Rather, their access

9. This is not a radical women's center but the Centre rennais d'information pour les femmes, "mis en place par les associations féminines" (*Dialoguer* December 1983–January 1984).

10. Renard is a UFCS member and political activist; Gros, sister of Jean-Jacques Servan-Schreiber, was a Radical party senator.

was eased by a climate of general social upheaval and questioning (44, 45). Support from husbands and children was seen as crucial, and the group stressed the importance of what they saw as egalitarian marriages as "trampolines" for public activity (23). They showed a moderate degree of political ambition: 36 percent would have liked to advance at least to their preferred level of the Conseil Général of the Department, though they had little interest in national politics. The 30 percent who flatly denied further political aspirations were likely to cite their lack of training as the major reason. The stress of the UFCS on *formation* seems highly relevant here. Finally, they overwhelmingly (80 percent) felt that being a woman had *facilitated* their involvement in politics. Many mentioned that they entered electoral politics on invitation from someone else; Jeane Kirkpatrick's sample of effective female state legislators in the United States, whom these women resemble in many ways, reported similar careers (1974). For social and economic reasons (basically, their availability) they were able to take these local jobs, and they found feminine psychology useful. Their specializations, again predictably, were in education, urbanization and environment, and the budget. The 10 percent who found being a woman disadvantageous tended to cite structural barriers rather than female qualities that might interfere with political effectiveness (46).[11]

We may compare Renard's 1965 study of women active in voluntary groups; many were members of the UFCS, and they are in effect Gros's respondents before they entered or were enticed into politics. Aware that the participation of women in public life has increased, Renard's respondents wanted and expected this process to continue. They reasoned: women are equal by nature (28.6 percent); because all things are connected, that is, presumably because women's special concerns are related to everything else (17.5 percent), because men and women are complementary (40 percent)(119–20). At the same time some 25 percent felt that in practice politics as it existed in France made it difficult for women to participate (121). Politics demanded combativeness and also background and specialized training, all things that women tended not to have; politics was too tiring and too hard on family life; finally, to succeed, women had to be better than men, for equal capacity was not enough. A difference resulting from intrinsic qualities or experience is clearly implied and, indeed, respondents went on to say that women's participation in politics should be different from men's, reflecting women's warmth, their intuitiveness, and their sense of detail and the concrete. Theirs is a traditional view of the role and nature of women and a social feminist logic for activism. We have no way of knowing if the minority views were held by the small proportion of this group which would take part in elected politics.

11. The demographics and attitudes are close to those of twenty-one Quebec *mairesses* interviewed in 1980 (Tardy 1982).

Ten years later, in Chantal Guérin's in-depth interviews with women who moved from such organizations to elected positions in municipal politics, the UFCS was astonishingly prominent, for four out of the seven interviewed referred appreciatively to their membership in the movement. In addition they noted, as does Guérin, that other women on municipal councils, including those elected under a party rubric, often turned to the UFCS for help after taking office. Training related to budgetary matters was mentioned with particular frequency. Madame E. discussed what she got from the UFCS sessions: technical competence, vocabulary, contact with a network of other individuals in the same situation, self-confidence, and the ability to express herself and to take the floor in discussions. Here the again are echoes of the Women's Co-operative Guild, and we may remember the role the Guild played in making it possible for women to move into municipal politics.

Guérin excluded from her sample women who were recruited by political parties or entered partisan politics through them, although anecdotal evidence in UFCS publications shows that many members did in fact enter politics by such a route. This preselection makes it unsurprising that her respondents showed uneasiness about political parties and connected that uneasiness with their general lack of enthusiasm for other elected positions. "We have the feeling of getting something done in a commune," said Madame F. (28). Madame D. noted that she was not like the "political operators who know how to cook up electoral stews" (25). These women did not think they had the necessary cunning for such activities, and they did not much want it. Indeed, most of these local officials did not see what they were doing as political. "Militancy" was something that happens in unions and political parties, with which they were not involved. Among those interviewed, the only one with possible political ambitions was uncertain whether she would run again. Madame G. was considering waiting until a substantial number of women could stand for office at the same time and then work together. She did see office-holding as important for improving the situation of women, however, and she had certainly become something of a feminist since taking office (though she did not use that term): "It took me a while to realize that what I do here could be done by anyone. Here I work like a man, I do urbanism like a man. . . . If you have a political career, you get gobbled up by the masculine world. It's not a matter of taking men's places. . . . Women have to contribute to creating a new humanity." She was dubious about the value of women's role in municipal politics: "Municipal problems are more and more often questions of administration . . . important matters are settled nationally or internationally, where men run things." And although she was most sympathetic to the Socialist party, she would not join it because "there's no place for women there" (30).

Guérin concluded by discussing the relationship of the women officials to the organizations from which they came. She noted that the training given by the UFCS, though it continued to center on specifics such as budgets, increasingly included what in another context would be called assertiveness training—learning how to take power, how to be comfortable with one's own forcefulness, and so on. Technical competence, which must be learned, was not enough, but fortunately the other skills could also be acquired. If women's interests and motivation came from their domestic role, the necessary political abilities could and must be deliberately learned. The UFCS previously urged dissimulation, suggesting ideas in such a way that men seemed to have originated them. Today, women neither believe nor pretend to believe that incompetence and limits follow from being female. Guérin also commented on the tensions that develop between elected officials and volunteer groups. The groups were serving as launching-pads, and one consequence was stress for elected women, who lost the solidarity of the group and could not replace it with solidarity among elected women or elected officials in general. Elected because they were women, the officials were nevertheless unlikely to support any "program of feminine action" (37). Guérin therefore perceived the election of women to office mainly as a means of integrating women into public life, analogous to the election of members of minority groups. However, she did suggest tentatively that women may in fact bring into politics not so much a prowoman program as a "sense of the real," a concern for running a community like a household. They would be superhousewives, or super-ménagères (37). The terminology is very close to Elsa Chaney's supermadres, the Latin American women in political positions who saw themselves as playing an expanded household role (1971, 1979).

The UFCS poll of 1983 supports the same conclusions. Directed to environmental policies, it used the occasion to ask some general questions about women and politics. About one-third of respondents had participated in collective activities related to the environment, and about one-fourth were active in associations for environmental protection; presumably those UFCS members who concentrate on direct entry of women into mainstream politics were underrepresented, as were those involved with training and retraining projects or more obviously feminist causes such as sexism or violence against women. The respondents appeared, however, to be typical UFCS members. More than a third were in the paid labor force, but only 14 percent had never worked for pay. Their occupations were "female" ones such as office work, medical or paramedical services, social services, and teaching. Their educational level was quite high: one-third had their high-school diploma (BAC), and 23 percent had more advanced degrees. They were slightly younger than respondents in the other studies, ranging from sixteen to eighty-two but with half under forty-two years old. A high percentage was married or in other permanent relationships (80 percent) and had children (half had two or three children, 11 percent had five or more); they linked their environmental concerns, especially health hazards, to their children. About one-fourth were involved in volunteer work, presumably in the UFCS itself.

This reasonably representative group of UFCS members felt, in an overwhelming majority, that at least sometimes women had a particular role to play in politics; only 36 percent disagreed with the proposition. To set these views in context we may look at responses to a similar question posed by a Eurobarometer survey in 1974: "Do you think that a woman should play the same role in politics as a man or a different role?" Overall in the European Community, 32 percent of women favored a different role. For Frenchwomen the figure was 41 percent, the highest in the Community (Rabier 1975:105–9). However, the surveys also found few Frenchwomen involved in any women's organizations (Rabier 1983:148), and only a small minority were members of two or more associations of any kind (Rabier 1979:204). UFCS respondents were thus clearly different, in activities and in views, from the majority of their countrywomen.

The principal exposition of the European data interpreted the "egalitarian" response (the same role for men and women) as more progressive and feminist. But scholars who performed a factor analysis of the same material pointed out how difficult it was to interpret questions about different roles for men and women in politics: "An obstinate traditionalist and deliberate liberationist might both think, for varying reasons, that men and women should play different roles in politics" (Inglehart and Inglehart 1975:190). And a 1978 cluster analysis of similar Eurobarometer data found the conviction that women would improve legislatures associated with other profeminist positions. The conviction was supported by arguments certainly implying a different role for women: women's problems would be handled better, and women would treat parliamentary life more seriously (Roche 1979:232). "Feminist" women with such a cluster of beliefs existed in every country of Europe.[12]

At issue are all the old, difficult distinctions between feminist and feminine, women's rights and women's issues, equity feminism and social feminism. All we can say here is that an identifiable group of women enters politics with backgrounds and motivations different from those of most (male) politicians. Being female has facilitated their recruitment into local politics; they were invited to run partly because of their experience in local affairs, partly as representatives of women, but mainly because, unlike men and women who are working for pay, they are available. Even more important, experience related to being female pro-

---

12. In 1987, 33 percent of the sample of European women told Eurobarometer they thought things would be better if there were more women in parliament. The question about different political roles for women and men was not repeated after the 1975 survey (Faits et opinions 1987:35).

duced an interest in policy that made them active in volunteer groups, including the UFCS. Their activism has not been prevented by their insistence that families come first and take precedence over public involvement—an involvement that originally derived from and was intended to serve those families. The UFCS is one of a number of groups that give such women a necessary apprenticeship in civic action and then mainstream politics, an apprenticeship that is informal and unconscious in most cases but relatively deliberate and formal in the case of the UFCS.

It is interesting to compare the present-day UFCS to its far more limited and conservative offspring, the Mouvement mondial des mères (MMM). In 1981 the MMM carried out a very extensive survey of members on the topic "Are the Roles of Father and Mother Interchangeable?" About two thousand responses were received, mostly from France but also from nine European countries, five African countries that were formerly French possessions, and seven other countries including Canada and the United States. Most of the respondents were under forty years of age (66 percent), two-thirds were female, most (66 percent) came from the countryside or from cities and towns (1). This group, we might think, ought to be conservative, even reactionary, given its close involvement with an unabashedly profamily organization of Catholic orientation.

Analysts of the survey obviously had trouble with the responses, which were not what they or we would expect, and they give only partial results. In a first section the analysts reported an overwhelming support of interchangeable roles for parents. Even for the care of very young children, over 90 percent felt both parents should be involved equally. A few individual responses are cited in the opposite direction, but even these favored a relatively egalitarian family structure: they would educate children the same way, they think it necessary for girls to be trained for a job as boys are, they divide or want to divide all household tasks equally (83 percent, even for infant care), and they think that such changes will improve family life. As the analysts reported somewhat plaintively, one young couple with two small children was "almost the only one to pose the question: 'Isn't the similarity of roles of Father and Mother going to pose problems for our children on the psychological level? Aren't there dangers related to identification?'" Among the young, those most strongly committed to role-sharing, "only one young man, aged 27, writes,'The authority of the Father will be diminished. The Mother will not longer have her role of love to play; she will be devalued'" (5).

It is obvious what answers were wanted, and the analysts managed to find them in the comments on single-parent families. Here respondents agreed overwhelmingly that children suffer in the absence of a parent.

Why they suffer is less clear. Certainly the task of child-rearing is almost impossible for one person, and certainly also there are problems with how the family is treated by others. The analysts chose to highlight comments that stated a need for a masculine or feminine model for sons or daughters. They concluded that tasks could and perhaps should now be shared, but a basic functional difference, not clearly expressed or understood, had something to do with establishing a sexual identity: "From their deepest nature, man and woman are different and complementary physically, psychologically, and intellectually." The key distinction was "between material tasks, which are interchangeable . . . and the deep nature of paternal and maternal roles, which are not" (15). For this male respondent, in fact, tasks were not really "interchangeable" at all, since he wished to retain their sex-linked differentiation. That is, the responsibility, the obligation, and the entitlement remain assigned to either mother or father, although on occasion the other parent may perform the tasks. The MMM agreed, as the early UFCS would have done. The present UFCS would not.

Men should perform female tasks when necessary. . . . In a clearly related way the message of the UFCS had originally been: Women must undertake male tasks now, because it is necessary. This position led to the conviction that such tasks were not masculine at all. Relevant specific changes include, of course, the rights of women so long neglected. But they include more importantly the human well-being of society, once a task of women in families, now a task that needs to be seen to by society as a whole. These were the arguments that moved the women of the UFCS into politics, whether partisan politics, or feminism, or volunteerism. The same processes occurred in the United States, where the League of Women Voters considered itself to be neither partisan, nor feminist, and even political. The League was certainly wrong on two of those counts.

PART IV

THE LEAGUE OF
WOMEN VOTERS

In 1915 Carrie Chapman Catt became president of the National American Woman Suffrage Association (NAWSA) and looked forward with her customary vigor to the imminent victory of the suffrage cause. "We must look for women who have political talent," she told the NAWSA convention. "We who have come down from the last generation are reformers, but reformers are bad politicians. Then let us strengthen our weaknesses by careful specialization" (Peck 1944:238). Her audience contained the last of a long succession of women responsible in fifty-two years of suffragist effort for four hundred eighty legislative campaigns for state suffrage, forty-seven state constitutional convention campaigns, thirty national political party convention campaigns to get woman suffrage into party platforms, nineteen campaigns in successive congresses to get the woman suffrage amendment submitted for ratification, and then the difficult ratification campaign itself (Peck 1944:5). Most people would consider what the suffragists had done as political. Catt did not.

Nor did she consider the suffragists' successors political. When asked in 1920 about the role of the new League of Women Voters (LWV) after enfranchisement, she replied, "In the League of Women Voters we have an anomaly; we are going to be a semi-political body. We want political things; we want legislation; we are going to educate for citizenship. In [the League] we have got to be non-partisan and all-partisan [and] to educate." She told women to join political parties and at the same time be active in the League: "You must convert your respective parties to have confidence in you and confidence in the League. I warn you that there is about one man in twenty-five who will be big enough to understand that a Democrat can work with a Republican in a non-partisan body and be loyal to their respective parties!" (Peck 1944:325). For her, as for so many others, political meant partisan. She helped set up the League of Women Voters to be different.[1]

1. I use "the League" and "LWV" to refer to the national organization, located in Washington, D.C., which more or less coordinates subsidiary branches. The national-level

241

Very few men—or women—managed to understand the resulting persistent nonpartisanship of the League. The organization became the stereotypical symbol of American women's limited capabilities for politics. For instance, the guidelines for equal treatment of the sexes that McGraw-Hill prepared for use in its publications warned editors and authors that women should not be "type-cast" in traditional jobs but "shown in a wide variety of professions and trades: as doctors and dentists, not always as nurses . . . as members of Congress, not always as members of the League of Women Voters" (reprinted in Eastman 1984:361). The League is seen as conservative, even reactionary, "the right wing of the women's movement" (Deckard 1982:284), and as part of a "regressive trend moving women away from the central area of professional politics." Although the League may be described as "the dominant voice for women in politics in the United States," such comments are likely to be part of its indictment for directing women's attention toward service rather than "the broader social, political, or economic system" (Stucker 1977:279–80). Even an analyst who approved of the group referred dubiously to allegations about the League's "political virginity" and felt it was "handicapped by being outsiders to the political process [and] by an inability to consider power as neutral, rather than innately bad" (Gruberg 1968:114).

Such critical comments, only a small sample of what has been said about the League,[2] present the familiar picture of women as politically marginal and inept. The only empirical study of the group characterized it as follows: "Still nonpartisan by charter, women members lobby for good government legislation and on behalf of issue positions they have thoroughly researched" (described in Baxter and Lansing 1980:120). Unusually, the author accepts the League as political and employs a sample of LWV board members to represent a group halfway between

---

group was called the League of Women Voters of the United States until 1944 when it became the National League of Women Voters, the title it retains. At this point the state leagues were abolished in their original form and became less influential—though I was told by League staff in Washington that the state leagues remain important in such major state-focused campaigns as support for the Equal Rights Amendment. In the interwar period the state leagues were the source of the social feminist reform measures approved by the national conventions. Some state leagues continued active in relation to both social feminist and equity issues during the period when the national was not involved. It also seems clear that other state leagues have been far more conservative than the national. But there is only indirect documentation on any of the state leagues at central headquarters. I do no more than refer to the state leagues.

2. Banks (1981:154) says dismissively that "in so far as it was political at all [the League] acted mainly as a pressure group to further a number of issues about which women might be expected to speak with a common voice." Evans identifies the League as one of a number of "political education societies" that inherited the remnants of the nonmilitant suffrage movements in various countries and writes contemptuously that the LWV "lacked a real cause. All that kept them going was institutional inertia—the unwillingness of their officials and leaders to abandon the organisational life, and their inability to find a role in conventional politics" (Evans 1977:212).

registered voters and party officials, "women participating more than minimally in politics." But even she condemned their nonpartisanship: "However intensely league members embrace politics, the impacts of their efforts are necessarily blunted because they choose not to participate in the selection, campaigns, or advisement of individual candidates, and it is these successful candidates and their appointees who hold the bulk of formal political power in this country" (120). Without discussing why the League adopted such a position, the analysis joins those which see nonpartisanship as characteristic of women, even women described as "sophisticated political activists." The only explanation offered is a reference to studies showing women to be relatively averse to conflictual relationships (120–21).

Inconsistent with the long history of struggle for women's rights, this approach is perilously close to attributing nonpartisanship to women's essential nature. In fact, substantial evidence suggests that the nonpartisanship characteristic of the League and of other women's organizations is a practical and appropriate response on their part to their experience in the public world of politics. But conventional analyses of politics, including those by equity feminists, provide no room for a definition that focuses on educational, pressure, and, above all, nonpartisan activities. By contrast, social feminism provides a rationale for women to act differently in politics and to reject its more characteristically masculine and undesirable aspects. By the time the League was established, the feminists knew what relationships with party politics would and would not work for them. Their subsequent experience only confirmed this knowledge.

For Americans, politics means partisan activity centered on elections. Issues enter politics mainly as arguments for selecting particular incumbents, who are then given considerable freedom to alter previous commitments in response to changing circumstances. Suffragists shared such perceptions, even though they themselves entered public life in support of specific policy goals. It is not surprising they believed themselves to be nonpolitical even after enfranchisement, as they continued their efforts to influence who would hold public office and what decisions they would make. The League of Women Voters was characteristic of suffragism's successor groups in its nonpartisan procedural preferences and the choice of issues it thought important—not because of its membership of women but because of its inherited feminist procedures and issues. This ideological and organizational continuity responded to the situation of women in relation to politics. Furthermore, the League was not just feminist but social feminist.

In the following pages I look at the origins and nature of the League of Women Voters' involvement with politics and at why the League has been so disparaged and misunderstood. Once again, it is the social feminist basis of the League's orientation to public life which has provoked such responses. In Chapter 13 I discuss the origins and early years of the LWV to show the way its nonpartisanship responded to feminist experience with party politics. Chapter 14 concentrates on the League's goals in the period immediately before the second wave of feminism, showing that Leaguers were social feminist even if they were not identified as such. Chapter 15 focuses on the League's feminism in an account of the movement of the League to support the Equal Rights Amendment and to reacquire feminist legitimacy. Finally, Chapter 16 assesses the organization's role in relation to electoral politics.

CHAPTER 13

Origins of
Nonpartisanship

Accounts of the League usually begin with its formal establishment in
1919, at the Jubilee Convention of the National American Woman Suffrage Association (NAWSA). Initially an auxiliary of the NAWSA, it
became independent the following year (Lemons 1975:49–50). This history pictures the LWV as direct descendant and inheritor of nonmilitant
suffragists in the United States. But though true in general spirit, the
account is not true in detail, for the League developed independently
and inherited a separate organizational history from suffrage efforts at
the state level. Nor did the League replace the suffrage coalition. Although the NAWSA itself had intended to wind up business with
ratification, the executive meeting in 1920 decided to continue until the
expiration of the articles of incorporation; at that point, in 1940, it chose
to carry on for five more years.[1] Carrie Chapman Catt insisted, however,
that the new League be separate from the start and that none of the old
suffrage officers should stay on. The first League president, Maud
Wood Park, had been active in the college branch of the movement and
then as a lobbyist in Washington but had held no NAWSA office; the
other officers had been working at the state rather than the national
level, and seven young regional directors were added (Peck 1944:326).

In addition, the League had direct predecessors somewhat separate
from the NAWSA, in the form of organized groups of women in the
enfranchised states. From 1911 to 1913 a National Council of Women

1. For one thing, it was necessary to administer the substantial sum of money left to the
NAWSA in 1914 by Mrs. Frank Leslie (Young 1929). Leslie money helped support the
Women's Joint Congressional Committee in the 1920s and paid in 1922 for foreign delegates to attend the first Pan-American Women's Conference held in Baltimore (Lemons
1975:168; Peck 1944:326). In 1940 a women's centennial congress was organized with
Leslie money for the hundredth anniversary of Lucretia Mott and Elizabeth Cady Stanton's being denied seats at the World Anti-Slavery Congress in London; it brought together representatives of all the major American women's organizations and heard reports
from commissions on five topics: the economy, the education of women, ethical and
religious values, government and politics, and peace through world organization (Peck
1944:221, 265, 356, 464).

Voters grouped and represented women in the five enfranchised western states; in 1913 it met in Washington and discussed how to use the threat of Republican votes by enfranchised western women to pressure the president (Morgan 1972:87). Prototypes and future components of the League also developed in unenfranchised states.[2] For instance, New York's Interurban Woman Suffrage Council became the New York Woman Suffrage party in 1909 and then, after winning the New York referendum in 1917, the New York League of Women Voters. Similarly, the Civic League organized in California after state-level victory in 1911 became the California LWV ten years later (Lemons 1975:50; Fowler 1986). Once America entered World War I in 1917, the state organizations, relatively unhampered by the need to support the war effort, were the main centers of suffrage activity (Morgan 1972:119). When they had been consolidated as the LWV, state groups of enfranchised women took as their first task the need to obtain ratification of the suffrage amendment in each state.[3] Since Congress approved the amendment in June 1919, in many cases this task meant obtaining a special session of the state legislature. These were difficult campaigns, though they were carried on by seasoned activists. The ratification campaigns confirmed suffragist hostility to partisan government, as the experience of new groups reinforced what had been learned in the suffrage movement.

The National American Woman Suffrage Association, which obtained the vote, was formed in 1890 when two societies that had been competing since 1868 merged: the American Woman Suffrage Association (AWSA) led by Lucy Stone and her husband Henry Blackwell, and the better-known National Woman Suffrage Association (NWSA) led by Susan B. Anthony and Elizabeth Cady Stanton. Both groups lived through embittering disappointments with political parties at both state and national levels. The NWSA was the first to reject efforts at party alignment, after the supposedly more progressive Republicans refused to support woman suffrage in the Kansas referendum campaign of 1867 and the New York constitutional convention of the same year. In the Kansas campaign an attempt by Anthony and Stanton to get party support briefly made them allies of the cynical and racist Democrat George Francis Train. By 1868 both the costs and the unreliability of partisan alignment were clear to the group that was to found the NWSA (DuBois 1978). The Boston-centered AWSA, reluctant to abandon the reform tradition of the Republican party after the Civil War, deliberately pursued a different route, but it pressed in vain for the inclusion of woman

2. Young notes that, beginning in 1912, a Mississippi Valley Conference of suffrage leaders of eighteen midwestern states met six times; the group included many future League activists (Young 1st version, 17).

3. Even in its status as auxiliary, the League was organizationally independent of the NAWSA; from 1918 to 1920 it was run by a Council of Presidents of groups in the enfranchised states, chaired by Mrs. Charles Brooks of Kansas (Young 1st version, 2).

suffrage in the GOP's party platform (Kraditor 1981, Wheeler 1981). Hundreds of workers in less well documented state campaigns had similar experiences (Strom 1975).

At the same time, on the positive side, the various segments of the women's movement learned in the years after the Civil War how to enlist inexperienced women for political action. The organizational activity involved in suffragism may have been more important than the ultimate suffrage victory itself:

> In retrospect we can see what suffragists only glimpsed in the 1860's, that it was women's involvement in the movement, far more than the eventual enfranchisement of women, that created the basis of new social relations between men and women. In other words, activity in the woman suffrage movement did precisely what Stanton and others had expected possession of the franchise to do—it demonstrated that self-government and democratic participation in the life of the society was the key to women's emancipation (DuBois 1978:201–2).

The empowering and educational effect of such shared activity must have been obvious to those involved; these women would apply the lessons they had learned when they organized the League.

All this suffragist effort was nonpartisan, and it was effective. By 1915 suffrage organization in New York is said to have been admired by Tammany Hall.[4] By 1915 the NAWSA had two million members in state groups, gross receipts per year of over \$750,000, and yearly headquarters expenditure of over \$100,000 (Morgan 1972:99). Even before the last push for the Nineteenth Amendment began, the message must have been clear: the governing parties were indifferent or even hostile to women's concerns, but women were able to muster on their own an independent and truly formidable political effort.

In 1917 Catt felt able to challenge the parties from a position of strength:

> It has been the aim of both dominant parties to postpone woman suffrage as long as possible. Many of us have deep and abiding distrust of all political parties; they have tricked us so often that our doubts are natural. We also know that your parties have a distrust of new women voters. Woman suffrage is inevitable—you know it. The political parties will go on—we know it. Shall we, then, be enemies or friends? There is one thing mightier than kings or armies, congresses or political parties—the power of an idea whose time has come to move. The idea will not perish—the party which opposes it may (Peck 1944:283).

---

4. Catt in turn apparently modeled her organization on Tammany, and the New York referendum was successful in 1917 when Tammany stood aside and allowed the large New York City majorities that approved the state franchise (Kraditor 1981:144; Peck 1944:169–72).

As woman suffrage moved to its victory, the hazards of partisan politics became even clearer. The Congressional Union attempted to apply in the United States the militant tactics of the Pankhursts and to blame the ruling party for the failure to achieve the vote. Their efforts were dramatic but had the same effect as in Britain: recruits flooded the more moderate suffragists while politicians used militant lawlessness as an excuse for inaction. President Woodrow Wilson had indicated his support of social policies dear to NAWSA members—particularly the Child Labor Law in 1916—but he nevertheless yielded to party pressures that delayed his public advocacy of the woman suffrage amendment. The NAWSA saw the disgraceful co-operation of southern and northeastern Democrats, in a Democratic Congress, refusing a Democratic president's request in 1918 to vote the amendment out for ratification. Then, in the ratification battle, members saw the political parties acting as agents for some of the powerful groups they most detested. Racism had animated the antisuffrage southern Democrats. Liquor companies and textile manufacturers now promoted opposition to ratification: the woman's vote was expected to support prohibition and improved working conditions for women and children in the factories of the northeast and the south. The crucial Tennessee ratification battle was referred to as "Armageddon" by the suffragists. There, the victory of good over evil finally turned on two votes.

The experience of European feminists also warned against putting trust in parties. In England, only very gradually had the mainstream National Union of Women's Suffrage Societies lost faith in the Liberals. Reluctantly, the Union shifted in 1912 to support the British Labour party, only to find Labour agreeing in 1917 to a limited enfranchisement measure that excluded those young working women whom they had claimed most needed the vote (Rover 1967, Pugh 1944). In France, feminist devotion to the republican parties (and explicit support of woman suffrage by the French Socialist party) produced a situation in 1922 where representatives of those parties defeated woman suffrage in the Senate; in 1936 the Popular Front did not even propose it (Sowerwine 1982, Hause and Kenney 1984). The American suffragists knew of these battles for they were actively involved in the International Woman Suffrage Alliance, of which Catt was the first president.

It is understandable that partisanship seemed both unhelpful and uncongenial. More positively, the suffragists' choice was appropriate, politically inspired, and effective: "By becoming centralized but remaining bipartisan, the National [American Woman Suffrage Association] had something to offer to every legislator at state and federal level" (Morgan 1972:186).[5] Avoidance of partisan commitment could be a way

5. Morgan (1972) is the only analyst of the American suffrage movement who has put it in its contemporary political context; he is highly laudatory of the suffragists' strategy and tactics.

to obtain political results. Certainly the League would not avoid contacts with parties in the way members' disillusion with antisuffragism might have suggested. Instead it was to attempt to prevail upon all parties to adopt the measures it believed desirable.

The LWV adopted this position from a sophisticated understanding of the party system in the United States. Even before enfranchisement, suffrage leaders had participated in efforts to modify the party system, in accordance with the argument that it was not the party system but the existing major parties that were unresponsive to feminists in the United States. The social measures of the traditional women's agenda—full legal equality for women, protection of women and children at work, feminist pacifism—could help provide the basis for a genuinely progressive party. Supporting the Progressive party's attempt to expand the party system so that issues of social welfare could become part of public business, Jane Addams seconded Theodore Roosevelt's presidential nomination and committed her tremendous prestige to campaign for him. In 1924 and again in 1928 a number of LWV leaders participated conspicuously and unproductively in national election campaigns. William O'Neill draws from these failures the conclusion that the naive and timid women reformers should instead have thrown their lot in with the American socialists since "the party system did not work" (1971: 165).[6] By O'Neill's own account, however, the leaders of the American feminists were hardly timid. They were less naive than he; among their prominent members was former socialist Florence Kelley, and many others possessed a clear understanding of the realities of both socialist and U.S. politics. As the years wore on, they were to find that, by and large, they had more sympathetic friends within the national Democratic than the Republican party. But they would never commit their organization to either.

Nor did they ever seriously consider the formation of a women's party or a voting bloc of women. They were well aware of the limited nature of the commitment of the millions of NAWSA members, and they witnessed the lack of success of the self-styled National Woman's party. Some critics apparently still feel the League missed the chance to organize former supporters of women suffrage into a single independent political unit; they do not take account of the actual conditions reflected in the low participation of women in the first postenfranchisement elections. The question of a women's party, however, is a minor one, an illusion born of a unique opportunity. Nor do most commentators suggest seriously that the League should have formed an alliance with a third party. They recommend, rather, a policy of systematic, selective endorsement of parties or candidates who adopt recommended policies.

6. The proof of his argument is the achievements of the "democratic socialists of northern Europe" who have "abolished poverty in countries whose resources do not begin to compare with those of the United States" (O'Neill 1971:165).

A typical response is that of a Kennedy administration aide who complained in 1964 of the League's refusal to publish names of those who supported its positions (Gruberg 1968:64). This the League has never done. Instead, it sees its role as influence on all parties through influence on the public.

This position was initially interpreted by observers as not just nonpartisan but hostile to and destructive of the party system itself. Even before the 1920 election Republican women activists deplored the establishment of the new League and attempted to block the transformation of the Illinois branch of the NAWSA into the Illinois LWV (Lemons 1975:52). The New York LWV nearly unseated Senator James Wadsworth and provoked at their next annual convention a blast from the governor: "There is no need for a League of Women Voters any more than for a League of Men Voters. . . . Any organization which seeks to exert political power is a menace to our institutions unless it is organized as a political party. Our institutions are so framed that party government is essential to their perpetuity, and a two-party system, if our representative system is to endure, is needed!" Carrie Chapman Catt was also present, to reply with a useful statement of the League's view of the party system:

> While it is true that ours is a government by parties, it is not the whole truth. The parties administer the government, but evolution is compelled by groups. I can recall no important change in our institutions which has been brought about by party initiative, and I can think of no policy more certainly destructive of normal progress than the dissolution of reform organizations. . . . No party adopts an idea until it believes it will gain more votes than it will lose by it—that is, not until the idea has already been made popular by a group (Peck 1944:404).

Clearly the League was not conceived as a means of bargaining with parties, offering support in return for advocacy of specific measures. As Catt went on to say, the intended role was more indirect and diffuse: "The League of Women Voters aspires to be part of the big majorities which administer our government, and it also wishes to be one of the minorities which agitate and educate and shape ideas today which the majority will adopt tomorrow" (Peck 1944:403). "Agitate and educate and shape ideas"—the League was to make this exhortation into a specific set of procedures. It was not compatible with the organization's giving even temporary support to any individual or party.

It was, however, compatible with the LWV's actively encouraging individual women to engage in partisan activity. It is generally believed that League attitudes toward partisan politics interfered with women's opportunities for individual participation in party organizations or electoral activity. This accusation persists in spite of the League's own stated policy, which reads: "The League is non-partisan: it neither supports nor opposes political parties but it does encourage members as individuals to participate actively in the party or campaign of their choice" (League of Women Voters 1985). In 1920 Catt had told the LWV that everyone should join and be active in parties (having noted wryly that the Republican women's attack on the League was a strange way to win women for the GOP): "Is it our intention to remain on the outside of those parties as we have been for sixty years?. Are we going to petition them as we have always done? . . . The only way to get things done is to get them done on the inside of the political party. . . . The next battle is going to be inside the parties, and we are not going to stay outside and let all the reactionaries have their way on the inside!" (Peck 1944:325).

It was not just Catt as an individual who held these views (ironically she never joined a political party). Although League members themselves retained a certain ambivalence about party membership and public office, League policy was clear. In 1924 the LWV added to its platform an explicit statement about the desirability of having qualified women elected to political office. As early as 1947, in the postwar years of the feminine mystique, a League pamphlet urged women to participate in electoral politics, citing the illustrious examples of such Leaguers as Emily Taft Douglas and Helen Gahagan Douglas. Ten years later the *National Voter*, in an article that shows the reality of the attitudes the League was blamed for encouraging, urged members to move into municipal office.

Headed "A Leaguer Becomes a Politico," the article is mainly a letter from a former League board member who is now an alderman in "a rather small city." The *National Voter*'s text insists the League is both a "training ground for real politics" (a view attributed to "practical politicians" with no League experience) *and* "something in itself" (the view of League members with no political experience). These functions of the League are not mutually exclusive; the techniques of League procedures can fruitfully be transferred to public life. Those who have gone from the League to electoral office, according to the *Voter*, "say that they would never have entered politics but for their League training, feel that they are better public servants for having learned 'the League way,' and adapt the League way to public office whenever possible." Such seemingly trivial techniques as advance distribution of an agenda and circulation of meeting minutes are significant, and LWV procedures of membership consultation translate into the attempt to maintain contact with constituents.

The alderman agrees: "The League of Women Voters is a training ground for political life," and she hopes to "encourage other women" to follow her example. "Without League training," she says, "I would never have undertaken a campaign." It seems clear she is correct. She has always thought of politics as something "dirty"; she is not a joiner—the League is her only organization—nor a leader: "Leadership was thrust

on me step by step rather than because I was a natural leader." Here is
the self-portrait of the rather unambitious woman politician so often
depicted by academic studies (Kirkpatrick 1974). Her motivation for
standing for election is implicit in a reference to her concern about "the
problems of a growing community." She clearly loves politics, even "enjoying reading zoning ordinances, the plumbing code, traffic reports,
etc." She adds, "My only wish is that more members of the League might
be encouraged to run for public office." And she ends with an apology
for having missed so many League affairs: "I am sure you know my
heart is always with you." Participation in electoral politics is obviously
satisfying for her, yet she sees the League as of continuing value, more
than merely a training ground.

The article hints at the League policy that partly explains why the
League is thought to bar members from partisan political activity. The
alderman is apparently a former president or board member. If she had
retained League leadership, she would indeed have been forbidden any
involvement with partisan politics. After an early period when League
officers participated conspicuously in political campaigns, the LWV
adopted an extremely stringent restriction, terrified lest it lose its nonpartisan reputation.[7] The limitations imposed by the policy can be seen
in the *National Voter* of March 15, 1954, where a member's query was
answered authoritatively to the effect that "to protect the League, Mrs.
Doe should have publicly resigned from the local Board *before* her husband announced his candidacy."

There was always some disagreement within the League about how
severe the prohibition should be. A 1956 survey of League and Board
members by the University of Michigan's Survey Research Center
showed that officers agreed with very narrow limits: 34 percent of the
presidents and 21 percent of the board members felt that an officer
(even a mere board member) should not belong to a political party, nor
should "members of her immediate family." Members, in contrast, were
prepared to allow (by 56 percent) that a board member could work
publicly for a party "as long as she makes it clear that she is acting as a
private citizen" (60–61). In practice, officers tended to involve themselves with partisan politics only after they had completed their very
time-consuming and absorbing terms at the League. But they would
then of course still be League members and remain close to the League
—like the alderman.

In 1972 the *National Voter* began to include substantial amounts of
material related to women in partisan politics. This was the year when

7. One study suggests that the League's nonpartisanship is a legal necessity, since its
nonprofit status bars "direct involvement in partisan races" (Carroll and Strimling
1983:99); this remark seems to be mistaken and indicates a confusion with the League of
Women Voters' Education Foundation, founded to gain tax advantages for donors. Here
knowledgeable analysts respond to a public image that produces the notion that the League
is nonpolitical.

the League moved to support the ERA, when it became involved with the National Women's Political Caucus (including in the *National Voter* of January–February a long interview with the NWPC's executive director), and when it published the results of a survey of League members serving in state legislatures (March–April). The article summarizing this survey begins by quoting Doris Meissner of the NWPC: "We've got to get more women running for public office." League members, says the *Voter*, "have traditionally served on the other side of the political fence—as informed and active voters—[but] many have opened the gate and moved on to become office holders." Their comments are fascinating.

We should note first that the League's politicos share the characteristics reported of other women in local office and, in particular, women in state office in the United States: the majority are married or widowed, with grown children; they agree on the need for supportive families; they are distributed by party affiliation in roughly the same way as the proportion in state legislatures nationwide. Most feel that there is indeed discrimination against women, particularly in respect to access to leadership positions within state legislatures. All note "the beneficial background supplied by their League work" and the help given their campaigns by League friends. This latter point may be important: the League will not endorse even its own members as candidates, but clearly an enormous amount of unofficial support is possible. The satisfactions of public office? serving the public good and the possibility of being more effective than as a Leaguer: "You know you count." All agree on encouraging political novices, one saying that League unit meetings require more intelligence and pose tougher questions than the state legislature. The echoes of Guild and UFCS reactions to politics are unmistakable.

The politicos' evaluation of the League experience is complex and indicates a considerable political sophistication. They comment that the League taught them how to acquire expertise in a policy area and how to demonstrate it in a way that commanded respect. But they feel also that the League is too rational, too idealistic, unaware of the emotion and compromise that characterize political life. Their conclusion is that more League members should participate in public office. "We spend days learning how to lobby," says one officeholder; "a more effective technique is to become decision makers." Comments contrast the "well meaning lady" with the "practical politician," and Leaguers are told that their obligation to public service includes an obligation to seek public office: "At other times of great crisis in America, our most competent people did seek office. Do they now? Will you?" The Leaguer's typical lack of concern with political reward is urged as an additional qualification. The League becomes more instrumental, a launching-pad and training ground—but its motivations must continue into partisan politics.

A year later (January–February 1973) a second article gave a less

systematic presentation of interviews with Leaguers who had been candidates for office, some successfully. The *National Voter* writer provides a
matter-of-fact (and accurate) account of the obstacles women encounter
when they seek public office and a list of sources for how-to information.
She includes also a useful statement on how the League sees itself as
relating to politics: "A political system is as good as its leadership [and]
it's obvious the League is a good training ground for political office. Of
course the League is issue-oriented and does not support political candidates or parties, but individual members take part in the democratic
process either by working for candidates of their choice or by running
themselves." Party membership is no longer stressed, nor is the changing
of party programs. Instead, women are urged to think of themselves as
capable of becoming rulers. The motivation, however, is unchanged. A
Leaguer who is a member of the South Carolina legislature puts it this
way: a candidate "should not run for public office just because she is a
woman but because she has something to contribute for the betterment
of our government. The League is a fine place to learn about that."
Another politician, a member of a city council, comments that "the nitty-
gritty arena of politics" is considerably more difficult than the idealistic
world of League study, but she nevertheless urges League members to
run for office in spite of all the difficulties and hard work involved. She
gives a powerful version of the arguments for the importance of local
politics, not just as a step in a career path but as a crucial setting for
political action: "It is at the local level that the most challenging problems
and decisions exist. It is closest to the people and most directly affects
our daily lives; recreation, transportation, affirmative action programs,
social and public services, land use planning, all hinge on the quality of
local government." She certainly does not see the League as either substituting for politics or inhibiting partisan involvement:"It is important
that more League members run and get elected to public office. They
know how to dig for facts and how to recognize one when they see it;
they aim at long-range goals and solutions rather than short-range
gains; they are reasonable, persuasive, and understand government."
Besides, she adds, "the city council is the most exciting job I have ever
held."

One striking aspect of such responses is an enthusiastic commitment
to both the League and the more conventional political activity that grew
out of it. Such responses are not what most critics ascribe to the "prosaic
LWV" whose "determined neutrality denied it the passionate loyalties
reserved for partisan organizations" (O'Neill 1971:274, 268).[8] Clearly
nonpartisan specifically does not mean "neutral." These women take
very seriously both the issues their group identified as important and the
larger issue of democratic process the LWV both embodies and pursues.

8. Interestingly, O'Neill is contrasting the League with the equally nonpartisan suffrage
leagues.

They are not neutral in their assessment of policies or of politicians' views. Members of Congress are rated regularly and publicly on an index called the Political Accountability Rating (PAR). The selection of significant votes is, of course, equivalent to judgments on what are important issues; the ratings themselves are anything but neutral, even if they are evenly applied to all legislators. Largely on commitment to such issues, League-trained politicians justify their movement into partisan politics.

For the majority of League members, however, the electoral route is not relevant. And it has never been entirely clear what political involvement grows for them out of the development of reasoned and accepted stances on public policy which is the main activity of the League. The many condemnations of the organization grow from impressions of how the League works for the ordinary member. Part of the problem is acceptance of the perceptions of League members.

League procedures are the same as those of all volunteer women's associations with a continuing interest in public policy. Topics the members find important, usually areas where they feel some need for government intervention, are studied until an understanding of the situation produces a notion of a preferable policy. This procedure is innocuous enough; it reproduces, in a group setting and at greater length, the process by which, ideally, the individual citizen comes to approve one or another party or candidate by her or his vote. Voter education programs such as those the League developed might perhaps carry out part of the activity for busy individuals, supplying study material as a basis for intelligent decision. The PAR is intended, in part, to perform such a function.

Because they lacked the vote, the predecessors of the League had lobbied as a result of their decisions about issues needing action. Later, because positions on issues were so strongly supported and because the issues themselves were felt to be so important, the League always felt substantial pressure to exert more direct, though not partisan, pressure. As soon as the League was established as an auxiliary of the NAWSA, even before it had its first separate delegate meeting, it established a Committee on the High Cost of Living which spent the next year preparing a report that condemned monopolistic practices in the meat-packing industry (Peck 1944:324). Surely the implication was some sort of action, at the very least taking a public stand and making widely available the information supporting it. And surely some sort of lobbying action was also indicated, if only in relation to the political parties and their elected representatives. This result led some analysts to describe the League as "a lobbying organization" (Gruberg 1968:91).[9]

But League members, as reports from their former members now

9. Jeffrey Berry (1977) uses the League as a major example of a public interest pressure group.

politicians indicate, tend to see this lobbying as part of a process very different from normal politics. They are likely to identify such activities as primarily educational.[10] At its most naive, the League sees even its contacts with elected officials as educational—teaching them the right thing to do. And education is always seen as a major part of the League's functions. In 1956 the SRC survey of League members found that almost all respondents believed that educational purposes were central to the League. These purposes included political education of the public, political education of women as a group, and political education of League members. Only 4 percent of members considered direct action on issues and legislation to be a main concern of the League (Survey Research Center Report I:41).

Interestingly, when the survey posed the same question to a sample of the public it found that the group's image was considerably more activist, even political: between one-eighth and one-fifth of the non-Leaguers thought the LWV supports specific candidates, tells people how to vote, or is otherwise politically partisan, and 17.6 percent thought of it as a "political action group" (Survey Research Center Report III:11–12). Closest to this view within the League were the 11 percent of members who had identified "encouraging women to participate in politics" as a major concern of the organization (Report I:41). The public perception, which corresponded neither to academic assessments nor to Leaguers' self-images, probably reflected reality rather more closely than either. The PAR does tell people who to vote for, and stances for and against issues such as the ERA are not taken in a scholarly and detached vacuum without consequences in "political action." At the same time, all can be considered part of the education of both Leaguers and public. But this is a committed and activist sort of education.

In 1974, two years after its commitment to support the ERA and its involvement with the NWPC, the League commissioned from the Kettering Institute an elaborate self-survey. Members were asked to identify the LWV's most important function from among three possible alternatives: "works to bring about changes by taking stands on important issues," "studies issues and educates the public," and provides "voter services." Respondents divided nearly evenly among the three, with 5 percent volunteering that all were of equal importance (Cantril and Cantril 1974:21). A more intensive study of four selected local leagues found it was the active members, especially the presidents and board members, who tended to translate education into political action and "look to the League as a vehicle for impacting on public policy" (10–11). Members, and especially officers, stressed their belief that the League's nonpartisanship was essential to its influence. By this time there was

10. This view is less often accepted by analysts, though Sarah Brumbaugh (1972) studies it as a means of "'democratic' education."

evidently more awareness of the political involvement of the organization, as the questions reflected.

Certainly some members of the League would prefer a more limited function for the group. Education for them is the only goal, perhaps extending to passing information to a larger public. In 1972 national board members spoke with dismay of their difficulties with members who talk "as if the goal of the League was to *study* issues, not to help solve problems. . . . We can't take effective action without study, of course. But we should choose program with *problem-solving* as our goal, not study" (*NV* November 1971). President Lucy Wilson Benson repeated this: "*The basic goal of the League program is ACTION!*" (*NV* November 1971, her emphases). And although the internal tension persisted, the balance had come down on the side of action. It seems clear that this was equivalent to politics.

The League was political because nonpartisanship had not prevented involvement—active involvement—with issues. It was also political, as well as feminist, because of the nature of those issues. Here we approach the central criticisms of the organization. Dismissal of the League reflects more than an assessment of the nature and importance of its characteristic methods. It also turns on evaluation of the group's central issues—its goals. These are not usually perceived as "radical" or even political, either in subject matter or in preferred outcome. As a result, the organization is barely recognized as part of the women's movement. Most significantly, the social feminist dimensions of the League stance are liable to brand it as reactionary and as having encouraged women in reactionary, even apolitical views: "On the right wing of the women's movement was the League of Women Voters. . . .The league did very little for women's rights and focused mainly on child labor laws, minimum wages and hour laws, pacifism, and many general reforms" (Deckard 1983:284).

Such analyses are likely also to attribute the League's failure to attract mass membership to its alleged neglect of "women's rights" in favor of "general reforms."[11] Certainly the official membership of the League has never been large, bottoming out in 1935 at 41,879, and not hitting 100,000 again until 1951; in 1980 the League was somewhat smaller than the Business and Professional Women's Clubs and about the same

11. Deckard's indictment continues: the League "advocated gradualism and attacked all sudden 'radical changes.' Because it never fought for women's liberation, used conservative tactics, and was generally dull, and because of the hostile political climate, it never gained the allegiance of most American women. Whereas NAWSA had about 2 million members in 1920, the League of Women Voters was down to about 100,000 by 1923" (1983: 284). Note the throwaway remark about "hostile political climate," which conceals the Depression and the red-baiting of women's groups in the 1930s (the League was one of the major targets). We might be surprised that the League survived at all under such circumstances.

size as the relatively new National Organization for Women (LWV 1980).[12] Obviously LWV members were and are a small percentage of American women, even of highly educated American women.[13] It is all the more paradoxical, therefore, that accusers decry the LWV's influence on the political opinions and behavior of American women. The underlying argument is that if most American women have not become political activists, let alone feminists or radicals, the fault must lie with the only relatively large women's group that has tried to influence or educate them politically. If that influence did not have the desired effects, it must have been because (a) the League did not make itself or its ideas attractive, or because (b) the League had the wrong ideas. That is, either the LWV had no impact or it had influence but in the wrong direction. Because it was a social feminist group, it encouraged women in passivity and inaction except when it encouraged conservative efforts. The argument is familiar: equity feminism is radical and social feminism is conservative.

However, criteria for policy are now often those of a second-wave equity feminism that favors revolutionary change. In addition, a direct challenge to "Victorian" ideas of role and of sexual morality is expected. On these grounds the equity feminist National Woman's party (NWP) is also criticized, for sharing the League's "lack of interest in the major social, economic, and racial issues" of the interwar period (Deckard 1983:284). The assumption is that the situation of women is not a major issue. After all, the ERA was developed, however correctly or incorrectly, as the solution for the economic and social disadvantages of half of the population. But for many analysts, defining a problem as related to women automatically marginalizes it.

More commonly, it is not issues but remedies that are discounted. The policies favored by women's organizations were reactions to unemployment on the one hand and the threat of war on the other. That is, they related to central issues of the era. But the focus of women's groups was

12. Limited and falling membership has been a problem for all mass membership voluntary associations as women move into the paid labor force. At the same time the contrast to the inexpensive, undemanding mass subscription to the NAWSA is misleading. We may also ask whether membership figures for the LWV are adequate indicators of the measure of support that American women are prepared to give to the League's methods and goals. The Survey Research Center found that 40 percent of those receiving the *National Voter* did not consider themselves members (1956 I:1); they presumably represent an even larger group who were informed and possibly influenced by the League but did not appear on the list of dues-payers. In addition, Kettering reported in 1974 that static membership figures of somewhat more than 100,000 conceal an annual turnover of about 20 percent joining *and* leaving (Cantril and Cantril 1974:4).

13. The reputation for hard work that is a basis of the League's legitimacy has the effect of discouraging potential members without college education (Breckinridge 1933, Lee 1977). The Survey Research Center report and the Kettering self-study both noted difficulties of recruitment and retention, suggesting they were related to the image but even more to the reality of the heavy demands, in both quality and commitment, made of League members.

different, and so their preferred policies were also different. For instance, in relation to unemployment, feminists like those in the League concentrated on the situation of women in the paid labor force whom they saw victimized by exploitative working conditions that unions did little to alleviate. The immediate solution was legislation to provide minimum wages and regulate hours, working conditions, and physical protection. LWV opposition to the ERA and to the groups supporting it was, precisely, an effort to prevent what the League saw as a threat to painfully won measures protecting largely nonunionized women in the industrial labor force. Both sets of feminists who saw the ERA as salient did so because of their focus on the situation of women.

Commentators have been reluctant to admit that attention to the specific situation of women is in itself political, as is the insistence on women's interest in and capacity to make judgments about policy. Furthermore, contrary to frequent published comments by uninformed analysts, the League continued to be involved with issues related to women's rights. Historical scholarship is now beginning to document League involvement in a series of unsuccessful campaigns to get women equal access and pay under programs such as the National Recovery Act (Ware 1982; Scharf 1983; Banner 1984; Cott 1987). LWV opposition to the ERA must also be seen as related to the issue of women's status. League defense of protective legislation for women was equivalent to the affirmative action goal of equality of results: what unions would not do for women, the law could.

The League's costly opposition to the ERA was a consequence of the group's expectations about how change occurred. These were reformist feminists. The actual policy recommendations made by the League fitted well with the progressive rather than radical nature of the New Deal, and we should note that the LWV was ahead of the administration in areas such as women's rights and pacifism.[14] Certainly the line-up for and against the ERA was significant: like leaders of the NWSA who aligned with George Francis Train, the interwar NWP had as companions the National Association of Manufacturers. Alice Paul, today revered for her unstinting devotion to the cause of women's equality, nevertheless could be seen in the 1930s to have learned from the Pankhursts more than their commitment and flair; like them, she refused to listen to the preferences of working women, and like them she ran an autocratic and unrepresentative organization unwilling to co-operate with other women's groups (Rupp 1985; Scharf 1983; Cott 1984; Rupp and Taylor 1987).

In policies about peace, the League showed a liberal but activist inter-

14. In more conventional contexts, Lemons sees the League as carrying on, almost single-handedly, the legacy of Progressivism; he points out that the LWV was "the only citizens' organization" to support the Tennessee Valley projects, and it played a major role in the adoption of that early experiment in public ownership (1975:131–33).

nationalism not very remote from its New Deal stance on domestic policy. Members certainly supported disarmament but even more strongly supported the use of international organization and negotiation. A long and intense campaign failed to produce American membership in the World Court. Support of the Kellogg-Briand Pact outlawing war helped obtain U.S. ratification of a symbolic statement thought important at the time. League support of reduction of World War I debts was more practical, as was its attention to the economic causes of war. Its pacifism was sufficiently complex that response to U.S. neutrality policies took the form of campaigns for policy that could distinguish among belligerents; Leaguers asked for discrimination against an aggressor and in favor of the victims of aggression (LWV 1959:29). This was hardly conservative in interwar America. But it was not conventionally radical in either tone or recommendation, in part because it built on the traditional commitment to peace of women's organizations.

Nothing in the League's interwar preferences in policy attracts those of revolutionary bent or those equity feminists who want a program focused on changing the relationship between women and men. The League loses credibility with nonfeminist radicals because of its membership (women) and its focus on women's situation. At the same time, because it is not explicitly aimed at changing women's or the world's situation, because its philosophy is gradualist or reformist and aimed at practical consequences, it is not seen by equity feminists as radical or, retroactively, judged to have been effectively feminist.

Carolyn Heilbrun joins this chorus of criticism, underlining feminists' main complaints: for her, the League's identification of problems is unacceptable, and its refusal to call itself feminist is offensive. She therefore identifies the League as an example of "the failure of women to bond . . . the failure of women to find 'support systems' among themselves" (1979:26). Comparing the League to the kind of group she approves of, Heilbrun asks, "Could anyone imagine a Black organization that refused to concern itself with Black problems?" She describes the League as follows: "From its inception until it felt the pressures of the current movement [the League] eschewed all questions concerned exclusively with women and refused to back candidates because of their stand on women's issues" (27). The League's opposition to the ERA does not count as attention to a women's issue; only support for the amendment is feminist.

But then, no one knows much about what the League has really been doing for over sixty-five years. It is a long and complicated story, one that can be only sketched here. But it is worth looking at.

CHAPTER 14

Goals as They
Changed Over Time

The goals and activities of the League are rather more complex than most observers realize. They have changed somewhat, as might be expected, over sixty-five years of existence. We are usually told that when Carrie Chapman Catt inaugurated the League, she said it would be needed for only five years (Lemons 1975:50). In fact she seems to have said that the League should be tried out for five years and then examined to see if it was still necessary. It is hard to believe she expected to see the organization's stated goals achieved by 1924 or 1925.

The resolution at the 1919 NAWSA Jubilee Convention establishing the LWV as an auxiliary noted the "low standards of citizenship found among men [which] clearly indicate the need of education in the principles and ideals of our government and methods of political procedure"; it accordingly urged the League to make "its first duty" the "political education of the new women voters (but not excluding men)" (Young, 1st version, 12). At that time Catt said the League was intended to foster education in citizenship, to promote for women and the public the discussion of civic reform, and to support needed legislation. It was also to continue the work of freeing American women from legal distinctions, as well as aiding women in other countries to obtain their rights (Peck 1944:306–7). A year later she specified the League's goals as

(a) the final enfranchisement of American women and "to reach out across the seas in aid of the woman's struggle" throughout the world;
(b) removal of legal discrimination against women at state levels; and
(c) "to make our democracy safe for the nation and so safe for the world that every citizen may feel secure and great men will acknowledge the worthiness of the American republic to lead" (quoted in LWV 1959:11).

Other statements make it clear that to Catt, education in citizenship and completion of enfranchisement meant the same thing: getting women legally and intellectually ready to be full citizens. She seems to have

261

hoped that in a few years women voters would be safely integrated into normal political processes.

Catt's anxieties about American democracy were undoubtedly based on what she had seen during the suffrage battles, including the way Tammany Hall had manipulated the immigrant male voters of New York. The crucial New York referendum had been won only when Tammany Hall stood aside—in anticipation, perhaps, of a new, even more malleable mass of freshly enfranchised (female) voters. One suffragist reaction to encounters with Tammany was to develop a notion of the "Americanization" of new citizens which was reflected in the civic education programs of the LWV. Once women voters had pulled level with the men, possibly raising the men in the process, an organization with the League's particular combination of purposes would no longer be necessary.

However, Catt always believed in the usefulness of women's groups that could pressure and educate in areas where mainstream political institutions were unresponsive. Women's rights at the state and international levels were such areas, as was another subject dear to her, peace. Catt continued her involvement with issues of women's rights through the NAWSA and the commission for the Leslie funds, as well as with the international suffrage movement through the IWSA. She was involved, with Jane Addams, in the founding of what became the Women's Peace party although, when the United States entered the war, she led the NAWSA war support programs (Fowler 1986). Once the LWV was launched, peace activities became the major focus of her prodigious energies, and she involved the League, and eight other national women's organizations, in seven years of study, meetings, and publicity around annual Conferences on the Cause and Cure of War. Completely forgotten now, these conferences were credited at the time with a large role in the American ratification of the Kellogg-Briand Pact (Peck 1944).

Catt identified the three areas of interest that would become central to the concerns of the LWV: civic education (especially for women), women's rights, and social feminist legislation. Women's legal rights, at the state level where the need was obvious, were central from the start. For Catt, peace replaced the program of domestic social welfare that motivated so many of the social feminists among the suffragists. As early as 1906 Jane Addams had converted the bulk of the members of the NAWSA to a "municipal housekeeping" view of politics, and inquiries into the meat-packing industry began shortly after. Catt had no personal experience with the urban poor, but she gave the League a mandate to improve the quality of American life, a mandate fully capable of accommodating the social policy agenda of the women's movement, including peace itself.

The initial purposes of the League were thus ambitious, complex, and possibly contradictory. They included the desire to "liberate women so that they could join men as equals in the political and social institutions of the country" and "the premise that females had a special set of interests which distinguished them from men and made it necessary for them to have a separate voice" (Chafe 1977:34). These two sorts of feminism had produced the NAWSA and the vote. In the League, as elsewhere, they coexisted. Now they produced a difficult practical agenda. How could one educate and train women in mainstream politics and at the same time pursue specific goals to which that same politics was indifferent, even hostile?

The tension is obvious in the wording of the League's 1924 decision to make the increased participation of women in public office a specific priority: "The League believes that qualified women in administrative office, upon boards and commissions, and legislative bodies, will contribute a necessary point of view to government in the United States and to its international relations. The League therefore urges the election and appointment of qualified women to positions in national, State, and local governments" (Young, 1st version, 7–8). In the word "qualified" lies the entire problem: once educated to political maturity and using all their (full) political rights, would women citizens differ from men? How was it possible to educate them so as to preserve the important difference? Perhaps it would be better to attempt to educate all citizens in "womanly" values—an education, however, that might well take a form different from instruction in the existing system of government and its values.

From the start the LWV leadership made the same response to all the goals it inherited—it combined them. The pursuit of women's rights and of social welfare could also become a means of civic education. The problem of gender specificity solved itself because men, as well as the established political mechanisms they continued to dominate, were visibly unresponsive to the issues in question. But it became increasingly clear that policies related to women and children and to the general welfare could motivate at least some women to a political activism they would not otherwise have undertaken. In the process they would learn the attitudes and skills necessary for moving into the greater world of normal politics. The League, as one analyst says in somewhat accusing tones, "retained a diffuse belief that females, by virtue of their sex, had a special concern with issues like social welfare" (Chafe 1977:35). Women in general also tended to retain that belief with the result that the League could appeal to them on just those grounds. But only at certain periods in its history did it formulate its purposes in such instrumental terms.

Catt did not approve of this approach. Her idea of citizenship training was far more abstract and specific, with academic experts instructing League officers who would then pass knowledge on to members of the local groups. After the inaugural meeting of the LWV in 1920, many of the new leaders stayed for a two-week School for Political Education, organized by Catt and run by University of Chicago professors directed by Charles Merriam; the material was then serialized in the feminist journal *The Woman Citizen* and afterward published as a book (Peck 1944:326). These sessions were followed by similar schools, three to seven days long, with copious handouts; more than a thousand women attended the sessions in 1920 (Young, 1st version, 28). But as time went on the training became less abstract. Indeed, from the very beginning it had included classes on such topics as marking a ballot and registering to vote.

Catt, who may have been less optimistic than the new LWV officers about getting the average woman to learn what was necessary, protested as early as 1922, "I do not agree that social welfare is a training [ground] for citizenship; getting rid of venereal disease has nothing more to do with the quality of citizenship than getting rid of the . . . common cold." Time was being wasted on such activities, she thought, time that could have been spent planning how to get more women on courts and into legislatures or influencing parties (Young, 1st version, 53). By contrast, the League as a whole accepted the argument that participation in the "working democracy" of the LWV was the best way to train citizens.

Maud Wood Park, the first president of the LWV, came to the organization after being coordinator of Washington lobbying for suffrage, and she moved with ease into organizing a coalition of women's groups to work for social legislation (the Women's Joint Congressional Committee). Park's training and her inclinations directed her toward both coalition activity and the use of education to change attitudes. But her background in the college suffrage societies made her relatively unresponsive to social feminist causes and inclined her to see them as of instrumental value. She believed that "the actual work of the League—the end for which organization supplies the means—is, first of all, training for citizenship" (LWV 1959:11). She could also say, without any sense of contradiction, that "we must teach legislators that the special concerns of women [have] to do with the conservation of human resources" (Young, 1st version, chap. 6). Similarly, the League's summary publication "Forty Years of a Great Idea" calmly accepted the legacy of the women's movement, saying the legislative concerns of the League's early years had already been studied for one hundred twenty years when the LWV was established and the flood of postsuffrage legislative projects was action logically accumulated during that period (1959:13).

At the beginning of the League, when progress was relatively easy in respect to the legislative agenda of the women's movement, potential conflicts of goals went unnoticed. During Catt's experimental five years there was progress on all policy fronts. Urged on by the Women's Joint Congressional Committee, Congress approved a long and long-desired series of measures. The 1924 convention of the League could rejoice in a congressional hearing on the World Court, the shift to permanent status of the Children's Bureau, congressional passage of the Child Labor

Amendment, the Cable Act (independent citizenship for women), the Lehlbach Civil Service Reclassification Act, the Packers and Stockyards Act, and the Voight Act (forbidding "filled" milk and establishing the Bureau of Home Economics). Most important of all was the Sheppard-Towner Infant and Maternal Welfare Act, passed in 1921, which established the beginning of a national system of child welfare; it had been "the first goal of newly enfranchised women" (Lemons 1975:155; Rothman 1978). On the state level, considerable progress had been made on women's rights in such areas as jury duty; the state leagues were very active and relatively successful here. Peace had been added to the organizational agenda: a campaign of support for U.S. membership in the World Court started in 1923, and an active Committee on International Cooperation to Prevent War was added the next year.

But as early as 1923 the process had begun to slow down, and opposition developed. From that year the social feminist women's groups felt obliged to combat the National Woman's party and its Equal Rights Amendment, which threatened the protective legislation so painfully won by trade-union women and reformers. Progress was slow in training women for civic activity. Women continued to vote in far smaller numbers than men, in spite of a major League campaign to get out the vote for the 1924 election. Few analysts were detached enough to recognize the effects of their being the first enfranchised generation. In 1924 the treasured Child Labor Amendment began to be defeated in the various states; it was never ratified. In a period of growing conservatism, it was increasingly clear that none of the League's specific goals was going to be achieved in the near future. More important, few of these goals were taken up by the men who still dominated the recognized political institutions. The few women in office could not be relied on. Alice Robertson, the only woman in Congress at the time, had been an antisuffragist; she voted against the Sheppard-Towner Act and opposed it actively (Lemons 1975:76, 157, 158).

Maud Wood Park was president until 1924, when Belle Sherwin, who had led the Ohio League, replaced her. Under Park, the League's program was essentially determined by delegates at annual conventions in a disorderly process that produced a large and widely proliferating series of specific goals and resolutions. Simple participation in this "town meeting" was thought to be the main form of civic education for members; they in turn carried on campaigns to enlighten the public. The League's definitive reaction to the low turnout by women voters in 1920 and again in 1922 was an attempt to involve more women in the organization itself. To this end, the constitution of the LWV was rewritten to speak of "improved" rather than "needed" legislation and to make the committees seem less controversial and more attractive to new members. Food Supply and Demand became Living Costs, American Citizenship became Education, Uniformity of Laws became Status of Women, Electoral Laws and Methods became Efficiency in Government, and Suffrage Research was terminated. At this point, also, programs were divided into two sections, separating reaffirmed policies from new ones, the latter in turn being divided into those from which action was to follow and those which were still being studied with a view to develop policy. The processes for passage of resolutions were tightened up; resolutions would be consolidated and a three-month period to study advance drafts was introduced; a period, usually several years, allowed the League to develop a consensus on new topics. But the dominance of members' initiatives and interests remained. Sarah Brumbaugh, who analyzed the League as an institution for adult education, approves of this period and particularly of its disregard of legislative effectiveness; for her, the process is the key (1972). Her perspective matches that of the next two presidents of the League.

The League had elected as its second president a woman with even less personal commitment than Park to the agenda of social feminism.[1] Belle Sherwin's first presidential activity was the extensive—and unsuccessful—campaign to increase the women's vote in the 1924 presidential election. She became convinced that citizen participation was affected less by motivation than by such institutional barriers as difficult procedures for registration, the poll tax, and literacy tests. In addition, nonvoters were ignorant of the impact of voting and of the potential of government action. Under her administration, the League developed a distinctive process of induction. A survey of local conditions was used to involve new members in supporting legislative action at the state level. Obviously the "Know Your Town" and "Know Your County" programs were likely to become mechanical, even manipulative; local conditions could not be reexamined de novo by each wave of new members. Similarly, women's issues became increasingly of instrumental value: "Voting is only interesting if the questions involved are understood and have some personal significance," wrote Sherwin in "Taking Part in Government" (quoted in Brumbaugh 1972:48). Voters' Service, facilitating voter participation, became a major part of League activity. In 1928–31 informational broadcasts were presented at the invitation of the National Broadcasting Company; these were the forerunners of the presidential and other candidate debates that are now an established part of LWV activities.[2]

Yet enthusiasm stayed high for issues that were parts or extensions of the traditional agenda of social feminism. For instance, the League had a

1. Young states, however, that Sherwin was much influenced by Canon Barnett of Toynbee Hall (1st version, 32).

2. In 1988 the League was, by invitation, coordinating voter registration publicized by rock stars Frank Zappa and Sting.

continuing, significant involvement with what became the Tennessee Valley Authority (TVA). Cost of living and domestic use of electricity were key to this LWV concern, based on the social feminist interest in household conditions and in the use of government for social welfare; such issues corresponded to consumers' interests. But Muscle Shoals and the TVA do not appear to have been seen in the League as women's issues. Under Sherwin's leadership identification with women diminished. Her own feelings are shown in response to a request (in 1926) to plan a program on "the civil rights of women" for the American Academy of Political and Social Science. The request itself suggests that the LWV was still seen as not just a women's but a feminist group. Sherwin, however, proposed "a better plan": "Why not move off the narrow base of 'equal rights' in which the fundamental difficulties have been largely solved to the larger question of 'constitutional expansion,' concerning the relationship of the government with a theoretically universal electorate, to the whole problem of allocating governmental responsibility for the public welfare?" (Young, 1st version, chap. 6). "Study without action is abortive" is given in "Forty Years of a Great Idea" as a summary of Sherwin's ideas about the League (1959:11). In her vision of the League, action had no content related either to social welfare or to women's rights. The goals of both sorts of feminism had been dropped. Yet Sherwin's main concern was still the feminist one of increasing women's autonomy. No move was made to include men in the citizen motivation and activity to which the League was now committed. Citizenship schools, "Know Your Town," questioning of candidates—all were still done by and mostly for women.

The year 1934 saw yet another LWV president, another unmarried woman, another woman committed to civic education rather than to feminism or social welfare. Marguerite Wells came from a state league (Minnesota), but her main experience had been with the legislative branch of the LWV in Washington. Her first initiatives were intended to streamline the procedures of the League in the interests of efficiency. Committees on areas of interest were drastically reduced in number and scope, concern with Social Hygiene (the double standard) being dropped in the process. Five topic areas resulted: government, foreign policy, economic welfare, social welfare, and education. Procedures were changed to provide more centralized organization, in order to allow the national board to focus attention on a small number of topics of yearly specialization. After 1927 the conventions became biennial, and only the council met nationally in between.

In 1938 Wells set out clearly her view of the LWV and of appropriate issues for its members. According to President Wells, the goal of the League was "a unique purpose . . . an effort to do no less than improve the operation of representative government and to foster the adequate functioning of government as a whole." Not a pressure group, the LWV worked in "the interests of good citizenship." Her version of history is interesting: initially the LWV had intended to educate new voters and to catch up on "certain social legislation long neglected because of the exclusion of women from the electorate." Only after these goals were achieved did the idea arise of "improving the electorate itself by providing more intelligent participation in politics" (7). She warns against a list of pitfalls including "artificial" (i.e., artificially high) standards of preparation and too extensive, insufficiently integrated programs. Coalition involvement is likely to lead the League to an inappropriate, ineffective focus on action, especially if related to "narrow" issues such as education, child welfare, women in industry, and peace (these are her examples). Consumer interests are acceptable: "'The consumer' is a shortcut for emphasizing citizen interest as paramount" (Wells 1962:12). But unlike the English Women's Co-operative Guild, she does not recognize that women have any specific role as consumers.

Within the League, leaders play the key role; they need to clarify the issues "until anyone of ordinary intelligence can grasp them . . . dramatizing them to catch the interest . . . [and] breaking them up into simple projects upon which budding citizens can cut their teeth" (19). The goal becomes a meaningful experience for each member at least once a year. The "easier choices," to be avoided, are to develop more experts or to become "a sort of eclectic pressure group on various subjects but restricted to governmental aspects" (21). "It is more important to teach one single citizen to take a first step in political activity than to teach a hundred citizens a great deal about government. . . . It is more important to help a hundred citizens to take a first political step than to penetrate far into the political process oneself" (19). Health, welfare, and education are identified by Wells as program topics that the League pursued in its early years: they are "subjects of universal concern, and involvement in them—as the League experience has demonstrated—leads the citizen and the organization on to ever broadening participation in government" (7). In 1940 the national section on Government and the Legal Status of Women was dropped as no longer necessary (Brumbaugh 1972:73).

Wells's manipulative and condescending view of the average citizen is appalling. It is, unfortunately, a continuing though not dominant dimension of the League. As late as 1962 the president of the League, "Mrs. John Glessner Lee," praised Wells's views as expressed in a reissue of the 1938 pamphlet. They are, she says, an "effective means to provide civic education and to stimulate responsible leadership." The League itself she describes as a model for "all truly democratic organizations which seek to prepare individuals to assume the full responsibility of leadership" (Wells 1962:1). No reminder appears either in 1938 or in 1962 that the organizations and individuals in question are or have relevance to women.

With the onset of war, the national executive became more and more directive. During the hostilities the League became a high-pressure distribution system for propaganda in favor of democracy and world government, and it temporarily put aside its wider educational function. In 1944 Wells prepared a slate of officers and a reorganization that would effectively have abolished the state leagues; she was obviously aware of the role of the state leagues in developing programs and in sustaining the organization's inherited lobbying and issue concerns. The state leagues rejected the proposals, although they recognized that after twenty-five years it was necessary to break loose from the last of the NAWSA structures and standardize the national-level policies of the League as a whole (Young, 2d version, 301–4). At this point the League structure was nationalized and centralized.

By the 1930s the League had disavowed its original rhetoric, and the agenda of social feminism should have ceased to be relevant. Meaningful and encouraging experience of politics could hardly be based on futile continuing attempts to produce equality for women, social welfare, and peace. Such attempts illustrated merely what the democratic system of government was incapable of. Nor could such issues provide dramatic, simplifiable inspirations for civic action. In addition, Marguerite Wells had explicitly rejected the untidy, nonhierarchical small groups and coalitions characteristic of the women's movement. Why then did the League not follow Catt's advice, voiced as early as 1922 in disappointment with the second nonresponse of women to their electoral opportunity—why did it not disband to form a new, general organization for civic education? At the least, why did it not turn to an agenda limited explicitly to education and directed to the whole population?

In institutional terms the answer is probably to be found in the ongoing activities of the state leagues, a history, as noted, that has not yet been written. The relationship between the state and national leagues always had an inherent tension. The state groups antedated the LWV itself and initially dominated on policy issues; at the start of the League's existence the state leagues appointed the chairs who drew up resolutions for the conventions (Young, 1st version, 21). At the state level the original impulses toward both sorts of feminism continued strongly, focusing both on social concerns and on equality for women. This was partly a matter of jurisdiction, since legislation regulating hours and conditions of work, including pay, was the business of the states. In the absence of a national ERA, state ERAs or their equivalent were possible, provoking the usual disputes about protective legislation. There were state courts and prison systems to be concerned with, state officials and legislatures to be targeted. Even practical arrangements for voting, increasingly a concern of the League, were legislated and administered by the states; Supreme Court decisions and constitutional amendments merely set limits on what was permissible. For constitutional change itself, such as the Child Labor Amendment, ratification was a state issue, and even voting an amendment out of Congress was accompanied by many glances toward constituency opinion of representatives and senators. In addition, the state leagues seem to have encompassed both the most reactionary and the most innovative elements of the LWV; they were the source of the proliferating policy suggestions that bothered national officers of the League and particularly Wells. In 1934 the process of developing resolutions was tightened up and the national officers enabled to select a focal topic or two; both charges served to reduce the influence of the state leagues and of feminist elements in the League.

Nevertheless, the national convention in 1936 approved no fewer than fifteen topics, including such traditional concerns as laws on pure food, drugs, and cosmetics. And strangely enough the new, businesslike League, intending to appeal to all citizens, selected as its national campaign subject a topic squarely within the social welfare tradition of the women's movement and of the League. The goal was a merit system for civil servants. A contest produced two slogans: "Good Government is Good Politics" and "Find the Man for the Job, not the Job for the Man" (LWV 1959:22). Admittedly, feminist sensibility was at a pretty low ebb to approve the latter slogan—but this happened before feminists became aware of sexist language. In keeping with new ideas, the issue was supposedly selected because it was dramatizable, simple, appealing, achievable, and could relate to the average individual; it ought to be able to give the woman citizen a satisfying experience connected with government.

This rationale for selecting the topic is clearly nonsense. Certainly corruption is dramatic, and certainly a merit system can be applied locally as well as nationally. But the facts are not what the average Leaguer could dig out at a local city council. Nor was it an issue whose unlikely successes would have an obvious appeal; who can work up enthusiasm about a change in the processes of hiring civil servants? In fact, the issue typified the civic concerns of social feminists. Concern about immorality and corruption in government and faith that citizen participation could produce necessary policy change are central to the views commonly stigmatized as indicating women's political naïveté, their moralism, their immaturity. Civic reform had been one of Catt's tasks for the League. The League had had considerable success already in cleaning up city government, often by promoting a nonpartisan or city management structure (Breckinridge 1933). In that sense the project of federal civil service reform grew out of local experience—but local league experience, not the experience of any general body of citizenry.

It is clear now, if it was not clear at the time, that employment conditions for women in the civil service were a central issue for the international women's movement between the wars—and that the merit system was crucial to women's access to jobs. Already in 1921 the Six Points Group chaired by Viscountess Rhondda had identified "equal opportunities for men and women in the Civil Service" as one of six areas where the law was blatantly discriminatory against women (Spender 1983). The 1930s saw married women dismissed from government jobs all over the world; such women had, in any case, worked in only limited areas and for fractions of the pay received by men in similar positions (Woolf 1938, Martin 1976). Women's organizations sprang to their defense. The Open Door Council and Open Door International groups (founded in 1927 and 1929) took up the cause, as did the International Alliance of Women, which had added economic equality to its list of concerns in 1920; by the 1930s the IAW included conditions of women in the public service as a related issue (Whittick 1979:124). These were essentially equity feminist groups; but although the League opposed them on the ERA and a number of other issues, it remained active in the IAW (a major arena for its struggles against the NWP) (Becker 1983). In addition, an effective merit system would help women in government and in particular the underpaid women staff of agencies of social policy such as the Women's Bureau and the Children's Bureau, which owed their existence to the activities of women's groups including the League.

The merit system campaign can best be understood as continuing the morality-and-purity campaigns that brought so many women into political activism and ultimately to the League's parent feminist organizations in the nineteenth century (Berg 1978). It seems likely that Leaguer response to this tradition contributed support to the campaign. Thus, although the rhetoric of the League in the 1930s paid no attention at the national level to the fact that the LWV was still a women's group, the organization was actively involved in issues clearly continuous with specific policy concerns of the historic women's movement.

After the war state leagues continued their activity on women's rights under the general mandates of the League's statement of purposes. Again, there is an unrecorded history of the development of equal pay legislation at the state level—the legislation that joined social and equity feminists in concern about the special difficulties of women's situation in the paid labor force.[3] In the LWV reorganization of 1944–46 the local leagues participated in developing new bylaws and a restatement of goals. The new president, Anna Lord Strauss, was a descendant of Lucretia Mott; what influence genealogy had is hard to tell. In any case, she oversaw a series of changes that stressed the role of nonexpert members of local leagues. The purposes now included "to promote political re-

3. Equal pay legislation was initially opposed by unions that wished the matter to be handled through collective bargaining; the National Woman's party perceived it as interfering with the ERA, but the Business and Professional Women's Clubs were active on the issue (Kenneally 1978; Rupp and Taylor 1986:145–46, 174–76).

sponsibility through informed and active participation of citizens in government"; the mandate of political education is not mentioned. The organization became activist and political: the League would now be able to "take action" on governmental measures and policies in the public interest by providing information, building public opinion, and supporting legislative measures.

On paper the reorganization was drastic. The national structure was reworked so that the national-level organization ceased to be a federation of state leagues. Members now belonged to local groups and also directly to the national; the state-level organizations were functionally defined, focusing on state-level problems and organized for that purpose by local leagues. But a whole series of possible new state-level mandates now responded to the continuing League principle of the "removal of legal and administrative discrimination against women" (Young, 2d version, 345). Here the campaigns for ratification of the ERA would be located. The restructuring recognized the need for more effective coordination at the national level; it left room for active continuing projects of the state leagues.

In this postwar period internationalism expanded; the guiding principle related to "domestic policies which will facilitate the solution of international problems," and it was used by the LWV to respond to the dropping of the atomic bomb (Young, 2d version, 310)[4] The League continued its support of international co-operation and therefore was an energetic backer of the United Nations. At first reluctantly and then with greater enthusiasm, it also took part in the establishment and activities of the United Nations' Commission on the Status of Women. Attention to consumers' concerns expanded and was joined by environmentalism; both developed from the long support of first the Muscle Shoals and then the TVA projects. Continued involvement with local conditions, especially in cities, and with citizen participation and civil rights led to increasing involvement with urban, racial, and native peoples' problems. It was officially in connection with this last cluster of issues that in 1972 a membership initiative moved the League to active support of the revived ERA; in 1954, like its close connection the Women's Bureau, the League had dropped its opposition to the amendment.

By the 1970s the second wave of the women's movement was well under way. Most commentators did not consider the League part of what they called a revival of feminism. Only when the group moved to support the ERA was it grudgingly admitted to the select company of supporters of women's liberation. By now most of the League's special concerns probably had little or no educational value as a training ground for general citizen participation through the normal channels of par-

4. This general survey of League policies is based mainly on Young's two manuscripts. Young was the U.S. informant for Duverger (1955).

tisan politics. But they were clearly feminist—if social feminism is accepted as part of the movement.

In the postwar period the League saw itself—and was seen—as a group intended to educate the whole citizenry. At the same time it continued to restrict its membership to women. The resulting contradiction itself provoked criticism. Sociologist Jessie Bernard said the LWV "was not designed for lobbying or exerting pressure on behalf of women's issues. It was, on the contrary . . . an educational organization for voters in general on behalf of issues of general not necessarily women's, concerns" (1979:281). This position she contrasted unfavorably with being "a strong female lobby to press for their own interests" (281). For Bernard, "public service" issues, though they counteracted machismo, were still not authentically women's own, since they had been defined for them by men (282).

To such criticisms the social feminist responds by asserting an autonomous commitment to distinctiveness, whoever initially defined it. And a group may assert such a position without recognizing anything feminist about its goals or nature. The League's most distinctive characteristic was what its members saw as a unique, disinterested commitment to the general welfare. The postwar League therefore lacked any initial identification with women. In particular, it did not see women as having special interests to defend. Accordingly, it did not adopt the male norm of the self-interested pressure group, nor did it perceive its altered policy in relation to the ERA as a significant change.

It is ironic that because it now supports the ERA, the League is praised for having moved to a new form of action, for lobbying for the first time on behalf of its members. Finally, say some commentators, the LWV is carrying on "normal" politics to advance the cause of women. Sheila Rothman pronounces such a judgment on women's organizations as a whole: as a result of experience with the ERA, "the women's movement is becoming another—and not altogether weak—vested interest group." She sees this as "novel and encouraging" and even goes so far as to rejoice that "this approach to social policy is likely to exacerbate tensions, to make an appeal to the common welfare still more obsolete" (1978:290). She is happy with a zero-sum world where compromise is unlikely and battle will be the appropriate metaphor for political discourse. The LWV, like all social feminists, rejected such an analysis of politics and instead had insisted on the possibility of finding a truly general good.

In effect the League is believed to have adopted equity feminism with its support of the ERA and is praised accordingly. This stance is irrational for Bernard, who is well aware of the importance of both the style and the content of social feminism, which fills what she calls the "redemptist role" (1979). What she correctly condemns is the pathology of female self-sacrifice, which cannot see women as deserving of decent treatment (Gilligan 1982). But of course social feminists have always wanted equality as well as a transformed environment; for them, equality is an essential precondition for change.

In the context of such hostile and often conflicting evaluations the League struggled with its feminist tradition. In postwar America, merely to be an all-women group or to make general interest arguments was to be stigmatized; self-interested arguments focusing on gender would have been unthinkable. Under these pressures the League stuck to its guns (to use a macho image): it retained its single-sex membership, it retained its commitment to the general welfare (including specific projects dear to the social feminist tradition), and it continued to work for women's equality.

CHAPTER 15

The League and
Its Feminist Identity

The best starting point in order to look at the postwar League is 1951. In this year all members became directly affiliated to the central federation, which was renamed the National League of Women Voters. For the first time all members received a League publication once a month. Respondents to the League surveys indicate that one attraction of membership is obtaining information; the *National Voter* (*NV*) is clearly a major source.[1] We can use this little magazine to see how the League deals with its self-image.

In the very first issue of the *National Voter* the League tackled the invidious implications of being a "women's organization." Policy themes are listed: economic development, inflation, U.S. security, the United Nations, individual freedom, voter service. The *Voter* assumes that this program will seem odd for a women's group; these are not traditional "women's issues," it claims, though in fact only women's organizations have ever taken voter service seriously, and some if not all of the other topics are public interest issues typically espoused by women's groups. The editor of the *Frankfurter Zeitung,* who had visited with the National Board, is quoted proudly as saying that the League represents "work by women but not for women." And the *Voter* notes that the editor was impressed by the five hundred (nonvoting) male members of the Atlanta League. "We are too!" is the arch comment (May 15, 1951).

However, the second issue of the *National Voter* shows with some precision just how the League defines its members. It is clear they have to be women; the Atlanta branch is a freak. An archetypal member is presented, Mrs. Dooley of "Mrs. Dooley Takes a Look": she is "methodical. She makes lists and she gets things done. Whether she's planning a Sunday school picnic, a Community Chest drive or how best to put over a school bond issue." She is an experienced civic activist, in short, with a

1. Initially a depressingly unglamorous pamphlet, the *National Voter* has become quite glossy and attractive, with effective layout and photographs; it consists of about thirty pages, 5.5 inches by 11 inches.

history of involvement with a church, in community charity, and in pressure activities related to education. She has followed the traditional volunteer route of the social feminist, and she epitomizes the activist woman who in 1951 was considered nonpolitical. The one area she apparently has not been involved in is partisan politics. Though there is no mention of it, she may have canvassed or worked in some other way in the nonpartisan world of municipal politics.

Mrs. Dooley is worried, and she is galvanized by her concern into activities beyond her immediate community. Her main anxiety is related to "the threat of communist aggression and the menace of inflation," which she sees as connected in a "vicious circle." Overseas and domestic problems are associated, and the situation is illuminated for Mrs. Dooley when she thinks about "friends using up their savings and buying on the installment plan." The metaphor is familiar from the Guild and the Union féminine civique et sociale: the world is, or could be, like a larger family. Her solutions are not complex, for she favors direct controls on prices, wages, and rent, as well as economic and military assistance to Europe "to strengthen the free world" and technical assistance for "underdeveloped countries." Her techniques are familiar: Mrs. Dooley is going off to consult her friends in preparation for "a busy summer ahead [when] big decisions would be made in Congress on aid to our Allies, taxes, and controls." She sets out confidently, for she "has seen things accomplished in her home town when groups have joined hands and worked for a school lunch program or an improved health department" (*NV* June 15, 1951).

This sort of approach is common in women's groups. The cozy tone and the allegorical citizen—"Mrs. Dooley squared her shoulders and put on her hat"—are characteristic. Mrs. Dooley is in fact a good representation of the League member. She has had children; they are not of an age to restrict her movements, but they were the reason for her moving into pressure group activity. A seasoned civic activist, she also understands the processes of national politics. She is now learning about international politics from a perspective where peace is the major goal and the family is the model. Obviously she is not currently in the paid labor force; if she "worked" at some stage in her life, the experience had no continuing impact on her. Finally, she feels no need to consult her husband about what policies to prefer and certainly not about whether she may engage in activities she does not think of as political.[2]

Mrs. Dooley, however, is atypical of the women members of similar groups in one important way. Her activism before she joined the League was related to home and children, but her present policy choices are not justified in terms of those presumably continuing concerns; she thus

2. Her non-WASP name is slightly surprising but may be echoing humorist Finley Peter Dunne's popular Mr. Dooley, who commented shrewdly on American politics before World War I (Hart 1965:240).

reflects the somewhat more academic tone attributed to League women and possibly their superior education. In addition, she projects from the domestic to a far more generalized social policy than most such activists do. And she does so in a way less responsive to women's specificities of situation. This point becomes clear if we contrast her to Mme. Jourdain, the heroine of the 1963 UFCS publication (Caron and Doneaud).

Mme. Jourdain, "a citizen without knowing it," is Mrs. Dooley before she became involved in public affairs. She demonstrates how a young mother can be drawn through her children into attention to all levels of politics. For her, support for the European Community comes from the realization that European integration makes it easier for a child to go on a summer study trip; world peace is important because it will save the children. The household is thus a direct motivation as well as an ana-logue or model. The process of becoming involved is accurately de-scribed. However, the end product is not a Mrs. Dooley but another French activist, Mme. Dubois. And Mme. Dubois continues to justify her activism in terms of her family. Mme. Jourdain, it should be noted, had to consult her husband about whether civic action was a good idea, and he counsels and educates her as she tries it. Furthermore, Mme. Jour-dain does not start with the ad hoc groups of Mrs. Dooley's (Ameri-can) experience but goes directly to the family-oriented, institutionalized UFCS.

In general, the UFCS distrusts formal political structures less than the League does, and differs from the League in its specific commitment to move its members into conventional politics. In addition, the UFCS is responsive to the situation and the organizational activism possible for women in the paid labor force. We infer this last point from the presence in Mme. Jourdain's life of a third woman who is also active in the UFCS: Mlle. Gilberte, a self-supporting single woman who is also a union mili-tant. For the UFCS, any organized group is potentially a locus for ac-tivity on behalf of and by women. The variety among women and their shared interests dictate this position. The family-oriented, explicitly "feminine" stance of the UFCS thus seems to have made it easier for the group to see itself as including all women and able to accept more easily the differences in the situation of those women. Women's shared charac-teristics, explicitly emphasized as the basis of the UFCS's distinctiveness, create a unity that does not need to be defensive.

In contrast, the League presents the confusing spectacle of an all-women organization, clearly dependent on female values and activities, that nevertheless works for the whole community and tries to think of women as just another, not particularly important segment of the popu-lation. In the interwar period women could be spotlighted as the latest among new citizens, not yet fully granted their rights and needing more education. In the 1960s women could be seen as another "minority." In the intervening period the social feminist inheritance survived, unrecognized, as an established agenda and procedures, retained on the pragmatic basis of effectiveness.

We can see the implications of the League's position of the 1950s in a statement made by the League president in September 1955 to the Constitutional Rights Subcommittee of the Senate Judiciary Committee (*NV* September 17). She had been invited to take part in a "survey of the state of constitutional rights," in which representatives of eleven classes of citizens were invited to "petition" the government. The groups concerned were a rather strange assortment: the lawyer citizen, the teacher citizen, the veteran citizen, the churchman citizen, the fraternal citizen, the Negro citizen, the businessman citizen, the workingman citizen, the farmer citizen, the newsman citizen, and the woman citizen. Percy Maxim Lee spoke for the last group; she was the only woman included.

President Lee began with a general preamble about the value of liberty and free speech and then provided a "frame of reference":

> Let me say at the outset that I do not presume to speak for all the women of America and not necessarily even for all the members of the League of Women Voters. Nor do I find it possible to look at the problem only as a woman for there is no such thing as a woman's point of view, as far as I can ascertain. The women of America live and work and think side by side with everyone else in the United States.

It is a pleasure to report that she went on to remind her audience that "when one speaks for educators, veterans, lawyers, business groups and so on, one is speaking for women as well as for men"; however, she expressed no concern that men were speaking for teachers and churchworkers, who include a majority of women, as well as blacks and farm families (50 percent women).

Why, then, Lee asked, should the League be consulted in relation to freedom of speech and expression? Her answer referred to the conventional history of the women's movement; she lacked either the knowledge or the will that would have invoked the difficulties the League and other women's organizations had in the 1930s with red-baiting very like the McCarthyism that explains the session she is attending. The League of Women Voters "was born when the last great stronghold of obstructionism to complete 'government by the consent of the governed' was abandoned. . . .The purpose of the League of Women Voters, founded in 1920 as a result of the granting of the franchise to women, is 'to provide informed and active participation of citizens in government.' By the very nature of its purpose and work it is the antithesis of totalitarianism." The central, giant nonsequitur goes unremarked; why should enfranchisement of women produce an organization whose goal is to increase the activity of "citizens"? Why the League of *Women* Voters? Historical accident is not a sufficient answer.

Lee then justified the association of the League with the First Amendment. The League typifies the voluntary organizations encouraged under that amendment, it has acted directly and indirectly to defend freedom of speech, and, most important, its own internal procedures exemplify the operation of freedom of speech: "As President of the League of Women Voters, I am convinced that the strict adherence of the organization to democratic principles and procedures is more important in the long run than are the causes which it pursues."

In fact, the subjects of League attention were neither arbitrary nor wholly neutral. The suffragists had wanted the vote in order to improve civic life; the successor movement retained that project. And the (female) membership of the group did affect choices of both tactics and causes, as can be seen in the December *National Voter* of the same year. The occasion was a presentation of the newly formalized process of "consensus." Under this process, which represents the League's proud claim to be a "grass-roots organization with a thoroughly democratic process," local boards recommend items for the national program. The list is then discussed and defined by the National Board; it is sent back as the Current Agenda section of the Proposed Program to the local leagues, which again discuss, suggest revisions, and prepare reports that become the basis for the "recommended" items of the Proposed Program to be presented to the biennial convention. The *National Voter*'s 1955 restatement of consensus was part of a summary of the League's revised procedures (after the revolt of the state leagues). The 1954 withdrawal of opposition to the ERA is explained as follows: the decision was taken "because of the time that had elapsed since the position was taken, and because many of the new members who had joined in the meantime had little background or little interest in the subject." The League had of course opposed the ERA vehemently throughout the 1930s, and the explanation seems disingenuous when we realize that the Women's Bureau also dropped its opposition in 1954. We may wonder also why this particular change receives prominence in the general discussion of procedural changes.

The explanation of the change is bland: "No voice had been raised in Convention against the traditional stand, but delegates chose to have the League stand uncommitted on this issue." A deliberate contrast is made with another withdrawn position, support for federal aid to education. In this case there was a "lack of a clear mandate from members," along with "lack of a paramount interest in the subject" (*NV* December 15, 1955). A striking contrast exists between two justifications of what is procedurally the same sort of decision. In relation to the ERA, there is no suggestion of lack of interest or concern; instead, we see a careful withdrawal from a contentious earlier position, with implied disagreement about the preferred alternative. The statement about federal aid to education sounds like the way a public interest lobby group with mixed membership might have disposed of the ERA. But would such a group have been either for or against the ERA in 1954? A quarter of a century later, this time remembering the 1930s, the League was prepared to defend its earlier opposition to the ERA in terms of "protection of tens of thousands of women working in non-unionized, unskilled jobs" (*NV* December 1980); in the 1950s process-oriented arguments were used to mask a significant policy change. Yet the policy change occurred.

Apart from the changed position on the ERA, the *National Voter* of the 1950s showed little that can be identified as ideologically feminist. The revised statement of principles did, it is true, retain the commitment to "removal of legal and administrative discrimination against women" (principle no. 10). Even this degree of explicit feminism was lost in the next decade. In 1964 the new human rights interests of the League were incorporated into the program, with the Current Agenda including an item on equality of opportunity in education and employment "for all persons." At the same time the principles were reworded, reduced to six, and put in the form "The League of Women Voters believes that. . . ." The old principle related to women's rights was assimilated: "The League of Women Voters believes that every citizen should be protected in his [*sic*] right to vote; that every person should have access to free public education that provides equal opportunity for all; and that no person or group should suffer legal, economic, or administrative disability." Discussing these agenda items, the *National Voter* gave illustrations related to age, poverty, and race but none related to gender (May–June 1964). However, a generalized commitment to activism on behalf of rights certainly permits state-level intervention on behalf of women. According to staff, such activity continued at an increasing rate. And the League continued to make proud if often vague and embarrassed references to its suffragist past.

Well before the revival of feminism the League took pride in its origins (*NV* July–August 1959, July–August 1961), though it also stressed its differences from the old National American Woman Suffrage Association, pointing out that the League had new officers and took on a wider, public affairs mandate. In 1961 the *National Voter* happily quoted an editorial from the Eugene, Oregon, *Register-Guard*: "The League may have been born of suffragette [*sic*] impulses, but it has matured to become one of the leading forces in the critical analysis of governmental problems and the general enlightenment of the public on these problems" (July–August).

As late as 1970 a brochure entitled "A Report to the Nation," part of the fiftieth anniversary drive for donations and intended to appeal to business, was stating defensively: "Too often, people think that because the word 'women' appears in the title of the League organization, its activities are confined to serving women. Of course this is not true. The League happens to be made up of women because its origins are found in the early suffrage movement. But the League exists to serve *people*— all the people it can reach, and it aspires to reach every citizen everywhere."

Yet the League continued to be a women's organization, and the implications of this decision are clear: topics of interest to women and neglected by other sorts of groups remain its top priorities. The organization's ambivalences about this commitment were fairly strong during the period preceding the second wave of feminism, but the identification with women and even with the women's movement was clearly present in the 1960s. For example, the *Voter* is happy to state that the League resembles the suffrage movement in its competence. It is more productive, however, for the suffrage movement "took many years to produce its first and only crop," while the League works on many fronts (*NV* July–August 1961). In 1963 the League president agrees with the president of Radcliffe College that "what most women want in addition to marriage and children is something they think is really important on which they would like to work very hard" (*NV* May–June). The next fall the League prepares for the elections by setting up a Women Voters Week, justifying it as follows: "The immediate aim of Women Voters Week is to get more women registered to vote in November, but its long-range goal is to promote more informed and active participation of citizens in government" (*NV* August 1964). The campaign focused on women because their voting rate was still 10 percent lower than men's.

The ambiguities are conspicuous at the fiftieth anniversary convention in 1970. Two young women are featured speakers—but they represent black and student militancy, not the new women's liberation movement. The report of the convention notes an attempt to have it "voice support of the women's liberation movement," an attempt defeated along with efforts to get conference condemnation of the Cambodian invasion and the Kent State University shooting. The justification for inaction is the wish not to break with the time-honored tradition of preparing positions through consensus. The Smithsonian Institution had arranged, on request, an exhibition in honor of the anniversary, with the theme of "Women in Politics." At the convention itself, Catherine Drinker Bowen, identified as "the well-known writer and feminist," argues in favor of greater participation by women in electoral politics (*NV* May–June 1970). Bowen may not have been the most radical or conspicuous feminist of 1970, but it is significant the League is prepared to use the term. The next convention, in 1972, featured Gloria Steinem.

By 1971 the *National Voter* shows that the ERA and related issues have become salient to members of the National Board. A dialogue about possible program items is presented, taped at a meeting held during the board's sessions. The ERA as a possible topic is discussed; one board member actually rejects it as a way of *avoiding* "getting involved in controversy . . . taking up the *real* issues . . . like equal pay for equal work, abortion, alimony, and such." The same number of the *National Voter* has a list of possible topics for the 1972–74 program. Concerned that members are insufficiently involved in the development of the famous consensus, the *Voter* asks them to send in coupons expressing preferences among the alternatives presented. These include a new area, "status of women." A summary of possible topics in that area includes the following questions, which suggest some of the feminist issues of which the League was aware:

> Would the ERA be an *effective* step toward improving the status of women? Should female candidates for public offices automatically be favored over male candidates? Should labor laws protecting women and restricting their work activities be repealed? Should employable divorced women receive alimony? Should courts routinely give mothers custody of their children? Are sex role stereotypes an essential ingredient of family stability?

The new Human Resources area now includes more attention to daycare, and in another article President Lucy Wilson Benson notes that the membership of the League is changing with changes in the situation of American women. Procedures must recognize that many members find it hard to attend meetings regularly (if they are working full time, for instance). Yet such members still have an interest in the organization and want a say in what it chooses to do. Perhaps a mail ballot or some other modernized procedure could be used to develop consensus? She adds: "And these approaches would also make it possible for the League to establish a position on issues of immediate and great importance." The list she gives includes the ERA (*NV* November 1971).

The reader of the *National Voter* may suspect some disagreement about moving so fast. Status of Women was not adopted as a program item. Nevertheless, the ERA did get approved for action at the 1972 convention, by a highly unusual procedure. Topics suggested but not included in the Proposed Program are listed as "non-recommended items," which the convention may by a two-thirds' vote substitute for recommended items. This almost never occurs, partly because the lengthy routine consultations do in fact tend to produce agreement. In addition, items are likely to be on the agenda for study for some considerable period before a stand requiring action is adopted. The ERA skipped all these preliminary stages; though listed only as "non-recommended," it was approved by a floor vote, and for action not just for study.

This endorsement of the ERA seems to have been a spontaneous effort by state leagues; staff members agree in this analysis, though I was told that at least part of the National Board was sympathetic. In the League as a whole, however, an overall awareness was only slowly developing. For instance, a major conference sponsored by the League that fall seems not to have seen the ERA as relevant or to have included any feminist perspective (*NV* September 1972). When, the next year, President Benson appealed again for procedural changes to make more action possible, her example was the way the League had operated in the 1930s: "A highly successful campaign [was organized] to get the merit system introduced into government. The campaign held League interest for nearly eight years, giving birth to such catchy phrases as 'Good Government is Good Politics' and 'Find the Man for the Job, not the Job for the Man'" (*NV* June–July 1973). Program guides a few years in the future would cite the merit system campaign as especially relevant for women; the League in 1973 had no sensitivity to this point, however, or indeed to anything limited about the second of the two catchy phrases.

By this time the League was seriously involved with the National Women's Political Caucus (NWPC) founded in July 1971 (Hole and Levine 1971:426–27). Six months after the caucus was formed, the *National Voter* published a page-long interview with its executive director. Is parity in politics a good idea? asks the League; "the goal of many people in the women's movement is to *eliminate* the distinctions made between men and women." The NWPC response defends parity, referring to "sex" as "the last unacceptable form of social discrimination that exists" (*NV* January–February 1972). The stance was comfortable for the League, which accepted the specificity of women and organization by and for women but also set an equity goal of liberal assimilation. When the NWPC opened a Washington legislative office early in 1973, the League was ready to assist (Costain 1982:26–27).

When Ruth C. Clusen became president in 1974, the League was more committed to involvement in political activity than it had been. During her presidency the League played a major role in activities for International Women's Year (1975). These were concerns no men's or mixed group would even have contemplated, and the same was true of the continuing, intensifying involvement with the ERA and with the NWPC. All the same, policy justifications that did not mention any special relevance for women still dominated. In 1976, for instance, a League intervention concerning spousal involvement in politics produced an *amicus* brief that focused on "strengthening citizen participation in government" and the electorate's right to pick its representatives as it chose. The issue was whether a judge's spouse may participate as a candidate in local politics, and the League did not mention that it is *wives* who are more likely to suffer from restrictive interpretations in such cases (*NV* Fall 1976).

In the meantime, however, the League had moved very strongly to support the ERA. The convention endorsement had taken a form that permitted immediate action by state and local leagues. By 1974 the League was part of state ERA coalitions in eight out of nine unratified states (Costain 1978:35n.40). The convention in that year gave the ERA "high priority" and explicitly approved "action to implement the principles" of the ERA, which had been endorsed in 1972; this motion was understood to approve of increased activity at the state level, where the campaign for ratification necessarily had its main centers.

This same convention, moved to Cincinnati, Ohio, from unratified Illinois, also saw approval of a program recommendation to admit men as voting members able to hold office. National television covered a heated debate, in the course of which the League's two feminist impulses stood clearly opposed. Equity feminist views saw the exclusion of men from full membership as discriminatory (they were allowed only as nonvoting associate members): "Equality of opportunity regardless of sex is an idea whose time has come. Let us show our leadership by establishing equal rights here and now in the League. Then, with our credentials untarnished, let us establish equal rights out there in the world." In contrast was the position that the League is "a unique place for women to develop leadership, talents, confidence and a sense of self-worth." Proponents of the second, unsuccessful position were prepared to invite men into the group but not until women had achieved equality. Neither position, it should be noted, saw any permanent place for women's organizations in an egalitarian world.

President Benson emerged from behind a television boom to accept a check from "an eager gentleman who wanted to become the first man to join under the new rule"—her husband. The vote, which some League staffers remember as close, was in fact more than the necessary two-thirds' majority (969 to 433) (*NV* Summer 1974). In 1976, however, a change of name dropping the word "women" was rejected, and the *National Voter* cites as persuasive a clearly feminist argument: "Why . . . are we reluctant to announce our commitment in our name? Why erase our feminine identity? We should refuse to change our name because we're proud to be an impressive, powerful, nondiscriminatory organization of women" (Summer). In 1980 the name was retained once more, but the *National Voter* commented only that the majority was "fearful of losing the instant recognition associated with the name" (Summer). By 1980 men were only 3 percent of the membership, and there was no evidence that the LWV was moving in either name or reality away from being essentially a women's group (LWV 1980).

It was a women's group, moreover, with a growing investment of resources and energy in the ERA and other issues clearly identified as both "women's" and "feminist." In 1977 a huge drive for funds for ERA support was coordinated through the state leagues, an unusual procedure justified because the state level was where the ERA action was.

Indicating the seriousness of the project, the drive was set up separately from the National Board, with the former president of the Pennsylvania League recruited as chair (*NV* Summer 1977). In the fall of the same year the *National Voter* for the first time featured "Women's Issues" in a double-page spread that included support of Medicaid for abortions, training for "displaced homemakers," affirmative action, and changes in credit and divorce laws. The next year saw the launching of a publication series on women with pamphlets on the job market and on daycare ("a pressing issue facing working mothers"). The League of Women Voters Education Fund, its nonprofit wing, now became involved in class-action suits related to women, such as women construction workers (*NV* Winter 1977). On paper these activities look like a small amount of the League's program. They were, however, costly in both money and personal commitment, and League staffers say that the ERA in particular became an obsessive issue that generated in the 1970s the classic feminist burnout.

At the 1978 convention, ERA chair Nancy Neuman voiced reactions to the prolonged and by now bitter campaign, and her statement reinforces the impression that the new activities themselves had a radicalizing effect. She saw the campaign as a basis for activating women politically. And she spoke as if all League members were women and feminists: the ERA battle "has opened our minds to the reality that everything else we do in our personal lives, our work and our involvement as citizen activists is diminished by the fact that we as women are not yet first-class citizens." In its argument that equality is necessary for women to be effective as reformers, this is pure social feminism. Yet it is also an equity argument. Social feminists do not feel that their status as citizens diminishes "everything else we do in our personal lives." She continued with another equity argument, one very characteristic of the League: "Our insistence that 51.3 per cent of the population, the females of this nation, be included in the U.S. Constitution is a continuation of the struggle to match this country's promises of democracy with the realities of daily life" (*NV* Summer 1978).

The next year the League Council, which met between conventions, established a new National Business Council for the ERA to operate at the state level (*NV* Summer 1979); it was part of an extensive pro-ERA campaign using business and media connections (LWV 1982–84:20–22). At the convention the League moved beyond its 1974 position, adopting an amendment from the floor that authorized using support of the ERA as a basis not simply for efforts to obtain ratification but for the far more ambitious program of "action to bring laws into compliance with the ERA":

(a) to eliminate or amend those laws that have the effect of discriminating on the basis of sex;

(b) to promote those laws that support the goal of ERA; and

(c) to strengthen the enforcement of such laws (LWV 1980–82:21).

Understandably, the League's sixtieth-birthday celebration differed in emphasis from its fiftieth. Nancy Neuman was now coordinator for the Human Rights area, under which the ERA was classified (called "Human Resources" in LWV 1980–82). She attempted to explain how the League had come to work on a "women's" issue; her version is probably close to how many other Leaguers managed to rationalize what they thought was a novelty:

> When the League first joined the battle to promote social justice for all, racism was the chief target. Over the years, the struggle has grown to encompass a number of other 'isms,' among them sexism. This contemporary angle of vision was a strong motif in a number of convention actions. And many Leagues will want to give special attention to the impact of Human Rights issues on women. It's an area where the League is already working actively (*NV* Winter 1980).

Neuman would have been aware of the League's long involvement with this and other issues of concern to women, but her knowledge of the League's history did not show in this statement. She was reiterating a familiar equity argument, with women's disadvantages justified by a generalized framework of concern about human rights. The League's main flyer for the ERA campaign does much the same. Glossy and colorful in bright blue and yellow, it mentions "women" only in the names of sponsoring organizations: "To set the record straight. . . . The ERA will affirm the nation's promise of equal rights for all before the law. That's *all* it will do." This is probably good politics, though it did not succeed in getting the ERA ratified.

In its internal communications, however, the League gave a rather different version of its feminist history. In what was told to League members, from 1976 on, about the history of the League's involvement with women's issues, the social feminist legacy reemerges.

The League publishes for each biennium a forty- to fifty-page booklet describing the program as adopted at the latest convention. It outlines policies, includes references to relevant League publications, and, most important for our purposes here, gives a history of each current issue. The ERA first appeared in the *Impact on Issues* (LWV 1972–74) as "ERA Ratification," which then became simply "ERA." The "Position in Brief" began as "Action to support equal rights for all and action in support of the Equal Rights Amendment" and changed in 1980–82 to "Action to support ratification of the Equal Rights Amendment and to bring laws into compliance with the goals of the ERA." The history given for the period prior to support for the ERA is interesting.

The first paragraph describes the adoption of the position, not mentioning that the ERA was "non-recommended," links it to congressional approval of the amendment ("only weeks after. . ."), and explains that the 1972 convention "saw it as a necessary extension of the League's long-term support for equal opportunity . . . [and] as one of the major ways to take action in support of H[uman] R[esources] positions. . . . With this decisive action, the League—a lineal descendant of the original women's movement—came full circle, to give priority support once again to equal rights for women and men."[3] The language is moderately feminist, referring to "the foremothers of the women's movement." One paragraph talks about the early movement and its "demand for unequivocal acknowledgement of women's equality before the law—the same demand they were making on behalf of blacks." The League is aware that these women "also put forward resolutions on many specific rights" and identifies the franchise as only one of many but the one that came to be seen "as the key that would unlock the door to the others." There is an unacknowledged echo here, of the Seneca Falls conference. League opposition to the ERA is defended as "a problem in priorities," and reference is also made to the "new and hard-won state labor legislation" the ERA threatened (a parenthesis reminds Leaguers that "organized labor took a similar position," with the AFL-CIO approving the ERA a year later than the League).

Then a paragraph asserts, still somewhat defensively, that "though it was an organization *of* women, the early LWV wanted to affirm strongly that its interests and lobbying activities were not *confined* to women's issues." The early League focused on "a broad range of social issues." A list follows of issues that "were, of course, of obvious concern for women," including the Sheppard-Towner Act, the removal of discrimination against women in immigration and naturalization, and equal pay for equal work. Action seeking "equality for women in the Civil Service Classification Act" has reemerged into the League's feminist consciousness, and so has the work of local and state leagues "to eliminate sex discrimination affecting jury duty, property rights, the treatment of women offenders and a wide range of other women's issues." The retention of the principle about women becomes a matter of pride; the anti-ERA position that was abolished in 1954 is described as "long dormant."

The League is thus delineated in terms of a feminist tradition, but neither the term nor the idea is used. The League's movement to a central emphasis on what are recognizably women's issues is described as follows: "Times change, but events have a way of repeating themselves. More than a century after the abolition fight, the civil rights struggle of the 1960s helped respark the women's rights movement. As the League became active in seeking civil rights for blacks, members became more acutely aware of the parallels between the status of women and that of minorities."

3. "Women and men" is the wording from 1978 on; 1976–78 had said "men and women." The quotations are from 1978–80.

The League wants to have it both ways, a tradition of feminism but also a superior, nongendered commitment to civil rights. The fore-mothers of the League would have been prepared to say that civil rights are a natural interest both of women and of women's organizations, the more so because men's groups have been inactive or ineffective in re-spect to such issues. They would also have been prepared to say that women's civil rights are particularly badly constrained. Instead, the LWV invokes an organizational tradition of concern with civil rights in general and women's rights in particular. But it is prepared to put major resources into the symbolically crucial women's rights issues for which it will not claim priority.

In short, the League will *act* like a feminist organization, it will claim a feminist history, but it will not talk like a first-wave let alone a second-wave feminist group.

Would the League be more effective if it explicitly identified with feminism? Most critics obviously believe it would. A more explicit com-mitment to feminism would today, it seems, be equivalent to the political engagement so long urged upon the League. It would have to include support of particular women or profeminist candidates, on the assump-tion that women as a group have interests that are competitive with those of others and need to be fought for.

Feminists studying the League today easily become impatient. The manipulativeness, the patronizing tone and attitudes, and the disavowal of feminist identity are infuriating. The notions of moral purity and co-operation, or education and general improvement, have a faintly alien air. Yet the energy, the commitment, the amazing range of issues and goals, and the ideals are all enormously appealing. Above all, the com-mitment to a grass roots–based women's community of activists seems to link with the core notions of feminism. The League's insistence on main-taining distance from the so-called real world of politics is understand-able. And it is hard to believe that the parallel and nourishing world of the League has constrained or damaged women in relation to politics. Rather, the LWV has extended the meaning of the key terms "feminist" and "politics." Most important, its version of politics is feminist in its insistence, for women, on a particular mode of exerting influence.

In fact the League has neither kept away from narrowly defined par-tisan politics nor kept women out. But Leaguers' involvement with poli-tics has been of a sort not usually recognized as political, much as its feminism has been unrecognized.

CHAPTER 16

The Politics of the
League of Women Voters

A 1981 assessment of the "new women candidate" of recent years reported that "all over the country, one hears political women echoing the remark 'I got my training in the League of Women Voters'" (Mandel 1981:137). Such awareness of the LWV's political role was new; the reality it reflected was not. League training and support of women in office, and the involvement of League members and former members in elected and appointed office can be seen in fragmentary form from the very earliest days. Sophonisba Breckinridge's contemporary survey of women's first ten years of citizenship in the United States even identified among women state legislators two who were drafted "by the League of Women Voters"; she noted severely in a footnote that they were drafted by "a branch not affiliated with the National League which discourages the policy of endorsing candidates" (1933:328). Breckinridge relied on the League for her information about women in local and county office, and her references show that the Minnesota, Wisconsin, Connecticut, and Michigan leagues made surveys of women in such offices in 1925, 1927, 1929, and 1930; she described these surveys "as the only available study of comparable offices over a period of years" (334). They imply considerable, sustained Leaguer involvement in local politics, at least as informed observers concerned with the role of women. Breckinridge also included an excellent three-page account of the LWV which underlines its focus on issues and notes that "with great earnestness it has supported a program of federal and state legislation" (66). She identified the League as "non-partisan" and recorded that "in some communities it has incurred the displeasure of local party leaders, [but] in general it is recognized to have an all-partisan membership." Noting successful work by Leaguers with city charters and with state legislation, she finally remarked that "naturally there is a great difference [among local leagues] in the attitude toward the study of political question and active participation in controversial issues" (67).

Martin Gruberg, in 1968, was the next person to think that an inventory of American women's political activity would be of interest. Like his predecessor, he took seriously the role of women's organizations, including the League, in politics. He noted explicitly the movement of LWV officers into political positions, quoting a League report that the organization was annually losing three hundred officers who went into politics: "Board membership is thus a springboard for entering a party" (91). In 1964 one out of every thirty-eight League members in Illinois was participating in government at policy levels including the state legislature as well as a large number of state and local commissions and boards.[1] To the extent that these are not elected offices, the Leaguers could continue to serve on League boards, as some 80 percent of them had (92).

Gruberg thus took a first look at the whole range of possibilities of appointment to public office which remained undocumented until the studies done in the 1980s by the Center for the American Woman and Politics (CAWP). Appointed office can be nonpartisan, and it has been of considerable importance in terms of women's opportunities for public service. Gruberg also inventoried politically active American women since their enfranchisement and included their organizational membership; a very large number were Leaguers, including Senator Maurine Neuberger and Eugenie Anderson, U.S. ambassador to Denmark and Bulgaria. More material about women in the 1920s and 1930s now fills in the networks of Leaguers' political activity, for example biographies of League members Eleanor Roosevelt and Frances Perkins and Susan Ware's work (1981) on women in government during the New Deal.

As systematic studies of women in politics finally began to accumulate, they revealed the role of the League in preparing women for elective office. In 1972, 40 percent of a sample of "effective" women state legislators had belonged to the League, and many cited the group as having trained them (Kirkpatrick 1974:44). In the same year the League reported that eighty-nine of its members were serving in thirty-two state legislatures, which is an astonishing 23 percent of all women legislators (*NV* March–April 1974, Werner and Bachtold 1974). In 1977, 18 percent of a sample of women party officials, (women centrally involved in partisan politics) were also members of the League, and 57 percent of a sample of League board members had participated in a political campaign (Baxter 1977:166). And in a 1983 summary of the CAWP projects assessing women in public office, the authors stated that "the League of Women Voters has emerged as critical to motivating women's candidacies." In their judgment, "the League of Women Voters, while a

1. Leaguers served on the state Commission on Human Relations, state Boards on Higher Education and Commission on Children, Governor's Commission on the Status of Women, Fair Employment Practices Commission, Election Laws Commissions, Board of Mental Health Commissioners, Northeast Illinois Metropolitan Area Planning Commission, Chicago Transit Authority, Chicago Commission on Human Relations, and other local bodies.

nonpartisan organization which does not support or endorse candidates, has stimulated many women to enter the political arena." About half of women legislators listed membership in the League; among women in county or local-level office, the League was the organization most frequently mentioned (Stanwick and Kleeman 1983:35).

The full CAWP study of women in state legislatures reported in 1983 that 57.5 percent of state senators and 49.7 percent of state representatives had belonged to the League at some time, as had 34.7 percent of women county commissioners, 17 percent of women mayors, and 17.9 percent of women in local councils. The data were displayed in a table headed "Except for Mayors, More Women Officeholders Belong to the League of Women Voters Than to Any Other Women's Organization" (Carroll and Strimling 1983:89).

These studies included only a small, select group of politically active women, those actually elected to office. We have no systematic information about unsuccessful candidates. When I wrote to the League about electoral activity of the eleven national presidents, I was told that none has held elected office; my correspondent, a League employee, noted that the current president was a candidate for the House of Representatives (Sorett 1982). The fact reminds us of all the unsuccessful attempts at office that Leaguers must have made. In addition, there is reason to think that Leaguers or former-Leaguers are well represented among the women appointed to governmental positions. In recent years two national presidents have served as federal appointees at the subcabinet level.[2] A CAWP study of women in cabinet and subcabinet positions and on the presidential or vice presidential staffs during the Carter administration showed the League as somewhat influential in having "helped [these women] to obtain appointments," though less influential than the National Women's Political Caucus and the National Organization for Women: 13 percent mentioned each of the latter, 8.7 percent the League (Carroll and Geiger-Parker 1983:39). These jobs are relatively partisan; no study was made of appointments to boards and commissions, an important area of influence on policy and likely to be congenial to those devoted to nonpartisanship.

The CAWP project on women in public office also included six group consultations with women actively engaged in public life, including novice and unsuccessful candidates for office and a small number of women appointees to high-level positions in the Reagan administration. Surveying the CAWP studies, the author declared flatly that "the League of Women Voters . . . has been the most important training ground for women in public life today" (Stanwick 1983:13). Women officials are quoted in the CAWP report on its consultations, making more concrete

2. Lucy Wilson Benson served as under secretary for security assistance, science and technology (appointed in 1977), and Ruth C. Clusen was assistant secretary for environment in the Department of Energy from May 1978 to January 1981 (Sorett 1982).

just how the LWV contributes to campaigns without losing its nonpartisanship. A councilwoman from California, for instance, states that "the League of Women Voters provided me with training on how to analyze policy issues"—this is standard—"and the public exposure that was invaluable when I ran for the council." Another local official in California is even more specific: "The League does provide excellent training on issues. In addition, the colleagues you develop in the League become volunteers and precinct walkers in your campaign. After they get involved in your campaign, they are encouraged to become active politically." Another council member notes: "The League of Women Voters gave me knowledge of government and an understanding of the situation and players in city hall" (13–14).

A picture of the active Leaguer begins to emerge as a woman with an interest in government processes which is more practical and focused than generalities about education for democratic government might suggest. The movement into actual electoral contests does not seem such a great leap into the unknown, especially at the local level, which is largely nonpartisan. The creation of networks of friends, supporters, and helpers itself extends political involvement. The League informally supplies volunteers to conduct telephone canvasses and to prepare and deliver campaign literature: "Individual members of these groups are entirely free to work on political campaigns. Not surprisingly, they are likely to sign onto campaigns with a candidate who belongs to the same organization in which they hold membership" (Mandel 1981:171).

It now seems undeniable that League members moved on in large numbers to contest and hold political office. Furthermore, the organization's nonpartisanship promoted this participation. Nonpartisanship as practiced in the League provided training in distinguishing among political issues, in deriving and supporting preferences among policy alternatives, in publicizing and lobbying for these preferences. Meanwhile, both deliberately, as part of an educational process, and unintentionally, as part of finding out about issues and promoting them, the LWV provided a great deal of information about the functioning of the political process. It also provided, for its officers, extended training in the practical procedures necessary within any mass-membership organization. Unpaid and demanding of time, it retained as active leaders only those who found such processes and above all such issues passionately important and absorbing. The quest for public office was a natural sequel. It should produce an officeholder without particular ambition but with a powerful commitment to the public good, to the issues that led her into politics, and to the public to whom she was responsible. Her fellow members would see themselves as continuing in the nonthreatening process of education; she would think she had now changed activity entirely. Both would overlook the continuity.

The CAWP analyses suggest that involvement with the ERA may have played an important role in the politicization of traditional women's groups, because it was a contest fought on a state level and one in which the absence of women officeholders had a clear impact (Stanwick 1983:14). Although such experience may have had some impact on the LWV, the League's role in training and generally encouraging women in relation to public office was already well-established by the time it moved to support the ERA.

The organization has always officially maintained a constraining view of its own proper relationship to politics, based on a concept of politics as narrow as that of any of its critics. Paradoxically, such views have in practice made available both for the League itself and for its members a wide range of activities related to politics. League President Ruth Clusen epitomized the LWV's position. In a 1979 article, "The League of Women Voters and Political Power," she restricted politics to the election of women to public office, but that, she said, was not the organizational goal of the League. "The greatest political gains in 'pushing women into the system'" were made as a result of the Education Fund's arrangement of presidential candidate debates, she believed: "That both presidential candidates agreed to debate under the aegis of the League of Women Voters was a testimonial from the highest level of politics to the viability and legitimacy of participation by women in public life" (1978:130). Yet she herself served in a federal subcabinet position and ran for election to Congress.

Clusen's account reserves for the League itself an odd and indirect role as involved in the structure but not the content, the process but not the outcome, of political competition. Politics, which operates within "the system," is part but not all of public life. The League's concern is the functioning of the system itself. It does not preclude individual women or Leaguers becoming active, even partisan participants, and in fact the specific form of the LWV's influence (toward democracy and openness) would facilitate women's access to politics. Finally, the League's visible role in the system made women's public participation more acceptable. But the organization's role was possible only if the League (not women necessarily) was perceived as nonpartisan and therefore nonpolitical.

In 1980 the writer of a letter to the *New York Times* presented a similar view, complaining that the League had refused to include third-party candidate John Anderson in the debates of that year. He thought it "unfortunate" that the "nonpolitical" LWV "jumps at the opportunity to play a major and *political* role in the outcome of the election" (Schenkman 1980). That is, he interpreted their action as intended to influence a political outcome and therefore pejoratively labeled it "political." Such a comment amounts to the severest possible interpretation of "nonpartisan." It would bar support not just for parties or candidates but also for issue positions. It would limit the League to a deliberately balanced and noncommittal examination of topics that might need citizen choices; the group would have to present evidence on both or all sides of each issue, and it would take action only to increase information and participation. Presidential debates would be acceptable in this view, but not support of the ERA. Advocacy would be excluded even in the relatively mild form of the Political Accountability Rating scales, since the very selection of topics for ratings bears with it a preference. The League would become a truly neutral educational organization; it would also become virtually unrecognizable.

For one thing, such a role would exclude lobbying, and the League certainly lobbies.[3] The LWV did not attempt to retain the tax-deductible status that prevents allocating a "substantial" portion of activities to lobbying (Berry 1977:50). Instead, it established the League of Women Voters Education Fund and the Overseas Education Fund, both of which confine their activities to education and litigation and receive substantial funds from foundations and from the government.[4] The LWV's success as an organization can be inferred from the fact that it is one of a handful of public interest groups that receive both enough small (not tax-deductible) contributions to support a lobbying wing and enough large donations to make tax-exempt foundations worthwhile.

The ERA campaign shows the range of activities that lobbying can include and the high level of energy and resources that the LWV can on occasion commit. Furthermore, this commitment was in terms of desired political outcomes. Although it can be interpreted as oriented toward process—democratization and equal citizen protection—the ERA goes far beyond neutral guarantees of citizen participation or government effectiveness, the ostensible goals of League efforts. Unlike such reforms as the movement to city managers or permanent voter registration, the measure lacks what have been pejoratively identified as the moralistic, abstract, and disinterested qualities of women's characteristic reformism (Lane 1965). In the case of the ERA the League took sides on an issue that normal politics cannot articulate adequately. Essentially, the ERA represents those issues of special interest to women which do not fit the established patterns of party politics. It is therefore political without being partisan in a formal sense (even though the Republicans now oppose it): conflicts of power and of preferred values are involved, and what necessarily follow are consequences in relation to control and policy. LWV convention discussions and decisions show that the organization was fully aware of the policy impact of the ERA on issues related to women. Perhaps the most useful way to understand the League's role overall is to focus on issues—issues that are inescapably political.

The League has never doubted its concern for issues; in question was the consequence entailed by orientation to issues. Within the League,

3. Even if analysts including Bernard (1979) are not aware of the fact.
4. The Leslie Suffrage Commission and the Carrie Chapman Catt Memorial Fund had been precedents, though they depended entirely on private donations.

where the principle of nonpartisanship was never seriously questioned, the tension between politics and apoliticism took the form of competition between study and action. In the prewar period the problem was solved by focusing on an overarching goal, citizen education intended to improve citizen participation. This educational process required action that would motivate citizens for learning. The resulting participation could be aided by reforms to improve the system of government and to make citizen action more effective. Working for a merit system combined all these goals, or should have: it educated citizens by guiding them in activities expected to produce a more responsive government. But such work did not appear political, since the subject, it seemed, was the environment of politics rather than politics itself.

If we look more closely at the question of the merit system, however, it becomes evident that efforts to improve structure or process can never be far removed from attempts to influence policy. The machinery of government is not neutral, and its reform has distinct consequences for particular groups and policies. Nepotism and favoritism in government had been used to restrict both services to women and the number and level of women employees. Any campaign to equalize treatment of civil servants was bound to have among its effects an increase in women's influence and an increased impact of women's interests and perspectives. The outcome would probably have partisan consequences, because government reform and expanded citizen participation tend to benefit the party not in office.

Even the apparently innocuous goal of education of the citizenry was bound to have effects upon the power relations that depend on citizens' failure to recognize their genuine interests (Lukes 1974). Since elite retention of dominance depends on citizens being unaware of alternative options, inattention to the decision-making system and its outcomes is crucial to continuing control over citizens. Public education about government structure and policy is therefore political because it is a potential disrupter of power. We may recall the indignation provoked when the League seemed to challenge the party system itself.

But the League, like the public in general, identified politics only as the direct operation of the electoral system and the choice of official actors. Attempts to increase citizen participation and education were certainly not seen as potentially able to change the structure or environment of power, let alone its distribution. Therefore they were not political—and from this conclusion has flowed all the criticism of the League for diverting women from politics. Leaguers' concentration on issues was interpreted as a refusal (perhaps an inability?) to accept the partisan method of identifying bases for disagreement and possible change; their emphasis on education and government structures was seen as compensation for their inability or unwillingness to play an effective role.

These considerations bring us to the crucial questions. The LWV, it seems clear, has not integrated women into the existing partisan and electoral arrangements. But should it have? Is it the fault of the League—or to its credit—that this integration has not occurred? And to what extent can this outcome be attributed to our— or the Leaguers'— definitions of politics?

The main "evidence" for the League's keeping women out of politics seems to be the scarcity of women in elected office in the United States. Many Americans think of the United States as the most advanced country of all in relation to women's civic status, the suffrage movement as having generated a vast potential group of women activists, and the League as having somehow diverted this potential in the years after 1920.[5] Most seriously, the LWV is thought to have encouraged in women a variety of attitudes incompatible with political activity and influence.

Until recently, political scientists took it as established that women actually holding political office were motivated differently from men, and therefore were less numerous and less successful. The "therefore" is the tricky part of this argument. As a classic article put it,

> Politics for the male leader is evidently more likely to be a vehicle for personal advancement and career advancement. But for the woman leader it is more likely to be a "labor of love," one where a concern for the party, its candidates, and its programs assumes relatively greater importance. If the male leader appears to be motivated by self-serving considerations, the female leader appears to be motivated by public-serving considerations (Constantini and Craik 1977:238).

The practical result of such an orientation is male dominance of politics, as the odd word "evidently" suggests. One of the major causes of such dysfunctional attitudes and career patterns is supposed to be the LWV.

John Stucker makes this accusation explicitly. To begin with, the League encouraged women to concentrate on "women's issues." In addition, "a second factor enhancing the isolation of women from professional political roles was the development of volunteerism in our society, a process which was symbolized by the growth of the League of Women Voters." Borrowing terminology from the National Organization for Women, Stucker consequently characterizes the LWV's activities as "service-oriented" rather than "political or change-oriented." Leaguers'

---

5. All dimensions of these assertions can be challenged, of course. We may begin with the ethnocentrism of the assumption of U.S. superiority in relation to the situation of women. Many indicators, including the timing of enfranchisement and the level and type of female labor force participation, cast doubt on U.S. claims of being advanced on the status of women. And it is fanciful to imagine that the League, with its limited membership, served as a substitute for politics for a significant number of interested women.

efforts were not "directed toward inducing change in the broader social, political, or economic system" (1977:279, 280). The "educational"
League, segregating women, encouraging them to think of themselves as
above or outside politics, has interfered with their political maturation.
The enormous amount of time and energy put into the League becomes,
paradoxically, part of the argument; no resources are left for "real"
politics. Note that, for Stucker, the alternative to "service-oriented" is not
ambition but "political or change-oriented."

Such arguments are suspect in their assumption that a deliberate will
to change, channeled through electoral politics, is essential for political
action. They are also undermined by newer research on the few women
who are unarguably part of politics, which shows that a voluntaristic or
public service orientation is not incompatible with entry into partisan
politics. A relatively traditional view of women's roles, which would encourage attention to women's issues, does not necessarily interfere with
involvement in conventional forms of politics. An analysis of women
delegates to the 1972 presidential conventions in the United States concluded that "the elements of politics which are thought to be unfeminine
are competition and *visible* dominance. If an activity is relatively non-
competitive, service oriented, and not in conflict with home and child,
we see no reason for the 'traditional women' to shy away from not only
general participation, but leadership positions" (Sapiro and Farah
1980:17–18). Especially at the level of local politics, a "citizenship duty–
voluntaristic" (18) approach is compatible with officeholding; this is, of
course, the level where the majority of women politicians is to be found.[6]

Another study, whose theme was that "privatization" keeps women out
of politics, found that under some circumstances concern for children
could serve as an activating force for community action by women—an
action classed as political. This study described the League as "one of the
largest political organizations in the United States outside the political
parties" and noted that "it has been devoted to citizen education and
mobilization for over a half century." (Sapiro 1983:135). The word "mobilization" here catches the League's often-overlooked exhortations to
citizen activism, a message directed first of all to women.

Looking at the much-examined 1972 convention delegates, yet another study found the women significantly different from the corresponding men only in their views about women in politics: "In brief,
among men and women who have everything but gender in common,
there was disagreement about the nature, situation, role, and future of
women" (Kirkpatrick 1976:478). Men were especially more likely to
deny discrimination and to see role conflict as disabling for women. The

6. Sapiro and Farah (1980) also cast doubt on questions that attempt to tap political
ambition by asking about hopes for future officeholding. Women like those they are
discussing move only gradually into politics and are unlikely to foresee running for office.

author, Jeane Kirkpatrick, concluded, "It is men rather than women who are most likely to oppose individual women's efforts to move into the more important roles in power processes" (488).

Earlier, Kirkpatrick had documented the movement into electoral politics at the state level by relatively traditional women, mainly devoid of political ambition but committed to public service. Her conclusion, in 1974, was that attitudes did indeed play a role in keeping women out of politics, but the relevant attitudes were those which enforced the primacy of domestic obligations. This is, of course, quite different from a preference for social welfare, a lack of personal political ambition, a lack of enthusiasm for partisan politics, or a fondness for women's organizations—the attitudes usually attributed to Leaguers and, more widely, to women. Women did indeed have such views, but those views were not what prevented their entry into politics. On the contrary, the ideology of social feminism often made potentially competitive roles compatible for women instead of disabling.

Kirkpatrick also emphasized the part played by discrimination in limiting women's access to political office. She thus draws attention to the large group of women who would like to hold office, a surprising number of whom demonstrate this wish by seeking it—usually without success. Every study that shows women to be less ambitious than men has also shown a pool of potential candidates large enough to have produced greater representation of women among candidates, let alone public officials, than in fact exists. For instance, one analysis of activists involved in suburban pressure politics found that about 60 percent of the women were reluctant to run for office, as contrasted with 40 percent of the men. Sixty women would consider electoral activity, compared to ninety men. Such figures do not fit comfortably with the actual number of women holding the relevant municipal offices: 13 out of 371 (3.5 percent) (Lee 1977:131, 127). Carrie Chapman Catt had foreseen barriers, warning women they would be unwelcome in what she called the "umbra" of politics, the inside of the parties among "the people who are picking the candidates, doing the real work that you and the men sanction at the polls. . . . You will see the real thing in the center with the door locked tight. You will have a long hard fight before you get inside" (Peck 1944:325). In 1933 the first cohort of women public officials told Breckinridge repeatedly that "the men do not want the women to come in, only to help on election day" (331). Politically minded women might not, as a group, wish to invest in such unpromising activities.

Nor is it necessary to postulate some feminine reluctance concerning competition to foresee enormous difficulties for women when they run for office. The new woman candidate of the 1970s, who had far greater chances of success than ever before, still faced special difficulties ranging from finances, clothes, and family conflicts to the greater liabilities of challengers and the disadvantage of being the second or third woman on a slate (Mandel 1981). Other problems related more directly to the current organization of government. A nonpartisan activist commented in 1977: as far as politics is concerned "it is not so much the amount of time—I can always hire a baby-sitter as long as I know some time in advance when I am needed. I can always plan my time around a League of Women Voters' meeting. But holding public office involves work at unpredictable hours, and I can't cope with this" (Lee 1977:130). The study from which this citation comes does not demonstrate any lesser sense of efficacy or any lesser commitment of time in the women studied. It does suggest, however, the existence of structural barriers related to the constraints on women's lives as they are currently lived. At best the woman in office will lack the domestic support system than most men can reasonably expect; the single or divorced woman who is a candidate or public official usually has no one with a regular commitment to cook, shop, clean, maintain a household, entertain, and run errands, and the married woman can expect little more than financial and moral support.

Considerable evidence now shows that American women are remarkable in their level of attention to and interest in politics, although their participation is not as high as that of comparable men (Verba, Nie, Kim, and Shabad 1978). In such a context, inhospitable to female participation in electoral politics except as voters, inhospitable also to the sort of issues with which organized women had been chiefly concerned, the League developed, not so much a substitute for partisan politics as a supplement for women. The activities of the League, like all social feminist insistence upon a distinctive role for women, can be cited as part of an ideological justification for excluding women from the mainstream of public activities. But this was not how Leaguers understood what they were doing, nor what they recommended. Nor does it seem reasonable to blame them for social structures that preceded their organization and made it necessary.

We need a more refined understanding of politics. When the women officeholders interviewed by the Rutgers University (CAWP) project described the LWV as "quasi-legal" or "quasi-governmental," grouped with the civil rights movement and "other community activities," they did not do so dismissively. The context was affirmative action in appointing women to public office; the demand was to treat League activities as equivalent to more common qualifications for appointive office (Stanwick 1983:6). Activities within such an organization are functionally equivalent to training for at least the appointive version of political office. The League thus has a role in relation to the political process.

At the same time the organization is still marginal, for these women officials continue to restrict the notion of politics to elective and appointive office. Similarly, League President Ruth Clusen, writing about the League just as larger numbers of women were starting to become officeholders, refused to include even pressure group activities in the category of politics: "The League of Women Voters has functioned as . . . a political lifeline for many women candidates. The League has re-emerged in the last decade as a strong citizen's lobbying group on national, state, and local levels of government, and as a result, is a natural training ground for women in politics" (Clusen 1979:112).

What Clusen writes is true, but the League is a good training ground because what it does is political (as all lobbying is), not because lobbying is a sort of antechamber to politics. In addition, the League increasingly carries out, though in a nonpartisan fashion, many of the functions normally performed by political parties. It trains, it recruits to politics, it provides funds and campaign workers. And it performs these functions in circumstances where parties continue to be unreceptive to women in general and to feminists in particular. The women interviewed by CAWP sound like the officeholders Breckinridge interviewed fifty years earlier: "Women will run in spite of the party, not because of the party," says one (Stanwick 1983:4).

Practical politicians, even when they are women, are aware of the conventional constraints of politics. "We've been issue-oriented . . . involved with issues," says one of the women interviewed by CAWP. "That's not what wins elections. It's the power that comes from being able to raise money, spend money, support other candidates with money" (Stanwick 1983:7). As another female officeholder, a California Republican, put it, "this is a time when our feminist philosophies are coming smack-dab face-to-face with our political philosophies" (Stanwick 1983:5). Experience in working the system is not a complete solution. A former (female) mayor observes that "no matter how well women learn to raise money, if women continue to represent the same types of issues they do now, they will never have the same access to money as men" (7).

But the last politician quoted does *not* proceed to suggest that women become "political" in the accepted way, shifting views to give them access to the parties and to funds. Instead, she concludes, "women will have to use the grassroots fund raising approach" (7). Or, as the CAWP study suggests, they will have to set up their own Political Action Committees and use their own organizations for recruiting, electioneering, and other support functions that parties and associated networks supply for men. Something along these lines seems to have happened in the 1970s and 1980s in Santa Clara County, with its exceptional networks of co-operating feminist groups (Flammang 1985). Beyond local and other nonpartisan offices, of course, the candidates will at some point have to work formally through the established parties. But they would do so from a position of far greater strength if skills, motivation, support system, and funds were already in place.

In short, women should not attempt to conform to the existing structures but instead should create alternatives that respond to their primary interests in issues and in public service. Any definition of politics must include such activities.

The League already provides training, motivation, and concrete support systems for women's movement into public office. It does so not in spite of its focus on issues but because those issues are central and strongly motivating to women volunteers. Public office becomes attractive to these women when they can see how tenure of such positions will help them realize the goals that drew them to the League. Issues must not be dramatic and educational or simply focused on the processes of democratic government. Instead they must be the "women's issues" that normal partisan politics cannot handle. Then women have every incentive not just to work on reforming the processes of politics, or to influence them through lobbying, but to move into the system for direct action—if only because under such conditions it is possible to enter politics without accepting its assumptions about acceptable issues and processes.[7]

The League values its nonpartisanship as a resource and will not give it up. However, it could, without contradicting nonpartisanship, put a higher priority on explicitly training women to move into public office and working with them once they are in office, as the UFCS does. It chooses not to, leaving the movement into public service to individual efforts. The CAWP analysts do not object, for they see a division of labor. The League's important role appears to be largely unplanned: "Large numbers of women officeholders have belonged to the League and have acquired important leadership skills through League activities" (Stanwick 1983:99). Such an analysis again removes the League from the structure of politics, making it no more or less important than any other voluntary group. It echoes the judgment that the suffrage movement was good for the women who participated (O'Neill 1971). And this is an inaccurate assessment of the League's role.

I have not discussed the League's influence on public opinion and on both the level and the quality of voter participation. Nor will I discuss further why analysts see that role as nonpolitical. I consider such influence a crucial part of politics because of its impact on agendas and on policies. Such activity is, at the least, a potential challenge to the estab-

---

7. Susan Tolchin and Martin Tolchin make the same point, but in a manner hostile to the LWV: "Relegated to voluntarism in the party, women with political interests often seek a more serious role for themselves in the League of Women Voters, where they can at least achieve some status to compensate for their distance from any real power and influence. Many fine women politicians are drained off by the league, which despite its value as an issues lobby has not changed its post-suffrage stance against noninvolvement in electoral politics, thus excluding itself and its members from gaining any real influence in the political world" (1974:82). As usual, they overlook the role played by the many Leaguers who have gone on to appointive and elected office, as well as the possible impact of information and structural change. But they do at least recognize the strong appeal of the League for "fine women politicians."

lished system of power. But let us put this matter aside, provisionally accepting the identification of the political with the control of policy making and execution that comes through election or appointment to an office controlled by the interplay of political parties. This view, let me repeat, the League shares with the public and with political analysts. In this context, I argue, the League has managed, in a nonpartisan way, to expand the political system by generating an issue-oriented route to both citizen activism and candidature for public office.

We may contrast the League with some of the other women's groups discussed here. The Women's Co-operative Guild and the Union féminine civique et sociale both started in a period when women did not have a recognized role as citizens in the public realm. Out of domestic considerations and obligations they generated a vocation that led, without detours, to citizen pressure and directly to partisan politics. Their members felt no need for nonpartisanship, since their ideological starting points gave them clear guidelines for selecting among parties. They were wary of the parties, as we have seen, even of those with which they had close connections, insistently evaluating them in terms of issues. But they had no problems with the basic idea of at least contingently endorsing candidates or parties whose policies they supported. They thus injected issues not usually central to party divisions into their relations with electoral politics. The WCG persisted in believing that a party could be influenced from within, and the UFCS was able to find parties or at least candidates it could support. The newly enfranchised Guild members had a home in the new Co-operative party, and the MRP welcomed the Union in terms of both personnel and issues. Disappointments came only later, after the habits of electoral involvement had been established. Partisan options, even if only instrumental ones, made sense.

The League, in contrast, started when women's entitlement to a public role was legally established if as yet untested. Its members were already accustomed to function as an effective pressure and education group in relation to public policy. Both major parties in principle supported women's partisan participation while in practice dismissing the issues most important to the women of the League. For this and other reasons, the League therefore recoiled from direct participation in partisan politics and, in its own and others' view, from any form of politics.

But the system of influence it established on the political environment, the nonpartisan zone of issues and structural change, was deeply political and more influential than has yet been recognized. In addition, as we are now beginning to realize, the League provided a prototype of an alternative training ground and support system for women in appointive and electoral office. More careful study of the political women of the interwar period will show an even greater influence by the League than has been suspected. And if we enlarge our view of politics to include these two neglected categories, the unsuccessful but (obviously) motivated candidate and the appointed official, we will find more evidence of the League's role. We will then be able to evaluate it properly as a feminist supplement to politics—to politics as both we and the League insist on defining it.

Or, better, we can redefine politics.

Of course, the problem is just how to proceed in this redefinition. The League experience can suggest to us that politics must and will come to be understood as including both the small-scale voluntary group and the individual and domestic goals that are characteristic of such a group. These goals include both the social and the moral aims typical of social feminism, along with its ideology of public service and the transformation of public life.

PART V

THE FUTURE: RISKS
AND POSSIBILITIES

The organizations studied in detail in this book resemble many other mass membership federations. For one thing, they all have a formal representative system, with presidents and other officers, votes, and resolutions. Of the multitude of such organizations, some have a significant number of women members. The groups I have examined differ importantly, however, in that they were organized expressly for a membership of women, have always been run independently by women, and accept a social feminist ideology. These group characteristics are related, for the social feminist belief in women's specificity entails single-sex organizations and guarantees their independence from male control.

The other characteristic shared by the three groups is their role in encouraging political activity by women. Again the impact of social feminism is crucial, for it makes it possible for women to change activity without changing self-image. An established domestic role can be extended rather than challenged, in the process showing the permeability of the boundaries between domestic and public life. The co-operative movement's interpretation of woman as consumer and household manager, which enabled the Women's Co-operative Guild to claim a major role in public life, was a specific version of the image of woman as nurturer and caregiver, an image that other social feminist groups have drawn on. The UFCS and the League of Women Voters similarly extended the Catholic concept of the mother as "queen of the household" and American images of women as educators and protectors of democracy.

The women involved in these activities did not necessarily identify their efforts as feminist or recognize them as likely to expand women's autonomy. Their "discourse" was conventional, even traditional. They were therefore able to continue to coexist with mainstream organizations, as well as the conventional systems of thought from which they increasingly diverged. Yet tensions were always present, if only in the women's assertion of the practical possibility of organizing by themselves for their own goals. As women's initial optimism about participation in public life encountered resistance from the political system, a crucial variable in the development of these social feminist groups became apparent: the degree to which the group was tied to existing, male-dominated political structures. The Guild, which had emotional and ideological as well as organizational links to the co-operative movement, was unable to maintain its feminist effectiveness. Its international links and its pacifism, so closely connected, were ignored, penalized, and in the end virtually destroyed by the co-operative movement. Its commitment to Co-operation fatally constrained its further expansion of women's autonomy. The Union féminine civique et sociale, by contrast, escaped the concrete and intellectual constraints of Catholicism. Its struggle to define a response to reproductive issues shows just how painful such liberation is likely to be. And the League has paid for its independence by enduring scorn, even hostility, for its nonpartisanship.

The development of three social feminist groups demonstrates how, in their different ways, these groups generated a viable and appealing political role for women. I now attempt a more general assessment of social feminism, looking at the risks imputed to it and at its possibilities. The risks, I argue, are organizational, and history suggests they are relatively insignificant. The possibilities, on the other hand, are on the theoretical side. Social feminism provides a basis for criticizing and re-evaluating, not just mainstream or sexist theory but equity feminism and the social system itself.

Here I move away from the organizational impact of social feminism, its concrete historical legacy. Social feminism, it should be recalled, is not usually thought of as having any theoretical significance. Even the most positive interpretations are likely to find the belief system's practical achievements flawed and dangerous precisely because of what is interpreted as atheoreticism or conservatism. I argue that, on the contrary, social feminism provides the most promising, the most powerful system of analysis now available for feminists.

CHAPTER 17

Organizational Lessons

The practical contribution of social feminism has to do with modes of political participation, with the development of a role in politics for women. Here "politics" means public life and particularly those areas of public life which relate to the authoritative allocation of resources—the selection of the personnel and policies of the state.[1] In the past two centuries women in modernized societies have moved from a role that was essentially domestic to a role that includes the entitlement to act in political life as freely as men. This is the political goal of equity feminism. In addition, I argue, women have begun the process of transforming political life by their participation—the social feminist goal. The activities of social feminist groups have had an impact in both ways, generating a practical activism that is now established and, as a result, beginning to change the shape of public life.

Even the analysts of suffragism concede the role of social feminism in obtaining civic rights for women, mainly because social feminism provided a rationale that enabled even conventional women to operate as volunteers and also as "normal" politicians at both the mass and the elite level. The continued paucity of women in high political office now owes very little to women's own inhibitions but much to attitudes among men and to practical barriers imposed by the continuing conditions of women's lives. Only a small number of citizens ever care to play an active political role, and in all modernized countries many women are now available to do so if permitted. And it is no longer a blanket prohibition, formal or informal, that restrains them.

The second contribution of social feminist groups is more subtle and more important. The legitimation of women's political activity combined with practical assistance was social feminism's crucial contribution histor-

---

1. I deliberately use a restrictive notion of politics here, a blend of notions suggested originally by Max Weber and adopted by Lasswell and Kaplan (1954) and Verba, Nie, and Kim (1978:46). In this book I am not interested in women's informal or illegal power but in the creation of an authoritative public role.

ically—but it was historically limited. The descendants of the suffragists no longer have to persuade anyone a woman can speak in public without fainting or being disgraced; eventually the descendants of today's reveiled women will achieve the same legitimacy (and I fully expect that social feminist arguments will assist them also). Women's mass participation increasingly approaches men's. Their participation will be equivalent when women's socioeconomic situation is equivalent to men's and when men cease to place obstacles in their way. These are not conditions we can expect in the near future. In the meantime, we can nevertheless expect a steadily increasing participation of women in politics. But those women will enter the flawed, hierarchical, partisan, competitive, and male-dominated public domain we know so well—Annie Leclerc's "stinking military world" that is marching blindly to self-destruction. Social feminist organizations, continuing after legal and practical emancipation, have provided the necessary resources for women to enter that masculine world. These resources include the potentially significant desire to change political life as well as a domestic model for changes. It is here the content of social feminist beliefs has direct significance for public life. Closely related to the rationale of women-only groups, social feminist beliefs generate an annex to or, better, an expansion of political participation.

The most obvious implications concern the role of political parties. Nonpartisanship is women's most innovative political response to a milieu that is still unresponsive to their concerns; it can accommodate active political interest and involvement along with a preference for basic change.[2] Social feminism seems to be basically unsympathetic to partisanship. Among the groups studied, only the League was formally nonpartisan, but even the Women's Co-operative Guild, devoted to a party it helped found, was prepared to give only contingent, issue-related support. Both the revolutionary and the interest-oriented party are bound to conflict with the social feminist orientation to politics, for the first disregards gender as a basis of social structure and the second can assimilate women only as an interest group. In either case the motivations that unite social feminist women's groups are excluded. For women's groups neither the apocalyptic future nor the self-interested play of power is acceptable as the criterion of policy. In addition, those women who are committed to the value of a women-only group cannot also make the required commitment to a party and its victory. Nor could social feminist groups make unquestioning commitment to an ideology other than their own.

Social feminism therefore precludes any unconditional involvement in

2. None of the political systems discussed here has room for a "women's party" on the model of existing ones. Even where such parties exist within multiparty proportional representation, their role is to serve as an extension of social feminist lobbying, as in Iceland. The so-called women's parties in West Germany and Canada are not interested in holding office (Lovenduski and Hills 1981).

a male or mixed-sex social movement. The organizations studied here were not equity organizations, female versions of a male model, whose members expected to merge into a larger whole. Instead, they postulated a particular and continuing mission for women. As a result, it is inaccurate to see the decline of the Guild as merely a mirror of the decline of co-operation, or the success of the UFCS as no more than a part of secularization in France. The Guild's self-image as the mothers' union related to a conception of co-operation, but it related also to an older image of the nurturing mother. The larger co-operative movement finally rejected both elements of the Guild's rationale, but the elements were too closely linked for the Guild to drop either one. What it dropped, in its old age, was the transformational element of social feminism, the drive to remake society in a domestic model through women's participation. The ideology and the organization it nested in were both too congenial, too close to what social feminists wanted. But the group's greatest successes in a feminist context were the activities that most bothered the englobing movement—when consumerism was expanded to become feminist reform including feminist pacifism and feminist internationalism.

The UFCS was in a quite different situation, in that Catholic expectations of women's organizational role could only with great difficulty encompass a group of women engaged in public reform. Social Catholicism, as I have suggested, provided an opportunity. But the activities even of the devout Andrée Butillard provoked criticism and hostility from Catholics. At the same time the apparent conventionality of a social feminist approach to social action reassured the rather traditional women who became involved in the group. The excesses of the Pétain era, when domesticity became a murderously confining constraint, helped enforce the split between UFCS activists and their church, as did the way in which the postwar Catholic church failed to evolve in relation to women's issues. The death of the MRP may have been the best thing that happened to the UFCS, for it removed the possibility of a confining alliance like that of the Guild with the co-operative movement and party.

The League provides a counterexample and a confirmation in the shape of a social feminist group that had no obvious organizational home. Its historical origins provided an example of independence which its experience then reinforced. The specifically American form of a woman's mission, the disinterested reformation of public life, supported a nonpartisanship that was crucial for the group's survival and growth and, above all, for its feminism. In the League we see the purest form of the specifically female political role: issue-oriented, directed at what is seen as the environment of politics, and treating political parties in a purely instrumental fashion. In the political systems discussed here, nonpartisanship is the most extreme form of a belief that women must act politically for goals they have articulated themselves.

The League has received continuing, virulent criticism for its nonpartisanship and its orientation toward women's issues. It is commonly described as apolitical, naive, and uninfluential. The most recent analyses of the LWV attempt to rehabilitate it by pointing out how many of the women now in elected office were trained in leadership by participation in the group. This is an equity analysis whose criterion for political influence is behavior and, presumably, beliefs like those of the present male incumbents. Social feminist analysis would ask not how many women but why and how they participate. What issues, what concerns, what goals do they have? What modes of political participation do they show, what modes have they developed?

It will be clear I am taking arguments that usually, critically, explain women's nonintegration into politics and making them positive. Social feminists' devotion to issues and to women's groups does not mean they reject politics but that they come at politics from a different perspective. I assume they are fiercely interested in politics—and indeed the members of my groups are, even if we define politics conventionally. I insist, moreover, that the issues to which social feminists devote their lives are political issues, in fact, issues that have the potential to transform political life.

I have not discussed the related and very interesting topic of the success of women's organizations in getting their political goals realized. Obviously, they have not yet had major successes, but they have gotten issues onto agendas—a necessary first stage. My focus instead has been the development of a political role for women—which means a different political role for women, related to a notion of women as different. And I hope I make it clear that *different* does not necessarily mean an acceptance of marginalization or inactivity. It means more than just equal—it means the possibility of improvement.

Social feminist theory does, of course, entail risks in organizational and practical political terms. Once we move past those criticisms which damn all women's groups for not conforming to existing mainstream models, we encounter other attacks aimed specifically at social feminism. Mainly posed by equity feminists, these attacks accuse social feminism of narrowness, of elitism, and of a separatism that works against women's interests.

Among European and North American feminists, the major criticism of the feminism of difference has been historical, that it misled the suffragists. At a moment of opportunity, it is alleged, the foremothers, perhaps for sound tactical reasons, perhaps out of profound bad faith, committed themselves to reinforce an outdated view of women's role and functions. This retroactive accusation owes part of its current force to an understandable feminist anxiety about the repressive power of what can no longer be viewed as outworn antifeminism. Social feminism is seen as playing once again into the hands of the Right. In a United States threatened by the Moral Majority and a Britain where the self-destructive Labour party has been helping deconstruct the welfare state, any praise of female domesticity seems dangerous (Stacey 1983, Eisenstein 1984).

And certainly a focus on difference can support a constraining view of women's potential. Recent feminist research on interwar Germany warns about the "dangers implicit in a feminism that celebrates separate spheres and differences between the sexes [and] glorifies motherhood and women's bodies" (Bridenthal, Grossmann, and Kaplan 1984:xiii). The same passage includes, however, some heartening suggestions about the conditions under which such a belief system is particularly risky. One crucial element is acceptance of the notion of impermeable boundaries between separate spheres. As Claudia Koonz notes, the majority of nineteenth-century feminist activists "endorsed women's entry into political and economic life as representatives of women's interests. In addition, they argued that women could enrich previously male spheres by contributing their superior morality and human concerns." Here women's roles reach across boundaries. In contrast, the Nazi women who enthusiastically supported Hitler on the basis of a separate spheres argument "saw little overlap at all between masculine and feminine worlds and endorsed a strong separatist policy on the 'woman question'" (Koonz 1984:200). They accepted the belief, incorrectly attributed to North American feminists, that the brutal male world would corrupt any woman who entered it (Elshtain 1973–74). Such self-isolation strengthens public/private boundaries and does indeed tend to make its version of feminism pathological.

The problem is how women's groups—and analysts—interpret the consequences of a female specificity related to the family. One key distinction made by Ellen DuBois is between difference of roles and difference of spheres. But the UFCS, in particular, suggests that some of DuBois's conclusions need to be reinterpreted.

In 1975, DuBois located the "radicalism" of the first-wave North American women's movement in the way "it bypassed women's oppression within the family, or private sphere, and demanded instead her admission to citizenship, and through it admission to the public arena" (63). Suffragism, she says, demanded for women "a kind of power and a connection with the social order not based on the family and their subordination within it" (64). The notion of spheres is crucial: DuBois writes of "sexual spheres," areas of activity separated by "absolute, sexually defined barriers"—the "public world of men [and] the private world of women" (65).

Certainly DuBois is correct that the equity demand for the vote denied such divisions in a key area. But the result was the development of a neutral zone closer to private than public because it was nonauthoritative, a zone where women's votes and women's work in the paid labor force are governed by rules other than those which govern the public world in general. This is the area of activity where women are allowed to participate but devalued as inferior or ignorant, undeveloped versions of men.

DuBois also points to sexual roles, the differentiated functions or activities believed to characterize the different sexual spheres. When social feminists extended functions—roles—from one sphere to another, they eroded the boundaries that confined women to the home. Such activities in practice broke down the sexually linked barrier between the two spheres. Public and private activities remained different, but henceforth they could be carried out by anyone with the required capacity. Some few socially necessary tasks remained female— childbirth, so far, and breastfeeding, where that was considered socially desirable. It is not clear that any tasks remained male. In practice, as long as males and females have different experience, their qualifications will vary somewhat along sex lines, as will their preferences, which should not be irrelevant. The key practical questions concern the desirability of this differentiated experience, as we have established it historically and enshrined it in institutions, and the possibilities for separating it from sex. We can then ask if androgyny is desirable, if it is possible, and what form or forms it might take.

DuBois correctly observed that it was radical for equity feminists to insist that the boundaries between sexual spheres should not limit women. But it is important to remember, without romanticizing the family, the extent to which family-oriented belief systems have historically served as sources of both personal and movement strength, as motivations for moving beyond the family. In such cases the denial of constraints comes from the domestic, rather than focusing on the public as an enabling device. The denial is social feminist, not a version of equity feminism. And it is obviously not separatist.

All logic focused on difference has some separatist implications and so shares similar possible consequences. Separatism itself is an abdication of influence that undercuts any possibility of real autonomy in a densely interactive world. At the same time, since the women's sphere is only metaphorically located outside the public realm, activist women tend to believe there is a role for women to play in public life, if only in the delineation of male and female activities and the state's involvement in the female sectors. In fact the Nazi women were unable to escape the obligation to serve male-defined goals of nationalism and national renewal. Contradictorily or not, they were unwilling to abdicate from administration of the areas allocated to women.

Separatism itself is clearly capable of enormous variation, for which the values held by both separatists and larger society are decisive. The Nazi women's organization was a "narrow and elitist women's movement that [expected] to participate in the administration of a socially unequal and hierarchical society" (Bridenthal, Grossmann, and Kaplan 1984:xiii). In many ways, theirs was more an equity than a social feminism, since they wished to adapt societal values to incorporate women. In contrast, today's feminist separatists are consistent in their active rejection of any possible role in the existing state; it would be both insulting and inaccurate to liken radical feminists to the women of the Nazi party. Any accusation of opting out of responsibility can be met by the response that such demands on women are part of the ideology that sustains an unacceptable, heterosexist society. The active assumption of a "place on the margins" certainly avoids active complicity in an unjust society (Zimmerman 1984:668).[3] But such a separatism, especially in the name of domestic or female virtues, necessarily strengthens the male monopoly on public life.

The large majority of social feminists have long discarded the notion of separate spheres except as a historical source of women's experience and values; only a tiny minority are separatist. But the possibility of narrowness and elitism remains a threat to feminism based on difference. For social feminists it is insufficient to retain the conventional democratic structures of the older women's groups, as in the Guild, the Union, and the League. Voluntary groups, however they may be structured formally, have their own hierarchies because only a few individuals have the time, the energy, and the ability to carry on the largely unrewarding activities required over the years. Possibly social feminism is less likely to tolerate the emergence of a truly dominant matriarch. Under the patriarchy, after all, women have had little experience of women with public authority. Among the groups studied here, it can at least be said that, if clearly in command, such social feminist leaders as Margaret Llewelyn Davies, Andrée Butillard, and Carrie Chapman Catt nevertheless combined long service with a commitment to democracy of structure.

More recently, in radical feminist groups, social feminists have made explicit attempts to avoid copying the structures of the society they hope to transform. This also has its hazards. Women's liberation groups have experienced great difficulties as a result of their avoidance of the male patterns of designated leaders, hierarchies, and tasks. Among these problems are media-assigned "star" leaders (and their subsequent rejection by the groups), the "trashing" of those members who seem especially competent or ambitious, and the existence of a covert system of power

3. Claudia Koonz picks up the history of the Nazi women when they had become clearly committed to separatism, arguing they were thus able to avoid "the contradictions that bedeviled liberals and conservatives" who were assimilationists claiming a role in the overall conduct of a society that increasingly rejected all their most important values (Koonz 1984:201). I think this is a misinterpretation; the problem for the German equity feminists was that under Nazism no viable model of resistance was developed by the groups they followed in ideology and might have followed in terms of action.

and exclusion based on friendship (Freeman 1975:119–28). Such circumstances can easily render political effectiveness or democratic responsiveness less important than correctness of structure and doctrine. In the name of internal differentiation, unrecognized elitism battles with tendencies toward schism. Such obsessions multiply within organizations doctrinally committed to self-definition.

The transformation of some second-wave feminist groups into feminist service agencies may represent an attempt to resolve the dilemmas of separatism and internal structure. Ideologically it makes sense, in that institutions such as rape crisis centers are, or can be seen as, particularly infused with female, domestic values. They represent a pragmatic and subjective response to a need peculiar to women, a practical extension of women's roles in the form of self-service institutions. Transition houses, women's health centers, feminist daycare, women's presses or media, producers of safe food or nonsexist clothing—all can be understood as comprising a new sort of politics, destined to influence the patriarchy by example if in no other way. The resemblance to the Co-operative Commonwealth is obvious, as is the continuing influence of the tradition of women's benevolent and charitable service.

At best, though, inventing the new society while changing the existing one demands enormous energy, making "burnout" and retreat from activism commonplace. It is obvious why cooption into existing structures and values is so great a continuing risk for those eager to transform public life by participating in it. Social feminist insistence upon the possible compatibility of male and female activities and values increases just such a danger. And avoidance may well carry the cost of becoming increasingly "narrow and elitist." A related danger is the refusal to accept other forms of feminism as legitimate. The Guild, most doctrinaire of the groups studied in this book, experienced the greatest difficulty in handling both the threat of cooption and the perceived risk of contamination. But its social feminist insistence on the shared situation of all women served to some extent as a counterbalance.

Feminist groups are never in a position to impose their preferences on any substantial scale. They seldom have much impact on the groups they are closest to, let alone on the larger society. The Nazi women lost influence precisely when their englobing organization gained power; the successful party had less need for its women's auxiliary and more resources to control it. In a very inexact parallel, the WCG women also saw their role decline within their organization when it became large and prosperous, at the point when Guildswomen might have expected influence on the workforce in the co-operative stores and on the Co-operative party and when, through the co-operative movement, they might have had some larger impact on the whole public sphere. Such powerlessness makes it likely that feminist groups' doctrinal judgments will impinge only on their relations with other feminisms. Equity feminists usually delimit their possible feminist partners in terms of nonfeminist reference groups; for instance, socialist feminists may ally with liberal feminists on occasion but only if socialists are acting in concert with liberals, and the splits within socialism itself are reflected in disagreements among socialist feminists (Picq 1986). Social feminists understandably distrust equity feminism's links with male groups. From a social feminist perspective, alliances should always be possible among feminists of any kind when shared issues indicate shared concerns and at least a degree of autonomy on the part of women. The UFCS, in spite of its Catholic commitments, demonstrated the reality of such openness.

A feminism based on difference has on occasion produced its own dogmatism of definition and exclusion. In France a continuing mutual hostility among feminists seems related to the insistence on female values and criteria espoused by the group originally known as Psych et po (Psychanalyse et politique). This group is now commonly and pejoratively called the "trademarked MLF" because it did, literally, trademark usage of that generic term both nationally and internationally. One American analyst now asserts, incorrectly, that the rest of the French women's movement perceives "the notion of difference as an instrument of oppression" (Kauffmann-McCall 1983:285). However, the Psych et po version of difference was ideologically a version of equity feminism, a projection of Lacanian psychoanalysis articulating women as the "absent," the "other."[4] This position is remote in content and source from the historic social feminism discussed here, which is both positive in goal and specific in delineating content for the female role.

Yet the core Psych et po notion is one we could extrapolate from the views of the social feminists: "Today Socialism and Feminism—pacifist, reformist and progressive or supposedly revolutionary—both heirs of Western humanism, are the two most powerful pillars of the patriarchy in decline" (Antoinette Fouque, quoted in Kauffmann-McCall 1983: 285). Andrée Michel and Elise Boulding, among many others, have expressed such views and included a condemnation of the way in which equity feminisms support the existing patriarchal system. The danger for social feminism lies in the tendency to dismiss all forms of equity feminism in the name of female values. Michel and Boulding avoid this trap; the trademarked MLF did not.

A further risk, today specifically a social feminist one, is the domination of an unstructured group by a mother-figure such as Psych et po's

---

4. Psych et po's Lacanian views about psychoanalysis and homosexuality provide the content of their version of sexual differentiation: "If capitalism is based on the sexual division of work, the women's struggle is based on sexual difference. The only discourse on sexuality that exists is the psychoanalytic discourse. Therefore the women's struggle must of necessity deal with the dialectical relationship between history and psychoanalysis. . . . Women's primary, fundamental homosexuality should only be a passage toward a rediscovered and truly free heterosexuality" (Antoinette Fouque, quoted in *Le nouvel observateur*, trans. Elaine Marks in Marks and de Courtivron 1980:118).

Antoinette (Fouque). The "mother" is less easily recognized as abusive than the matriarch who replicates male power within a structured organization. Certainly radical feminist structurelessness seems to facilitate a quasi-maternal dominance, but the history of the American National Woman's party suggests that the role of both ideology and structure is more complex. The NWP, equity feminist in belief and formally democratic in structure, was completely dominated by Alice Paul. Paul's lifelong devotion to the cause of women has won her admiration even from those feminists who think her misguided; her almost brutal control of a narrowly defined movement is a warning (Becker 1981; Cott 1984; Rupp 1985; Pfeffer 1985). In the national League of Women Voters some national presidents would have liked to have gone the same route but were thwarted by the continuing influence and final revolt of the state leagues. In organizational terms the two groups were similar, though the League was of course far larger. Perhaps the key feature of the League was the combination of a large-scale and decentralized organization, formally structured, with the ideology of social feminism; in such a setting the domestic ideal supported a less domineering style of leadership.

Nevertheless, the typical social feminist commitment to self-defined and subjective values, to private sphere and experience, can produce a repulsive self-satisfaction and complacency, including a bland acceptance of male domination. As an example, let us take Arianna Stassinopoulos (Huffington), whose small public fame is due to a recent, best-selling biography of Picasso.[5] She has also written a deservedly neglected book, *The Female Woman* (1973), an attack on what she always calls "Women's Lib" as exemplified by the early writings of Kate Millett, Germaine Greer, Juliet Mitchell, and Shulamith Firestone. "Libbers" such as these promulgate a doctrine that "attacks the very nature of woman and, in the guise of liberation, seeks to enslave her" (11).[6] "Liberation" she sees as the demand for "achievement of equality through identical patterns of behaviour"; her own preferred goal, "emancipation," "insists on equal status for distinctively female roles" (15).

Stassinopoulos exhibits just those "slave" vices which separate spheres can produce (Woolf 1966–67 IV:174). After demonstrating her hostility to other women's formulations of possible ways of life, she validates her arguments by consultation with male friends who are asked *inter alia* whether it is more desirable for women to be "attractive" or "intelligent." She quotes the following comment:

5. Stassinopoulos was born in Athens in 1950, won an exhibition to Girton College, was president of the Cambridge Union, and graduated "with honours in Economics" in 1972.

6. Western overpopulation explains this success of the movement, but the problem is now solved, "a development that will greatly help to restore the status of the maternal role. Women will regain their self-confident femaleness and Women's Lib will fall on even deafer ears" (163).

The only quarrel I have with the questionnaire is that it separates attraction and intelligence at all—even conceptually. . . . Intelligence is attractive—directly physically attractive. Have you met Barbara the philosophy student? I was discussing my research with her yesterday and she took something I'd said, and analysed it, clarified it. . . . The effect on me was as if she'd taken her skirt off. It was exciting, wildly exciting. I wanted her more than I ever had before (55–56).

She adopts not just male criteria but male sexualization of women's activities. Such views are related to another serious risk of any feminism based on difference: a separatism that rejects male authority but accepts male definition of femininity, developing a notion of women based on male fantasies (Rossanda 1979). Stassinopoulos is unaware of such dangers, citing her "euphoric feeling" in response to the "everyday chivalry of men," calling female dependence a myth "that leads to pleasure and satisfaction. . . . It is the same feeling that I got when I was told on the phone by a [male] friend of mine who was away: 'Take care of yourself until I come back! after that, I'll take care of you.' The fact that we both knew that I was perfectly capable of taking care of myself and that I was unlikely to die of starvation or be attacked by Red Indians didn't make the euphoric feeling any less real" (134). Any feminist must allow Stassinopoulos her erotic turn-ons. She demonstrates effectively and depressingly how a feminism of difference can produce hostility to other feminists, even other women, as well as encourage female conservatism and passivity.

The Female Woman makes clear why so many equity feminists of the second-wave reject with horror any link between difference and feminism. Contemporary equity feminism has found it extremely difficult to deal with the manifestly feminist views of radical feminists and particularly those who moved to a lesbian separatism. Its solution has been to posit separatism and political inactivity as necessary consequences of social feminism. Central to the analysis is the implication that such feminism, when not in servile compliance to male formulations, is actively hostile to men.

Jo Freeman's analysis of second-wave social feminism—not under that name—in the United States was among the earliest and most influential. She emphatically rejected classification of feminism's two branches as "reformist" and "radical" on the grounds that "some groups often called 'reformist' have a platform that would so completely change our society [that] it would be unrecognizable. Other groups called 'radical' concentrate on the traditional female concerns of love, sex, children, and interpersonal relationships (although with nontraditional views)" (1975:50–51). She thus recognized the historical roots of the new groups that considered themselves radical rather than socialist feminists. But she was unresponsive to the beliefs of social feminism in its second-wave incarnation as radical feminism; the phrase "traditional female concerns" is dismissive of women's historical experience and of social feminism. In her book radical feminists appear only in the section on the "younger" or liberationist branch, under the heading "The Gay/Straight Split," with a focus on the emergence of lesbian feminism, followed by a brief section on "cultural nationalism." "This view," she writes, "sees men [as] at worst destructive and at best irrelevant" (1975:142). For Freeman, such analyses reinforced the existing gender system with its distinctions between men and women and its unavoidable gender hierarchy: "Starting from the traditional belief in the difference between the sexes, sexism embodies two core concepts: . . . that men are more important than women . . . [and] that women are here for the pleasure and assistance of men" (1984:553). The liberation of women entailed the obliteration of sex-role differences: "Our history has proved that institutionalized *difference* inevitably means *inequality*" (1984:555) The emphasis is Freeman's; another commentator might prefer to emphasize the word "institutionalized."

Joan Ringelheim summarizes in the mid-1980s a similar judgment of "cultural feminists," already encapsulated in that somewhat pejorative label: "Cultural feminism . . . shifted the territory of liberation from an insistence on the need for changing material conditions to a belief in changing the inner life, consciousness, culture, and so on" (1985:753). Like Freeman, Ringelheim interprets cultural feminism as a rejection of analyses of the women as an oppressed class and of the corollary insistence that revolutionary social change is necessary for women's liberation. Such self-styled feminists would therefore reject all forms of political action. For Ringelheim, there are even more serious consequences; writing about women and the Holocaust, she questions in more general terms the political effectiveness of feminine values of community and coping. Her conclusion is that social feminism has facilitated not just patriarchy but extermination. This is equity feminism with a vengeance, making social feminism equivalent to the most extreme acceptance of marginalization and even extinction.[7] Freeman, for her part, does not believe that radical feminists can wish to interact with or affect men: for radical feminists "integration with men is neither necessary or possible; the only solution is female autonomy" (1975:142). The charge is that for

7. Anna Coote and Beatrix Campbell give a similar analysis in the context of the British women's movement, which they divide into "socialist" and "radical" feminists. Radical feminists accept differentiation and consequently accept withdrawal and ineffectiveness: "A precept which united all radical feminists was that the fight for women's liberation was primarily *against men:* they saw it as overriding all other struggles and were deeply suspicious of any attempt to link it to a wider political strategy." Coote and Campbell use the following central distinction: whether the goal is to "destroy *masculinity* as a social construct, and so transform men as human beings, with a view to developing a harmonious relationship in which [men] wielded no power over women; or whether one seeks to end the necessity of the biological distinction by establishing ways of living and reproducing which are entirely independent of men" (1987:25–26).

radical feminists—social feminists—"autonomy" means isolation from and therefore implicit toleration of a sex-role system that is intrinsically oppressive to women.

Although the basic disagreements between socialist and radical feminists are not entirely clear, one element stands out: the former's equity feminist refusal to accept that women's own experience and values, both privately and in the women's movement, can produce change and provide guidance for a new society. Ringelheim represents most equity feminists in her perception of reliance on difference as evasive, self-serving, conservative, a way of avoiding political action that is dangerous but potentially generative of revolution and liberation. She is reacting against a sentimental consolation that she and many others had drawn from realizing that women survived the death camps somewhat better than men because of their capacity for female solidarity. But did this solidarity stop or hamper the Nazis? she asks. Can women's culture alter the patriarchy? asks Freeman. Can social feminism change the expectation of male dominance or the dependence of capitalism on exploitation of women's productive and reproductive labor?

Here questions of context and setting become crucial. It is indispensable to understand the relative capabilities of the groups wanting change and the systems denying it. Usually we are not dealing with the absolute, deranged bureaucracy of extermination. As Ringelheim herself notes, it is not obvious even under those circumstances when resistance is the appropriate response or if survival is an illusory goal. Nothing done by victims of the Holocaust had any impact on the outcome; it was "a story of loss, not gain" (1985:757). The alternative to mutually supportive (and therefore nonresistant?) women was not, either historically or analytically, successful armed revolt. Rather, it was masses of isolated individuals who were deliberately deprived of identity and thereby doubly destroyed. The alternative, some form of effective individual physical resistance, is itself a sentimental fantasy—and a male one at that.

If we move back to the less horrifying dilemmas of everyday feminism, we find, similarly, that the alternative to an assimilative equity feminism is not cultural isolationism but the activism of social feminism. A feminism of difference may produce separatism and with it a rejection of political activism. But it need not, and historically it has not usually done so. Traditional views and behaviors have produced a version of feminism that has on occasion been a source of change for women—if only by making group interaction and the development of a practice of public involvement possible for them. Under other conditions the doctrine of difference has been a basis of individual survival. Under still others, it has indeed been conservative, even reactionary in its impact. But it is not intrinsically so.

The problem for the feminist analyst is to understand conditions of effectiveness in terms of the cultural and political context of a given social system. And the best way to do so is not, as Freeman does, to extrapolate from what should theoretically be useful for all human beings. It is instead to examine the available data, such as Freeman's own history of the American second wave, for conditions under which women and women's groups have had some degree of success. This is, of course, what Freeman in practice does.

Freeman rejects the "egalitarian ethic" of the mainstream American women's movement because it means that women will simply become like men and demand "their piece of the pie, without questioning whether that society is worth participating in" (1984:555). Instead, she favors the "liberationist" commitment to a total revolution that will free all people equally. The "liberation ethic looks at the kinds of lives currently being led by men as well as women and concludes that both are deplorable and neither is necessary. . . . Women cannot become equal to men without the destruction of these two interdependent, mutually parasitic roles" (1984:555). Then, surprisingly, she inserts an assertion of difference: "It is erroneous to assume that [women's] interests are identical to those of men. . . . There has yet to be created by any political or social theorist a revolutionary structure in which women were equal to men and their needs equally considered" (556). If women's needs are privileged in this way, it is because they have, in however limited a way, some distinctive character (other than the need of all not to be oppressed by other individuals or groups). Freeman is not asserting women's distinctiveness as a transitional or temporary expedient, for she has redefined difference as appropriate and not disadvantageous differentiation on a basis of actual need.

We may ask why Freeman's ideal society includes not only androgyny but also special attention to women, identified as a group with specific needs. We may also ask why she decided to analyze in detail the feminism she had lived. She is after all not one of those analysts who deny they have a commitment to the women's movement. The answer seems to be that she learned from her activism the lesson that women are indeed different and that both their repression and their responses are distinctive, even valuable. Her research delineates a social movement that is not quite like the others. It also indicates ways in which women's groups are producing innovative political solutions as well as substantial impact on institutions (1981). Here we may look at Freeman's own account of "rap groups" (1975:116–19) and at her discussions of the pitfalls of "structurelessness" and possible remedies (1974). These accounts have been influential in helping to develop institutional structures that can be nonhierarchical yet effective.

There is now a substantial feminist literature on topics related to feminist organization and effectiveness, such as Charlotte Bunch's "The Reform Tool Kit," which concludes that "evaluations of reform will come out of our ongoing experiences as feminists" (1987:117). Freeman's projection of the future incorporates a genuinely social feminist perspective, based on her own experience of the student Left: women's liberation is the necessary condition of a better society for all.

All feminist literature about the content of the desired new society starts by specifying the absence of sexism. But for positive goals it has to turn to the only human existence not identified with patriarchal rule: the lives and experience of women. The problem is that the goals of women under the patriarchy can be interpreted as instruments of their subjugation, whose function is to keep them devoted to men. Yet women's distinctive preferences can also be identified as an alternative human tradition, developed practically rather than theoretically under the particular conditions experienced by women.[8] The processes, goals, and institutions identified there can also be found among men, but they are unacceptable as central social values under patriarchy. The men who espouse domestic values are stigmatized as womanlike or simply ignored. But the fact that such goals have on occasion been articulated or experienced by men suggests that no biological essentialism underlies them, that these are indeed alternative human values encouraged by certain structures and experiences. It seems reasonable to say that some of these experiences have historically had biological links to female characteristics, either directly or indirectly—but not all.

Nurturing in the simplest sense might best be interpreted as biologically encouraged by the dependence of the fetus and the newborn but by social or environmental influence historically confined mainly to one sex.[9] Peacefulness, on the contrary, might be seen as entirely contingent on conditions. Deliberate social policy could attempt to produce situations conducive to both nurturance and peacefulness. This is what Virginia Woolf was struggling to articulate in *Three Guineas,* and the political implications of such views are activist.

Such a position is not cultural feminism in the sense of a turning inward to a private life in some sort of community of women (a preference for which Woolf herself has incorrectly been given both praise and blame). Ringelheim voices a characteristic criticism of social feminism for rejecting the "belief that genuine liberation must deal with power first and foremost" (1985:754). Such versions of feminism, she says, encourage the delusion that patriarchy can be transformed without "violent revolution; without confronting the state, family, marriage, or orga-

8. This is the argument made by Carol Gilligan (1982) and Nel Noddings (1984), by the analysts of "mothering" (e.g., Thorne and Yalom 1982), and most recently by M. F. Belenky et al. in their study of "women's ways of knowing" (1986).

9. Alice Rossi provoked a storm of hostile response when she suggested that some female characteristics, such as attachment to infants, may continue to be characterized by biological preconditions (1977; Gross et al. 1979). Observers translated the suggestion into an exclusive connection of biological mothering with nurturing and ignored Rossi's suggestion that it might be socially desirable to inculcate nurturance in the sex that was less predisposed to it and to encourage it in those women less inclined that way—in sum, that the ideal society would enable everyone to take responsibility for the welfare of children.

nized religion; and without eliminating institutions intent on keeping women in their place" (754). Her statement assumes that change can only be violent, politics only confrontational—that women must adopt the tactics radical men have traditionally used. Many other feminist critics concur that a feminism of difference must accept powerlessness and ineffectiveness.

The historical evidence suggests that a social feminist analysis focusing on difference can generate both a reality and a theory of power that are far from ineffective. We should not overlook the sources of women's power within the household, highlighted by the doctrine of difference, however variable and limited that power is (and note that it is a power without much reliance on violence) (Collier 1974). Even more important is women's potential power outside the home, projected and extended from that domestic experience which is perceived as characteristically female. The theoretical justification for such an expansion is weak; the world as larger household is an ideologically appealing metaphor that means, at most, the world can be made more like (though not entirely like) a household in certain important respects. Nevertheless, when extrapolated beyond the family, the doctrine of difference has served far better to support than to oppose change in the patriarchy. It has created and legitimated conditions under which women can in practice and in good faith work for changes, including equality of a sort that the theory of difference would seem to rule out. "Social feminism" refers to that argumentation and process, in which feminism is able to use the doctrine of difference not to obliterate differences of kind but to change a society that uses difference as a basis of exclusion.

On a theoretical level, furthermore, social feminism is able to supply the grounding crucial to feminists' attempts at an explicit critique and reformulation of social policy. In broad theoretical terms, a preference for reliance on practice or experience rather than theory holds the potential for a major impact on the conduct and content of public life.

CHAPTER 18

Theoretical Lessons

Historically, equity feminism, whether liberal or socialist, has attributed primary importance to the activity of constructing theory. Theory building is a way in which women can assert similarity of competence and equivalence of function with men. Following their male mentors, socialist feminists argue that the most important need of women is a theoretical understanding of the world and their situation. For liberal feminists the required theoretical activity is simpler: feminist theory as such is not necessary. Instead, liberal theory must be expanded to include those humans who were formerly excluded. And since such an enterprise is best initiated by those whom personal experience has made aware of the omissions, a primary mandate of feminists is the explicit elaboration of theory. Equity feminist analysts expend major energies on demolishing preceding or competing forms of feminist theory, and particularly any that are social feminist in emphasis. They feel obliged to correct social feminism in theoretical terms as well as to criticize any practical or policy achievements it may have to its supposedly atheoretical credit. Social feminism, they concede, has produced concrete gains, but only in a way that is theoretically deficient and therefore ultimately disadvantageous. With this destructive project they have had some success. On the other hand, such endeavors, derived from existing mainstream approaches, are hard put to advance any new way to assess social conditions.

In contrast, social feminism, which has very little interest in theory building as such, embodies an alternative to existing (patriarchal) social arrangements and generates new ones. It is therefore, increasingly, the basis of an alternative social critique. Today, as a result, although different sorts of equity feminism animate reform movements of varying effectiveness, we have reason to doubt the likely outcome of their efforts, in both theoretical and practical terms. Social feminism is beginning to provide an explicit theoretical basis for analyzing the reform achievements of activists—not what would have been expected from the "nonideological" and "conservative" social feminists.

Contemporary analyses continue the twofold division of feminism, as analysts either accept or reject the concept of difference. Equity feminists, whether socialist or liberal, attempt to place women among or beside other groups that have been discriminated against. In a context of minority rights it is hard to argue that feminism has an ideological base or, indeed, any compelling claim. Organizations of women do not resemble closely any other groupings of the dispossessed (Black 1986). They rarely seem more than an aggregation. American theorists who see feminism as a solvent of the patriarchal family explain it as the acceptance by women of an individualism demanding equal rights. They are likely to lament the feminist "failure" to challenge the family in theoretical terms. Yet their version of feminism is, in fact, intrinsically incapable of addressing any dimension of social life apart from the denial of women's claim to be and be treated as the atomistic individuals of classic liberal theory (Degler 1980). Such analysis produces a definition of feminism as campaigns to produce "an end to sexist practices and attitudes and full equality for women in all areas of life" (Fulenwider 1980:30).[1] In this context any separatist mode is a temporary expedient (34). So defined, feminism is unable to provide any innovative basis for criticizing public life as we currently experience it. The criterion for policy is simply its success or failure to provide equal roles for women.

This is a reductive if fairly common form of equity feminism. Janet Radcliffe Richards provides perhaps the most popular and extreme example, defining feminism as the belief that "women suffer from systematic social injustice because of their sex" (1982:13–14) and, more generally, as the movement to eliminate sex-based injustice. This definition has the virtue of specifying explicitly what other equity feminisms only imply: the only injustice at issue is what women as such endure. There is no ideology here; "feminism" has become pejorative and is reserved for beliefs held by those who today identify themselves as feminists in a way different from Richards. Their ideological stances Richards identifies in order to reject them: "The oppressiveness of the family, the inherent equality of the sexes (or the superiority of the female) and the enslavement of women as the root of all oppression" (14). "The inherent equality of the sexes" rings oddly in this list: surely Richards accepts this notion? But in fact she does not, except in the sense that gender itself is no justification for disadvantageous treatment.

1. In contrast to Degler, Fulenwider (1980) claims to have delineated a feminist "ideology," which she sees as increasingly influencing the voting behavior of American men and, especially, women. This ideology is the belief system demonstrated by responses to questions about male and female roles. Underlying Fulenwider's inductive procedure and dictating the choice of questions examined is the assumption that sex-linked difference of roles is oppressive. The key question in her study contrasts two beliefs: "Women should have an equal role with men in running business, industry, and government," and "Women's place is in the home" (1980:43). This is a muddling of role and sphere which nevertheless opts against difference.

One reason for Richards's considerable success is her ability to criticize other feminists tellingly. Speaking as a self-identified feminist, she can locate where, from the perspective of liberal beliefs, equity feminism falls down. Effectively detaching style from substance, she can deflate the pretensions of self-styled feminists to represent the perspective of all women. For instance, she points out that arguments about clothing are not what they claim to be: "A feminist whose main motivation was to put as little time and money into [clothes] as possible should presumably go around in the first and cheapest thing she could find at a jumble sale, even if it happened to be a shapeless turquoise Crimplene dress with a pink cardigan" (225). "The regulation blue jeans," she suggests, are appropriate only for "feminists whose daily life calls for their being prepared to shift a ton of coal at a moment's notice" (226). We may shelve arguments about skirts vs. trousers and related questions of footwear and underclothes, for Richards is not really interested in the long-established campaigns for rational female clothing. She has earlier identified as an extraneous, damaging part of alleged feminism the "forswearing of femininity of appearance and demeanour" (as well as a commitment to consciousness-raising and nonhierarchical organizations) (14). Her concern in discussing feminist views of clothing is to argue for the intrinsic value of attractive garments. Concern for appearance may have been imposed on women by the need to appeal to men, she says, but it has nevertheless a positive, objective significance of its own.

By her own criteria, unfortunately, she is no longer speaking as a feminist. Her argument about physical attractiveness has no more validity than the one about functional clothing which she scorns; neither relates to women's experience of social injustice. Both, in fact, implicitly criticize the bases on which men and women alike select their clothing, devoting time and energy to satisfy social expectations. What is, after all, the function or the attraction of a man's tie or the buttons on his jacket sleeve? The unisex uniform of blue jeans should please Richards, for it represents, in part at least, a female attempt to adopt young males' relative lack of obligation to dress "suitably." She is correct in finding the feminist rejection of ornament willful; her version of feminism, however, is unable to recognize there an assertion of female autonomy.

Richards has, in this case, used an argument very close to those of social feminists, for her implicit standards are based in women's experience. We do not find among middle-class men the extreme contrast of the economical grubbiness of the woman in the home and the ornamental finery of her nights on the town. Unabashed cheapness and economy of effort, bodily adornment as art—neither is characteristic of the (male) public world of today. But Richards has not used the example to criticize current modes of dress. Her goal is instead to criticize self-styled feminists as trivial and essentially irrelevant.

Here she is in tune with many contemporary critics of feminism. Like them, she finds women's specific activities unappealing; in general she accepts current judgments on women. Housework she dismisses, in the context of an argument that the measure of doing good is the number of people affected, as essentially degrading (209, 221). The public world is therefore more important, and equality of treatment within it the goal. When both men and women suffer injustice, then feminism has nothing to contribute. And all of women's experience, because private and limited in scope, is at best of secondary value. If men and women are indeed alike, who can argue with her? Where can the volition for eliminating shared injustice come from? The answer seems to be shared activity based on shared experience, and women can contribute to the enterprise only numbers that make action more significant.

This argument removes any priority from the cause of women, of course, and Richards makes the point explicit. Structural injustice is to be remedied in the public realm. Its cause is nothing to do with the exclusion of women. Let us first get the good society and then be concerned to increase the number of its active participants: equality for women, certainly, but only as a means to honor more adequately one of the underlying principles of a society that is already excellent in all but detailed execution of rules. This is a common version of arguments about justice, extended into an equity feminism that makes virtually no specific claims for women. It excludes the large majority of historical feminists, but it feels familiar and persuasive to the progressive liberal.

So do analyses that will not call "feminist" even those women who achieved the vote in the United States: "Twentieth century suffragists abandoned feminism, the belief that men and women are equal, by accepting differences between the sexes. . . . These women fought for women's concerns, including the vote, but they were not feminists, since they did not believe that men and women are or should be equal" (Klein 1984:14).[2] The author of such an analysis may be aware of the social feminist critique of the public realm:

> Women do not want to become men. The tension between home and work is not merely spatial: it is also one of values. The workplace currently emphasizes traditionally masculine values, such as self-control, logical and objective thought, and an emphasis on efficiency, at the expense of the quality of human relationships. Traditionally female qualities, such as patience, nurturance, and an emphasis on interpersonnel [*sic*] relationships, are seen as impediments to success (171).

This is an argument from difference, once difference is seen as at least in part socially constructed, but in its equity context it cannot be used as a

2. Klein can find the necessary association of "ideology" (equality) with "mass movement" only in 1970, with the Women's Strike for Equality, which marks the emergence of "the first social movement to push for demands to ensure women's equality" (2). This identification is hardly helpful to those who wish to build on the very considerable achievements of the historical activists whom Klein excludes from the women's movement.

basis for criticizing and reconstructing the male reality of the workplace. One traditional value has no claim against another. In this case the dilemma is solved by an appeal to another male model: women's "discomfort" with a workplace "hierarchically structured and concerned with profit" is legitimized by assimilation into "the current failure of the hierarchical, impersonal management of American business, as compared to the less hierarchical, personnel-focused practices of Japanese business" (171).[3] Women have neither distinctive perspectives nor distinctive solutions to offer.

In a similar vein wages for housework may be suggested as a progressive feminist goal: "The concept of sex equality need not presume that the development of a public workplace identity is superior to women's private family one." This sentence sounds a bit like social feminism, as does the observation that "the integration of women into the labor force . . . threatens to suppress the traditional female world and female identity." The solution: "Receiving wages for housework is one way for women to gain economic independence and maintain their separate sphere. It is important to recognize that some women may not want to integrate into a male economy and male culture" (Klein 1984:172). But, of course, such a solution makes housework into wage labor and by that fact alone destroys an essential aspect of the so-called separate sphere, assimilating women into the male world.

Such analyses all acknowledge a debt to Aileen Kraditor and William O'Neill. All recognize that two sorts of social activists have called themselves feminists and that two realms of activity and sets of roles have been delineated. All choose to identify equity feminism as authentic, the public realm as the goal and standard. All finally notice and praise the values of the private realm but can understand them only as consequences of an inequality that must now be eradicated. If feminism as they define it has been incompletely successful thus far, their assessment is by and large positive. The policy implication of these analyses is that women can and should move into conventional political action, consciously joining the search for allies and the acquisition of influence. In short, the "male economy and male culture" continue to set standards and procedures (Klein 1984:172).

Social feminists, some of whom have been examined in this book, present a striking contrast. Clearly they wanted and continue to want equality in the sense of having as much autonomy as men have to define options. At the same time, for them equality or equal roles were not ideologies in the sense of dominant belief system, of empowering slogan,

3. This line of argument is increasingly popular in the United States. Japanese workers may well be surprised to learn that Japanese business practices are less concerned with profit, less imbued with formal authority than American ones; Japanese women, effectively excluded from the command structures, would be astonished to learn they would find them comfortable.

or even of mystification. Instead, the doctrine of difference serves all these functions. Its most important function, I have argued, was to legitimize women's activity in the public sphere and thus to create a political role for them. In the process the theoretical and practical boundaries between public and private were effectively eroded. But the doctrine of difference, as understood by activists, can hardly be described as a theory, nor was it articulated as such. Instead, it served to motivate activists and was employed as a justification when it seemed appropriate.

What social feminism has not provided is any explicit feminist theory of a sort clearly distinguishable from conservative versions of the notions about sex-based differences. I believe it would have been inappropriate for social feminists to privilege theory building in an extension of those mainstream judgments which awarded these activities to men and praised them over the practicalities of everyday life. A feminist "theory" of feminism should be pragmatic and action-oriented, uninterested in typologies and divisive distinctions. Yet it is appropriate to use social feminist perspectives to judge policy and social structure with a view to practical improvement. It is even more appropriate to use such perspectives to judge the consequences of equity feminist reforms. And now feminist analyses are beginning to construct social feminist theory.

The most conspicuous examples are the feminist critiques of mainstream methodology I outlined in discussing a feminist perspective on social science. These studies attempt to challenge mainstream intellectual orientations and assumptions from a perspective grounded in women's experience. Related to such discussions are attempts to make the notion of difference both more rigorous and more usable in practical ways. Finally, some critiques focus directly on those dimensions of contemporary society which have been most influenced by the ideas of equity feminists. I take these social feminist critiques in reverse order, starting with the analytical equivalent of the focus on policy which is historically characteristic of social feminism. This is the direction social feminism is taking today: without abandoning the reform action that is its justification, it is beginning to develop a theoretical structure that can challenge the consequences of equity feminism and even provide some analytical alternatives.

Let us therefore look at the arguments of feminist scholars Elizabeth Wolgast and Ann Scales, at Italian discussions of difference including Rossana Rossanda's, and finally at one aspect of the work of Catherine MacKinnon. These theoretical approaches tell us where social feminism is going—where the logic of *Three Guineas* leads. These thinkers might not identify themselves as social feminists, but that is what they are.

Elizabeth Wolgast's *Equality and the Rights of Women* (1980) has in effect been dismissed for making the obvious point that equality does not mean the same as equivalence—an unpopular argument to make in the American political context where *Brown vs. Board of Education* identified "separate but equal" as discriminatory. Wolgast starts from the manifest lack of success that an "atomistic egalitarian model" has had in dealing with women's specific needs (16). She argues that denial of the importance of sex difference is closely related to "our view of human nature as spiritual and rational, our disdain for what counts as animal or merely physical about us" (15). Woman's distinctiveness has physical bases; "equality" assimilates women into a view of human nature that is inaccurate also for men and destructive for all humans. Instead, we need a "bivalent" view of human nature and, as a result, a society "that gives emphasis to human connections, to forms of human interdependence, and to the needs that lead to them "(16). Such a society would be adapted to the needs of infants for love and care, the inability of the elderly to support themselves, and the unselfish dimensions of child-rearing. It would be more than merely the context of family life, resembling a family in that it would be more than an association of "individuals who join together for their mutual benefit" (17). The family thus becomes at least in part the model for the state; the services a family can provide, for which women have characteristically been responsible, are also central to the public realm.

Wolgast concludes her introductory section with a statement that is pure social feminism: "If men and women have somewhat different perspectives and concerns, . . . then it seems reasonable that a new model of society would profit from contributions by women, even though some of these contributions may be ajar with tradition" (17). She ends the book with a discussion of "different life forms" that women might find attractive: "wife and homemaker," "career woman," "the woman who pursues a part-time career," "the woman whose career begins late," and "the divorced mother." In this list no items correspond to male models, for even "career men" usually have supportive wives and probably children; even a dual-career marriage nearly always leaves domestic responsibility, if not all domestic chores, to the wife. As Wolgast notes, "To acknowledge the legitimacy of these different life forms requires a different vision of society." She adds: "This may be the most important mission of the movement for women's rights. For since their demands cannot fit into the framework ready at hand, it is up to them to help create a new one. . . . The perspectives of both sexes need representation, not just in the political arena, but in the very conception of what society is" (157–58). More specifically, in good social feminist terms she justifies women's claims by reference to "a fact that individualism obscures, that one of society's chief and rudimentary concerns is that the children in it, and the families who care for the children, and the mothers who are their primary parents, have the best support it can provide" (158).

Wolgast manages to combine a feeling for maternity and the family with a considerable flexibility in defining how these are to be organized. The family is certainly not identified with any traditional form, particularly not with patriarchal domination over women. Most important, the variants she suggests are developed by women and, she believes, likely to be chosen by women if they are given social support. Her ideal society would encourage similarly wide ranges of options for men.

This is a very modern version of social feminism. In it, self-protection is the strongest motivation for women's legitimate demands. Wolgast does not accept some earlier social feminists' implicit concession that women's inequality or exploitation would be acceptable if society as a whole benefited. Women are not asked to sacrifice themselves for their children or for the public good. Rather, they are to work for a society where social support removes the demand for anyone to make sacrifices. In that society, so-called equality will no longer eliminate due consideration of sexuality and particularly women's sexuality. Here Wolgast is close to Germaine Greer (1986) and Annie Leclerc and also, of course, Virginia Woolf. Similarly, her low-keyed reminder that "the fairness of an atomistic society fails utterly to represent what is fair in a human one" echoes radical feminists who argue for the superiority of the domestic (family, co-operative) over the public (impersonal, competitive) (1980:154). Her feminism, beginning from women's perspective, thus moves inexorably to criticize the most basic elements of current social organization.

Similar consequences can be found in Ann Scales's careful analysis of the legislative and judicial treatment of pregnancy in the United States (1980). Measures relating to women during pregnancy and childbirth are at present the only area of protective legislation supported by both social and equity feminists.[4] Maternity has generally entered labor law under the rubric of disability or sickness; in Canada it is treated as unemployment. Scales demonstrates that judicial doctrine acts as if "women need only be treated as persons when they are not engaged in their childbearing function." That is, "there is some quality in the phenomenon of pregnancy that justifies isolating women from the social mainstream and forcing them to be dependent on others" (398). Underlying this judgment, she suggests, is a belief "that a woman's role is to bear children and that women should bear the cost of childbearing just as they have always done" (399). She rejects Wolgast's suggestion that bivalent women should have special rights related to their distinctive characteristics, as well as the equal ones available to all; this claim would encourage continuation of the stereotyped and paternalistic interpretations that have historically limited women's options.

Instead, Scales proposes what she calls an "incorporationist" approach, which would extend notions of antidiscrimination: "The new approach

4. A very few equity feminists continue to reject the notion of maternity-related benefits as a limit on women's right to contract their labor and as a social endorsement of inferiority.

should carefully account for the historical exclusion of women based on the basic difference in reproductive capabilities and argue for the inclusion of women, with due regard for their reproductive capabilities, in every aspect of society" (434). This ideal of equal treatment would generate what she identifies temperately as a "legislatively-mandated and judicially-enforced restructuring of many institutions" (438). In fact, her list of legislative applications of the incorporationist version of equality is staggering, ranging from flexible hours of work to a complete reformulation of family law.[5] But this is just the beginning. Stronger versions of appropriate legislation would include, for instance, a right to breast-feeding at the workplace, with the onus on the employer to show why it was impracticable, and even some sort of "parents' preference" resembling "veterans' preference." In the United States, Scales sees these measures as requiring national schemes of health and pregnancy insurance and a new, sex-neutral, positive national policy for the family and childcare (438–42).

In short, starting with women's disabilities and asserting a positive evaluation of those female characteristics which underlie them, she produces a restructured state. "The law," she writes, "can participate in the future rather than dwell in the past . . . by taking a hand now in the creation of new institutions which will accommodate the real needs of real citizens. . . . Governments should be concerned with facilitating the experiences of motherhood and fatherhood and with providing a healthy environment for children." Uniqueness, she notes, "is a 'trap' [for women] only in terms of an analysis which assumes . . . that maleness is the norm." What is at stake is *"not a right to be free of classification, but rather a right not to be classified in a degrading manner"* (435).

This is a feminist analysis because it assumes that women should determine the bases of classification. It is social feminist because it attempts to delineate criteria related to women's historically specific experience and values—and to extend these values as a basis on which to reconstruct society as a whole. Recommended measures include and expand those policies for which social feminists have historically worked.

A related pattern of analysis is advanced by European feminists whose work has received little attention in North America, particularly Italians such as Rossana Rossanda and those in Collective no. 4.[6] Rossanda and the

5. Other measures include reduction of the work week below forty hours, extension of regulation of hours worked to include managerial and professional employees, giving legal status (including pension coverage) to unpaid private work, requirement of equal benefits for part-time work, insurance providing maternity and other benefits for pregnant workers, regulations providing and encouraging paternity leave and parental leave, provision of an adequate system of combined public and employer daycare, and allowances to prevent disadvantage for domestically caused absence from the workplace.

6. This material is apparently not available in English. Texts published in *Sottosopra, Orsaminore,* and *Via Dogana* in early 1983 were summarized in the French journal *Les cahiers du CRIF* at the end of 1983, and Rossanda's *Le altre* (1979) was published in translation as *Elles, les autres* by Editions des femmes in 1983. The English translations given here are mine.

collective have taken on the same theoretical task: to define the terms in which female experience can relate to the larger world. Without labeling their own beliefs, they agree on the necessity of avoiding "emancipation-ism," their term for an assimilationist equity feminism. Rossanda describes herself as having been one of the "emancipated": she was in a better situation than her mother's generation and the unliberated women of her own but still as uncomfortable as a frog out of water (1983:15). The collective captures Rossanda's feelings: "Emancipation . . . inserts us into the social game with words and desires which are not our own" (Del Re, Coyaud, and Veauvy 1983–84:4).

Feminism responds to this lack of fit by withdrawal, but women also desire to reenter, to "be at ease" in, society. This is Rossanda's goal. She fears that otherwise, men and women will

> partition the world. . . . The sphere of power will remain his. She, the great mother, the principle of the earth, will cease perhaps to tolerate the other, but she will not be able to change him because she will not be able to understand him, she will not wish to impose on him her own vision of the world, and she will not be able to disentangle alone the knot of vipers which our civilization has fabricated (1983:57).

Both Rossanda and Collective no. 4 seem to assume that society accurately reflects the reality of masculinity, which is based upon the nature of male sexuality. As Rossanda puts it, sounding like a more intellectual Edna O'Brien,

> In him, the act of will and of violence without which he cannot have any relationship with the other sex entailed—inevitably?—an affirmation of individuality, of power, of organization of relationships (beginning with the ones with women) as hierarchical and consequently a construction not only of political values but also of political language as an infinite projection and a reflection of masculinity (1983:47).

The word "inevitably" suggests a skepticism the collective does not feel, as well as greater optimism about the possibilities of changing both men and society. But all of these Italian feminists agree on the radical separateness of women from men. Women, unlike other minorities, do not have in common with their (male) oppressors even a "shared code of conflictuality" (Rossanda 1983:48).

Rossanda and the collective nevertheless disagree about how feminine values can become a model for remaking society. Collective no. 4 is convinced that the battle against "the social misery of women" is pretty much won, that male prejudice is not the issue and neither, therefore, is discrimination. It is time to move out from the static separatism of "finding oneself among women." Now the collective's project is to create within the existing society a "web of preferential connections among women, a shared world of women" (Del Re, Coyaud, and Veauvy 1983–84:4). Within this system it is necessary to accept inequality among women, without damage to mutual respect and love; the model is relations between mother and daughter. As recounted in *Les cahiers du CRIF*, the collective has little to say about how society as a whole will be changed; presumably incorporation of a female sector organized on feminist principles will have some significant effect.

Responses by other Italian feminists focus on the transformation of the whole social order: How is the proposed women's world to avoid being merely another pressure group or a ghetto? Binaca Beccalli reminds us that Italian feminism has not, by and large, been either separatist or committed to an encapsulated women's world: "We did not simply criticize male supremacy but we also wished to change social life. Feminism has tried to promote other values; we must not lose this heritage" (Del Re, Coyaud, and Veauvy 1983-84:6). Similarly, Margareta Repeto of the long-established Union of Italian Women (UDI) refused to accept Rossanda's suggested distinction between two stages of feminism, emancipationism that focused on entry into public life and liberation that concentrated on private life:

> We have always been aware that we could not simply make ourselves a place in the world of men and that in the feminine specificity was implicit a revolutionary specificity which could not affirm itself if all the rest did not change too. That finally a woman was not the equal of a man, she was different, and had to impose her difference on society as a qualitative transformation. (Rossanda 1983:352–53).[7]

Collective no. 4 was struggling to model a female alternative in positive terms where context defines women in negative contrast to men. With the mother-daughter model the collective has done something innovative, attempting to find a structure of social dynamics and interaction in the women's world rather than a simple audit of characteristics. The characteristics implied, however, seem to be those conventionally accepted for women. Rossanda sums up such a feminist approach as accepting proudly the feminine identity men have given women: "affectivity, corporeality, emotion, non-violence . . . exaltation of feminine sexuality (tender, diffuse, undifferentiated, receptive), even . . . rediscovery of maternity as destiny." (1983:49). But she suggests that such an approach is, at best, misleading, as well as dishonest, even manipulative: "To retranslate what pleases him as my pleasure so that we are

---

7. Other Italian feminist commentators objected that women's economic problems were not yet solved or that it was too soon to move from redefinition of private life to reformulation of public life (and they cited what they see as the U.S. choice between lesbian separatism and traditional familialism as a warning). But the most significant responses were to the maternal model. The ideas of inequality and trust were found alarming, implying hierarchy, potential discrimination, and envy.

happy together without him knowing that I am escaping him—isn't this the ultimate lie we can tell ourselves?" (Del Re, Gadant, and Veauvy 1984:12).

On the other hand, says Rossanda, if we reject this image of femininity as "a projection of the other's identity, a fantasy complementary to masculine sexuality," the result is a void: "If a class defines itself by its alienation, its dispossession, its reification, its reduction to merchandise, how can it become the active subject of a revolution, the active principle of a society founded on other values?" (1983:49). Separatism within or outside society can today be a sort of careerism or simply a retreat and resignation from influence. Rossanda therefore has little interest in separatism except as a means for women to develop awareness of their radical difference from men. But she does not see feminism's task as to complete or correct the current state of affairs: "The culture of feminism is a true critique and therefore unilateral, antagonistic, denying the other culture. It doesn't complete it, it puts it in question" (371).

Avoiding self-deception, avoiding bad faith, feminism of this sort has great difficulty in operating creatively to change social structures and social values. Rossanda outlines with precision the problems that Collective no. 4 is wrestling with: the incompatibility with current society of any imaginable alternative to male definitions of the feminine.

At the same time Rossanda, like the collective, insists that some form of integration is possible, that in at least some areas of the current and future social order women will be able to feel effective and at ease. Like the collective, she suggests something like a halfway house. Here we will find the emancipated—like her?—sufficiently integrated into society to be effective, sufficiently feminist to be the most drastic force yet for change. The emancipation of women "could even end up in true revolution, as revolution has been imagined, and not just in the practice of workers' movements, but in the most radical of liberating trends." Feminism, for its part, could "limit itself to serving as an accelerator of the movement for emancipation . . . the cutting edge" (1983:56). As both emancipation and feminism continue, women can be seen as not just the Other but the Contradiction, "the obscure embryo of a critique of politics, as the revolutionary working class was of economics" (57). Like Collective no. 4, she is looking for a reconciliation, the beginning of a "reunited vision" (1983:58).

Unlike the collective, Rossanda cannot suggest even social structure let alone values that are to animate the reunited social order. But she reminds the feminist reader that "the world is bisexual even if culture . . . the way of thinking about it and organizing it, is not." The "sex that is not one" also determines the other sex through its fantasies (Del Re, Gadant, and Veauvy 1984:11-12). That is, women also play a role in the construction of the world. And for Rossanda, looking at Italian politics, it is women's marginalization from partisan (or normal) politics which has produced both the most important parts of feminism and the crisis of Italian politics.

This feminist formulation grew out of Marxism and long experience of participation in politics. It is equally a radical feminist formulation, one that sees sexism (a term used by neither Rossanda nor Collective no. 4) as immemorial and therefore prior to any oppression imposed by capitalism. Its Italian context is a world where feminists combine activism in feminist and in mainline political groups ("double militantism"), where fascism and communism are political history rather than abstract ideologies. Rossanda's own history is indicative: a Resistance activist, she was after the war a member of the Central Committee of the Italian Communist party, then the center of a party fragment, and finally expelled to continue as an independent leftist. Later still she became a nonparty feminist and founder of the feminist journal *Orsaminore*. Her history does not replicate the American pattern of feminist schism from a leftist pressure group, though her feminism is in some sense a criticism of politics as she experienced it. In Italian terms her political experience has been mainstream; she describes herself as a highly successful honorary man. Without knowing just what sort of feminist group she now belongs to, we can see that even today she does not feel the marginalization characteristic of feminists in so many other countries.[8]

Rossanda writes of how unaware of women she was as a Communist militant, how hostile she was to anything identifiable as a woman's perspective or problems. The rebirth of feminism excluded her. Afterward, gradually, women became visible to her as a group:

> From the moment when the language of women not longer appeared to me as something incomplete and imposed, a lag, but rather something incomplete and chosen, a signal—a condition inscribed and accepted, flowering, rationally self-aware or not, but still determined in its revolt, its happiness and sadness—I could no longer not see them. The sex which is not one became it for me now (1983:52).

The echo of Luce Irigaray is clear, but the conclusion is not Irigaray's. Everything looks different now, Rossanda says, and Marx brings her a final consolation: "Humanity only poses questions it can resolve" (1983:57).

Virginia Woolf's concerns in *Three Guineas* are alive and well; her Society of Outsiders attempts to handle the tension between separatism and integration in a way similar to what Collective no. 4 suggests. Rossanda's questions about the impact of sexuality and sexual fantasy pick

8. Collective no. 4 has no history available in English or French. In contrast to Rossanda, collective members report a feeling of alienation and ineffectiveness in relation to public life. They seem to be a separatist collective that has in the past been involved in feminist service activity. They are likely to be considerably younger than Rossanda, with direct memories only of the postwar era.

up problems posed by the theorist who wrote in *A Room of One's Own* that women served as an enlarging mirror for men to see themselves in, who cried out in defense of women's culture but knew that only the pork butcher's daughter (owner of "a share in the pig factory") could speak with confidence and have a chance of being listened to (Woolf 1982:298).[9] Woolf can be seen as one of the earliest to formulate a critique of current society as intrinsically or structurally hostile to women and women's values—a critique picked up in a different context by the theorists of violence against women. These also, I argue, are social feminists who derive their arguments from women's perspectives and values. If we are mindful of its specifically Anglo-American context, Catherine MacKinnon's analysis can serve as a final example of how social feminism is entering feminist discourse with more theoretical relevance than it had in the past.

MacKinnon is an original theorist who has attracted some notoriety because of the policy implications of her views, implications she has actively pursued. This is not the least of the ways in which her approach is typical of a significant element of social feminist theorizing today. MacKinnon's arguments are directed to social disjunctures that affect women, beginning with rape and pornography. She is concerned with social features harmful to women which the "progressive" elements in (male) society are prepared to tolerate. As a result, her policy concerns now are often thought to show that feminism, or at least social feminism, is reactionary, in part because conservative groups on occasion share the social feminists' targets (though not their logic).

MacKinnon identifies rape and pornography as issues "central to women's survival," along with battery, prostitution, sexual harassment, sex discrimination, and abortion (1982:643).[10] These areas will not be affected by increased juridical equality for women, for they follow from the nature of the patriarchal and therefore oppressive state. They are problems that equity theorists are unable to recognize, and they are linked to a thoroughgoing rejection of the underlying assumptions of both the modern state and modern scholarship. MacKinnon sums up her position thus: "The state's formal norms recapitulate the male point of view on a level of design" (1983:655). "Feminism, on this level," she writes, "is the theory of women's point of view" (1982:535). Analysis is therefore inseparable from activism. She concludes that reforms will not change women's situation. Treating women "equally" will not eliminate the essential antifeminism of the state, even if reforms make "police more sensitive, prosecutors more responsive, judges more receptive and

9. Ironically, Rossanda mentions *Three Guineas* as an example of first-wave feminism's preoccupation with inequalities of power, its identification of women as being like other oppressed groups in a sex-neutral world into which they could be integrated (1983:48). Her misreading does not invalidate the theoretical continuity.

10. She also includes, for the United States, the ERA. However illogically, this is the touchstone issue for U.S. feminists.

the law, in words, less sexist" (1983:643). Yet in the world of activism she has not opted for separatism but instead actively involved herself with, for instance, the Minneapolis bylaw that would enable women to lay charges treating pornography as an identifiable source of damage to them.

MacKinnon's position is a paradox, as well as a double militantism, similar to that of contemporary Italian theorists. It echoes Virginia Woolf's assertion in *Three Guineas* that the most committed and even disinterested members of the elite are the worst because of their unavoidable support of patriarchy. Woolf's solution was to recommend to feminists that they gain mainstream credentials while remaining apart in the Society of Outsiders; MacKinnon's stance is similar.

Here we see, in new versions, the contradiction inherent in social feminism, which, in the name of the home and the private sphere, has moved women out of the home and into the public sphere. The tensions between separation and integration, cooption and critique, are inescapable. MacKinnon's analysis can provide no solution, but she claims more than most social feminists would for the impact of a properly developed feminist theory. For her, women have the world-historical role attributed to Marx's proletariat: to understand and thereby "explode" the reality by which its life is "determined." Note the contrast with Rossanda's explanation; perhaps the latter's Marxist experience makes her dubious about the direct impact on society of theoretical argument. MacKinnon's is thus very much a male model, against which she herself warns and which in practice she disregards, concentrating on action by women in areas they themselves have identified as important.

MacKinnon's analysis finally leaves the reader face to face with the basic dilemmas of feminist analysis: In respect to feminist actions, if the test is women's own consciousness and choices, how can any feminist be condemned as inauthentic? In respect to social change, if women's nonparticipation is part of existing social structures, how can women possibly be agents of change? Were the feminisms of the past false consciousness or bases of empowerment—or both? And what about our own analyses and actions?

I have suggested that a truly feminist perspective would look for answers in the experience of women and in their own formulations of goals and evaluations of change. This is what MacKinnon is presenting in her own highly intellectualized version of women's point of view. This is what Wolgast, Scales, Rossanda, and Collective no. 4 are trying to work out. They are thus providing theoretical counterparts to the ideology and actions of the women I have called social feminists. It is in accounts of specific groups that such theories can be substantiated, and that is what I have tried to do in this book.

In addition, and possibly most important of all, the doctrine of difference can direct feminists to a more accurate and serviceable notion of power than any equity feminism can. Neither a call for violent revolution nor one for enrollment in existing "progressive" ranks will enable women to change the world. To say that politics is concerned with power is not the same as saying that politics, or change, depends on violence in general or revolution in particular. To keep the notion of politics from encompassing all of life, we customarily limit it to social structures larger and more impersonal than the family. The most convenient way of designating that level of organization is to identify it with the authoritative, delegated use of force. This is the basis of Max Weber's definition of politics as the legitimate monopoly of force. Underlying his definition are familiar assumptions about a contrast between a bureaucratized public realm and a personal private one, the first the locus of male activities, the second mainly of female but with men also involved. Similarly, the legitimate force that defines realms is monopolized not just by government but by men, and only they can take it into the household or use it to defend the household. It is not surprising that under such circumstances women understand power as involving a "zero-sum game of domination, control and denial" defined and carried on by men (Flammang 1983:1).

Nor is it surprising that feminists wish to redefine power so that it remains effective but is transformed into "interpersonal relations of reciprocity, ability and energy" (1983:1). An easy, sentimental rhetoric is then likely to speak of substituting empowerment for domination. A relatively sophisticated version may be responsive to "the tension between using our organizations as instruments for taking and transforming power in a society structured by power understood only as domination, and using our organizations to build models for a new society based on power understood as energy and initiative" (Hartsock 1974:16–17). But even here the terminology of "taking" power implies a direct and likely forceful conflict, and it is unclear how transformation will then be possible.

Nancy Hartsock says correctly that "what we mean by political change is structural change" (1974:17). But she and other equity feminist analysts of power seem uninterested in mainstream discussions of power that have been available for a generation and more. As early as 1954 Harold Lasswell and Morton Kaplan suggested that power is relational, derived from seven sorts of resources including respect and affection as well as the capacity for violence. Robert Lane (1955) neutralized power even further, arguing that it is best understood as the ability to produce desired consequences; he followed Lasswell and Kaplan in including positive inducements ("indulgences") as well as negative ones ("deprivation"). He noted that threat may be absent, control being exercised through the weaker party's anticipation of some future consequence. Analyses focusing on citizen groups rather than on elites have demonstrated how disagreements may be stopped from becoming issues, so that no competition is ever necessary. Control thus need never involve force or even threat (Bachrach and Baratz 1962, 1963). More recent discussion of "hegemony" has postulated a more subtle form of control in which potential conflict is not subjectively visible because the powerful structure the environment. Dissatisfaction is not even felt, let alone expressed, pushed to confrontation, or triumphant (Lukes 1974).

This combined model fits male-female relationships far better than any simple assumption that power means visible exercise of strength. It explains why male dominance has been so persistent historically: men monopolize not just the instruments of physical control but also those instruments of ideology and communication which sustain hegemony. It also explains the ability of women to cope and survive: they have resources that, in a specific context, may have a significant impact. Less encouragingly, this notion of power suggests also that the decrease of overt violence or confrontation in male-female relationships may indicate a greater rather than a lesser degree of control. Furthermore, it makes clear that energy, initiative, and reciprocity are not new meanings for power but instead are options among possible bases and forms of power relationships.

International relations embody the versions of power relationships most characterized by brute force and explicit confrontation. Here recent analyses are even more pertinent to feminist wishes and hopes. Structural analyses of power now focus on international regimes, including those characterized as "interdependence." Interdependence is an attractive term, and if its meaning is not quite the feminist utopia of the end of force, still it represents a system in which gain is shared by the parties involved and in which consent plays a larger role than coercion. Within this setting, power is divisible and interchangeable, reputational, variable, diffuse, and based on many facets of a relationship. The englobing relationship, in turn, involves partners who are mutually influential and mutually vulnerable, able to inflict costs even after measures short of terminating the relationship are undertaken (Keohane and Nye 1977). A related notion is the "security community," a relationship lacking domination and in which it is not expected that force will be used (Deutsch et al. 1957). In the historical examples, the European Community and North America, power bases are markedly uneven and there is a past history of often bloody conflict.

These are non-zero-sum versions of power related to the structures of interaction. Analytically coherent, they also have historical referents. They are important from a feminist perspective as evidence that it is possible to change and adapt ongoing relationships valued by all parties. International examples are crucial because the units, nation states, always have as a primary goal the protection of their differences and their independence of decision making. The models of the integrating system, which will merge nations together into larger units, is not helpful, but a genuine and close peaceful coexistence is (Black 1974).

Power needs, in short, not so much to be redefined as to be better understood. It makes sense to look at the structural conditions that enable human beings to live together in conditions combining autonomy and mutual gain. Students of community and international power have directed considerable attention to the conditions—relative and relational—under which both less and more benign versions of nonviolent, mixed-motive relationships are created and continue.

At this point the feminist might well look more closely at the semi-metaphoric use of zero-sum and non-zero-sum games. Those who identify the current practice of politics and power as zero-sum are slurring over the real meaning of the game theory they are using. The actual structure of male-female power is not zero-sum. Instead, it resembles a series of games that continue because over time they amount to a mixed-motive competition. This is another way of saying that all but acutely pathological versions of politics take place as part of a continuing relationship: the gains and losses of the players are not entirely in conflict. Even under current circumstances the interests of men and women are not completely incompatible, and certainly their relationships can be expected to continue. Any plan for transformation must take this situation into account.

The feminist may well object that this and preceding observations about power are part of an intellectual analysis that masks or palliates a situation in which women, knowingly or not, consistently do less well than men. At fault (but this also is a game-theoretic observation) are both the structure of interaction and the distribution of resources. That is, women as such are oppressed, however subtle and varying the forms of interaction and male domination may be. Part of the domination is the denial of anything unusual in women's actual or potential relationship to power.

This criticism is reasonable. Since the theories of power outlined here relate power to specificities of resources and relationships, however, the inclusion of women (as related to men) does not deny the uniqueness of women's situation. Furthermore, the feminist use of the notion of zero-sum competition has *already* incorporated women into the same analytic model. Closer attention to the implications of game theory has the advantage of supplying the concept of the mixed-motives game, which may provide a basis for designing a preferable future.

An analysis using game theory also directs attention to the goals of the women's movement, posing the problem of their compatibility both internally and with the goals of men, of male society, and, more broadly, of society as a whole. The goods available may make certain incompatibilities irreducible. The solution, however, is not to redefine power, but to redesign the social system in which choices have to be made between incompatible alternatives. Only wishful thinking can suggest that at some point no incompatibility will exist between nurturance and creativity. But we are talking of *mixed*-motive relationships, not of wholly co-operative ones (as would be possible if there were no autonomously defined competing claims), and it is also possible to construct acceptable tradeoffs.

Social feminism, with its emphasis on the experience of women in the home—and by extension, in women's groups—directs our attention to the most immediate examples of ongoing mixed-motive interactions. What we need to discover is the conditions under which such groups can become examples or agents of the change that will make the larger society more like them. Janet Flammang suggests one necessary element: that change be attained through "reeducation and informed consent, not the intimidation and coercion associated with male politics" (1983:71–72). "Intimidation and coercion" may characterize politics as we know it today, but even today's politics include other dimensions. "Reeducation and informed consent" do sometimes occur; they are precisely what we need to dissolve the mystification that is a key element of domination.

We can probably agree that all of the groups discussed in this book have had such an impact on their members, have reeducated them and in the process produced their informed consent to a range of social reforms. Some feminists, thinking this was enough, would set as a goal the transformation of women as a group. But the organizations studied here did not see women's transformation as their goal. Rather, they wished to produce significant change in the whole structure of society. They had the ambition, in Flammang's words, of "redistributing resources and reordering public priorities" (1983:71).

If the organizational risks of social feminism are related to the dangers of narrowness and elitism, separatism and essentialism, then its possibilities are related to this ambition for social change. Individual women and the theory of feminism are now positioned so that they can hope for progress greater than what has occurred. These possibilities come directly from the conception of female difference or specificity.

Social feminism is best discussed as an ideology, an organizational and personal motivator. But social feminism, as I suggested in earlier chapters, also functions as a theoretical construct, a basis from which to reorganize theories about feminism. This role I find compatible with an insistence that the goals and promises of feminism are not theory building but action. Similarly, I argue that social feminism currently offers not just a continuing practical, organizational context for social change but also a theoretical critique and guide to analysis.

CHAPTER 19

Conclusions

We write about feminism with extraordinary confidence that our knowledge extends across all its possible varieties. In spite of the accusation that feminists mistake their own situation for a universal one, feminists are aware by now of the risk of indifference to other women's disadvantages of class or race, of age or bodily capability. We are less conscious of theoretical variety unless reminded by an encounter with Italian feminism through the French or by sudden awareness of what is going on in, say, Brazil, remote from North Americans in language and experience (Goldberg 1986). The best antidote is the social feminist emphasis on difference itself, with its corollary concern for the specificities of groups and individuals within the encompassing category of women. In the pragmatic, action-oriented context of social feminism, this emphasis can provide practical guidance. Analytically, however, the warning does not take us far. In particular, the understanding of social feminism as originating in notions about male/female differences means only that women's distinctiveness provides a basis for social action and for social criticism. The doctrine of difference can then produce feminist strategies of either separatism or integration; neither is simple or takes a single form.

If parent theories are the most important sources of illumination for equity feminisms, then the political, social, and cultural contexts of specific groups are the most important in explaining social feminist beliefs. Even then it is not easy to distinguish among theoretical orientations. Linda Gordon and Ellen DuBois have illustrated this point in their studies of the American women's movement and the struggle for reproductive control; their shared argument is more explicit in a joint article on the movement's responses to female sexuality and sexual violence against women (DuBois 1978; Gordon 1976; DuBois and Gordon 1983). The old notion of "voluntary motherhood" through abstinence sounds odd today, though it has important affinities with current attitudes about contraception (a concept abhorred by most nineteenth-century

342

feminists). Yet in both cases feminists accept a difference between male and female sexuality, and in both they want women to keep control. The differences lie, perhaps, in changed reproductive technology and in women's changed political and economic status. They may also be due in part to changes in the women's movement itself, so that the enduring feminist condemnation of, for one example, wife battering, changes meaning over time. The Women's Christian Temperance Union is not the same as Women against Violence against Women (WAVAW), even if both see men and women as different and domestic violence as male and reprehensible.

Even archetypes of female nature vary, contrary to the beliefs of social feminists. Studying a number of simple societies, researchers found women socially identified as "sexy partners" to hunters rather than as mothers of children (Collier and Rosaldo 1981). As a result Michelle Rosaldo, who had influenced feminist anthropologists to define the private sphere in terms of female, child-centered units, warned against projecting the seemingly natural images of our own everyday life onto other cultures, in a search for mothers and the Great Mother (1980). We are more sophisticated in our use of explicitly academic imagery. Here the private sphere is the domestic pole of a whole series of oppositions. Jessie Bernard identified at least six oppositions in the academic literature but preferred to focus on *agape,* a notion that placed her own analysis squarely within the Judeo-Christian tradition from which the other notions also come (1981:23–36). Ranging from *Gemeinschaft* to "integry," these extraordinarily varied notions of the domestic differ from the self-definitions of active social feminists, definitions that in turn change and develop over the years.[1] Reproductive and now sexual differentiation remains at the core, more or less explicitly, but the rest of the beliefs also differ substantially. I have stressed their similarities; their differences matter too.

The next task of the student of feminism is therefore to look more closely at a large number of differing historical social feminisms, seeking their explicit and implicit ideologies. The necessary basis is studies of specific groups and activists, like the ones recounted in this book for groups of social feminists in England, France, and the United States.

The delineation of feminist beliefs becomes a difficult, even delicate undertaking when, within social feminism, the analyst begins to look at the causes and nature of specific belief systems. I have been able to do no more than sketch belief systems for three social feminist groups. Starting from ideology and looking superficially at setting, we can see how such an analysis might proceed for Italian feminists such as Rossana Rossanda

1. Bernard discusses Maine's status (in contrast to contract), Tönnies' *Gemeinschaft* (*Gesellschaft*), Kropotkin's and Spenser's mutual aid (competition), Ruth Benedict's Apollonian (Dionysian), Mancur Olson's sociology (economics), and Kenneth Boulding's integry (economy).

and Collective no. 4. They developed in a place where the relationship between politics and male perspectives is particularly obvious, concrete, and specific. Italy historically never adopted an equal rights liberalism that might generate the ideology of liberal equity feminism. Here the pervasiveness of masculine control was made explicit and brutal by fascism; here unionists and thugs together embody the sexual identity of public life. In addition, in Italy nonutopian Marxist alternatives compete with liberalism and conservatism, and the church is the survivor of a Concordat; the central feminist issues of divorce and abortion have played a role in partisan disputes. These and many other specificities shape the Italian version of social feminism at the same time as, apparently, they truncate the possibilities of equity feminism. To go further, we would need to know far more both about Italy and about the ideas and structures of Italian feminism.

Even without such information, we can see significant contrasts with the development of feminism in the Anglo-Saxon countries where equal rights made up the political tradition and context. For this and other reasons, feminists in Britain and North America could have a reformist impact relatively easily. Changes could occur where the centrality of the issues considered was muted. Thus in the United States easier divorce procedures could be accepted and incorporated into law as an extension of civil liberties, and the decriminalization of abortion could be interpreted as simply a logical consequence of the right to privacy. Similarly, in bilingual, multicultural Canada, women's "voice" could be compared to that of francophones or the country's multiple ethnic groups in arguments that women ought to keep their own identity (Marsden 1980, McCormack 1984). Furthermore, women's group action draws in such settings on an established reformist tradition of managing group differences. These environments make even notions of difference and the assertion of women's values less confrontational. Social feminist theory, such as it was, accordingly tended to focus on specific difficulties generated by equity reforms as well as on those women's problems to which a feminism couched in equal rights terms had not responded. Its ideology, never very explicit, became less so, but its power for generating political action and its usefulness as a basis for analyzing or reanalyzing women's activities remained great.

In this book I have only suggested the usefulness of the concepts associated with social feminism. Groups animated by such an ideology can be found all over the world, and more will appear. Seeing them as social feminist makes clearer their impact and also illuminates the general situation of women in politics. To underline this point, it is worth looking at a final example of a social feminist women's organization, a modern Third World group: the Malaysian Kaum Ibu, as described in 1977 by Lenore Manderson. The Kaum Ibu was the women's section of a political party and so had some resemblance to the relationships of the

Guild to the Co-operative movement and the UFCS to the MRP. The case suggests why other groups, such as the League, preferred greater independence. It also suggests the usefulness of a social feminist perspective as a basis for analyzing women's political activities.[2]

The Malay women of what is now Malaysia became prominent in conventional politics in response to British attempts to reassert authority after World War II. There was a "mushrooming" of women's organizations which can be divided into women's "social and welfare" associations and others that were "expressly political" (213). These latter took two forms: equity feminist groups, such as the Malay Women's Emancipation Association, and the Kaum Ibu (women's auxiliary) groups formed specifically to support male Malay associations in nationalist protests.[3] The Kaum Ibu shared the mainstream anticolonialism of the time, and their women leaders were apparently involved in founding the United Malays National Organization (UMNO), a "conservative communal party with mass grass-roots support" (Manderson 1977:227). At a later date they federated Kaum Ibu groups into a single organization affiliated with UMNO; Manderson cites effectiveness in assisting and influencing UMNO as reasons for the reorganization. At unified Kaum Ibu's first separate meeting, however, a third cluster of concerns was discussed: problems of easy divorce and arranged marriages, the need for Malay women in the Department of Welfare, and issues of women's education. Later, at UMNO conferences, the women were to obtain party approval of resolutions dealing with divorce, religion, prostitution, social welfare, and increased participation of women in civic and political life. This is the agenda of social feminism.

Manderson recounts a series of unsuccessful efforts by Kaum Ibu to obtain guaranteed representation and influence within UMNO as well as slightly more successful attempts to get Kaum Ibu women fielded as legislative candidates. She stresses the way the women backed away from confrontations about intraparty standing; for instance, they did not carry through on a threat to boycott elections because of the absence of women candidates. She attributes this failure to three factors: along with the "subordinate status of the section to the party proper" and "its limited representation within the party machine" there was, revealingly stated, "the interests of the majority of [Kaum Ibu] membership." The result was "greater attention to social rather than political activity" and

2. I rely here on Manderson (1977); she makes it clear that Malay politics was extremely complex in the period 1945–1972, and a neophyte certainly cannot hope to untangle it. I suspect also that the history of the Kaum Ibu is less clear-cut than she suggests. Yet if we use the outline she offers, the account is suggestive and bears directly on the relation of women to mainstream politics, as well as on the difficult question of how to analyze social feminism.

3. Manderson implies in passing a fair amount of earlier activity among women, but she does not take up the point.

hence, she infers, less concern to force the issue of representation. The day-to-day activities of Kaum Ibu "centered on the interests of its members as wives and mothers." They also "occasionally" included political courses and seminars and, around election times, "concentrated political activity" that included political education of an uninformed electorate and canvass of votes for UMNO (227). Malays, both men and women, turned out in very large proportions for elections, and Kaum Ibu was given credit.

It is always hazardous to rely on material presented in only one truncated version. But it is possible to interpret Manderson's account differently. Manderson concludes with the familiar equity feminist demand for an explicit focus on status of women, with the usual implied slur on the political capability of social feminists: "Kaum Ibu's general acceptance of its status within the party and national politics illustrates the entrenchment of social attitudes regarding the role of women and attests that participation in the public sphere without reassessment of those attitudes does not effect a changed role" (228). However, along with male resistance to more than token representation of women in public and party office, she also shows a female elite that was active in conventional politics at a surprisingly early date. The level of political activity among Malay women in general (turnout rates were equal to men's, unlike the predictably low rates among Indian and Chinese women) suggests also a fairly wide Malay acceptance of women's political role; women still lag behind men in voting rates in countries with a much longer experience of woman suffrage. We may hear echoes here of the early experience of the League of Women Voters.

Two elements are missing from Manderson's account of the final decision of Kaum Ibu not to press to the point of electoral boycott its demand for a share of party offices and candidatures for the legislature: the substantive policy interests of members, and women's own crucial role in UMNO victories. The interests of grass-roots members, which Manderson implicitly dismisses as nonpolitical, seem to correspond to the standard package of social feminist policies and seem also to have been shared by the leaders. A "conservative communal party with mass grass-roots support" is precisely one that would incorporate such policies into its program. It resembles Christian Democratic parties in just that appeal to women voters—and to women activists. It seems safe to say that UMNO therefore attracted female support because of issues. These are, of course, issues usually labeled domestic or social, and they are also, in my view, political.[4]

For ideological or programmatic reasons, UMNO was bound to hold the loyalty of women activists as long as those women did not renounce party politics. Kaum Ibu members would be acting against their own

4. Manderson does not tell us what the opposition parties had to say on these topics; I assume they were not interested.

interests to push their demands to the point of defeating the party, as they could have done. And if the party paid little attention to resolutions relating to the status of women, at least it approved such resolutions, as well as others relating to social reforms of special interest to women— because of the influence of the Kaum Ibu.

The dilemma was that of the Guild: once commitment was made to a party, on the basis of the available options most auspicious for women, how could women then oppose or even influence it? Exit would be possible if the key issues ceased to be important. But they have not yet. And Manderson notes the extent to which the Kaum Ibu, like the Guild, was increasingly inhibited from such a break by personal and family associations.

The women of the Kaum Ibu were clearly politically active, especially if we include among political goals the welfare measures that focus on the situation of the "wife and mother." They were also active in normal politics—but not as elected or appointed public officials. The reason seems to be opposition from male party members, that is, by male politicians who controlled the parties including access to party office and to political candidature. For ideological reasons—because of the party loyalty women are believed not to have—the women could not leave or effectively pressure their party. But it was not women's roles or their inability to reassess or restructure their roles that produced this situation. Rather, the cause was men's refusal to incorporate women fully into the political process. We can say exactly the same of the Guild, and the women of the Union féminine report similar perceptions. We can see why incorporation was a situation the League was eager to avoid, and we can see why the loss of the MRP actually benefited the Union.

Why do men impose these obstacles? In the assimilationist, equity model the reason is men's refusal to accept women as legitimate rivals and their use, unconsciously as well as consciously, of the doctrines of difference and social feminism to justify their refusal. A more friendly interpretation sees men as socialized to a view of women that does not include political activity. Women, for their part, are inhibited from competition and therefore politics, and their reticence encourages men's resistance. This version, like Manderson's analysis, puts the onus on women to change their interests and modes of behavior as well as their sphere of activity. In the process their distinctive issue preferences are, as we have repeatedly seen, labeled unpolitical and unprogressive, subjective and mistaken.

Social feminism derives male refusal to accept women as active politicians from the structure of male politics and related ideas about proper goals and behavior in public life. Even when significant areas of domestic policy—such as issues of health, education, and welfare in general and of international co-operation, development, and peace—are correctly recognized as political, conventional policy options are truncated and deformed. In addition, partisan structures and competitive processes, organized around the principles of hierarchy and violence, exclude women and women's issues. The very subordination of career to impact on social policy—central to any distinctively female role in politics—is excluded by the attitudes and structures of partisan politics. "Normal" politics therefore resists those who, if at all different, bring with them issues and attitudes subversive of the norm.

The submission or subordination of women to men within conventional politics is almost certainly motivated (in women) not so much by a sense that men are more competent or women less so as by concessions to the demands of the existing system. Women manifest loyalty to party or movement because of issues. Social feminists are convinced that their policy priorities will be successful in human terms; they are not likely to produce successful electoral results or to fit comfortably into the conventions of existing social policy. Hence the reluctance of parties to support them; hence also the support social feminist activists give to those few parties and movements which respond to social feminist goals or even individuals. It is not surprising that Choisir and a very large number of Frenchwomen support the Socialists, the first party to give anything like a feminist response to issues of reproduction. But it is understandable that women wish to retain at least a separate organizational base within the party. It is also understandable why women's organizations continue to exist alongside the organizations of mainstream politics even when individual women are highly integrated into the political system and the groups' overall membership is deeply involved in issues of social policy.

Equity feminist analysis cannot provide such insights; social feminism has some chance of doing so. It can also provide some practical guides for women to organize their lives and reorganize the public realm to which social feminism continues to provide an entry for even quite conventional women—as most of us are.

No system as fluid and inexplicit as social feminism can be tidily circumscribed. Nor should it be. But it is worth trying to see what it is likely to mean for the future. As a starting point, we may note that social feminism relies not just on an assertion of difference (between sexes) but also on an assumption of compatibility. This is not the same as subordination or complementarity, which together characterize existing relationships of the sexes. As to goals, social feminists believe that a bisexual society is both desirable and possible. As to methods, they believe such a society can be produced without revolutionary transformation. Male/female conflict is therefore a short-run problem, inevitable as women assert their role in constructing the necessary new institutions. After all, the major change predicted is male loss of the exclusive power of decision. Analytically, there is certainly an incompatibility between the existing public order and the one that has not yet come into existence, between those who benefit disproportionately at present and those who wish to redistribute power and gain. But gender relations are not intrinsically zero-sum or purely competitive in nature; rather, their conflicts can be resolved over time by adaptation and mutual accommodation. To see male-female differences about practice and goal as implying confrontation, battle, and final triumph of one side or the other—that is characteristic of male values and of the public world as we know it, still relatively untouched by the influence of women.

Social feminism's model for a new social order is the family, that institution so maligned by equity feminists. The family is the locus of the experience we can identify historically as being female. Although the modern family is imperfect, it has changed for the better from the institution that gave the ancient patriarchs a literal power of life and death. Unlike other forms of feminism, social feminism thus uses women's experienced standards to assess possible male-female relationships in a nonsexist world. Instead of the abstract intellectual models of class and caste, the ideal image is one encountered by all, in however defective a form. Although the family has been a poorer protection for women and children than observers have supposed, it has been able to accommodate major alterations in technology, social environment, ideology, and relative power both internal and external. Both the myth and the demonology of the family grow out of women's experience, and at the same time both reflect and respond to larger social groupings. Laws about marital rape and wife and child abuse, as well as regulations about public education, sanitation, taxation, and charity, all indicate social consensus on what the family should be like. Feminists have demonstrated how such state intrusions have subordinated the family to a conflictual and sexist public order, making it serve the interests of class and gender domination (Land 1980). But social feminists have nevertheless been able to use the family in its private aspects as a basis for critiques of the public realm and values derived from the family as a basis for remodeling public life.

What is different, what remains different about the domestic sphere— these are the crucial elements of social feminism's critique of society. Here battles are not supposed to be fought to the death, here conflicts can be put aside or outgrown, here change is gradual but also inevitable. In the idealized modern family, where economic and psychological dependency is either mutual or else to be outgrown, "war" is avoidable because the parties have shared interests as well as conflicting interests and because all have, eventually, the option of leaving.

The family thus serves both as a concrete model and as a metaphor with an originality that is by definition impossible for the central concepts of equity feminism, derived as they are from systems of analysis based on the differentiated perspectives and experience of men in the public sphere.

Class analysis, the most salient dimension of modern political discourse, has only two choices in analyzing the specificity of women's situation: to deny it exists, or to see any emphasis on it as producing an incompatibility between the sexes analogous to that between economic classes. But women, even if identified as a "sex-gender" class, cannot possibly be about to generate a successful world-historical struggle for change. Therefore any analysis based on class must regard any grouping of women as either a threat to working-class unity or a challenge to the organized working class to recognize women's genuine grievances, which can be incorporated into the appropriate strategy of the workers. This last argument is strengthened by the fact that nearly all women now spend some considerable period of their lives in the paid labor force. Their grievances—lack of economic independence, double day of wage and domestic labor, reproductive dependency—can now be seen as flowing from conditions of work or at least remediable by improvements there. Feminist demands directed to men as a group are deprived of legitimacy, and so, in the long run, are feminist organizations. If the only possible source of social and political progress is the working class's successful battle against employers, feminism is a bourgeois phenomenon basically antithetical to progress but instrumentally useful when working-class organization is unable to respond to women's situation. Feminism is thus valuable as a "goad to the workers' movement." But it is nothing more significant: "Wishing to replace the solidarity of workers by the solidarity of women, [feminism] would contribute to prolonging the exploitation of men by men, and in that way the exploitation of women. . . . There is no feminine solidarity as such, [because] it cannot exist except as solidarity in face of a particular problem" (Zylberberg-Hocquard 1981:220).

Feminist solidarity is thus suspect among leftist analysts, including Marxist and socialist feminists. Feminist solidarity within the leftist model of uniform agreement and action on a shared material basis is likely to become both sentimental and essentialist. The search for shared material bases for sex-gender solidarity is likely to end up with biology (maternity or potential for it) or some relational quality such as "sexage," the control of women's labor power by men (Guillaumin 1981; 1981a; 1985). These are illusory bases for co-operation, no better than the emotional bonding some of the "progressive" feminists felt they had created with conservative women at the 1977 Houston conference. Such solidarity has virtually no impact on perceptions or policy preferences (Rossi 1979:43).

It may well be, however, that Marxists' dismissive analysis of female group action has inadvertently identified the form of organization appropriate for feminists: overlapping and shifting alliances in response to problems perceived by specific groups of women. These problems, not all of them related to wage labor, can be seen in turn as part of the structural problem that is male dominance, as it appears in the different lives and life-stages of women. At the Houston conference, Rossi was able to identify overlapping issues and interests among the wide variety of feminist groups represented. Among these organizations were many whose energies were directed to relatively narrow ranges of women's issues. But overall there was solidarity, in the sense that most were unwilling to drum out of the women's movement those groups and individuals who were dissident or inactive even on certain key issues. Thus over half accepted as feminist those women who opposed abortion, and one in three even accepted opponents of the ERA (1979:93).[5] Their concerns and their actions, aggregated rather than unitary, overlapping and mutually tolerant, had in common both perspectives and goals corresponding to women's domestic experience.

There is no need to repeat that physical experiences and social situations are neither universal nor uniform among women. However, some response to some experience of male dominance is present or potentially present in all women. It is articulated in order to deal with specific resulting problems. These problems, in turn, repeat and cluster, generating over time an identifiable repertoire of feminist agendas, whatever the disagreement about rankings.

These agendas of "women's issues" marginalize women in relation to mainstream politics and in the political discourses out of which equity feminisms grow. "Normal" politics has only two ways to handle the feminist agendas. On the one hand, women's concerns can be treated as a version of something recognizable in the existing public world—and obliterated as far as distinctiveness goes. On the other hand, distinctiveness can be preserved at the cost of withdrawal and separatism. Neither version has served women well. The social feminist response is some sort of women's group that relates to existing political structures while attempting to change them, at least to the degree of putting social feminist issues and preferences on the policy agenda.

For the social feminist, separatism that is unrelated to the male, public world is without interest. But separatist organizing, in women-only activist groups, can provide a basis for transforming society, first of all through an alteration of the process of change itself. A distinction must be made between the conventional domestic sphere of women, however helpful their mutual support is, and "a strong, public female sphere" (Freedman 1979:513). The first realm, loving and supportive, assists the individual woman to cope but encourages self-limitation and acceptance of male domination. The second can become a powerful mechanism for

5. 53.1 percent in the first category, and 33.9 percent in the second (93).

social transformation. The social feminist has ambitious goals, after all. She wants to see women more integrated into all aspects of society, if only to be able to change it. At the same time she wants to see society profoundly changed, and not just by the incorporation of women. Separate women's organizations become crucial: they can integrate women into politics while ensuring that integration means female influence and, above all, the influence of female values and procedures.

We are beginning to accumulate evidence about the historical role of women's organizations, especially in Europe and North America, and about their analogues in the present-day Third World. Further, we are beginning to see the outlines of a continuing role for such groups even when women are technically fully integrated into politics. Janet Flammang writes about the interaction of feminist groups and individual feminists who have taken office in Santa Clara County, California, the "feminist capital." She attributes the election of a women-majority county council to the "grassroots feminist activists" supporting women candidates (1985:90). Her account underlines the point of the CAWP studies of American women in politics, that women in office rely heavily on women-only groups who will support them with money and personnel without undercutting a shared commitment to feminist procedures and goals (Stanwick 1983). Ruth Mandel (1981) also documents the increasingly concrete role of women's groups in support of women candidates. Women's political action committees, for instance, can mean independence from party or other pressures concomitant on funding. This is a modern, specifically political continuation of a process, first identified by feminist historians, in which women and women's groups have had an ongoing impact on American public life. In 1984 Anne Firor Scott made the point emphatically in her presidential address to the Organization of American Historians. "No one has yet begun to trace in detail all the ways in which the work of women's associations shaped and changed society and social values [in the United States] over 120 years," she commented, "but what we know so far suggests that when that detailed work is done, their influence will be seen to reach into every corner of community life as well as into state and national politics" (1984:19). The starting point of her discussion was her own experience in the League of Women Voters in the postwar years, when conventional wisdom viewed that organization as moribund.

Social feminism obviously does not see women's interests as identical with men's, nor the relation of the sexes as nonconflictual. But it does not envisage that conflict as cumulative, as producing confrontation and eventually revolution. Rather, it sees the possibility of using the existing male-dominated system, of working within it in a way that serves women's interests—which include a transformation of the entire system. As the case of Kaum Ibu shows, such a perspective can generate a reinterpretation of much of the scholarly analysis of the role (or nonrole) of women in political life. In social feminist analysis, women's organizations are part of the political process, what encourages or assists women to respond to the specific problems posed for women by the patriarchy.

Women's autonomy, the defining goal of feminism, is the immediate, necessary instrument for action, but the goal is not the end of the oppression of women. There are many goals, varying, separate, and specific. Group response amounts to a tacit recognition of points at which the personal is political and therefore has to be dealt with by collective rather than individual actions. Women's group action implies that difficulties arise not from personal deficiencies but from systemic conditions— which can be changed, but only by changing the system. In the experience of other women and other women's groups, women can see the limits and possibilities of change in a way and in a form not included in the (male) norms of political change. For the prevailing ideas about politics include the assumption that women cannot affect public life or their own situation.

The women's liberation movement felt it was engaged in a radical and radically new activity when, through consciousness-raising groups, the analysis moved from individual to systemic dimensions of women's activities. It is easy to read back a group formulation onto the past, reconstructing personal history so that it conforms with "a rigorously logical political theory" (Zimmerman 1984:667). Separatism, and particularly lesbian separatism, was one logical implication of female specificity. That choice was shaped by Leftist—male—assumptions that change occurs only by irreconcilable, revolutionary confrontation. By the 1960s only a quietist could avoid adopting this male recipe for change—at the cost of acquiescing in male dismissal of any female role in politics. In earlier generations, action groups of women had available a more useful characterization of women: a differentiated identity that obligated them to assist those in society who were worse off. This role was certainly perceived by men and women alike as marginal to politics and social change. But it became a mission of transformation based on shared responses to problems, shared values, and shared experience.

The resulting "solidarity" was very different from the solidarity postulated in conventional social and political theory, which saw (and sees) objective grievance or advantage as a basis of joint consciousness that in turn produces collective action. Only intermittently does such an attitudinal and emotional solidarity exist among women. However, in the past century and a half women have repeatedly formed into groups to protect themselves or others in the name of women's specific duties and capabilities. They were able to tap a recurring pattern of shared attitudes, responses, situations. In the process they established a political role for women and identified issues that, in some cases, they succeeded in making political. They thus provided agendas and procedures for future generations of feminists.

"The most revolutionary of all," reflected Pierre Mendès-France, "is to want the revolution to succeed." His comment suggests domestic criteria of effectiveness as well as feminist criticisms of male styles of political action. But such a formulation still accepts violent and explicit conflict and confrontation. We may modify it: the most revolutionary of all is to have a successful revolution—without its being recognized. The most feminist action of all would be to invert the primacy of theory over practice without disavowing the importance of understanding and analysis, and then to look for guidance to the successful practice of feminist foremothers.

The feminism of difference grew out of an essential part of the ideological foundation of patriarchy. Its wicked stepsister is the reactionary Nazi Woman; her companions are the Total Woman, the Superwoman, and the Mother of Twenty. Social feminists, like everybody else, have been racist, classist, heterosexist, natalist, and just plain stupid, not to mention ineffectual. They have also given major assistance to opponents of all the ugly ideologies. And they have refused to accept either the "reactionary" or the "progressive" version of patriarchy's conflictual notion of how social change occurs; how could they, when women differed from men precisely in their lack of capability for public conflict, whether learned or intrinsic?

If change comes from confrontation, women must either become like men or stay on the sidelines. Equity feminists opted for the first alternative; social feminists could not logically accept either. So, illogically, they changed constraints into empowerment. What they did is not dialectical, it is not transcendental. It is like what happens in pregnancy—predictable, analyzable, ultimately mysterious but still mostly reliable. This is politics as a craft, not a theory. Social feminists are the midwives of history. And, thanks in large part to social feminism, we can now evaluate midwives more accurately.

References

Abensour, L. 1923. *La femme et le féminisme avant la révolution*. Paris: Ernest Leroux.

Abzug, B., with M. Kelber. 1984. *Gender gap: Bella Abzug's guide to political power for American women*. Boston: Houghton Mifflin.

Albistur, M., and D. Armogathe. 1977. *Histoire du féminisme français du moyen âge à nos jours*. Paris: Editions des femmes.

Anderson, K. 1985. "Commodity exchange and subordination: Monragnais-Naskapi and Huron women, 1600–1650." *Signs* 11:1, 48–62.

Azuzias, C., and A. Houel. 1982. *La grève des ovalistes, Lyon, juin–juillet 1869*. Paris: Payot.

Bachrach, P., and M. S. Baratz. 1962. "Two faces of power." *American Political Science Review* 56, 947–52.

——. 1963. "Decisions and non-decisions: An analytical framework." *American Political Science Review* 57, 632–42.

Backstrom, P. N. 1974. *Christian socialism and co-operation in Victorian England: Edward Vansittart Neale and the co-operative movement*. London: Croom Helm.

Bacon, M. H. 1980. *Valiant friend: The life of Lucretia Mott*. New York: Walker.

Banks, J. A., and O. Banks. 1964. "Feminism and social change: A case study of a social movement." In *Explorations in social change*, ed. G. K. Zollschan and W. Hirsch, 547–69. Boston: Houghton Mifflin.

Banks, O. 1981. *Faces of feminism: A study of feminism as a social movement*. Oxford: Martin Robertson.

——. 1986. *Becoming a feminist: The social origins of "first wave" feminism*. Brighton, England: Wheatsheaf.

Banner, L. W. 1984. *Women in modern America: A brief history*. New York: Harcourt Brace Jovanovich.

Barry, K. 1981. "International feminism: Sexual politics and the world conference of women in Copenhagen." *Feminist Issues* 1:3, 37–50.

Bashevkin, S. 1985. "Changing patterns of politicization and partisanship among women in France." *British Journal of Political Science* 15:1, 75–96.

Baxter, S. K. 1977. "Women and politics: The parties, the League of Women Voters, and the electorate." Ph.D. diss., Sociology, University of Michigan.

Baxter, S., and M. Lansing. 1980. *Women and politics: The invisible majority*. Ann Arbor: University of Michigan Press.

Becker, S. 1983. "International feminism between the wars: The National Woman's Party versus the League of Women Voters." In *Decades of discontent: The women's movement, 1920–1940*, ed. L. Scharf and J. M. Jensen, 225–42. West-port, Conn.: Greenwood.

——. 1981. *The origins of the equal rights amendment: American feminism between the wars*. Westport, Conn.: Greenwood.

Beckwith, K. 1987. "Response to feminism in the Italian parliament: Divorce, abortion, and sexual violence legislation." In *The Women's movements of the United States and Western Europe*, eds. M. F. Katzenstein and C. M. Mueller, 153–71. Philadelphia: Temple University Press.

Belenky, M. F., B. M. Clinchy, N. R. Goldberger, and J. M. Tarule. 1986. *Women's ways of knowing: The development of self, voice, and mind*. New York: Basic Books.

Bellamy, J., and J. Saville, eds. 1972, 1974. *Dictionary of labour biography*. London: Macmillan.

Bem, S. 1983. "Gender schema theory and its implications for child develop-ment: Raising gender-aschematic children in a gender-schematic society." *Signs* 8:4, 598–616.

Benstock, S. 1986. *Women of the left bank, Paris, 1900–1940*. Austin: University of Texas Press.

Berg, B. 1978. *The remembered gate: Origins of American feminism*. New York: Oxford University Press.

Berger, S. 1969. "Corporative organization: The case of a French association." In *Voluntary associations: Nomos XI*, ed. J. R. Pennock and J. W. Chapman, 263–83. New York: Atherton.

Bernard, J. 1979. "Women as voters: From redemptist to futurist role." In *Sex roles and social policy: A complex social science equation*, ed. J. Lipman-Blumen and J. Bernard, 279–86. Santa Barbara, Calif.: Sage.

——. 1981. *The female world*. New York: Free Press.

——. 1987. *The female world from a global perspective*. Bloomington: Indiana University Press.

Berry, J. M. 1977. *Lobbying for the people: The political behavior of public interest groups*. Princeton: Princeton University Press.

Bers, T. H., and S. G. Mezey. 1981. "Support for feminist goals among leaders of women's community groups." *Signs* 6:4, 737–48.

Bidelman, P. K. 1982. *Pariahs stand up! The founding of the liberal feminist movement in France*. Westport, Conn.: Greenwood.

Birotheau-Coussy, A.-M. 1977. "Approche d'un mouvement féminin: L'union féminine civique et sociale, 1925–76." Thesis, Law and Political Science, University of Nantes.

Black, C. 1915. *Married women's work*. London: G. Bell.

Black, N. 1980. "Feminism and integration: The European communities' surveys 'European men and women.'" *Journal of European Integration* 4:1, 83–103.

——. 1981. "The future for women and development." In *Women and world change: Equity issues in development*, ed. N. Black and A. B. Cottrell, 265–86. Beverly Hills, Calif.: Sage.

——. 1983. "Virginia Woolf and the women's movement." In *Virginia Woolf: A feminist slant*, ed. J. Marcus, 180–97. Lincoln: University of Nebraska Press.

——. 1986. "Le fossé des sexes: société dimorphique et état monomorphique." In *Minorités et état*, ed. Pierre Guillaume et al., 215–32. Quebec City: Presses de l'Université Laval.

Blair, K. 1980. *The clubwoman as feminist: True womanhood redefined, 1868–1914*. New York: Holmes & Meier.

Blaszak, B. 1981. "Raising the standard of living and the consciousness of mar-ried working class women: The Women's Co-operative Guild, 1883–1921." Paper presented at the Berkshire Conference on Women's History.

Blumberg, R. L. 1976. "Kibbutz women: From the fields of revolution to the laundries of discontent." In *Women in the world*, eds. L. B. Iglitzin and R. Ross, 319–44. Santa Barbara, Calif.: Clio.

——. 1981. "Rural women in development." In *Women and world change: Equity issues in development*, ed. N. Black and A. B. Cottrell, 32–56. Beverly Hills, Calif.: Sage.

Bolotin, S. 1982. "Voices from the post-feminist generation." *New York Times Magazine,* 12 October.

Bondfield, M. 1944. "Tribute to Margaret Llewelyn Davies." *Labour Woman,* July.

Boneparth, E. 1982. "A framework for policy analysis." In *Women, power and policy*, ed. E. Boneparth, 1–14. New York: Pergamon.

Boserup, E. 1970. *Women's role in economic development.* London: Allen and Unwin.

Bostick, T. P. 1980. "Women's suffrage and the press and reform bill of 1867." *International Journal of Women Studies* 3:4, 373–90.

Bouchier, D. 1979. "The deradicalisation of feminism: Ideology and utopia in action." *Sociology* 13, 387–401.

Boulding, E. 1976. *The underside of history: A view of women through time.* Boulder, Colo.: Westview.

Bourque, S. C., and J. Grossholtz. 1974. "Politics as unnatural practice: Political science looks at female participation." *Politics and Society* 4:2, 225–66.

Boy, M. 1936. "Les associations internationales féminines." Diss., Law, University of Lyons.

Boyd, N. 1982. *Josephine Butler, Octavia Hill, Florence Nightingale: Three Victorian women who changed their world.* London: Macmillan.

Bradbrook, M. C. 1975. *Barbara Bodichon, George Eliot, and the limits of feminism.* Oxford: Holywell.

Brault, E. 1967. *La franc-maçonnerie et l'émancipation des femmes.* Paris: Derry.

Brennan, T., and C. Pateman. 1979. "Mere auxiliaries to the commonwealth: Women and the origins of liberalism." *Political Studies* 27:2, 183–200.

Bridenthal, R., A. Grossmann, and M. Kaplan, eds. 1984. *When biology became destiny: Women in Weimar and Nazi Germany.* New York: Monthly Review Press.

Brimo, A., 1975. *Les femmes françaises face au pouvoir politique.* Paris: Montchréstien.

Brittain, V. 1980. *Testament of experience: An autobiographical story of the years 1925–1950.* London: Fontana/Virago. (Originally published 1957.)

Brown, W. H. 1928. *A century of London co-operation.* London: Education Committee, London Co-operation Society.

——. 1944. *The Rochdale Pioneers: A century of co-operation.* Manchester: Co-operative Union.

Brownmiller, S. 1975. *Against our wills: Men, women, and rape.* New York: Simon & Schuster.

——. 1984. *Femininity.* New York: Ballantine.

Brumbaugh, S. 1972. *Democratic experience and education in the National League of Women Voters.* New York: AMS. (Originally published 1946.)

Bulkin, E., M. B. Pratt, and B. Smith. 1984. *Yours in struggle: Three feminist perspectives on anti-semitism and racism.* Brooklyn, N.Y.: Long Haul Press.

Bunch, C. 1987. "The reform tool kit." *Quest* 1:1, 37–51. In *Passionate politics: Feminist theory in action*, 103–117. New York: St. Martin's.

Burton, H. 1949. *Barbara Bodichon.* London: John Murray.

Bussey, G., and M. Tims. 1965. *The Women's International League for Peace and Freedom, 1915–1965: A record of fifty years' work.* London: Allen & Unwin.

Butillard, A. 1942, 1945. *La femme au service du pays.* Paris: Union féminine civique et sociale.

Cameron, J. M. 1981. "Dorothy Day (1897–1980)." *New York Review*. 22 Jan.

Camus, A. 1972. *Neither victims nor executioners*. Chicago: World without War Publications.

Cantril, A. H., and S. D. Cantril. 1974. "The Kettering study—The League of Women Voters: A statistical overview; The view of members; The view of former members; A look at four leagues: pre-testing the study guide technique; National opinion survey—the public's view." Ann Arbor: University of Michigan Survey Research Center.

Carbery, T. F. 1969. *Consumers in politics. A history and general review of the Cooperative Party*. Manchester: Manchester University Press.

Carden, M. L. 1977. *Feminism in the mid-1970s: The non-establishment, the establishment, and the future*. New York: Ford Foundation.

Caron, H., and T. Doneaud. 1963. *Madame Jourdain: Citoyenne sans le savoir, ou la participation de la femme à la vie sociale*. Paris: Fleurus.

Carroll, B. 1976. "Mary Beard's *Woman as force in history*: A critique." In *Liberating women's history: Theoretical and critical essays*, ed. B. Carroll, 26–41. Urbana: University of Illinois Press.

Carroll, S. J. 1985. *Women as candidates in American politics*. Bloomington: Indiana University Press.

Carroll, S. J., and B. Geiger-Parker. 1983. *Women appointed to the Carter administration: A comparison with men*. Rutgers, N.J.: Center for the American Woman and Politics.

Carroll, S. J., and W. S. Strimling, 1983. *Women's routes to elective office: A comparison with men's*. Rutgers, N.J.: Center for the American Woman and Politics.

Ceadel, M. 1980. *Pacifism in Britain 1914–1945: The defining of a faith*. Oxford: Clarendon Press.

Chafe, W. H. 1977. *Women and equality: Changing patterns in American culture*. New York: Oxford University Press.

Chambers, R. C. 1954. "A study of three voluntary organizations." In *Social Mobility in Britain*, ed. D. V. Glass, 383–407. London: Routledge & Kegan Paul.

Chaney, E. M. 1981. "Women in Latin American politics: The case of Peru and Chile." Diss., Political Science, University of Wisconsin—Madison.

———. 1979. *Supermadre: Women in politics in Latin America*. Austin: University of Texas Press.

Charlot, M. 1980. "Women in politics in France." In *The French National Assembly elections of 1978*, ed. H. R. Penniman, 171–191. Washington: American Enterprise Institute.

Charlton, S. E. M. 1984. *Women in Third World development*. Boulder, Colo.: Westview.

Charnas, S. M. 1979. *Motherlines*. New York: Berkley.

Charzat, G. 1972. *Les femmes françaises, sont-elles des citoyennes?* Paris: Denoel Gonthier.

Chester, G. 1981. "I call myself a radical feminist." In *No turning back: Writings from the women's liberation movement, 1975–80*, ed. Feminist Anthology Collective, 67–78. London: Women's Press.

Clarke, P. 1978. *Liberals and social democrats*. Cambridge: Cambridge University Press.

Cleverdon, C. L. 1974. *The woman suffrage movement in Canada: The Start of Liberation, 1900–20*. Toronto: University of Toronto Press. (Originally published 1950.)

Clusen, R. C. 1979. "The League of Women Voters and political power." In *Women organizing*, ed. B. Cummings and V. Shuck, 112–32. Metuchen, N.J.: Scarecrow.

Cohen, N. E. 1960. "The volunteer and social change." In *The citizen volunteer*, ed. N. E. Cohen, 219–28. New York: Harper & Row.

Cole, G. D. H. 1944. *A century of cooperation*. Manchester: Co-operative Union.

Collectif des associations aixoises. 1975. "Contraception et avortement à Aix." Flyer distributed by a group of organizations including the MLAC, Planning Familial, and the UFCS.

Collier, J. F. 1974. "Women in politics." In *Woman, culture, and society*, ed. M. Z. Rosaldo and L. Lamphere, 86–96. Stanford: Stanford University Press.

Collier, J. F., and M. Z. Rosaldo. 1981. "Politics and gender in simple societies." In *Sexual meanings*, ed. S. Ortner and H. Whitehead, 275–329. Cambridge: Cambridge University Press.

Constantini, F , and K. H. Craik. 1977. "Women as politicians: The social backgrounds, personality, and political careers of female political leaders." In *A portrait of marginality: The political behavior of the American woman*, ed. M. Githens and J. L. Prestage, 221–46. New York: David McKay.

Conway, J. 1971. "Women reformers and American culture, 1870–1930." *Journal of Social History* 2, 164–177.

Cook, B. W. 1979. " 'Women alone stir my imagination': Lesbianism and the cultural tradition." *Signs* 4:4, 718–39.

Co-operative Union. 1905, 1915. Reports of annual co-operative congresses. Manchester.

———. 1982, 1987. An outline of the Co-operative Movement. Manchester.

———. N.d. Flyer on the co-operative movement. Manchester: Education Department.

Co-operative Women's Guild. 1975. Program, National Service of Dedication, 25 September. London.

———. 1980. Training manual. London.

———. 1984. Newsletter. London.

Coote, A., and B. Campbell. 1982. *Sweet freedom: The struggle for women's liberation*. London: Picador.

Cope, D., and J. Gaffin. 1985. "Workshops on women in the Co-operative Movement." Typescript. London.

Corlieu, C. de. 1937. "Tribune Libre, Les conditions du progrès." *La française*, 5 June.

———. 1959. "Le conseil international des femmes." Talk to L'association des femmes diplômées d'université, Paris.

———. 1970. *Carnets d'une chrétienne moderniste, de 1870 à nos jours*. Toulouse: Privat.

Costain, A. N. 1982. "Representing women: The transition from social movement to interest group." In *Women, power, and policy*, ed. E. Boneparth, 19–37. New York: Pergamon.

Cott, N. F. 1984. "Feminist politics in the 1920s: The National Woman's Party." *Journal of American History* 71:1, 43–68.

———. 1987. *The grounding of modern feminism*. New Haven: Yale University Press.

———. 1982. Review. *Signs* 7:4, 897–900.

Cott, N. F., and E. H. Pleck, eds. 1979. *A heritage of her own: Toward a social history of American women*. New York: Simon & Schuster.

Dangerfield, G. 1961. *The strange death of liberal England, 1910–14*. New York: Capricorn.

Danguy, M.-L. 1946. *Les femmes et l'action syndicale*. Paris: R. Royer.

Dansette, A. 1957. *Destin du catholicisme français, 1926–1956*. Paris: Flammarion.

Davis, K. N.d. "Margaret Llewelyn Davies." Typescript. Hull University Library, Hull, England.

Davies, M. L. 1899. *Co-operation in poor neighbourhoods.* Kirkby Lonsdale, Westmorland: Women's Co-operative Guild.

——. 1904. *The Women's Co-operative Guild, 1883–1904.* Kirkby Lonsdale, Westmorland: Women's Co-operative Guild.

——. 1921. "Women as organized consumers." Manchester: Co-ooperative Union.

——. N.d. "Death or life? A call to co-operative women." London: Women's Co-operative Guild.

Davies, M. L., ed. 1915. *Maternity: Letters from working women.* London: G. Bell.

——. 1931. *Life as we have known it.* London: Hogarth.

Davis, K. N.d. Typescript notes on Margaret Llewelyn Davies. Hull University Library, Hull, England.

de Lauretis, T. 1986. "Feminist studies/critical studies: Issues, terms, and contexts." In *Feminist studies/Critical studies*, ed. T. de Lauretis, 1–19. Madison: University of Wisconsin Press.

de Lauwe, C., et al. 1962. "Images de la femme dans la société." *International Journal of Social Science* 14:1, 7–78.

De Lesseps, E. 1981. "Female reality: biology or society?" *Feminist Issues* 1:2, 77–102.

Decaux, A. 1972. *Histoire des françaises, II: La révolte.* Paris: Librairie académique Perrin.

Deckard, B. S. 1983. *The women's movement: political, socioeconomic, and psychological issues.* New York: Harper & Row.

Decroix, C. 1975. "Un mouvement féminin: L'union féminine civique et sociale." *Les Cahiers de l'Animation* 10:4, 39–44.

Degler, C. 1965. "Revolution without ideology: The changing place of women in America." In *The Woman in America*, ed. R. J. Lifton, 193–210. Boston: Beacon.

——. 1980. *At odds: Women and the family in America from the revolution to the present.* New York: Oxford University Press.

Del Re, A., S. Coyaud, and C. Veauvy. 1983–84. "Les reflexions féministes menées en Italie dans les années 80." *Bulletin du CRIF* 4, 3–10.

Del Re, A., M. Gadant, and C. Veauvy. 1984. "Les reflexions féministes menées en Italie dans les années 80: Deuxième partie 'Sur la question de la culture féminine.'" *Bulletin du CRIF* 5, 3–12.

Delhaye, A.-M., and N. Dunand. 1969. "Comparison de la conception qu'ont Jeunes Femmes et L'union féminine civique et sociale de l'éducation permanente." Thesis, Sociology, University of Paris.

Delphy, C. 1981. "Women in stratification studies." In *Doing feminist research*, ed. H. Roberts, 114–128. London: Routledge & Kegan Paul.

Deutsch, K. W., et al. 1957. *Political community in the North Atlantic area.* Princeton: Princeton University Press.

Diamond, I., and N. Hartsock. 1981. "Beyond interests in politics: A comment on Virginia Sapiro's 'When are interests interesting? The problem of political representation of women.'" *American Political Science Review* 75:3, 717–21.

Dogan, M., and J. Narbonne. 1955. *Les françaises face à la politique: Comportement politique et condition sociale.* Paris: Armand Colin.

Drath, V. H. 1984. "Foreign policy views of the 'Greens.'" In *Power and policy in transition: Essays presented on the tenth anniversary of the National Committee on American Foreign Policy in honor of its founder, Hans J. Morgenthau*, ed. V. Mastny, 73–88. Westport, Conn.: Greenwood.

DuBois, E. 1975. "The radicalism of the woman suffrage movement: Notes toward the reconstruction of nineteenth-century feminism." *Feminist Studies* 3:1/2, 63–71.

——. 1978. *Feminism and suffrage: The emergence of an independent women's movement in America, 1848–1869.* Ithaca, N.Y.: Cornell University Press.

DuBois, E., et al. 1980. "Politics and culture in women's history: A symposium." *Feminist Studies* 6:1, 26–64.

DuBois, E., and L. Gordon. 1983. "Seeking ecstasy on the battlefield: Danger and pleasure in nineteenth-century feminist sexual thought." *Feminist Studies* 9:1, 7–25.

Duchen, C. 1986. *Feminism in France: From May '68 to Mitterrand*. London: Routledge & Kegan Paul.

Duchen, C., ed. and trans. 1987. *French connections: Voices from the women's movement in France*. Amherst: University of Massachusetts Press.

Dumont, M., M. Jean, M. Lavigne, J. Stoddart (Le Collectif Clio). 1982. *L'histoire des femmes au Québec depuis quatre siècles*. Montreal: Quinze.

Dunn, M. M. 1979. "Women of light." In *Women of America*, ed. C. R. Berkin and M. B. Norton, 114–36. Boston: Houghton Mifflin.

Dupeux, G. 1960. "France." In *La participation des citoyens à la vie politique*, ed. S. Rokkan, 46–58. *Revue Internationale des Sciences Sociales*, 12:1.

Duverger, M. 1955. *The political role of women*. Paris: UNESCO.

Dye, N. S. 1980. *As equals and as sisters: Feminism, unionism, and the Women's Trade Union League of New York*. Columbia: University of Missouri Press.

Dykewomon, E. 1982. "The fourth daughter's four hundred questions." In *Nice Jewish girls: A lesbian anthology*, ed. E. T. Beck, 148–60. Trumansburg, N.Y.: Crossing Press.

Eastman, A., et al., ed. 1984. *The Norton reader: An anthology of expository prose*. New York: W. W. Norton.

Edwards, I. 1977. *Pulling no punches: Memoirs of a woman in politics*. New York: G. P. Putnam's.

Eisenstein, H., and A. Jardine, ed. 1980. *The future of difference*. Boston: G. K. Hall.

Eisenstein, Z. 1981. *The radical future of liberal feminism*. New York: Longman.

———. 1984. *Feminism and sexual equality: Crisis in liberal America*. New York: Monthly Review Press.

Eisenstein, Z., ed. 1979. *Capitalist patriarchy and the case for socialist feminism*. New York: Monthly Review Press.

Ekman, R. 1983. "Women and the changing norms of health and disease." In *Women's studies and the curriculum*, ed. M. Triplette, 77–84. Winston Salem, N.C.: Salem College.

Elgin, S. 1984. *Native tongue*. New York: Daw.

———. 1987. *The judas rose*. New York: Daw.

Elshtain, J. B. 1981. *Public man, private woman: Women in social and political thought*. Princeton: Princeton University Press.

———. 1987. *Women and war*. New York: Basic Books.

Enfield, A. H. 1927. *Co-operation: Its problems and possibilities*. W. E. A. Outline Series. London: Longman Green.

———. N.d. "The importance of women for the Co-operative Movement. London: International Women's Co-operative Guild.

Epstein, B. 1981. *The politics of domesticity: Women, evangelism, and temperance in nineteenth-century America*. Middletown: Wesleyan University Press.

Evans, R. J. 1977. *The feminists: Women's emancipation movements in Europe, America and Australasia, 1840–1920*. London: Croom Helm.

Evans, S. 1980. *Personal politics: The roots of women's liberation in the civil rights movement and the new left*. New York: Random House.

Faits et opinions. 1987. *Women and men of Europe in 1987. Women of Europe* Supplement No. 26.

Fauré, C. 1981. "The twilight of the goddesses, or the intellectual crisis of French feminism." *Signs* 7:81–86.

Fawcett Society and Women in Media. 1980. *Women's action day*. London: Onlywomen Press.

Feminist Anthology Collective. 1981. *No turning back: Writings from the women's liberation movement, 1975–80.* London: Women's Press.

Ferraru, A. T. 1974. "Transnational political interests and the global environment." *International Organization* 28, 31–60.

Firestone, S. 1970. *The dialectic of sex: The case for feminist revolution.* New York: Morrow.

Flammang, J. A. 1983. "Feminist theory: The question of power." *Current Perspectives in Social Theory* 4, 37–83. Greenwich, Conn.: JAI Press.

——. 1984. "Filling the party vacuum." In *Political women: Current roles in state and local government,* ed. J. A. Flammang, 87–113. Beverly Hills, Calif.: Sage.

Flammang, J. A., ed. 1984. *Political women: Current roles in state and local government.* Beverly Hills, Calif.: Sage.

Flanagan, D. 1969. *1869–1969, A centenary story of the Co-operative Union of Great Britain and Ireland.* Manchester: Co-operative Union.

Flexner, E. 1959. *Century of struggles: The women's rights movement in the United States.* Cambridge, Mass.: Belknap Press.

Fogarty, M. 1957. *Christian democracy in western Europe, 1820–1953.* London: Routledge & Kegan Paul.

Forbes, G. 1982. "Caged tigers: 'First wave' feminists in India." *Women's studies International Forum* 5:6, 525–36.

Forster, M. 1984. *Significant sisters: The grassroots of active feminism, 1839–1939.* New York: Alfred A. Knopf.

Fowler, R. B. 1986. *Carrie Catt: Feminist politician.* Boston: Northeastern University Press.

Fox, B., ed. 1980. *Hidden in the household: Women's domestic labour under capitalism.* Toronto: Women's Press.

Franklin, U., ed. 1984. *Knowledge reconsidered; A feminist overview.* Ottawa: Canadian Research Institute for the Advancement of Women.

Freedman, E. 1979. "Separatism and strategy: Female institution building and American feminism, 1870–1930." *Feminist Studies* 5:3, 512–29.

Freeman, J. 1973. "Origins of the women's liberation movement." *American Journal of Sociology* 4, 792–811.

——. 1974. "The tyranny of structurelessness." In *Women in politics,* ed. J. S. Jaquette, 202–214. New York: John Wiley.

——. 1975. *The politics of women's liberation: A case study of an emerging social movement and its relation to the policy process.* New York: David McKay.

——. 1983a. "On the origins of social movements." In *Social movements of the sixties and seventies,* ed. J. Freeman, 8–32. New York: Longman.

——. 1983b. "A model for analyzing strategic options of social movement organizations." In *Social movements of the sixties and seventies,* ed. J. Freeman, 193–210. New York: Longman.

——. 1984. "The women's liberation movement: Its origins, structure, activities, and ideas." In *Women: A feminist perspective,* ed. J. Freeman, 543–56. Palo Alto, Calif.: Mayfield.

Friedan, B. 1976. *It changed my life: Writings on the women's movement.* New York: Random House.

——. 1981. *The second stage.* New York: Summit.

——. 1985. "How to get the women's movement moving again." *New York Times Magazine,* 3 November.

Frye, M. 1983. *The politics of reality: Essays in feminist theory.* Trumansburg, N.Y.: Crossing Press.

Fulenwider, C. K. 1980. *Feminism in American politics: A study of ideological influence.* New York: Praeger.

Gaffin, J. 1977. "Women and cooperation." In *Women in the labour movement: The British experience,* ed. L. Middleton, 113–42. London: Croom Helm.

Gaffin, J., and R. Hollingsworth. 1977. "The Women's Co-operative Guild: A historical bibliography." Typescript. London.

Gaffin, J., and D. Thoms. 1983. *Caring and sharing: The centenary history of the Co-operative Women's Guild.* Manchester: Co-operative Union.

Galey, M. 1976. "The neglected majority: An international perspective." Paper presented at the Annual Meeting of the International Studies Association.

Gallagher, O. R. 1957. "Voluntary organizations in France." *Social Forces* 36, 153–60.

Gallup Opinion Index. 1976. *Women in America.* Report no. 128, March.

Canley, L. N.d. "History of the Women's Co-operative Guild." Typescript. Hull University Library, Hull, England.

Gardiner, J. K. 1983. "Power, desire, and difference: Comments on essays from the *Signs* special issue on feminist theory." *Signs* 8:4, 733–37.

Garmanikow, E., D. H. J. Morgan, J. Purvis, and D. Taylorson, eds. 1983. *The public and the private.* London: Heinemann.

Gearhart, S. M. 1982. "The future—if there is one—is female." In *Reweaving the web of life: Feminism and nonviolence,* ed. P. McAllister, 266–84. Philadelphia: New Society Publishers.

Gelb, J., and M. L. Palley. 1982. *Women and public policies.* Princeton: Princeton University Press.

Gennari, G. 1965. *Le dossier de la femme.* Paris: Librairie Académique Perrin.

Giddings, P. 1984. *When and where I enter: The impact of black women on race and sex in America.* New York: William Morrow.

Gilligan, C. 1982. *In a different voice: Psychological theory and women's development.* Cambridge: Harvard University Press.

Gilman, C. P. 1979. *Herland.* New York: Pantheon. (Originally published 1915.)

Gimenez, M. 1980. "Feminism, pronatalism, and motherhood." *International Journal of Women's Studies* 3, 215–40.

Giroud, F. 1977. *La comédie du pouvoir.* Paris: Fayard.

Githens, M. 1984. "Women and state politics: An assessment." In *Political women: Current roles in state and local government,* ed. J. A. Flammang, 471–99. Beverly Hills, Calif.: Sage.

Goldberg, A. 1986. "Femmes, recherches, féminismes au Brésil: Un ordre de facteurs qui altère le produit." *Bulletin du CRIF* 10, 3–12.

Goode, W. J. 1982. "Why men resist." In *Rethinking the family: Some feminist questions,* ed. B. Thorne and M. Yalom, 131–50. New York: Longman.

Goot, M., and E. Reid. 1975. *Women and voting studies: Mindless matrons or sexist scientism?* Santa Barbara, Calif: Sage.

Gordon, L. 1976. *Woman's body, woman's right: Birth control in America.* New York: Grossman.

———. 1986. "What's new in women's history." In *Feminist studies/Critical studies,* ed. T. de Lauretis, 20–30. Madison: University of Wisconsin Press.

Gorham, D. 1976. "The Canadian suffragists." In *Women in the Canadian mosaic,* ed. G. Matheson, 23–56. Toronto: Peter Martin Associates.

Gould, S. J. 1984. Review of R. Bleier, *Science and gender: A critique of biology and its theories on women. New York Times Book Review,* 12 Aug.

Greenfield, G. 1982. "Shedding." In *Nice Jewish girls: A lesbian anthology,* ed. E. T. Beck, 5–27. Trumansburg, N.Y.: Crossing Press.

Greenstein, F. L. 1965. *Children and politics.* New Haven: Yale University Press.

Greer, G. 1986. *The madwoman's underclothes: Essays and occasional pieces, 1982–1985.* London: Picador.

Grimes, A. P. 1967. *The puritan ethic and woman suffrage*. New York: Oxford University Press.

Groombridge, B. 1960. "Report on the Co-operative Auxiliaries." Co-operative College Paper no. 7. Stanford Hall, Loughborough; Education Department, Co-operative Union.

Gros, B. 1975. *Qui sont ces femmes élues dans les Yvelines?* Mimeo. Meulan.

Gross, H. H., et al. 1979. "Considering 'A biosocial perspective on parenting.'" *Signs* 4:4, 695–717.

Gruberg, M. 1968. *Women in American politics: An assessment and source book*. Oshkosh, Wis.: Academia.

Guérin, C. 1975. "De la bénévole à l'élue locale." *Cahiers de l'Animation* 10:4, 17–37.

Guilbert, M. 1966. *Les femmes et l'organisation syndicale avant 1914*. Paris: CNRS.

Guillaumin, C. 1981a. "The practice of power and belief in nature, part I: The appropriation of women." *Feminist Issues* 1:2, 3–28.

———. 1981b. "The practice of power and belief in nature, part II: The naturalist discourse." *Feminist Issues* 1:3, 87–109.

———. 1985. "The masculine: Denotations and connotations." *Feminist Issues* 5:1, 65–73.

Gusfield, J. R. 1955. "Social structure and moral reform: A study of the Women's Christian Temperance Union." *American Journal of Sociology* 61, 221–32.

Guyol, M. A. P. 1976. "Mary Ann Page Guyol's story." In *Making do*, ed. J. Westin, 279–83. New York: Follett.

Halimi, G. 1978. *Choisir, la cause des femmes: Le programme commun des femmes*. Paris: Grasset.

———. 1981. *Quel président pour les femmes?* Paris: Gallimard.

Hansen, S., L. Franz, and M. Netemayer-Mays. 1975. "Women's political participation and policy preferences." *Social Science Quarterly* 56, 576–90.

Harding, S. 1986. *The science question in feminism*. Ithaca: Cornell University Press.

Harding, S., and M. Hintikka, ed. 1983. *Discovering reality: Feminist perspectives on epistemology, metaphysics, methodology, and philosophy of science*. Dordrecht, Netherlands: D. Reidel.

Hart, J. D. 1965. *The Oxford companion to American literature*. New York: Oxford University Press.

Hartsock, N. 1979. "Feminist theory and the development of revolutionary strategy." In *Capitalist patriarchy and the case for socialist feminism*, ed. Z. Eisenstein, 56–77. New York: Monthly Review Press.

———. 1981. "Political Change: Two perspectives on power." In *Building feminist theory: Essays from Quest*, ed. C. Bunch, 3–19. New York: Longman.

———. 1983. "The feminist standpoint." In *Discovering reality*, ed. S. Harding and M. Hintikka, 283–310. Dordrecht, Netherlands: D. Reidel.

Hause, S. C., with A. R. Kenney. 1981. "The limits of suffrage behavior: Legalism and militancy in France, 1876–1972." *American Historical Review* 86, 781–806.

———. 1984. *Women's suffrage and social politics in the French Third Republic*. Princeton: Princeton University Press.

Hayden, D. 1981. *The grand domestic revolution: A history of feminist designs for American homes, neighborhoods, and cities*. Cambridge: MIT Press.

Heilbrun, C. G. 1973. *Toward a recognition of androgyny*. New York: Alfred A. Knopf.

———. 1979. *Reinventing womanhood*. New York: W. W. Norton.

———. 1986. "Women, men, theories, and literature." In *The impact of feminist research in the academy*, ed. C. Farnham, 217–25. Bloomington: Indiana University Press.

Hellman, J. A. 1987. *Journeys among women.* New York: Oxford University Press.

Hewlett, S. A. 1986. *A lesser life: The myths of women's liberation in America.* New York: William Morrow.

Holcombe, L. 1983. *Wives and property: Reform of the married women's property law in nineteenth-century England.* Toronto: University of Toronto Press.

Hole, J., and E. Levine. 1971. *Rebirth of feminism.* New York: Quadrangle/New York Times.

Holsti, O. R., and J. N. Rosenau. 1982. "Foreign policy beliefs of women in leadership positions." In *Women, power and policy,* ed. E. Boneparth, 238–62. New York: Pergamon.

Holton, S. 1986. *Feminism and democracy: Women's suffrage and reform politics in Britain, 1900–1918.* Cambridge: Cambridge University Press.

Holyoake, G. J. 1900. *The history of the Rochdale Pioneers, 1844–1892.* London-Swan.

Hooks, B. 1984. *Feminist theory: From margin to center.* Boston: South End.

Hull, G. T., P. B. Scott, and B. Smith, ed. 1982. *All the women are white, all the blacks are men, but some of us are brave.* Old Westbury, N.Y.: Feminist Press.

Hume, L. P. 1982. *The National Union of Women's Suffrage Societies, 1897–1914.* New York: Garland.

Huston, N. 1986–87. "Les enfants de Simone de Beauvoir." *Lettre internationale* 11, 58–60.

Imray, L., and A. Middleton. 1983. "Public and private: Marking the boundaries." In *The public and the private,* ed. E. Garmanikow et al., 12–27. London: Heinemann.

Inglehart, M., and R. Inglehart. 1975. "Factor analyses and multicriterion analysis of the answers." In *European men and women: A comparison of their attitudes to some of the problems facing society,* ed. J.-R. Rabier, 186–95. Brussels: Commission of the European Communities.

International Co-operative Alliance. 1982. Co-operative principles as established by the Rochdale Pioneers and as reformulated by the 23rd congress of the International Co-operative Alliance. Manchester.

International Co-operative Women's Guild. 1944. The guild movement in war and peace. Manchester.

International Council of Women. 1966. *Women in a changing world: The dynamic story of the ICW.* London: Routledge & Kegan Paul.

Irving, R. E. M. 1973. *Christian democracy in France.* London: George Allen & Unwin.

Israeli, D. N. 1981. "The Zionist women's movement in Palestine, 1911–1927: A sociological analysis." *Signs* 7:11, 87–114.

Jaggar, A. 1983. *Feminist politics and human nature.* Totowa, N.J.: Rowman & Allanheld.

Jaggar, A., and P. Struhl. 1983. *Feminist frameworks: Alternative theoretical accounts of the relations betwen women and men.* New York: McGraw-Hill.

Jaggar, A., and P. Rothenberg. 1984. *Feminist frameworks: Alternative theoretical accounts of the relations between women and men.* New York: McGraw-Hill.

Jancar, B. 1981. "Women in communist countries: Comparative public policy." In *Women and world change: Equity issues in development,* ed. N. Black and A. B. Cottrell, 139–58. Beverly Hills, Calif.: Sage.

Jaquette, J. S. 1982. "Women and modernization theory: A decade of feminist criticism." *World Politics* 34, 267–84.

Jennings, M., and B. Farah. 1981. "Social roles and political resources: An overtime survey of men and women in party elites." *American Journal of Political Science* 25, 462–82.

Jenson, J. 1987. "Changing discourse, changing agendas: Political rights and reproductive policies in France." In *The women's movement of the United States and Western Europe*, ed. M. F. Katzenstein and C. M. Mueller, 64–88. Philadelphia: Temple University Press.

Kauffmann-McCall, D. 1983. "Politics of difference: The women's movement in France from May, 1968 to Mitterrand." *Signs* 9:2, 282–93.

Keller, E. F. 1985. *Reflections on gender and science*. New Haven: Yale University Press.

Kelly-Gadol, J. 1976. "The social relations of the sexes: Methodological implications of women's history." *Signs* 1:4 , 809–23.

———. 1977. "Did women have a renaissance?" In *Becoming visible: Women in European history*, ed. R. Bridenthal and C. Koonz, 137–64. Boston: Houghton-Mifflin.

Kenneally, J. J. 1978. *Women and American trade unions*. Montreal: Eden.

Keohane, R., and J. Nye. 1977. *Power and interdependence*. Boston: Little, Brown.

Kerber, L., et al. 1986. "On *In a different voice*: An interdisciplinary forum." *Signs* 11:2, 304–33.

Kirkpatrick, J. 1974. *Political woman*. New York: Basic Books.

———. 1976. *The new presidential elite: Men and women in national politics*. New York: Russell Sage Foundation.

Klein, E. 1984. *Gender politics: From consciousness to mass politics*. Cambridge: Harvard University Press.

Kome, P. 1982. *Somebody has to do it: Whose work is housework?* Toronto: McClelland & Stewart.

Koonz, C. 1977. "Mothers in the fatherland: Women in Nazi Germany." In *Becoming visible: Women in European history*, ed. R. Bridenthal and C. Koonz, 445–73. Boston: Houghton Mifflin.

———. 1984. "The competition for women's *Lebensraum*, 1928–1934." In *When biology became destiny: Women in Weimar and Nazi Germany*, ed. R. Bridenthal, A. Grossman, and M. Kaplan, 199–236. New York: Monthly Review Press.

Kraditor, A. 1970. *The ideas of the woman suffrage movement, 1890–1920*. New York: W. W. Norton.

Kraditor, A., ed. 1970. *Up from the pedestal: Selected writings in the history of American feminism*. Chicago: Quadrangle.

Krieger, D. M. 1971. "The another mother for peace consumer campaign—A campaign that failed." *Journal of Peace Research* 8, 163–66.

Labour Woman. 1941. "International Co-operative Women's Guild."

Land, H. 1980. "Social policies and the family: Their effect on women's paid employment in Great Britain." In *Equal employment policy for women: Strategies for implementation in the United States, Canada, and Western Europe*, ed. R. S. Ratner, 366–87. Philadelphia: Temple University Press.

Laot, J. 1977. *Stratégie pour les femmes*. Paris: Stock.

Lash, J. P. 1972. *Eleanor: The years alone*. New York: W. W. Norton.

Lasswell, H., and A. Kaplan. 1954. *Power and society*. New Haven: Yale University Press.

Le Garrec, E. 1976. *Les messagères*. Paris: Editions des femmes.

Leach, W. 1980. *True love and perfect union: The feminist reform of society*. New York: Basic Books.

League of Women Voters. 1959. "Forty years of a great idea." Washington, D.C.

———. 1969. "Fifty years of a great idea." Washington, D.C.

———. 1970. "A report to the nation: Towards a more responsible and responsive society." Washington, D.C.

———. 1970–84. "Impact on issues, 1970–72, 1976–78. 1980–82, 1982–84." Washington, D.C.

——. 1980. "Membership records." Mimeo. Washington, D.C.

Leclerc, A. 1974. *Parole de femme*. Paris: Grasset & Fasquelle.

Lee, M. M. 1977. "Towards understanding why few women hold public office: Factors affecting the participation of women in public office." In *A portrait of marginality: The political behavior of the American woman*, ed. M. Githens and J. L. Prestage, 118–38. New York: David McKay.

Léger, D. 1982. *Le féminisme en France*. Paris: Sycomore.

Lehmann, A. 1960. *Le role de la femme française au milieu du XXe siècle*. 2d ed. Paris: Ligue française pour le droit des femmes.

Lemons, J. S. 1975. *The woman citizen: Social feminism in the 1920s*. Urbana: University of Illinois Press.

Lerner, G. 1979. *The majority finds its past: Placing women in history*. New York: Oxford University Press.

——. 1986. *The creation of patriarchy*. New York: Oxford University Press.

Levin, T., and J. Miller-Goeder. 1984. "Feminist teaching in a military setting: Co-optation or subversion?" *Women's Studies Quarterly* 12:2, 13–15.

Lewis, J. 1975. "Beyond suffragism: English feminism in the 1920s." *Maryland Historian* 7, 1–17.

——. 1980. *The politics of motherhood: Child and maternal welfare in England, 1900–1939*. London: Croom Helm.

Liddington, J. 1984. *The life and times of a respectable rebel. Selina Cooper, 1864–1946*. London: Virago.

Liddington, J., and J. Norris. 1978. *One hand tied behind us: The rise of the women's suffrage movement*. London: Virago.

Little, C. J. 1975. "Moral reform and feminism: A case study." *Journal of Interamerican Studies and World Affairs* 17, 386–97.

Lovenduski, J. 1986. *Women and European politics: Contemporary feminism and public policy*. Brighton, Sussex: Wheatsheaf.

Lovenduski, J., and J. Hills, eds. 1981. *The politics of the second electorate: Women and political participation*. London: Routledge & Kegan Paul.

Lukes, S. 1974. *Power: A radical view*. London: Macmillan.

MacGill, E. G. 1981. *My mother the judge*. Toronto: PMA Books.

MacKinnon, C. A. 1982. "Feminism, Marxism, method, and the state: An agenda for theory." *Signs* 7:3, 515–44.

——. 1983. "Feminism, Marxism, method, and the state: Toward feminist jurisprudence." *Signs* 8:4, 635–54.

——. 1987. *Feminism unmodified: Discourses on life and law*. Cambridge: Harvard University Press

Mainardi, P. 1970. "The politics of housework." In *Sisterhood is powerful: An anthology of writings from the women's liberation movement*, ed. R. Morgan, 447–54. New York: Vintage.

Manceaux, M. 1974. *Les femmes de Gennevilliers*. Paris: Mercure de France.

Mandel, R. B. 1981. *In the running: The new woman candidate*. New Haven, Conn.: Ticknor & Fields.

Manderson, L. 1977. "The shaping of the Kaum Ibu (women's section) of the United Malays National Organization." In *Women and national development: The complexities of change*, ed. Wellesley Editorial Committee, 210–28. Chicago: University of Chicago Press.

Mansbridge, J. 1986. *Why we lost the ERA*. Chicago: University of Chicago Press.

Marks, E., and I. de Courtivron, eds. 1980. *New French feminisms*. Amherst: University of Massachusetts Press.

Marsden, L. 1980. "Brave new women: The generation of the 1960s." Paper presented to the Royal Canadian Institute. Toronto, Canada.

——. 1981. "'The labour force' is an ideological structure: A guiding note to labour economists." *Atlantis* 7:2, 57–64.

Martin, C., D. Hine, and R. E. M. Irving. 1974. "Divorce—Italian style." *Parliamentary Affairs* 27, 333–58.

Martin, G. 1976. *Madam secretary: Frances Perkins.* Boston: Houghton Mifflin.

Maruani, M. 1979. *Les syndicats à l'épreuve du féminisme.* Paris: Syros.

——. 1985. *Mais qui a peur du travail des femmes?* Paris: Syros.

Maruani, M., coord., 1986. "Femmes, Modes d'emplois," *Nouvelles Questions Féministes* nos. 14–15.

Marwick, A. 1977. *Women at war, 1914–18.* London: Croom Helm.

Mattelart, M. 1980. "The feminine version of the coup d'état." In *Sex and Class in Latin America*, ed. J. Nash and H. Safa, 279–301. South Hadley, Mass.: J. F. Bergin.

McAllister, P., ed. 1982. *Reweaving the web of life: Feminism and non-violence.* Philadelphia: New Society Publishers.

McBride, A. B. 1976. *The married feminist.* New York: Harper & Row.

McClung, N. L. 1972. *In times like these.* Toronto: University of Toronto Press. (Originally published 1915.)

McCormack, T. 1975. "Toward a nonsexist perspective on social and political change." In *Another voice: Feminist perspectives on social life and social science*, ed. M. Millman and R. M. Kanter, 1–33. Garden City, N.Y.: Anchor.

——. 1981. "Good theory or just theory? Toward a feminist philosophy of social science." *Women's Studies International Quarterly* 4:1, 1–12.

——. 1984. "Two(b) or not two(b): Feminism and freedom of expression." In *Se connaître: Politics and culture in Canada*, ed. J. Lennox, 64–83. North York, Ontario: Robarts Centre for Canadian Studies, York University.

McFadden, M. 1984. "Anatomy of difference: Toward a classification of feminist theory." *Women's Studies International Forum* 7:6, 495–504.

McMillan, C. 1979. *Women, reason and nature: Some philosophical problems in feminism.* Princeton: Princeton University Press.

McWilliams-Tullberg, R. 1975. *Women at Cambridge.* London: Victor Gollancz.

Melder, K. E. 1977. *Beginnings of sisterhood. The American woman's rights movement, 1800–1850.* New York: Schocken.

Meyer, D. 1987. *Sex and power: The rise of women in America, Russia, Sweden and Italy.* Middletown: Wesleyan University Press.

Meynaud, J. 1958. *Les groupes de pression en France.* Paris: A. Colin.

Michel, A. 1979. *Le féminisme.* Paris: Presses Universitaires de France.

——. 1985a. "Introduction." In *La militarisation et les violences à l'égard des femmes*, ed. A. Michel, 5–8. *Nouvelles questions féministes* nos. 11–12.

——. 1985b. "Le complexe militaro-industriel et les violences à l'égard des femmes." *La militarisation et les violences à l'égard des femmes*, ed. A. Michel, 9–86. *Nouvelles questions féministes* nos. 11–12.

Michel, A., and G. Texier. 1964. *La condition de la française d'aujourd'hui.* Geneva: Gonthier.

Michy, J. 1975. "Les mouvements féminins et les mouvements féministes." *Pourquoi* 106, May.

Midgley, M., and J. Hughes. 1983. *Women's choices: Philosophical problems facing feminism.* London: Weidenfeld & Nicolson.

Mill, J. S. 1970. "The subjection of women." In *John Stuart Mill and Harriet Taylor Mill: Essays on Sex Equality*, ed. A. S. Rossi, 123–242. Chicago: University of Chicago Press. (Originally published 1869.)

Mitchinson, W. 1979. "The WCTU: 'For God, home and native land': A study in nineteenth-century feminism." In *A not unreasonable claim: Women and reform in*

Canada, 1880s-1920s, ed. L. Kealey, 151–67. Toronto: Women's Educational Press.

Moi, T., ed. 1987. *French feminist thought: A reader.* Oxford: Basil Blackwell.

Morgan, D. 1972. *Suffragists and democrats: The politics of woman suffrage in America.* East Lansing: Michigan State University Press.

Morgan, D. 1981. "Men, masculinity, and the process of sociological enquiry." In *Doing feminist research,* ed. H. Roberts, 83–113. London: Routledge & Kegan Paul.

Mossuz-Lavau, J., and M. Sineau. 1978. "Sex, social environment, and left-wing attitudes." *International Journal of Sociology* 8:3, 38–55.

——. 1980. "A proposal of the French secretary of state for women: The quota of 20%. Opportunities, content and consequences." Memorandum prepared for presentation at the Florence Joint Sessions of the European Consortium for Political Research.

——. 1983. *Enquête sur les femmes et la politique en France.* Paris: Presses Universitaires de France.

Mouvement mondial des mères. N.d. "Les roles du père et de la mère sont-ils interchangeables?" Mimeo. Paris.

Mueller, C. 1982. "Feminism and the new women in public office." *Women and Politics* 2:3, 7–21.

Nash, R. 1904. "A working women's organisation." *The Speaker* 24 September, 585–86.

——. N.d. "Margaret Llewelyn Davies." Typescript. Hull University Library, Hull, England.

National Council of Civil Liberties. N.d. "Women's rights: Notes prepared and written for the Co-operative Auxiliaries' branch programme theme 1978–79." London.

Neville, K. 1987. "Peace games." *Sunday Observer,* 22 Feb.

Newman, K. 1981. "Women and law: Land tenure in Africa." In *Women and world change: Equity issues in development,* ed. N. Black and A. B. Cottrell, 120–38. Beverly Hills, Calif: Sage.

Noddings, N. 1984. *Caring: A feminine approach to ethics and moral education.* Berkeley: University of California Press.

Noonan, L. 1970. *France: The politics of continuity in change.* New York: Holt, Rinehart & Winston.

O'Brien, M. 1981. *The politics of reproduction.* London: Routledge & Kegan Paul.

O'Neill, W. L. 1971. *Everyone was brave: A history of feminism in America.* Chicago: Quadrangle.

——. 1986. "The fight for suffrage." *Wilson Quarterly* 10, 99–109.

Oakley, A. 1981. *Subject women.* Oxford: Martin Robertson.

Offen, K. 1987. "Women and the politics of motherhood in France, 1920–1940." *EUI Working Papers* No. 87/293.

——. 1988. "Defining feminism: A comparative historical approach." *Signs* 14:1, 119–57.

Olin, U. 1976. "A case for woman as co-managers: The family as a general model of human social organization." In *Women and world development,* ed. I. Tinker and M. Bo Bramsen, 105–28. Washington, D.C.: Overseas Development Council.

Olsen, T. 1965. *Silences.* New York: Delacorte Press/Seymour Lawrence.

Ortner, S. 1974. "Is female to male as nature is to culture?" In *Woman, culture, and society,* ed. M. Z. Rosaldo and L. Lamphere, 67–85. Stanford: Stanford University Press.

Pateman, C. 1980. "Women, nature, and the suffrage." *Ethics* 90, 564–75.

Patterson, C. M. 1982. "New directions in the political history of women: A case study of the National Woman's Party campaign for the equal rights amendment, 1920–27." *Women's Studies International Forum* 5:6, 585–97.

Paul, H. W. 1967. *The rapprochement between church and state in France in the twentieth century.* Washington, D.C.: Catholic University of America Press.

Peck, M. G. 1944. *Carrie Chapman Catt: A biography.* New York: H. W. Wilson.

Pennock, J. R. 1969. "Epilogue." In *Voluntary associations: Nomos IX*, ed. J. R. Pennock and J. W. Chapman, 285–91. New York: Atherton.

Perkins, J., and D. L. Fowlkes. 1980. "Opinion representation vs. social representation; or, Why women can't run as women and win." *American Political Science Review* 74:1, 92–103.

Petchesky, R. 1980. "Reproductive freedom: Beyond 'a woman's right to choose.'" *Signs* 5:4, 661–85.

Phillips, M. 1980. *The divided house: Women at Westminster.* London: Sidgwick & Jackson.

Picq, F. 1986. "Bourgeois feminism in France: A theory developed by socialist women before World War I." In *Women in culture and politics: A century of change*, ed. J. Friedlander et al., 330–43. Bloomington: Indiana University Press.

Pintasilgo, M. de L. 1980. *Les nouveaux féminismes: Questions pour les chrétiens?* Paris: Cerf.

Pleck, E. 1983. "Feminist responses to 'crimes against women,' 1868–1896." *Signs* 8:3, 451–70.

Porter, M. C., and C. Venning. 1976. "Catholicism and women's role in Italy and Ireland." In *Women in the world: A comparative study*, ed. L. B. Iglitzin and R. Ross, 81–103. Santa Barbara, Calif.: Clio.

Poujol, G. 1975. "Les pratiques socio-culturelles des femmes." *Cahiers de l'Animation* no. 10, 3–15.

Prentice, A., P. Bourne, B. Light, G. C. Brandt, W. Mitchinson, and N. Black. 1988. *Canadian women: A history.* Toronto: Harcourt Brace Jovanovich Canada.

Pugh, M. D. 1944. "Politicians and the women's vote, 1914–1918." *History* 59:197, 358–74.

Rabaut, J. 1978. *Histoire des féminismes français.* Paris: Stock.

Rabier, J.-R. 1975. *European men and women: A comparison of their attitudes to some of the problems facing society.* Brussels: Commission of the European Communities.

———. 1979. *Femmes et hommes d'Europe en 1978: Attitudes comparées à l'égard de quelques problèmes de société.* Brussels: Commission of the European Communities.

———. 1983. *European women and men in 1983.* Brussels: Commission of the European Communities.

Rapp, R. 1982. "Family and class in contemporary America: Notes toward an understanding of ideology." In *Rethinking the family: Some feminist questions*, ed. B. Thorne and M. Yalom, 168–87. New York: Longman.

Rathbone, E. 1936. "Changes in public life." In *Our freedom and its results*, ed. R. Strachey, 15–76. London: Hogarth.

Reeves, J. 1944. *A century of Rochdale cooperation.* London: Laurence & Wishart.

Renard, M.-T. 1965. *La participation des femmes à la vie civique.* Paris: Editions ouvrières.

Rendel, M. 1977. "The contribution of the Women's Labour League to the winning of the franchise." In *Women in the labour movement*, ed. L. Middleton, 57–83. London: Croom Helm.

Rhonnda, M. H. 1933. *This was my world.* London: Macmillan.

Rich, A. 1976. *Of woman born.* New York: W. W. Norton.

———. 1980. "Compulsory heterosexuality and lesbian existence." *Signs* 5:4, 631–60.

———. 1982. "Split at the root." In *Nice Jewish girls: A lesbian anthology*, ed. E. T. Beck, 67–84. Trumansburg, N.Y.: Crossing Press.

Richards, J. R. 1982. *The sceptical feminist: A philosophical enquiry.* Harmondsworth: Penguin.

Ridings, D. 1984. "Parties are unfit to sponsor TV debates." Letter to the editor. *New York Times*, 10 June.

Ringelheim, J. 1985. "Women and the holocaust: A reconsideration of research." *Signs* 10:4, 741–61.

Roberts, H., ed. 1981. *Doing feminist research.* London: Routledge & Kegan Paul.

Robinson, L. 1978. "Who's afraid of A Room of One's Own?" In *Sex, Class and Culture*, ed. L. Robinson, 97–149. Bloomington: Indiana University Press.

Roche, B. 1979. "'Pro-feministes' et 'anti-féministes': Un essai d'analyse typologique." In *Femmes et hommes d'Europe en 1978*, ed. J.-R. Rabier, 214–38. Brussels: Commission of the European Communities.

Rollet, H. 1955. *Sur le chantier social.* Lyons: Chronique Sociale de France.

———. 1958. *L'action sociale des catholiques en France.* Paris: Boivin.

———. 1960. *Andrée Butillard et le féminisme chrétien.* Paris: Spès.

———. 1975. *La condition de la femme dans l'église: Ces femmes qui ont fait l'église.* Paris: Fayard.

Rosaldo, M. Z. 1974. "Woman, culture, and society: A theoretical overview." In *Woman, culture, and society*, ed. M. Z. Rosaldo and L. Lamphere, 17–42. Stanford: Stanford University Press.

———. 1980. "The use and abuse of anthropology: Reflections on feminism and cross-cultural understanding." *Signs* 5:3, 389–417.

Rosaldo, M. Z., and L. Lamphere, eds. 1974. *Woman, culture and society.* Stanford: Stanford University Press.

Rose, H. 1983. "Hand, brain, and heart: A feminist epistemology for the natural sciences." *Signs* 9:11, 73–90.

Rossanda, R. 1983. *Elles, les autres.* Paris: Editions des femmes.

Rossi, A. 1964. "Equality between the sexes: An immodest proposal." *Daedalus* 93, 607–52.

———. 1977. "A biosocial perspective on parenting." *Daedalus* 106, 1–31.

———. 1982. *Feminists in politics: A panel analysis of the first national women's conference.* New York: Academic Press.

Rossi, A., ed. 1973. *The feminist papers: From Adams to de Beauvoir.* New York: Bantam.

Rossiter, M. L. 1986. *Women in the resistance.* New York: Praeger.

Roth, P. 1984. "A conversation with Edna O'Brien: 'The body contains the life story.'" *New York Times Book Review*, 18 November.

Rothman, S. M. 1978. *Woman's proper place: A history of changing ideals and practices, 1870 to the present.* New York: Basic Books.

Rothschild, J. 1976. "Taking our future seriously." *Quest* 2:3, 17–30.

Roudy, Y. 1985. *A cause d'elles.* Paris: Albin Michel.

Rover, C. 1967. *Women's suffrage and party politics in Britain, 1866–1914.* London: Routledge & Kegan Paul.

Rowbotham, S. 1977. *Hidden from history: 300 years of women's oppression and the fight against it.* London: Pluto.

Rowbotham, S., L. Segal, and H. Wainwright. 1980. *Beyond the fragments: Feminism and the making of socialism.* London: Merlin.

Ruddick, S. 1980. "Maternal thinking." *Feminist Studies* 6:3, 343–67.

Rupp, L. J. 1981. "'Imagine my surprise': Women's relationships in historical perspective." *Frontiers* 5:3, 61–70.

——. 1985. "The women's community: The National Woman's Party, 1945 to the 1960s." *Signs* 10:4, 715–40.

Rupp, L. J., and V. Taylor. 1987. *Survival in the doldrums: The American women's rights movement, 1945 to the 1960s.* New York: Oxford University Press.

Ruthven, K. K. 1984. *Feminist literary studies: An introduction.* Cambridge: Cambridge University Press.

Sabrosky, J. A. 1979. *The evolution of feminist ideology.* Westport, Conn.: Greenwood.

Safilios-Rothschild, C. 1974. *Women and social policy.* Englewood Cliffs, N.J.: Prentice-Hall.

Salt, C., P. Schweitzer, and M. Wilson. 1983. "Of whole heart cometh hope. Centenary memories of the Co-operative Women's Guild." London: Co-operative Retail Services.

Sands, D., J. Smith, and J. Thompson. 1983. "A feminist Chautauqua for a rural state." In *Learning our way: Essays in feminist education,* ed. C. Bunch and S. Pollack, 210–18. Trumansburg, N.Y.: Crossing Press.

Sapiro, V. 1979. "Women's studies and political conflict." In *The prism of sex: Essays in the sociology of knowledge,* ed. J. Sherman and E. T. Beck, 253–65. Ann Arbor: University of Michigan Press.

——. 1980. "Memo from the front: Inter-sex and inter-generational conflict over the status of women." *Western Political Quarterly* 33:2, 260–77.

——. 1981. "Research frontier essay: When are interests interesting? The problem of political representation of women." *American Political Science Review* 75:3, 701–16.

—— 1983. *The political integration of women: Roles, socialization, and politics.* Urbana: University of Illinois Press.

Sapiro, V., and B. Farah. 1980. "New pride and old prejudice: Political ambition and role orientation among female partisan elites." *Women and Politics* 1:1, 3–36.

Sarah, E. 1982. "Toward a reassessment of feminist history." *Women's Studies International Forum* 5:6, 519–523.

Sargent, L., ed. 1981. *Women and revolution: A discussion of the unhappy marriage of Marxism and feminism.* Boston: South End.

Sauter-Bailliet, T. 1981. "The feminist movement in France." *Women's Studies International Forum* 4, 409–20.

Sayers, J. 1982. *Biological politics: Feminist and anti-feminist perspectives.* London: Tavistock.

Scales, A. C. 1980–81. "Towards a feminist jurisprudence." *Indiana Law Journal* 56, 375–444.

Scharf, L. 1983. "'The forgotten woman': Working women, the New Deal, and women's organizations." In *Decades of discontent: The women's movement, 1920–1940,* eds. L. Scharf and J. M. Jensen, 244–59. Westport, Conn.: Greenwood.

Scharf, L., and J. M. Jensen, ed. 1983. *Decades of discontent: The women's movement, 1920–1940.* Westport, Conn.: Greenwood.

Schenkman, E. 1980. "A nonpolitical League's political act." Letter to the editor. *New York Times,* 18 October.

Scott, A. F. 1984. "On seeing and not seeing: A case of historical invisibility." *Journal of American History* 71:1, 7–21.

Scott, H. 1976. "Feminism and the methodology of women's history." In *Liberating women's history: Theoretical and critical essays,* ed. B. Carroll, 369–84. Urbana: University of Illinois Press.

Sebo, K. 1976. "The women's movement as a transnational phenomenon." Paper presented at the Annual Meeting of the International Studies Association, Toronto, Canada.

Segal, J. C. 1982. "Interracial plus." In *Nice Jewish girls: A lesbian anthology*, ed. E. T. Beck, 55–8. Trumansburg, N.Y.: Crossing Press.

Seigfried, C. H. 1985. "*Second Sex*: Second thoughts." *Hypatia* (3), a special issue of *Women's Studies International Forum* 8:3, 219–30.

Sherman, J., and E. T. Beck, eds. 1979. *The prism of sex. Essays in the sociology of knowledge*. Ann Arbor: University of Michigan Press.

Smith, D. S. 1973. "Family limitation, sexual control, and domestic feminism in Victorian America." *Feminist Studies* 1:1, 40–57.

Smith, D. 1987. *The everyday world as problematic: A feminist sociology*. Toronto: University of Toronto Press.

Smith Rosenberg, C. 1979. "Beauty, the beast, and the militant woman: A case study in sex roles and social stress in Jacksonian America." In *A heritage of her own*, ed. N. Cott and E. Pleck, 197–221. New York: Simon & Schuster.

Sochen, J. 1973. *Movers and shakers: American women thinkers and activists, 1900–1970*. New York: Quadrangle/New York Times.

Soldon, N. C. 1978. *Women in British trade unions, 1874–1976*. Dublin: Gill & Macmillan.

Sorette, F. 1982. Letter to author. 7 September.

Sowerwine, C. 1982. *Sisters or citizens? Women and socialism in France since 1876*. Cambridge: Cambridge University Press.

Spare Rib. 1984a. "'She goes on and on, you can't kill the spirit!' Women's involvement in older peace movements." May, 25–27.

———. 1984b. "Why peace and not feminism?" May, 26.

Spender, D. 1980. "Report on the 'alternative' Copenhagen conference." *WRRC Newsletter* 5.

———. 1983. *There's always been a women's movement this century*. London: Pandora.

Spender, D., ed. 1981. *Men's studies modified: The impact of feminism on the academic disciplines*. London: Pergamon.

———. 1983. *Feminist theorists: Three centuries of key women thinkers*. London: Women's Press.

Stacey, J. 1983. "The new conservative feminism." *Feminist Studies* 9:3, 559–83.

Stacey, M., and M. Price. 1981. *Women, power and politics*. London: Tavistock.

Stanwick, K. A. 1983. *Political women tell what it takes*. Rutgers, N.J.: Center for the American Woman and Politics

Stanwick, K. A. and K. E. Kleeman. 1983. *Women make a difference*. Rutgers, N.J.: Center for the American Woman and Politics.

Stassinopoulos, A. 1973. *The female woman*. London: Davis-Poynter.

Stiehm, J. 1976. "Invidious intimacy." *Social Policy* 12–16.

———. 1982. "The protected, the protector, the defender." *Women's Studies International Forum* 5:3/4, 367–76.

Stocks, M. 1970. *My commonplace book*. London: Peter Davies.

Stott, M. 1978. *Organisation woman: The story of the National Union of Townswomen's Guilds*. London: Heinemann.

———. 1983. "Why not a co-op at Greenham Common?" *Manchester Guardian*, 9 May.

Strachey, R. 1927. *Women's suffrage and women's service: The history of the London and National Society for Women's Service*. London: London and National Society for Women's Service.

———. 1974. *The cause: A short history of the women's movement in Great Britain*. Bath: Cedric Chivers. (Originally published 1928.)

Strasser, S. 1982. *Never done: A history of American housework*. New York: Pantheon.

Strom, S. H. 1975. "Leadership and tactics in the American woman suffrage movement: A new perspective from Massachusetts." *Journal of American History* 62, 296–315.

Strong-Boag, V. 1976. *The parliament of women: The national council of women of Canada, 1893–1929.* Ottawa: National Museums of Canada.

———. 1986. "'Ever a crusader': Nellie McClung, first-wave feminist." In *Rethinking Canada: The promise of women's history,* ed. V. Strong-Boag and A. C. Fellman, 178–90. Toronto: Copp Clark.

Strumingher, L. S. 1979. *Women and the making of the working class: Lyon, 1830–1870.* St. Alban's, Vt., and Montreal: Eden Press.

Stucker, J. 1977. "Women as voters: Their maturation as political persons in American society." In *A Portrait in marginality: The political behavior of the American woman,* eds. M. Githens and J. L. Prestage, 264–83. New York: David McKay.

Sullerot, E. 1977. *Le fait féminin.* Paris: Fayard.

Survey Research Center. 1957. *Report III: Some problems of League membership. Cross-sectional membership and member activity.* Ann Arbor: University of Michigan Press.

Swerdlow, A. 1984. "Woman's peace festival, June 2, 1873." *Women's Studies Quarterly* 12:2, 29.

Tardy, E. 1982. *La politique: Un monde d'hommes? Une étude sur les mairesses au Québec.* Quebec City: Cahiers du Québec.

Terborg-Penn, R. 1983. "Discontented black feminists: Prelude and postcript to the passage of the nineteenth amendment." In *Decades of discontent: The women's movement, 1920–1940,* ed. L. M. Scharf and J. M. Jensen, 261–78. Westport, Conn.: Greenwood.

Thorne, B., and M. Yalom, ed. 1982. *Rethinking the family: Some feminist questions.* New York: Longman.

Thornton, A. P. 1966. *Habit of authority: Paternalism in British history.* London: George Allen & Unwin.

———. 1977. *Imperialism in the twentieth century.* Minneapolis: University of Minnesota Press.

Tolchin, M., and S. Tolchin. 1974. *Clout: Womanpower and politics.* New York: Coward, McCann & Geoghegan.

Toronto Star. 1986. Poll on housework. March 10.

Trevelyan, J. 1923. *The life of Mrs. Humphry Ward.* New York: Dodd, Mead.

Turbin, C. 1979. "'And we are nothing but women': Irish working women in Troy." In *Women of America: A history,* ed. C. R. Berkin and M. B. Norton, 202–19. Boston: Houghton Mifflin.

Uglow, J. 1983. "Josephine Butler: From sympathy to theory." In *Feminist theorists: Three centuries of women's intellectual tradition,* ed. D. Spender, 146–64. London: Women's Press.

Union féminine civique et sociale. 1960. "Promotion de la femme? Eléments de réponses pour 1960." *Fiches documentaires d'action sociale et civique* no. 1. Paris.

———. 1961a. *Dossier:* "Régulation de naissance et méthodes de contraception." Paris.

———. 1961b. *Fiche documentaire:* "Services familiaux de la halte d'enfants aux conseillères ménagères." Paris.

———. 1969. *Statutes.* Paris.

———. 1971a. *Dossier:* "Les choix face au droit à la vie." Paris.

———. 1971b. Report of Commission nationale de la famille: "La maternité: Une fonction specifique; Vers un statut social de la mère." Paris.

——. 1972. "Note concernant la législation sur l'avortement." Paris.

——. 1973a. "Positions de l'UFCS sur le problème des crèches." Paris.

——. 1973b. "Les femmes en France." Cahier d'éducation civique no. 24. Paris.

——. 1973c. *Dossier*: "Les partis politiques et le statut de la femme." Paris.

——. 1976. "Notes sur 'Les projets pour les femmes, 1976–1981.'" Paris.

——. 1977. *Dossier*: "Présentation de l'UFCS." Paris.

——. 1978. "Femmes et féminisme." Cahiers d'éducation civique nos. 45/46.

——. 1979. "Le statut juridique de la femme." Cahier d'éducation civique no. 48.

——. 1980a. "Rapport des activités, 1979–80." Paris.

——. 1980b. Letter to the membership about the consultation, 16 May.

United Nations. 1985. Report of the world conference to review and approve the achievements of the United Nations decade for women: Equality, development and peace. A/Conf. 116/28.

Verba, S., N. H. Nie and J.-O. Kim. 1978. *Participation and political equality: A seven-nation comparison.* Cambridge: Cambridge University Press.

Verba, S., N. H. Nie, J.-O. Kim, and G. Shabad. 1978. "Women and men: Sex-related differences in political activity." In *Participation and political equality: A seven-nation comparison*, S. Verba, N. H. Nie, and J-O. Kim, 234–67. Cambridge: Cambridge University Press.

Vickers, J. M. 1982. "Memoirs of an ontological exile: The methodological rebellions of feminist research." In *Feminism in Canada: From pressure to politics*, ed. G. Finn and A. Miles, 27–46. Montreal: Black Rose.

Vlastos, G. 1978. "Was Plato a feminist?" Paper delivered at the University of Toronto, 12 November.

Walters, F. P. 1952. *A history of the League of Nations.* London: Oxford University Press.

Ward, Mrs. H. 1914. *Delia Blanchflower.* New York: Hearst's International Library.

Ware, S. 1981. *Beyond suffrage: Women in the New Deal.* Cambridge: Harvard University Press.

Ware, S. 1982. *Holding their own.* Boston: Twayne.

Webb, C. 1927. *The woman with the basket: The story of the Women's Co-operative Guild.* Manchester: Co-operative Wholesale Society.

Webb, I., D. Paskin, and S. King. 1987. "People who care. A report on carer provision in England and Wales for the Cooperative Women's Guild." Watford, Herts.: Watford Printers.

Weekend Magazine (*Toronto Star*). 1979. "Weekend poll: Women's lib." 3 Mar.

Weiss, L. 1946. *Ce que femme veut: Souvenirs de la IIIe République.* Paris: Gallimard.

Weitz, M. C. 1978. "The status of women in France today." *Contemporary French Civilization* 3:1, 29–48.

Welch, S. 1975. "Support among women for the issues of the women's movement." *Sociological Quarterly* 16, 216–27.

——. 1980. "Sex differences in political activity in Britain." *Women and Politics* 1:2, 29–47.

Wells, M. M. 1962. "A portrait of the League of Women Voters." Washington: Overseas Education Fund. (Originally published in 1938.)

Werner, E., and L. Bachtold. 1974. "Personality characteristics of women in American politics." In *Women in politics*, ed. J. S. Jaquette, 75–84. New York: John Wiley.

Westin, J, ed. 1976. *Making do: How women survived the '30s.* Chicago: Follett.

Wheeler, L. 1983. "Lucy Stone: Radical beginnings." In *Feminist theorists: Three centuries of women's intellectual tradition*, ed. D. Spender, 124–36. London: Women's Press.

Wheeler, L., ed. 1981. *Loving warriors: Selected letters of Lucy Stone and Henry B. Blackwell, 1853 to 1893*. New York: Dial.

White, L. 1951. *Non-governmental organizations: Their purposes, methods, and accomplishments*. New Brunswick, N.J.: Rutgers University Press.

Whittick, A. 1979. *Woman into citizen: The world movement towards the emancipation of women in the twentieth century with accounts of the contributions of the International Alliance of Women, the League of Nations, and the relevant organizations of the United Nations*. London: Atheneum with Frederick Mueller.

Wilson, E. 1977. *Women and the welfare state*. London: Tavistock.

Wolgast, E. H. 1980. *Equality and the rights of women*. Ithaca: Cornell University Press.

Womanpoll. 1986. "Women's roles and rights." *Chatelaine* May, 42.

Women's Action 1982. 1982. "Organisations supporting women's action day." Typed list. London.

Women's Co-operative Guild. Various dates. *Annual reports*. London.

——. 1920. "The Women's Co-operative Guild: Notes on its history, organisation and work." London.

——. 1926. "New model branch rules." London.

——. 1931. "The ABC of the Women's Co-operative Guild." London.

——. 1943. "Woman of tomorrow." London.

——. 1948. "A new approach to guild education." London.

——. 1949. "The woman of today steps out." London.

——. 1957. "Speakers' notes." London.

——. N.d. "A new approach to guild education." London.

——. N.d. "Would you like to know?" London.

Women's Leader. 1927. "The 'mothers' international.'"

Women's Studies International Forum. 1985. Issue on reproductive and genetic engineering 8:6.

Woolf, L. 1921. *Socialism and co-operation*. London: National Labour Press.

——. 1967. *Downhill all the way: An autobiography of the years 1919 to 1939*. London: Hogarth.

Woolf, V. 1928. *A room of one's own*. London: Hogarth.

——. 1931. Introductory Letter to *Life as we have known it*, ed. M. L. Davies. London: Hogarth.

——. 1938. *Three guineas*. London: Hogarth.

——. 1966. "Thoughts on peace in an air-raid." In *Virginia Woolf: Collected essays*, vol. 4, ed. L. Woolf, 173–77. London: Hogarth.

——. 1979. *The sickle side of the moon. The letters of Virginia Woolf*, vol. 5, ed. N. Nicolson and J. Trautman. London: Hogarth.

——. 1982. *The diary of Virginia Woolf*, vol. 4, 1931–1935, ed. A. D. Bell. London:

——. 1984. *Leave the letters till we're dead. The letters of Virginia Woolf*, vol. 6, ed. N. Nicolson and J. Trautman. London: Hogarth.

Young, L. N.d. "History of the League of Women Voters." Typescripts, National Headquarters of the League, Washington, D.C.

Youssef, N. 1974. *Women and work in developing societies*. Berkeley: University of California Press.

Zimmerman, B. 1984. "The politics of transliteration: Lesbian personal narratives." *Signs* 9:4, 663–82.

Zylberberg-Hocquard, M.-H. 1981. *Femmes et féminisme dans le mouvement ouvrier français*. Paris: Editions ouvrières.

APPENDIX

Sources

None of the groups studied here has yet received full scholarly analysis, although I am indebted to Stanley Lemons's study of the first two decades of the LWV (1975) and the centenary history of the WCG by Jean Gaffin and David Thomas (1983). In addition, the Guild has three official histories, though one of them never got past typescript. These provide in often tedious detail the resolutions and activities of the group year by year through 1957 (Davies 1904, Webb 1927; Ganley n.d.). For the LWV, two versions of a draft history (Young n.d.) take the organization through 1970. This history provides invaluable detail about LWV policies and activities; Greenwood Press will publish a shortened version under the title *In the Public Interest.* These official histories have been very helpful for locating relevant documents, and I appreciate the groups' willingness to let me consult them. It remains the case that very little has been written on any of these organizations. Increasing interest in the period between the suffrage victory and women's liberation, however, has produced some attention to the League from historians dealing with topics to which it is relevant (Fowler 1986, Cott 1987, Rupp and Taylor 1987). For the UFCS, one particularly important volume is the biography of its founder, Andrée Butillard, written by a close collaborator (Rollet 1960); this takes the UFCS through 1955.

Only the UFCS has some consistent form of internal publication directed to members. Its *Bulletin périodique* or *Circulaire*, a single sheet folded in four, appeared every two months from September 20, 1925 to April 1927, when it became *La femme dans la vie sociale* (*LFVS*, Woman in society). *LFVS*, in newspaper format ranging from eight to twenty pages in length, appeared every month with occasional issues covering two or three months. Its publication was interrupted during the war, resumed shortly after, and continued until 1966 when the journal was renamed *Dialoguer* (To carry on a dialogue), its current name. *LFVS* was accompanied by other periodicals, difficult to identify because the UFCS has held onto only scattered copies. These include two-sheet monthly news-

377

papers for the less-educated members who were organized into the Groupes d'action populaires. They were published in the 1930s under varying titles (*Notre Feuille, Notre Journal, L'Entr'aide populaire dans la vie sociale, L'Entr'aide populaire féminine*) and seem to have been eventually incorporated into *La femme dans la vie sociale*. An international version of *LFVS* was published from 1948 to 1956. The other major UFCS publication I used was the *Cahiers d'education civique* (Civic education workbooks), actually a series of substantial, well-researched, and fully referenced pamphlets sold widely. I did not study systematically the *Dossiers* and *Notes* produced by the UFCS for internal use.

The WCG published its own journal for only one year, and I have used the 1939 issues of *The Guildswoman*. As the main continuing source for the Guild I have relied on its annual reports (prepared with the members as the main audience). Unfortunately, there is no longer any complete run of these in existence, and for the years before World War I, I have had to rely on the accounts given by Jean Gaffin (1977, Gaffin and Thoms 1983) and the versions to be found in the Reports of the Annual Meetings of the Co-operative Union. I supplemented these sources with pamphlets and handbooks designed to be distributed to members and potential members. Beginning in 1951, the League has published *The National Voter*, which goes to all members four times a year; this has been a major source. The League also produces a very large amount of pamphlet material for members and potential members.

I visited and consulted documents at the headquarters of each of the organizations studied. For the UFCS I interviewed paid workers at the national headquarters during the period 1977 to 1981, among them some of the survivors from the early postwar period who knew the founder of the group. During my brief stay at LWV headquarters in 1981 I interviewed paid workers, who helped enormously in setting the written material in context. I cannot express adequately my gratitude to those busy women in the three groups who welcomed and helped me, putting their archives and memories at my disposal.

I urge anyone interested in studying these groups to get to work as soon as possible. Only the League has its records stored safely in an accessible form (earlier material is in the Library of Congress), and even for the League explanations by old-time members are indispensable for making sense out of what is available. The UFCS material has been sorted and is easy to work with, but its repository is a historic mansion in the Marais and the paper is literally moldering away. The Guild has recently misplaced the only complete run of annual reports for the period preceding World War I, and its remaining material is unsorted and in poor physical condition; a good deal of it, however, is stored safely and catalogued in the library at the University of Hull, where the staff are both knowledgeable and hospitable. Microform Ltd. has recently put some valuable WCG material onto microfilm. Any substantial study of particular groups will have to interview members systematically, which I did not attempt.

Index

Library of Congress Cataloging-in-Publication Data

Black, Naomi, 1935–
   Social feminism.

   Bibliography: p.
   Includes index.
   1. Feminism—England. 2. Feminism—France. 3. Feminism—United States. 4. Wom-
en's Co-operative Guild. 5. Union féminine civique et sociale. 6. League of Women
Voters (U.S.) I. Title.
HQ1599.E5B57   1989   305.4'2   88-47937
ISBN 0-8014-2261-2 (alk. paper)
ISBN 0-8014-9573-3 (pbk. : alk. paper)